A Practical Guide
to the
Evaluation of
Child Physical Abuse
and Neglect

To the memory of CJ, a little boy I first met in May of my pediatric internship year. His death came 2 months later at the hands of his abusive caregivers. My involvement with the subsequent murder investigation and trial taught me a great deal about the "system" that failed CJ so terribly. It was in large part this experience that crystallized my resolve to work toward a better system. This book represents a small step toward that aim.

APG

To my parents, husband, and girls, for all their love.

CWC

To my parents and grandmother, who together created a home for my brother and I that was filled with constant and unconditional love.

ERG

A Practical Guide to the Evaluation of Child Physical Abuse and Neglect

Angelo P. Giardino, MD, MSEd
Cindy W. Christian, MD
Eileen R. Giardino, PhD, RN, MSN

SAGE Publications
International Educational and Professional Publisher
Thousand Oaks   London   New Delhi

For information address:

 SAGE Publications, Inc.
2455 Teller Road
Thousand Oaks, California 91320
E-mail: order@sagepub.com

SAGE Publications Ltd.
6 Bonhill Street
London EC2A 4PU
United Kingdom

SAGE Publications India Pvt. Ltd.
M-32 Market
Greater Kailash I
New Delhi 110 048 India

Printed in Canada

Library of Congress Cataloging-in-Publication Data

Giardino, Angelo P.
    A practical guide to the evaluation of child physical abuse and neglect / Angelo P. Giardino, Cindy W. Christian, and Eileen R. Giardino.
        p.   cm.
    Includes bibliographical references (p.) and index.
    ISBN 0-8039-5426-3 (cloth: acid-free paper)
    1. Battered child syndrome. 2. Abused children—Medical examinations. I. Christian, Cindy W. II. Giardino, Eileen R. III. Title.
RA1122.5.G53 1997
362.7'6—dc20   96-35623

97 98 99 00 01 02 03 10 9 8 7 6 5 4 3 2 1

Acquiring Editor:	C. Terry Hendrix
Editorial Assistant:	Dale Grenfell
Production Editor:	Diana E. Axelsen
Production Assistant:	Denise Santoyo
Typesetter/Designer:	Andrea D. Swanson/Dick Palmer
Indexer:	Virgil Diodato
Cover Designer:	Ravi Balasuriya
Print Buyer:	Anna Chin

Contents

Foreword

The study of the condition we label child abuse and neglect is the study of all parents' struggle to raise their children and, in particular, the study of those who went wrong in some way. Parenting is a complex and sometimes frustrating role. It is a job for which there is no single charted pathway; there are many unexpected twists and turns, often few external supports, and always high societal expectation for competence. It is no wonder that some parents go astray and end up hurting their offspring rather than nurturing them. In fact, recent statistics indicate that more than 1 million children were abused or neglected in 1994, and more than 1,100 died as the result of abuse.

In 1969, as a medical student, I attended a grand rounds given at St. Christopher's Hospital for Children in Philadelphia. The speaker was Ray Helfer, MD. The topic was child abuse. Dr. Helfer described his formulation of the etiology and pathophysiology of child abuse. There were three required elements: a vulnerable child, an abuse-prone parent, and a family stressor. It was described so simply, and it was analogous to the fuel, oxygen, and spark triad of the elements of fire. It was a captivating lecture, and one that stayed with me as I left medical school and went on to pediatric residency. Dr. Helfer had passed down a parcel of information and understanding in the best tradition of the great medical educators (of which he was a part).

In my 25 years of pediatric practice since that time, I have found that simple paradigm both true and untrue. It is true at its core, and the concepts have held up over time. But the study of child abuse and neglect has proven to be so much more. It has been more complex, more intricate, and more enigmatic than I ever imagined. The parents I have met along the way have been varied beyond description, from homeless unemployed to wealthy professionals. The children have presented every imaginable form of injury, from mild cutaneous trauma to traumatic death. They have varied in age from newborns to adolescents. Their stories have been remarkable in many ways and often tragic in that they could have been avoided. The family stresses have also been many, and they also have changed over the course of time, including economic stress, substance abuse, and relationship problems. As background to the triad of abuse, there has been a societal factor: constant violence. Violence is woven through the entire cloth of our culture. Violence is so much a part of our daily lives that it is no wonder that our children are also its victims.

Throughout my career as physician and teacher, I have tried to impart an interest in and respect for the phenomenon that we recognize as child abuse. It is a study that has proven worthwhile for me, and although it is not at as global a level as that of the late Dr. Helfer, I have been pleased to see some younger colleagues pick up the banner.

Such is the case of the book that follows. It is an excellent work of several young and dedicated authors who have themselves studied child abuse and now stand ready to help others. The book stresses the recognition and initial management of child abuse. It is written clearly and succinctly. It follows a logical pattern that helps the practitioner in what is often a difficult and emotionally charged clinical situation. Although it is a compact reference, it is comprehensive and meticulous in its attention to detail. It is a book that will help the reader, just as that simple formulation of Ray Helfer's helped me so many times.

I congratulate the authors on their outstanding accomplishment and the publisher on its continued dedication to helping the helping professionals deal with the complex and challenging field of practice. All have helped children and their parents— there can be no more noble or important goal.

Stephen Ludwig, MD

Preface

As a pediatric intern, I learned then [1968], from [C.] Henry Kempe, that child abuse and neglect is not just a medical problem, a social problem, or a legal problem. It is ultimately a child's problem and a family's problem, and solving it requires each of us in medicine, social work, law enforcement, the judiciary, mental health, and all related fields to work together for that child and family.

Krugman (1991)

Despite the growth of the child protection movement, a steady increase in the professional literature dealing with child abuse and neglect, increased public awareness of the issues surrounding child maltreatment, and the promulgation and enactment of model legislation, child abuse and neglect remain a major problem facing children and families today. This manual, *A Practical Guide to the Evaluation of Child Physical Abuse and Neglect*, is a resource for the health care professional to help increase knowledge of abuse and provide easy access to basic information concerning the evaluation of a child suspected of having been physically abused or neglected. The manual provides a framework from which to comprehensively evaluate the child.

The intended audience for the manual includes health care providers and related professionals who work with abused children, including physicians, nurses, nurse practitioners, clinical social workers, mental health professionals, and child protection workers. Law enforcement personnel and attorneys may use the manual as a resource when working with children and families. To provide practical information, there is a balance between the areas of content and the comprehensiveness of material included. The authors include clinically relevant information to guide the initial interview, examination, and the accurate documentation of the evaluation of a child who may have been physically maltreated. Toward that end, the ultimate goal of this manual is to assist the professional in performing and documenting a complete and accurate evaluation.

The terms *health care professional* and *health care provider* are used interchangeably throughout the text in recognition that many disciplines provide care to abused and neglected children and their families.

The manual is organized as follows. Chapters 1 and 2 provide an overview on the phenomenon of child abuse and neglect and offer a general approach to the evaluation of the maltreated child. The need for a systematic and comprehensive approach in the evaluation of suspected child maltreatment cases is highlighted. In addition, the authors support an interdisciplinary evaluation to enhance attention to both physical and psychosocial aspects and to facilitate the development of comprehensive treatment plans that build upon each discipline's different skills and perspectives.

Chapters 3 through 8 address specific forms of maltreatment. Each of these more focused chapters addresses mechanisms of injury, characteristic findings, clinical approach, differential diagnosis, and proposed treatments where applicable. Some information is repeated in several chapters to allow for those providers who may need to use a specific chapter as a reference when working with a child with a given symptom or finding. When more detailed information is available in a related chapter, the reader is referred there as well.

Finally, Chapters 9 and 10 cover the psychosocial assessment and legal issues. These chapters are intended to give more detail regarding these critically important issues.

This manual will assist the health care provider in performing a systematic evaluation of the child suspected of abuse or neglect. As the clinician develops greater expertise in the evaluation of the maltreated child, he or she will recognize patterns suggestive of physical abuse and neglect more easily, be better able to complete the appropriate medical and psychosocial evaluations of the child, and become more cognizant of the ultimate responsibility to work with other professionals and agencies to ensure the safety and recovery of the victimized child. We believe that the needs of the child and family are best served by knowledgeable health care professionals who clearly understand their role as health care provider and child advocate.

Authors' Note

Every effort has been made to ensure that information concerning the recommended ordering of laboratory and diagnostic tests, the interpretation of laboratory values, and suggested drug dosages and usages stated in this manual are accurate and conform to the accepted standards at the time of publication. However, the reader is advised to consult printed information on each test or drug prior to ordering a study or administering any medication, especially when ordering unfamiliar tests or using infrequently used drugs.

Acknowledgments

We would like to thank the following for their assistance in the production of the manual and their willingness to share their materials:

Paul DefOhannesian, JD
Mark Ells, JD
Lori Freedman, MD
Charles F. Johnson, MD
Paul K. Kleinman, MD
Alex V. Levin, MD
Eric Marx, JD
Toni Mauro, MSW
Suzy Kravitz Miller, MD
Gary F. Purdue, MD
Ryan Rainey, JD
Robert M. Reece, MD
Irving Robinson, MD
Anthony L. Rostain, MD
Donald Schwarz, MD, MPH
Toni Seidl, MSW
Howard M. Snyder, MD
Catherine Stephenson, JD

The Advisor, American Professional Society on the Abuse of Children
Pediatrics
W. B. Saunders
Williams & Wilkins
Churchill Livingstone
Guilford Publications
American Journal of Pathology
Ross Products Division, Abbott Laboratories
American Prosecutors Research Institute

Margi Ide, Photography and Graphic Art (Medical Education Center, The Children's Hospital of Philadelphia, PA)

Ruth Joray, Illustrations, Philadelphia, PA

Pediatric, nursing, and social work staff, The Children's Hospital of Philadelphia, PA

Donna Moore, Administrative Assistant, Health Partners of Philadelphia, Philadelphia, PA

Renea Jones-Coleman, Administrative Assistant, Children's Seashore House, Philadelphia, PA

Linda Tedeschi, Administrative Assistant, The Children's Hospital of Philadelphia, PA

Rebecca Press, Reasearch Assistant, University of Pennsylvania

Jata Ghosh, Director, Medical Library, The Children's Seashore House, Philadelphia, PA

Natalie Gorvine, Library Assistant, The Children's Hospital of Philadelphia, PA

Maraget G. Riviello, Typist

We thank the following reviewers:

Randall Alexander
    University of North Carolina at Chapel Hill
Charles Felzen Johnson
    Director Child Abuse Program, Children's Hospital, Columbus, Ohio
Bob Reece
    Massachusetts Society for the Prevention of Cruelty to Children
John Myers
    McGeorge School of Law, University of the Pacific
Amy Richardson
    Child Protection Program, Rainbow Babies and Children's Hospital, Cleveland, Ohio
Jean Smith
    University of North Carolina at Chapel Hill

1 Introduction to Abuse and Neglect

Child abuse and neglect is a major threat to the health and well-being of children throughout the world. Maltreatment occurs primarily in the family setting and is a problem firmly rooted in the caregiving environment (Ludwig & Rostain, 1992) (see Figure 1.1). Historical review indicates that caregivers have maltreated children in all cultures and nations of origin (Hobbs, Hanks, & Wynne, 1993a; Korbin, 1987; Lazoritz, 1992; Levinson, 1989; Radbill, 1987; Solomon, 1973).

Despite increasing societal and professional attention to this problem, large numbers of children remain at risk to the dangers of abuse and neglect. Maltreatment may result in physical injury and potential impairment of growth and development.

It is the responsibility of the health care professional to diagnose the child's condition accurately and to focus attention on the caregiving environment. Ensuring proper medical and community action involves treating the child's existing injuries and ensuring protection from future injury.

The focus of this book is on the evaluation of children who are suspected of being, or who have been, victims of physical

FAMILY DYSFUNCTION		
TASK	**DYSFUNCTIONAL INADEQUACY**	**DYSFUNCTIONAL EXCESS**
Supplying Physical Needs		
Protection	Failure to protect Child abuse	Overprotection and overanxiety
Food	Underfeeding Failure-to-thrive	Overfeeding, obesity
Housing	Homelessness	Multiple residences "Yo Yo"/vagabond children
Health care	Medical neglect	Excessive medical care Munchausen syndrome by proxy
Providing Developmental Behavioral, Emotional Needs		
Stimulation: developmental and cognitive	Understimulation Neglect	Overstimulation "Hothousing" Parental perfectionism Overindulgence "spoiled child"
Guidance: approval and discipline	Inadequate approval Overcriticism Psychological abuse	Overindulgence "spoiled child"
Affection: acceptance intimacy	Inadequate affection Emotional neglect Rejection Hostility	Sexual abuse Incest
Socialization		
Intrafamilial relationships	Attenuated family relationships Distanced parents	Parenting enmeshment Overinvolved relationships
Extrafamilial community relationships	Boundaryless families Deficiency in training in extrafamilial relationships	Insular families Excessive restriction from extrafamilial relationships

Figure 1.1. Family dysfunction.

Note: Dysfunction in families may occur through either excessive or inadequate attention to normal family tasks (Ludwig & Rostain, 1992). Used with permission.

abuse and neglect. This text does not address the complex and multiple issues of sexual abuse because the authors have published a similar text devoted specifically to sexual abuse. Throughout the text, the term *parenting* is often subsumed in the term *caregiving* to indicate the practices and actions to which the child is subject. The book guides the health care provider in understanding the immediate problems related to abuse and neglect and then completing the medical and psychosocial evaluation of the child suspected of having been physically abused or neglected.

Definition

Child Abuse   *Child abuse, maltreatment,* and *victimization* are interchangeable terms that refer to a complex social phenomenon in which the caregiver fails to provide for a child's health and well-being. A comprehensive definition of child abuse draws upon information from a number of disciplines (see Figure 1.2). This phenomenon has diverse medical, developmental, psychosocial, and legal consequences. Child abuse and its synonyms describe a wide range of situations. It involves caregiver acts of commission or omission that had or are likely to have injurious effects on the child's physical, developmental, and psychosocial well-being. Child maltreatment is categorized into (a) physical abuse, (b) sexual abuse, (c) emotional/psychological abuse, and (d) neglect. Neglect is further subcategorized into specific areas, such as physical, supervisional, educational, and emotional/ psychological (see Chapter 7).

There are a variety of definitions of abuse and neglect used among practitioners in various fields. Definitions that guide the practice of professional disciplines may vary (Giovannoni & Becerra, 1979; Valentine, Acuff, Freeman, & Andreas, 1984). For example, physicians and nurses commonly focus on medical aspects of injury, clinical social workers tend to focus on family and caregiving systems that gave rise to abuse, and law enforcement officers and attorneys may concentrate on the evidence that determines guilt or innocence of the suspected perpetrator of the abuse. Definitions are purposely broad to encompass the many different etiologies, presentations, and clinical manifestations of abuse or neglect cases (Azar, 1991; Bourne, 1979; Helfer & Kempe, 1987; Hobbs et al., 1993a; Ludwig, 1992a; Wissow, 1990a). Clinical situations may vary widely, ranging from a child who is tortured to death by a psychotic caregiver to a toddler who sustains a bruise to his or her buttocks during the application of corporal punishment (see Table 1.1 for definitions used in pediatric and child abuse textbooks). The unifying theme in all definitions of intrafamilial child maltreatment is that abuse and neglect occurs in the context of either active or passive caregiving behavior that is destructive to the normal growth, development, and well-being of the child (Ludwig, 1993).

Regardless of personal or professional preference for a specific definition, it is important that health care providers understand

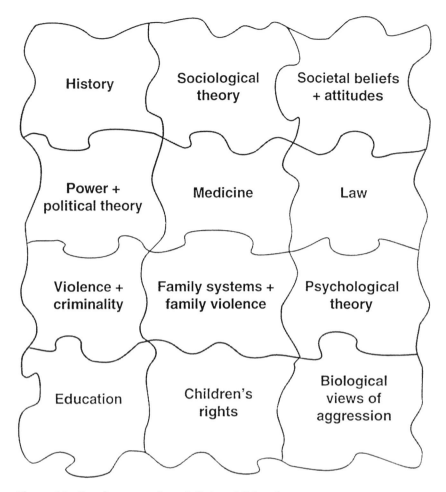

Figure 1.2. Puzzle approach to defining child maltreatment.

Note: Hobbs and colleagues' conceptualization uses a puzzle to define child abuse and neglect. They suggest that each piece represents a body of knowledge and insight into the problem, and only through fitting these diverse but related pieces together can one arrive at an accurate definition of child maltreatment (Hobbs, Hanks, & Wynne, 1993). Used with permission.

and comply with the definition of child abuse contained in the state laws governing the geographical area in which they practice. Most state laws define child abuse by the federal government's Child Abuse Prevention and Treatment Act (Wissow, 1990a). The law is as follows:

> The physical and mental injury, sexual abuse, negligent treatment or maltreatment of a child under age of 18 by a person who is responsible for the child's welfare under circumstances which indicate that the child's health and welfare is harmed or threatened thereby. (p. 1)

Physical Abuse and Neglect

Physical abuse occurs when a child has suffered injury at the hands of his or her caregiver. *Physical neglect* describes inadequate parenting or caregiving where there is potential for injury

Table 1.1 Definitions of Child Abuse

Citation	Definition
Avery and First (1989)	Child abuse is "any form of physical maltreatment of children" (p. 1306).
Chadwick (1991)	"An intentional act of commission or omission by another person that harms or threatens to harm a child in a significant way. The term 'non-accidental' is often used in place of 'intentional,' because it is sometimes difficult to be very certain about just what an abusive caretaker intended to do when he or she produced the injury that is seen. The term 'inflicted injury' may be the best one to describe what physicians can diagnose as abusive physical injury" (p. 839).
	Classifies abuse as "physical abuse, neglect, sexual abuse and emotional abuse" (p. 839)
Helfer (1987)	"Any interaction or lack of interaction between family members which results in non-accidental harm to the individual's physical and/or developmental states" (p. 61).
Ludwig (1990)	Child abuse describes "many different parental behaviors. . . . Abuse is used to describe a parent who repeatedly beats, starves, and confines the victim. It also describes a parent who leaves a child unattended for a short time and a parent who loses control on one occasion while attempting to instill the child with admirable values. Any behavior that results in injury to the child may be considered as abusive" (p. 319).
Ludwig (1992a)	"The precise definition of abuse remains elusive and difficult to grasp . . . it is a complex set of parental behaviors and child responses. It is multifaceted: personal, familial, community, and societal phenomena" (p. 1).
	"A symptom of family dysfunction in which the child sustains injury, be it physical, emotional, developmental, or sexual, rather than looking for 'good parents' versus 'bad parents' " (p. 6).
Ludwig (1993)	Uses Pennsylvania law definition of physical abuse:
	Injury primarily caused by an act of omission which (1) significantly jeopardizes the child's safety, (2) significantly impairs the child's physical functioning temporarily or permanently, or (3) is accomplished by physical evidence in a continuous pattern of unexplained injuries. (p. 1430)
	And uses National Center on Child Abuse and Neglect (1988) definition of physical abuse:
	Child abuse which results in physical injury, including fractures, burns, bruises, welts, cuts and/or internal injuries. Physical abuse often occurs in the name of discipline or punishment, and ranges from a slap of the hand to use of objects. (p. 1430)
Schmitt and Krugman (1992)	"Child abuse is any maltreatment of children or adolescents by their parents, guardians, or other caretakers" (p. 78).
Wissow, L. S. (1990b)	Physical abuse is "the inflicting of physical injury through malicious, cruel, or inhumane treatment. . . . Punishments that result in injury, that is, leave marks, break the skin or bones, or involve real or perceived threats to life or health, are generally regarded as abusive" (p. 589).

resulting from omissions on the part of the caregivers. Poor hygiene, exposure to the elements, lack of compliance with medical therapy, and forms of malnutrition related to parental control over feeding constitute physical neglect.

Levels of Definition

Ludwig (1992a) describes three levels of definitions related to child maltreatment: legal, institutional, and personal. Legal definitions are laws that define abuse. Kempe states that abuse is what the law says it is (Hobbs et al., 1993a). Health care providers must understand the laws of the geographical area in which they practice because they are mandated to comply with them. They are also required to report suspected cases of child abuse and neglect.

Institutional definitions refer to organizational policies and procedures that guide local clinical practice. They are designed as a reference for a facility's personnel to follow. Interpretations of institutional standards vary depending on the institution and its mission in protecting children, although compliance with legal definitions is necessary.

Finally, personal definitions encompass an individual's assessment of what defines appropriate caregiving behaviors. Personal definitions are subject to factors such as family rearing practices, parenting experience, socioeconomic status, religious beliefs, cultural practices, and personal idiosyncrasies. Aspects related to the abusive event that may help to explain individual responses to maltreatment are one's perception of the (a) effect on the child, (b) intention of the perpetrator, and (c) sociocultural context used to judge the situation (Starr, Dubowitz, & Bush, 1990) (see Table 1.2). An example of disparity in personal definitions of abuse is the acceptance or rejection of corporal punishment as an acceptable form of discipline. A discussion of corporal punishment and its potential for maltreatment follows.

Corporal Punishment

Corporal punishment is a discipline method that uses physical force or the threat thereof as a behavior modifier (Hobbs et al., 1993a). Its use is widespread, is universal, and has been practiced for generations (American Humane Association, 1994). It stems from cultural, religious, and societal views of how children should be disciplined. Acts included are pinching, spanking, shoving, shaking, choking, excessive exercise, confinement in closed spaces, and denial of bathroom privileges (Grossman, Rauh, & Rivara, 1995). In the United States, forms such as slapping, spanking, paddling, and general hitting of children by adult caregivers are widely accepted (Hyman, 1990; Straus & Gelles, 1988). It is estimated that 10,000 to 20,000 students per year require treatment and/or medical evaluation as a result of corporal punishment (Society for Adolescent Medicine, 1992).

Physical punishment to decrease the frequency of child misbehavior uses force that carries a risk of injury to the child "to teach a lesson." One may question the value of a discipline program oriented toward the use of physical force and inflicted pain as a behavior modification technique (Gelles, 1982; Justice & Justice, 1976; Straus, Gelles, & Steinmetz, 1980). A review of

Table 1.2 Aspects of the Abusive Event That Shape Individual Definitions

Aspect	Description
Effect	The effect of abuse on the child is central to the child's overall evaluation, and the therapeutic plan is dependent on accurate assessment of injury and potential for further harm. The degree of force or negligence involved is clinically useful in assessing a child's injury and may reflect upon his or her potential risk for further damage if returned to his or her current environment. Furthermore, the determination of the level of external intervention needed to ensure the protection of the child is related to the degree of injury incurred and potential for harm. The nature and severity of the child's injury affects the health care provider's assessment of the seriousness of the caregiver's omission or commission (Giovannoni & Becerra, 1979).
Intention	The decision of the health care provider to report an injury as abuse may be affected by his or her perception of the perpetrator's intention to harm the child (Gelles, 1982). The health care provider's distinction between an accidental or inflicted injury is affected by his or her perception of the caregiver's intention as well (Herzberger & Tennen, 1988). Finally, health care providers are likely to label as intentional and abusive those injuries that are repetitive in nature, are associated with other injuries, or do not match the history provided (Newberger & Hyde, 1975). Whether the parent or caregiver meant the event to lead to such injury is of secondary importance when an injured child presents to the health care professional for care.
Sociocultural norms	The sociocultural norms are important in that they help define levels of responsibility and culpability. What is considered abusive in one cultural context may be acceptable in another (Korbin, 1987). For example, male circumcision is an accepted part of religious and cultural practice for some, whereas it is regarded as a painful mutilation by others. Likewise, a light spanking is considered a suitable form of punishment by many Americans, whereas it is illegal in Sweden (Deley, 1988).

60 references found no credible evidence for the continued use of corporal punishment as an effective way to modify behavior (McCormick, 1992). However, proponents of corporal punishment claim that it is a valid discipline that leads the family "to live in harmony and love toward each other" (Nelson, 1991, p. 17). In cases where undesired behaviors are repeated after corporal punishment, the caregiver may become angry and frustrated and reapply the punishment. There is increased potential to lose control while angry and to engage in violent behavior toward the child. Often, well-meaning parents, "for the child's own good," inflict punishment and pain in the same way their parents did to them.

Child discipline aims for limit setting, helping the child learn right from wrong, assisting in appropriate decision making, and assisting the child's development of self-control (Christian, 1992). Therefore, opponents of corporal punishment believe that discipline is best achieved through consistent, nonviolent discipline techniques such as time out, loss of privileges, parental disappointment, and grounding, which are not associated with significant potential for physical harm (American Humane

Association, 1994; Drabman & Spitalnik, 1973; Hyman & Lally, 1982; Poole et al., 1991). There is little to support the effectiveness of corporal punishment over non-pain-oriented forms of discipline. In fact, there are deleterious effects from promoting violence as a problem-solving strategy (McCormick, 1992).

Caregiver reliance on corporal punishment is a significant risk factor for physical abuse (Berger, Knutson, Mehm, & Perkins, 1988; Straus, 1987). Punishment becomes child abuse when the correction causes bodily harm. Findings such as hematomas, ecchymoses, fractures, muscle injury, intracranial bleeds, and death may result from punishment that becomes uncontrolled. When a child manifests signs of abuse, the health care provider is legally mandated to report the caregiver for physical abuse regardless of his or her initial intention (Straus et al., 1980).

Despite negative outcomes, corporal punishment remains a socially acceptable form of punishment (Socolar & Stein, 1995). Graziano and Namaste (1990) found that 93% of college students studied reported being spanked at some time in their childhood. Sixty-four percent believed the effects of the spankings were helpful to very helpful. Generally, violence in society is illegal with the exception of warfare, self-defense, necessary force by law enforcement, and corporal punishment directed at one's children (Graziano & Namaste, 1990).

Nations that have outlawed corporal punishment in schools include Austria, Belgium, Cyprus, Denmark, Ecuador, Finland, France, Great Britain, Holland, Iceland, Israel, Italy, Japan, Jordan, Luxembourg, Mauritius, Norway, Philippines, Portugal, Russia, and Sweden (Hobbs et al., 1993a; Wessel, 1980). Sweden even banned corporal punishment by parents (Deley, 1988; Starr et al., 1990; Wessel, 1980). Presently, 27 states in the United States have banned the use of corporal punishment in schools (Hyman, 1994) (see Table 1.3). A survey study found a lower prevalence of corporal punishment in those school districts that banned its use as an acceptable means of punishment (Grossman et al., 1995).

National organizations that voice opposition to corporal punishment in one form or another include the American Academy of Pediatrics (AAP), Parent Teachers Association (PTA), American Psychological Association (APA), National Education Association's Task Force on Corporal Punishment, American Public Health Association (APHA), Executive Sub-committee of the AAP's Section on Child Abuse, and the Surgeon General's Workshop on Violence and Public Health (Christian, 1992; McCormick, 1992; Wessel, 1980).

Reporting   The health care provider uses clinical skills and judgment to decide if a child's injuries are due to abuse and/or neglect. They are mandated reporters of suspected child abuse and neglect

Table 1.3 States That Ban Corporal Punishment in Schools (as of 1995)

By Statute	By State Regulation	By School Board
California	Alaska	Rhode Island
Connecticut	New Hampshire	South Dakota
Hawaii	New York	
Illinois	Utah	
Iowa		
Maine		
Maryland		
Massachusetts		
Michigan		
Minnesota		
Montana		
Nebraska		
Nevada		
New Jersey		
North Dakota		
Oregon		
Vermont		
Virginia		
Washington		
West Virginia		
Wisconsin		

Source: Hyman (1994).

and are obligated in all jurisdictions to comply with the law (see Chapter 10). If available, clinical social workers are an excellent resource for helping health care professionals understand specific child abuse reporting laws and guidelines.

Scope of the Problem

Epidemiology The incidence of child maltreatment (the number of new cases identified in a 1-year period of time) is often determined through research using data sources from reports of abuse and neglect. The data sources represent those cases known to social service or law enforcement agencies. The flaw in determining incidence by this method is that not all abuse is reported, and not all reports are considered to be actual abuse or neglect after investigation. Aggregation and comparisons among studies are problematic because reports often originate from reporting standards that vary. For example, a legal standard that holds up to rules of evidence governing an adversarial courtroom situation would likely yield different results than a social services' standard

Table 1.4 National Incidence Study "Levels of Knowledge" of Abuse and Neglect

Level	Description
Level 1	Included those children reported to child protective services as possibly being abused and/or neglected.
Level 2	Included those children known by other investigatory agencies, such as law enforcement or public health officials. This group was not in the child protective services system but may have had overlapping responsibilities with the child protective services. Although investigatory officials know the children because of involvement with situations such as domestic disputes, assaults, delinquency, or nutrition or hygiene problems, they may not be considered as significantly abused and/or neglected as the Level 1 children. As such, interventions are not directed specifically at their maltreatment.
Level 3	Included abused and neglected children known to professionals in major community institutions such as schools, hospitals, day care centers, or mental health agencies but not known by the agencies in Levels 1 or 2. Because of definitional ambiguities and assumptions on the part of professionals, a child may not be reported to official investigations because the involved professional may have felt that he or she was in the best position to handle the situation and the child's needs. Professionals at Level 3 who fail to comply with obligatory reporting standards run the risk of personal liability.
Level 4	Included abused and/or neglected children recognized by someone outside of Level 3 such as a friend, neighbor, or family member. A key point is that the abuse or neglect was not disclosed to anyone at Levels 1 through 3. Included in Level 4 are the perpetrator and the child.
Level 5	Included those cases not known to anyone because of lack of recognition or awareness about abuse and neglect. The perpetrator may have regarded his or her behavior as nonabusive or "appropriate discipline," and no one outside observed or recognized the behavior as maltreatment.

Source: National Center on Child Abuse & Neglect (1988).

for abuse, which is less strict and allows the investigator's judgment as well as physical evidence to be used.

Major Studies   There are three major sources of national data that provide a basis upon which to estimate the number of children who are maltreated each year. These sources are collected and reported by the following: (a) the National Committee for Prevention of Child Abuse (NCPCA) uses data compiled from officially reported statistics provided by the states; (b) the National Center on Child Abuse and Neglect (NCCAN), using data from its two commissioned National Incidence Studies on Child Abuse and Neglect (Study Findings, 1988, NIS-1 and NIS-2) (National Center on Child Abuse and Neglect, 1981, 1988b), estimates the incidence of child abuse and neglect using a five-level model of "knowledge" about the abuse (see Tables 1.4 and 1.5); and (c) epidemiology and social science investigations use a variety of survey methods on representative samples of U.S. households. The surveys attempt to characterize children's risk for violence and abuse at the hands of caregivers (Gil, 1971; Straus & Gelles, 1986).

CHILD PHYSICAL ABUSE AND NEGLECT

Table 1.5 National Incidence Study Sociodemographics

Parameter	Description
Gender	Female children are more likely to experience child abuse than are male children, largely because of the increased likelihood of female children being sexually abused. The increased risk for female children is present even in the subanalysis done for only physical abuse and neglect. There is a positive correlation between the age of the child and risk for physical abuse and neglect.
Age	Children of both sexes appeared to be more at risk for physical abuse with increasing age. Concerning fatal abuse and severe injuries, serious injury was more common in younger children (less than 2 years old), whereas moderate injuries were more common in older children. In comparing NIS-1 to NIS-2, the increased incidence of physical and sexual abuse in older children was thought to represent an increased recognition of maltreatment rather than an increase in actual occurrence (National Center on Child Abuse and Neglect, 1981, 1988b). Regarding race and ethnicity, there was no significant relationship identified between the incidence of maltreatment and the child's race or ethnic origin. Race and ethnicity are challenging parameters to analyze because of concerns that minority groups may be more likely to be reported to child protective service agencies (Hampton, 1985; Pelton, 1978).
Socioeconomic status	Low family income was significantly associated with a higher risk of abuse. In 1986, children coming from families whose income was less than $15,000 per annum were more likely to be maltreated in all forms of abuse than were children with higher family incomes. Lower-income children also suffered more severe injury than did those with higher income. Children from families earning less than $15,000 had three times the number of fatalities, seven times the number of serious injuries, and five times the number of moderate injuries, and were nine times more likely to be neglected. Children coming from families of four or more children were more likely to be physically abused (36/1,000) or neglected (14/1,000) than were children from families with fewer siblings (20/1,000 for physical abuse and 9/1,000 for neglect) (National Center on Child Abuse and Neglect, 1988b).
Metro status	Finally, no reliable variation of risk for abuse or neglect could be explained based on county characteristics related to the metro status—urban, suburban, or rural.

Source: Cappelleri, Eckenrode, and Powers (1993); National Center on Child Abuse and Neglect (1988b).

Magnitude   *Official Reports*

The magnitude of the problem of child abuse and neglect can be estimated only because of definitional heterogeneity, methodologic variation, and analytic disagreements. The estimates and extrapolations generated, using sound epidemiologic principles and these statistics, guide health care professionals in recognizing the scope of the problem (Leventhal, 1981). In 1994, the NCPCA estimated that 3,140,000 reports of suspected child abuse and neglect were made to child protective services or a public social service throughout the United States (see Figure 1.3) (American Humane Association, 1995). The reporting rate was 47 per 1,000 children in the United States.

The following is the 1994 breakdown of substantiated child abuse reports by type of abuse: 49% neglect, 21% physical abuse,

11% sexual abuse, 3% emotional abuse, and 16% miscellaneous forms such as abandonment, educational neglect, dependency, and other unspecified situations not included in other headings (American Humane Association, 1995). Approximately 1,036,000, or 33%, of the child abuse reports were confirmed for abuse and/or neglect (American Humane Association, 1995).[1,2] This represents an abuse rate of 18 cases per 1,000 children in the United States. An estimate, using the subcategory breakdown from above, translates into 498,972 neglected children (8/1,000) and 278,496 children who have been physically abused (4/1,000). NIS-2 estimates that approximately 72% of physical abuse cases known to child protection agencies represent moderate injuries, 15% serious injuries, and 12% mild injuries.

In 1994, 1,271 children were known to have died from abuse and/or neglect (American Humane Association, 1995). This figure, based on data from 34 states, is undoubtedly an underestimate of the homicide rate related to abuse. Data from 19 states showed that 45% of those children who died from maltreatment between 1992 and 1994 were known to child protective services systems through current or prior reports and services (American Humane Association, 1995; McCurd & Daro, 1993). NCPCA data from 1992 indicate that overall reporting of child abuse and neglect has increased by 50% since 1985 (see Figure 1.3). Comparisons between two National Incidence Studies reveal increases in "countable" cases occurring between 1980 (NIS-1) and 1986 (NIS-2) (National Center on Child Abuse and Neglect, 1988b). One possibility for the rise is that the incidence of abuse and/or neglect increased. A second possibility is that greater professional awareness of the issues may have increased reporting behavior (National Center on Child Abuse and Neglect, 1981, 1988b). Finally, methodological differences between the two studies may account for different estimates between NIS-1 and NIS-2 (Ludwig, 1992a; Starr et al., 1990). There has been a steady increase in the reporting of severe injuries. Starr et al. (1990) argue that increased reporting stems from expanded professional awareness and recognition of abuse and/or neglect. They cite a significant increase in the reporting of moderate injuries, which are those most likely observed and diagnosed as abuse by heightened professional awareness and improved judgment (Starr et al., 1990).

Social science studies have contributed to the estimation of child maltreatment. In 1965, Gil (1971) interviewed 1,520 adults in a random sample of the U.S. population and surveyed U.S. newspapers and periodicals over a 6-month period for reports of abuse. He compared these data to reporting data from official sources available in 1967 and 1968, a period during which all 50 states were not yet mandated to provide such reporting to the federal government. Gil (1971) found more nonofficial sources

Number in Thousands

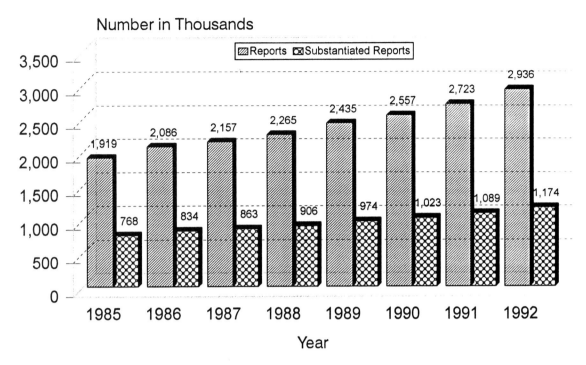

Figure 1.3. Child abuse and neglect statistics.

Note: Data are from national sources that show the annual rise in the number of child abuse and neglect reports along with the approximate number of substantiated reports (using a 40% substantiation rate) (Maternal and Child Health Bureau, 1994).

reporting abuse than he did official sources. Nonofficial sources were asked if they knew any families who had hurt a child intentionally. The study estimated that 2.5 million to 4.1 million children had been injured that year (Gil, 1971). Gil's methods were criticized, and reanalysis with methodologic correction estimated the incidence of physical abuse more conservatively at 500,000 per year (Light, 1973). Perhaps most concerning, Gil (1971) found that 60% of the children reported as abused or neglected had a prior history of being abused. He concluded that physical abuse was part of a pervasive pattern in a large number of families.

Straus and Gelles (1986) conducted two national household surveys, 10 years apart, on parental and familial violence. They surveyed two-parent households with at least one child between 3 and 17 years old. The researchers asked about parental behavior directed toward the child that involved beating (more than one punch), biting, grabbing, hitting with a fist or object, kicking, pushing, shoving, slapping, spanking, and/or threatening with or using a knife or gun. The methodologies differed between the two studies,[3] but a comparison of findings showed that exposure to overall violence remained about the same. However, there was a lower incidence of severe violent acts in

1985 as compared to 1975 (defined as the child being kicked, bitten, hit with a fist, hit or almost hit with an object, beaten up (more than one punch), or being threatened or attacked with a knife or gun.

Studies where individuals recall or disclose abuse are open to confounding effects, such as respondents' ability to recall the events in question and willingness to report a stigmatized behavior that carries well-publicized criminal and civil sanctions. There are questions as to the honesty of telephone survey respondents in reporting information that society views negatively and that has legal consequences. However, even if the actual incidence of severe violence did decrease between 1975 and 1985, the lower incidence remains at an unacceptable level.

Etiology of Physical Abuse and Neglect

Models for Abuse

There is no single cause of physical abuse and neglect. Therefore, theoretical approaches and conceptual models help to organize the complex issues involved with child abuse and neglect. An early typology of physical abuse containing 17 subtypes of circumstances that lead to physical abuse has been condensed to a smaller list of four subtypes (Gil, 1971; Wissow 1990a). (See Table 1.6 for a typology of physical abuse cases.) Each subtype clarifies the heterogeneity of perpetrator involvement in the physical abuse of children.

A jigsaw puzzle approach captures the multifactorial nature of child abuse and helps to explain causes (Hobbs et al., 1993a). This approach incorporates diverse knowledge and understanding from a variety of sources including anthropology, child advocacy, criminology, education, history, law, medicine, political science, psychology, and sociology (see Figure 1.2).

Early theories and models based on the existence of psychopathology in the parent (usually the mother) have evolved into more holistic cognitive and ecological models that try to account for factors involved in child maltreatment (Gil, 1975; Newberger & Newberger, 1981; Steele, 1987). At present, cognitive and ecological models are most accepted and focus more on what the abuser has learned and experienced and how these forces may predispose him or her to function in a family context (Zuravin, 1989). These models describe the cause of abuse as multilevel and interactive involving the individual, the caregivers, the

Table 1.6 Typology of Physical Abuse

Subtype	Description
One	This results from an angry and uncontrolled disciplinary response to real or perceived misconduct of the child. The parent either loses control during the punishment or views him- or herself as a stern disciplinarian who justifiably applies firm punishment.
Two	This revolves around the caregiver's rejection of the child and stems from the caregiver's own psychological impairment. There is a sense of resentment toward the child rooted in a variety of reasons or a perception of the child as provocative and different.
Three	This arises from a child left in the care of an abusive baby-sitter.
Four	This is seen when the child is injured as a result of entanglement in a dispute involving the caregiver and another person (Gil, 1971; Wissow, 1990a).

community, and the global sociocultural context (Gil, 1975; Newberger & Newberger, 1981).

The ecological approach is associated with the seminal work of psychologist Urie Bronfenbrenner (1977). It defines child development in the context of an interacting, dynamic system. The ecology for child development includes family (microsystem), the community in which the family exists, forces applied to the system (exosystem), and sociocultural values that overlay the community and its families (macrosystem) (Bronfenbrenner, 1977). Garbarino (1977) applied ecological principles to the study of abuse and neglect, thus introducing the interactional nature of the roles of the parent and child, family, social stress, and social and cultural values (Belsky, 1980; Justice, Calvert, & Justice, 1985).

Clinically Useful Approaches

Helfer (1973, 1987) provides a clinical and developmental perspective to abuse and neglect. He states that the caregiver and child interact around an event or in an environment where the end result is that the child is injured or put at significant risk of injury or neglect. Helfer's (1987) approach accounts for the caregiver, the child, and triggers and stressors of the event or environment.

The Helfer (1973, 1987) model uses caution in defining the child's contribution to an abusive interaction. A child needs parenting, and nothing a child does, says, or thinks is reason to inflict injury on that child. However, personality or physical characteristics can be predisposing factors to child abuse or neglect. The most frequently cited characteristics associated with abuse or neglect are prematurity and disability (Breslau, Staruch, & Mortimer, 1982; White, Benedict, Wulff, & Kelly, 1987). Proposed reasons why premature infants are at higher risk for abuse and neglect include decreased bonding between child and parent, medical fragility of the child, and stress associated with the level of medical care that prematurity requires (Sameroff & Abbe, 1978). Proposed reasons that physically and mentally challenged children are at increased risk center around the high demand that special needs place on the caregiver (Frisch & Rhodes, 1982). The health care provider can identify child factors that may place the child at risk for injury and provide to the caregiver ongoing anticipatory guidance related to these stressors.

A 1995 government study reported the following data concerning the incidence of abuse among children with disabilities (U.S. Department of Health and Human Services, 1995):

- The incidence of maltreatment (number of children maltreated annually per 1,000 children) among children with disabilities was 1.7 times higher than the incidence of maltreatment for children without disabilities.
- For 47% of the maltreated children with disabilities, Child Protective Service (CPS) caseworkers reported that the disabilities led to or contributed to child maltreatment.
- CPS caseworkers reported that a disability led to or contributed to maltreatment for 67% of the maltreated children with a serious emotional disturbance, 76% of those with a physical health problem, and 59% of those who were hyperactive.
- The incidence of physical abuse among maltreated children with disabilities was 9 per 1,000, a rate 2.1 times the rate for maltreated children without disabilities.
- Among maltreated children with disabilities, the incidence of physical neglect was 12 per 1,000, a rate 1.6 times the rate for maltreated children without disabilities.
- The incidence of emotional neglect among maltreated children with disabilities was 2.8 times as great as for maltreated children without disabilities.

Stress, defined as internal anxiety related to a perception of an inability to meet external demands, is often cited as a factor in abusive interactions (Selye, 1956). Because stress is subjective, what is stressful to one individual may or may not be stressful to another. Coping strategies may mitigate the amount of stress experienced in a given situation. Subsequently, caregiver stress and frustration figure prominently in the occurrence of child abuse (Straus & Kantor, 1987). Stressors most often related to child abuse are those associated with poverty, significant life events, caregiver-child interaction patterns, and caregiver role conflicts (Justice & Justice, 1976; Straus & Kantor, 1987).

The way that a family functions is a key factor that lends to the child being at risk for injury and abuse (Ludwig & Rostain, 1992). The factors that lead to dysfunctional inadequacy and excess include social stressors and even child characteristics.

Figure 1.1 lists tasks that take place in a family and examples of dysfunctional inadequacy and excess.

Helfer (1973) cites the following as factors associated with potential abuse or neglect:

Caregiver Factors

- Personal history
- Personality style
- Psychological functioning
- Expectations of the child
- Ability to nurture and assist the child's developmental progress
- Rearing practices modeled during the parents' own upbringing
- Degree of social isolation characteristic of the parent
  — His or her ability to ask for and receive help from other individuals in the social network
- Support of the caregiver's partner in assisting with the parenting role
- Ability to deal with internal and external difficulty and coping strategies

Child Factors

- Prematurity and disability
- Poor bonding with caregiver
- Medical fragility
- Level of medical care of premature children
- Special needs of physically and mentally disabled children
- Child perceived as "difficult"

Environmental Factors

- Poverty
- Significant life events
- Caregiver-child interaction patterns
- Caregiver role conflicts

Effects

The physically abused or neglected child may sustain physical, emotional, and developmental effects. Injured or neglected children experience physical consequences that vary in severity depending on the type of injury, organ systems involved, and extent of tissue damage inflicted. Physical effects of abuse are discussed separately in subsequent chapters.

Maltreatment also may have negative effects on the child's behavior, development, and psychosocial functioning. Studies using "clinical" populations of seriously disturbed individuals found a high correlation between maltreatment and poor behavioral, psychosocial, and developmental outcomes (Lamphear, 1985; Oates, 1982; Parish, Myers, Brandner, & Templin, 1985). However, reliable, consistent predictions concerning the effects of maltreatment are difficult to make, and this remains an active area of research interest. Well-designed, longitudinal studies of the long-term effects of physical abuse and neglect point toward a complex relationship between child maltreatment and subsequent development. The impact of victimization on development hinges on "mediating" factors that mitigate against the negative effects of abuse and neglect on the child (Augoustinos, 1987; Crittenden, 1992; Martin & Elmer, 1992). Possible mediating variables identified are the child's personality characteristics and coping strategies, available resources in the environment, the child's perception of how responsive people are to his or her plight, and the modeled adult behavior that the child observes during the aftermath of the abuse (Augoustinos, 1987).

Despite evidence that points to the potential to intervene positively after abuse has occurred, many victimized children and their families do not receive adequate social and psychological services (American Humane Association, 1993). Among approximately 1.2 million cases of substantiated abuse identified in 1992, less than 66% received therapeutic or supportive services after the investigative phase of the case was completed (American Humane Association, 1993). This indicates that more than 500,000 abused children and families received no such services.

A child's development builds upon interactions with people and events in his or her environment (Wissow, 1990a). Environments that do not provide positive, nurturing interactions may impair the child's accomplishments in a wide range of psychomotor, cognitive, psychosocial, and emotional capacities (Liebert & Wicks-Nelson, 1981; Sroufe & Rutter, 1984). For instance, a child whose abusive environment prevents the attainment of an internal sense of safety and trust may have difficulty achieving developmental tasks such as cooperation and group play (Wissow, 1990a). Potential developmental manifestations of abused or neglected children include

- behavioral problems related to self-control such as aggression, violence, and juvenile crime
- social and cognitive difficulties such as decreased academic and socioeconomic achievement
- emotional and psychologic disorders related to attachment formation, empathy, and self-esteem (Allen & Oliver, 1982; Egeland,

Sroufe, & Erickson, 1983; Wodarski, Kurtz, Gaudin, & Howing, 1990)

Widom (1989a) found a higher rate of adult criminality and arrests for violent behavior in victims of child maltreatment when compared to controls who were not abused or neglected. However, she notes that the majority of abused and neglected children do not become delinquent, criminal, or violent (Widom, 1989b). Interestingly, the abused and neglected group did not have a higher adult arrest rate for child abuse or neglect offenses when compared to the controls (Widom, 1989a). This finding helps dispel the belief that abused children grow up to become abusive parents. Although abusive parenting occurs in some cases, abused children do not inevitably become abusive parents. One study estimates that approximately 25% to 35% of children subjected to all forms of child abuse will go on to abuse their own children as compared to controls who were not abused (Kaufman & Ziegler, 1987). Martin and Elmer (1992) found that although some abused children are at risk of becoming abusive toward their own children, the majority of such survivors do not go on to abuse their children.

The potential long-term effects of abuse on mental health are significant. Only recently have the pervasive effects of maltreatment on adult functioning come to light. Briere (1992) developed a framework from which to view the mental health implications of abuse and neglect. He describes three stages of potential impact that maltreatment may have on the child: (a) initial reactions that include posttraumatic stress, alterations in normal development, painful affect, and cognitive distortions; (b) accommodation to ongoing abuse, including coping behaviors intended to increase safety and/or decrease pain; and (c) long-term effects and ongoing accommodation that reflect on the initial reactions and accommodations and that are rooted in the ongoing coping responses (Briere, 1992). Briere (1992) describes a number of serious mental health problems found in abuse survivors that, at the extreme, include posttraumatic stress and dissociative disorders. Although the majority of survivors of abuse will not experience the most extreme impairment, Briere (1992) contends that a large number of victims experience some level of dysfunction. Therapeutic efforts that are focused on the coping strategies of the child or adult can help the survivor's healing process (Briere, 1992).

In summary, physical abuse and neglect may have far-reaching implications for the child victim. Research describing outcomes from abuse and neglect shows that deleterious effects from exposure to child abuse can be mitigated if supportive, responsive people and systems respond to the child victim in a substantive manner. It is important that the health care provider appreciate that children who are abused are not "doomed," and that the child needs to be nurtured and supported in a safe environment for healing and normal development to occur.

In Brief

- Child maltreatment is categorized into (a) physical abuse, (b) sexual abuse, (c) emotional/psychological abuse, and (d) neglect.
- There is no single cause of physical abuse and neglect.
- The result of abuse and neglect is a child who either sustains injury or is at risk for injury, and whose growth and development may be impeded.
- Maltreatment primarily occurs in the family setting and is a problem firmly rooted in the caregiving environment.
- Corporal punishment ends and child abuse begins when the punishment inflicted by the parent causes bodily harm.
- Approximately one third of fatally abused children were known to child protective services systems through current or prior reports and services (American Humane Association, 1993; McCurd & Daro, 1993).
- When a child manifests the signs of abuse, the health care provider is legally mandated to report the caregiver for physical abuse regardless of the caregiver's intention.
- Health care providers are mandated reporters of suspected child abuse and neglect and are obligated in all jurisdictions to comply with the law.
- Health care providers must understand and comply with the definition of child abuse in the state laws governing the geographical area in which they practice.
- Health care providers understand that children who are abused need to be nurtured and supported in a safe environment for healing and normal development to occur.
- The most frequently cited child characteristics associated with abuse or neglect are prematurity and disability (Breslau et al., 1982; White et al., 1987).
- Stressors related to child abuse are those associated with poverty, significant life events, caregiver-child interaction patterns, and caregiver role conflicts (Justice & Justice, 1976; Straus & Kantor, 1987).
- Injured or neglected children experience physical consequences that vary in severity depending on the type of injury, tissues involved, and extent of damage.
- Of approximately 1.16 million cases of substantiated abuse, less than 66% received therapeutic or supportive services after the investigative phase of the case was completed (American Humane Association, 1993).

- Therapeutic efforts focused on the child's and/or adult's coping strategies can help the survivor live in a satisfying and productive manner (Briere, 1992).

Notes

1. A child abuse report is considered substantiated if investigation yields a determination that the child has been abused or is at significant risk of being abused or neglected. Substantiation implies a degree of certainty on the part of the child protective services (CPS) agency that the abuse occurred or that the child is at significant risk of such. Although not necessarily a court-issued determination, substantiation of a report generally warrants intervention. Substantiation occurs in approximately 40% (in a range between 35% and 50%) of all child abuse and neglect reports (American Association for Protecting Children, 1989; Maternal and Child Health Bureau, 1994). Some states add a middle tier—indicated reports—between substantiated and unsubstantiated reports. Indicated reports include those reports that are not clearly unsubstantiated and "reason to suspect" is uncovered during the investigation. These reports also warrant some level of surveillance and intervention.

2. The issue of duplicate reports remains a difficult problem during analysis. Duplication occurs when a family or child previously reported is counted again when a subsequent report is made. The second report added to the total count for that calendar year may inflate the estimate of children abused or neglected (American Association for Protecting Children, 1989). A survey of six states that remove duplicated cases from their reports suggests that duplication may add 30% more reports in a calendar year. In other words, the actual number of children abused may be only 70% of the number of substantiated reports. A Massachusetts study found the percentage of duplication highest in neglect cases, with 25% being duplicate reports. Cases of physical and sexual abuse followed with a 14% incidence of duplicate reports, and emotional maltreatment was lowest with a 10% incidence (National Center on Child Abuse and Neglect, 1993).

3. In the 1975 study, 1,146 currently cohabiting people were interviewed using face-to-face, 1-hour interviews to explore violence directed at a child aged 3 to 17 years. The 1985 survey conducted 35-minute telephone interviews on 1,428 households with two caretakers present and a child aged 3 to 17 years. In reporting results, the investigators made distinctions between the level of violence to which the child was exposed (Straus & Gelles, 1986).

2 Evaluation of Abuse and Neglect

Approach to the Medical Evaluation

It may be difficult to identify children who are victims of physical abuse. Many injuries are not pathognomonic, and the diagnosis may not be obvious. The history given by the caregiver may be misleading or incomplete, causing a delay or mistake in diagnosis. In addition, victims of abuse often are too young to provide a history. Although only a small percentage of injuries seen by health care professionals are the result of abuse, there are a number of historical and physical findings that should raise the suspicion of nonaccidental trauma.

Diagnosing child abuse requires knowledge of child development, the epidemiology of trauma, mechanisms of injury in children, and the differential diagnosis of various forms of injury. The medical evaluation includes a history, physical examination, indicated laboratory and diagnostic studies, and observation of the caregiver-child interaction. The recognition of abuse stems from the "building block" approach, which synthesizes data from each part of the clinical evaluation to develop and confirm a suspicion of abuse (Ludwig, 1993) (see Figure 2.1a, b, and c). Completing a detailed history and physical

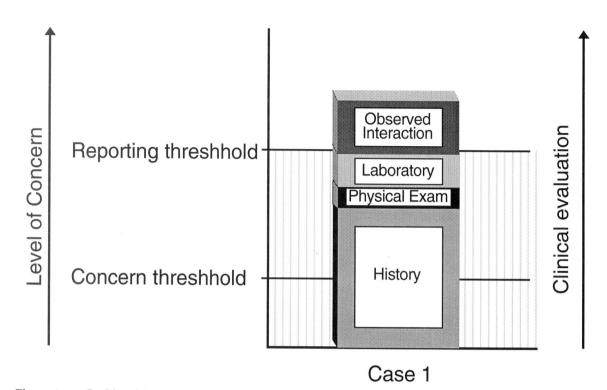

Figure 2.1a. Building block approach to diagnosis of child maltreatment.

Source: Ludwig, 1993. Used with permission.

Each component of the clinical evaluation is viewed as a building block that, as they are stacked during the process of the evaluation, can lead to higher and higher levels of concern. At a certain point, the stack of blocks may lead to a reporting threshold for the clinician.

examination is paramount because many cases of abuse are first detected by identifying discrepancies between the history and physical findings. It is ideal for two health care providers, such as a physician and nurse or social worker, to obtain a history together. The likelihood that important questions will be missed decreases if more than one person is present to interview the family. In addition, information can be recorded by one person while the other asks questions. After the interview, the questioners can review information for accuracy.

The History and Interview

A complete history helps determine whether an injury is the result of abuse or an accident. Professionals who evaluate injured children and their families consider the possibility of abuse when evaluating all pediatric injuries. Although the majority of childhood injuries seen by medical personnel are accidental, missing a case of child abuse puts the patient at great risk for future injury. It is important to be thorough yet nonac-

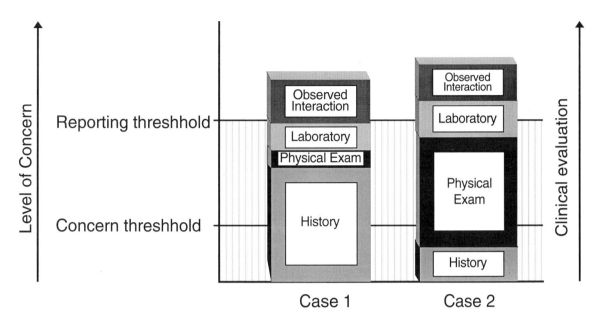

Figure 2.1b. Building block approach to diagnosis of child maltreatment.

The blocks may be of different sizes depending on how much of a concern the information is that is uncovered during that component of the evaluation. In Case 1, the history is very much of a concern for abuse and contributes a great deal toward reaching the clinician's reporting threshold. In Case 2, the history is of minimal concern, but the physical examination contributes a great deal toward reaching the clinician's reporting threshold.

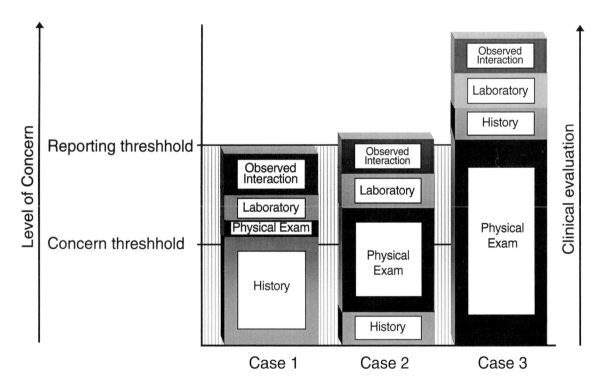

Figure 2.1c. Building block approach to diagnosis of child maltreatment.

Case 3 demonstrates how one component can be so much of a concern that it alone causes the clinician to reach a reporting threshold (e.g., the physical findings of loop marks on a child's skin)

cusatory during the evaluation. Health care providers do not apportion blame. The interview is conducted professionally, without displays of anger or reproach that would serve only to alienate the caregiver and not improve the condition of the child.

Documentation

It is essential to complete a detailed medical record in cases of suspected physical abuse. A standardized form can be used to document the evaluation (see Appendix 2.1). Health care providers are asked to justify the medical diagnosis more commonly in child abuse cases than for almost any other pediatric condition. County social workers, law enforcement officials, and attorneys often become involved in cases of child abuse, and details regarding the medical findings are necessary for their evaluations. Health care professionals are often asked to testify in criminal or civil court regarding the child's injuries and the basis for the diagnosis of abuse (see Chapter 10).

A complete and thorough medical record is essential because court proceedings may occur 1 to 2 years after the child is injured. Although the health care professional may have some independent memory of the case, it may be difficult to recall details months or years after the examination was completed. A health care provider who has had the painful experience of reviewing a record in court that is incomplete or substandard recognizes the need for meticulously documented information as it relates to the abused child.

The details of the history and interview are documented in the record using quotes to indicate exact responses of the child whenever possible. Because the record is a legal document that may be used in legal and court proceedings, it is necessary that statements reflect the nonleading and unbiased nature of the questions asked in the history, interview, and examination. The record is written clearly to document all significant history related to past and present occurrences of abuse or neglect. The record should contain the date and time of injury, the identity of the caregivers who bring the child for care, and any denials of any known trauma to the child.

The Caregiver-Child Interaction

An essential component of the child abuse evaluation is the observation of how the caregiver and child interact with one another (Schmitt, Grosz, & Carroll, 1976). Of great concern to the health care provider are caregivers who seem unaware of the seriousness of the child's injuries, are indifferent to the child's needs, or appear unsupportive of the child. Additional concern arises when the caregiver belittles the child, is overly directive in his or her communication, and is inattentive to the child's requests. Children who interact with their caregiver in an unusual manner and do not look to their caregiver for emotional

Table 2.1 Central Questions Related to the Injury

What was the date and time of the injury?
Where did the injury occur?
Who was caring for the child at the time of the injury?
Did the caregiver witness the injury?
What events preceded the injury?
What was the child's reaction to the injury?
What did the caregiver do after the injury occurred?

support are also of concern. Caregivers and children vary in their response to stress and trauma and may not be behaving normally in an emergency setting. Caution is taken to avoid overgeneralizing and attributing meaning or blame to these observations in the acute clinical setting.

History Related to Injuries

The history is integral in establishing the diagnosis of child abuse. A thorough approach to history taking in all cases of trauma identifies injuries that may have been inflicted. A standard format for gathering medical data is used that includes chief complaint, history of present illness, review of symptoms, and past medical and psychosocial history. Family history related to bleeding disorders, osteogenesis imperfecta, or other injury-related disorders is important to include. Children who are verbal often can provide a history of injury, unless they are developmentally impaired, in a great deal of pain, or frightened. As a general rule, separating the caregivers and verbal child helps to obtain a more reliable history from the child. For injured infants and young children, it is common for the caregiver to provide the history. The improvement of verbal abilities in children as they reach school age is reflected in the details that the child describes regarding an injury. A school-aged child who cannot remember how a significant injury was sustained may be a victim of abuse, except for those children with head injuries.

Regardless of who provides information, the history begins by asking for a narrative of the injury. The interviewer then asks questions to clarify confusing statements and fill in missing details in the story. It is important to ask open-ended, nonleading questions. The following are questions that should be explored in all evaluations (see Table 2.1).

1. What was the date and approximate time that the injury occurred?

   In some cases, a history of injury cannot be provided, either because the adult with the child was not present at the time of the injury or because there was no known trauma to the child. In this situation, it is important to know when the child last seemed perfectly well. For example, an infant who sustained a femur fracture may have been injured by a parent prior to being dropped off at the baby-sitter, only to be recognized by late morning, when the caregiver noted swelling of the leg. A history of irritability throughout the morning would support this scenario, whereas a history of playfulness and well-being all morning would not.

2. Where did the injury occur?

   Abusive injuries are most commonly sustained in the privacy of the home rather than in public places. Accidental injuries that occur in public often have been witnessed by unrelated adults who may provide information to police or emergency medical technicians (EMTs). This information can corroborate an accidental mechanism of injury.

3. Did the caregiver witness the injury?

   In an attempt to provide a history of trauma, caregivers sometimes provide a likely scenario for an injury they did not actually witness. Determine whether the injury was witnessed or unwitnessed. Both can be accidental. Ask detailed questions regarding the injury, such as approximate distance the child fell, the surface onto which the child fell, the position in which the child landed, parts of the body that appeared to be injured, and whether there were any objects in the path of the fall.

4. What events preceded the injury? What were the child and caregiver doing just before the injury?

   Search for signs of chaos or stress, which may be related to abusive injuries. For example, an infant who sustains abusive head injury may have kept a tired caregiver up all night and then refused a bottle that was meant to quiet the baby. Beware of claims that a child with major injury went for hours or days without pathology or changes in behavior.

5. What was the child's reaction to the injury?

   Determine whether the child's reported behavior after the injury is compatible with the disability or pain caused by the injury.

6. What did the caregiver do after the injury?

   Determine when the caregiver first noted the injuries and what treatment was given to the child prior to being seen by a health care provider.

7. How much time elapsed between the injury and the time the child arrived for medical care?

   If significant time elapsed, determine what occurred during that time and the reason for the delay. If there was a delay in seeking care, determine why the caregiver chose this time to bring the child for evaluation.

Past Medical History

The past medical history of the child may help to identify suspicious injuries and medical conditions that can be mistaken for abuse. In evaluating suspicious injuries, the interviewer asks about the child's health to reassure the caregiver that he or she is interested in the child's well-being and not merely trying to apportion blame for an injury. The interviewer explores the child's general health, previous hospitalizations, operations, and any past significant trauma. Document what the caregiver states in the initial history about trauma and the child and if the caregiver denies any recent or past trauma to the child. It is essential to obtain phone numbers and addresses of the caretakers and family members for future reference.

It is important to determine former injuries that the child sustained and where the child was treated. In abuse, there may be evidence of old and unexplained injury. This is accomplished by asking the caregiver and by checking past records within the same hospital, at other hospitals, and at facilities or offices where the child has been treated. The history uncovers whether the child receives regular health care with a single provider or has been to multiple physicians. Abusive caregivers often bring children with inflicted injuries to multiple medical care providers in an attempt to avoid the recognition of abuse. Although seeking care with multiple health care providers may indicate abuse, it is not a definite indicator. The interviewer explores reasons for using multiple health care providers and then reviews old records.

The past medical history reflects information about the mother's pregnancy and the child's birth. Family history explores the health of family members and inheritable diseases that may affect the diagnosis of the child, such as osteogenesis imperfecta, bleeding and bone disorders, and Ehlers-Danlos syndrome.

A developmental history of the child is obtained that includes the child's present level of abilities and the age at which the child reached standard developmental milestones. For school-aged children, it is important to know if the child requires any special education and how the child functions in school. An understanding of normal child development is essential in evaluating injuries that are said to be self-inflicted. In addition, a child's slow development may be a source of frustration and stress for a caregiver, thereby increasing the risk for abuse in some situations (see Table 2.2).

Finally, the social history of the family is explored, including family composition and individuals living in and outside the home. The social history includes financial and emotional supports for the family and recent or chronic family stresses. Caregivers are screened for alcohol and/or drug abuse and a history of domestic violence (see Chapter 9).

Histories That Raise the Concern for Abuse

There are a number of historical clues that raise suspicion of abuse. None is used in isolation to diagnose maltreatment. The health care professional considers the complete history when evaluating children with injuries. The following are factors that raise the suspicion for abuse:

- History of trauma that is incongruous, inconsistent, or not plausible with the physical examination

Table 2.2 Developmental Milestones

Age	Physical characteristics	Social-emotional intellectual characteristics
0 to 3 months	Has birth reflexes—sucking, grasping, frequent arm-leg movements, lifts head when held at shoulder. Develops own rhythm in sleeping, feeding, eliminating.	Is concerned with satisfaction of needs. Smiles responsively ("social smile") Likes to be held and rocked. Vocalizes sounds (coos). Cries in different ways when cold, wet, hungry, in pain. Is fearful of loud or unexpected noises, situations, or people.
3-6 months	Can roll over stomach to back. Holds head up when held in sitting position. When on abdomen, can lift head and look about. Begins to reach for and grasp objects.	Distinguishes primary caretaker from others but will socialize with anyone. Smiles responsively. Laughs aloud. Turns head to voice. Follows with eyes. Coos, gurgles, chuckles, laughs, squeals. Has expressive noises. Anticipates food on sight.
6-9 months	Rolls from back to stomach. On back, can lift head up. Sits with some or no support. Beginning attempts to creep or crawl. Stands with hands held. When sitting, reaches forward to grasp without falling.	Prefers primary caregiver. Has separation anxiety. May cry when strangers approach. Puts everything in mouth. Likes to do things over and over. Responds to name. Begins to understand familiar words such as *eat, bottle, bye-bye, mama, doggie.* Imitates sounds. Has single consonants, such as *ba, ka, ma.*
9-12 months	Crawls well. Sits alone steadily for more than 10 minutes. Stands holding onto furniture. Walks, holding onto a hand or furniture. Learns to grasp with thumb and finger.	Friendly and affectionate with caretakers. Has initial stranger anxiety, continued need to feel sure someone will care for him or her. Extremely curious about everything. Likes to interact in play with adult. Plays peek-a-boo and patty cake. Waves goodbye. Likes to drop objects deliberately. Will talk using babbling sounds. Says "mama" and "dada." Understands "no" or inflection of "no!"
12-18 months	Can get to standing position alone. Walks alone well by 18 months. Can stoop and recover object. Creeps up stairs. Rolls or tosses ball. Finger feeds. Drinks from cup on own. Uses spoon (messy). Seats self on chair.	Begins to indicate wants by pointing, reaching, and so on. Has to touch and mouth everything. Imitates some words, has 3 to 5 words. Looks at pictures in a book. Points to one body part. Follows one or two directions (e.g., take a ball to . . .)
18-24 months	Walks. Runs stiffly.	Is still very attached to primary caretaker— makes regular overtures to seek approval,

Table 2.2 Continued

Age	Physical characteristics	Social-emotional intellectual characteristics
	Walks up and down stairs with one hand held. Jumps with both feet. Hurls ball. Can kick a ball or object. Uses spoon, spilling very little. Can tower two or more 1-inch blocks.	ask for help, and be comforted. Begins to assert independence. Is at beginning of "no" stage. May begin temper tantrums. Turns pages of a book. Can point to two or three body parts. Imitates words. By 24 months is combining two-word phrases. Understands a lot more than he or she can say.
2-3 years	Is highly mobile. Can walk up stairs without hand held. Can jump from bottom step. Can jump in place. Can throw a ball. Has muscle control sufficient to begin toilet training. Uses spoon to feed self.	Appears self-reliant but continues to need active caregiving. Displays affection, especially toward caretaker. Difficulty containing impulses. Responds negatively to limits placed on activity. Is very emotional—laughs, squeals, throws temper tantrum, cries violently. Can anticipate need to urinate or defecate. Does simple tasks. Can occupy self for short time period. Can be fearful of loud noises, large animals, or mother's departure. Identifies more than parts of own body. Is very verbal—enjoys talking to self and others. By 3 years, has a vocabulary of 100 to 300 words.
3-4 years	Alternates feet when going up stairs, rides a tricycle, swings, and climbs. Uses toilet consistently. Is beginning to dress and undress self. Builds with blocks. Is very interested in own body, especially genitals. Has lots of energy. Is fearless, will try anything.	Continues developing independence and self-reliance. Has a strong need for love, praise, and approval from adult caretakers. Sees self as part of family unit. Likes to be "big" and achieve new skills. Uses imagination and fantasy play (e.g., may blame misdeed on fictional character). Plays alongside other children and begins to interact with them. Notices difference between men and women. Knows name, sex, age. Frequently asks "why" questions. Engages in conversations. Begins to use reasoning abilities. Knows rhymes and songs.
4-5 years	Runs well and turns. Is beginning to skip. Walks down stairs one foot to each step. Has improved finger dexterity—uses pencil, cuts with scissors, brushes teeth, uses spoon and fork.	Often exhibits aggressive, demanding, threatening, name-calling behavior. Displays extremes in behavior within short period of time—bossy and belligerent one minute; crying, shy, and clinging the next. Can separate easily from mother.

(continued)

Table 2.2 Continued

Age	Physical characteristics	Social-emotional intellectual characteristics
	Prefers to talk or play rather than eat. Can dress self with little supervision. Is very active—constantly on the go.	Identifies with parents and likes to imitate them. Learns to share, accept rules, take turns. Plays cooperatively. Increasingly aware of right and wrong. Talks incessantly. Asks many questions. Has a vocabulary of over 1000 words. Can name 3 to 4 colors. Can answer questions like "What do you do when you're cold . . . hungry . . . tired?"
5-6 years	Skips on both feet alternately. Can catch a bounced ball. Can walk heel to toe on a line. Dresses and undresses self without supervision. Able to care for toilet needs independently. May be able to print a few letters.	Is sensitive to how others view him or her. Is easily embarrassed. May tell untruths or blame others for wrongdoing because of desire to please others. Engages in elaborate dramatic play. Is interested in babies and where they come from. May develop nervous habits such as nail biting, sniffling, stuttering. May experience stomachaches, nausea, and other physical symptoms if he or she doesn't like school or is fearful of new task. Understands cause and effect relationship. Names coins, counts 10 objects. Asks questions about the meaning of words.

Note: Used by permission, courtesy of Lori Freedman, MD.

- History of minor trauma with extensive physical injury
- History of no trauma with evidence of injury (magical injuries)
- History of self-inflicted trauma that is incompatible with child's development
- History of the injury changes with time
- Delays in seeking treatment
- Caregiver ascribes blame for serious injuries to a young sibling or playmate

History Incongruous With the Physical Examination

History of Minor Trauma With Extensive Physical Injury

Infants and young children are relatively resistant to injuries from both common household falls and free falls of low-moderate heights. *A history of minor trauma that results in serious or life-threatening injury to a child should be suspect, and an evaluation for possible abuse should be performed.* A number of studies have examined the consequences of minor trauma (Chiaviello, Christoph, & Bond, 1994; Helfer, 1977; Joffe & Ludwig, 1988; Lyons & Oates,

1993; Nimityongskul & Anderson, 1987). Joffe and Ludwig (1988) analyzed pediatric stairway injuries. Of 363 consecutive children seen in a pediatric emergency department after falling down stairs, none had life-threatening injuries or required intensive care. A majority of patients sustained minor soft tissue injuries such as abrasions and contusions. Seven percent of the children fractured one bone, most commonly the skull or a distal extremity. Only three children required hospitalization, all for observations after head trauma. Stairway falls did not result in abdominal visceral injuries, multiple fractures, intracranial hemorrhages, or cerebral contusions. Overall, stairway injuries resulted in occasional significant injuries, but much less than free falls of the same vertical distance. Severe, truncal, and proximal extremity injuries did not occur in this population.

Chiaviello et al. (1994) reviewed 69 children less than 5 years of age who fell down the stairs. The majority of injuries were minor and involved the head and neck. Injuries to more than one body area did not occur. In contrast to Joffe and Ludwig's (1988) findings, a few children sustained significant head injury, including one child with a subdural hematoma, one with a C-2 fracture, and two with cerebral contusions.

In separate studies, Helfer (1977), Lyons and Oates (1993), and Nimityongskul and Anderson (1987) reviewed injuries sustained to children who fell out of bed while in the hospital. Of approximately 450 children who fell out of beds or cribs from a height of less than 4.5 feet, none was seriously injured. Most sustained no identifiable injuries. All injuries were minor, such as contusions, small lacerations, or an occasional skull or clavicular fracture. Whereas falls from single beds result in minimal injury, bunk bed injuries tend to be more severe. Selbst, Baker, and Shames (1990) prospectively studied children seen in a pediatric emergency department after bunk bed injuries. Lacerations (40% of patients) and contusions (28% of patients) were the most common injuries. One percent of patients sustained a concussion, and 10% of patients fractured a bone. Although 9% of patients required hospitalization, no life-threatening, internal-abdominal, neck, or genital injuries or deaths resulted from bunk beds in this study.

A number of studies examined the relationship between the height of free falls and injury and death in children. These studies show that the predominant injury in falls from heights occurs to the head and skeleton. Musemeche, Barthel, Cosentino, and Reynolds (1991) reviewed the outcomes of children who fell more than 10 feet (or at least one story). Of the 70 records reviewed, the majority of children fell from one to three stories. Head (54%) and skeletal (33%) trauma were common, but no deaths occurred. Chadwick, Chin, Salerno, Landsverk, and Kitchen (1991) reviewed the outcome of 317 children with a reported fall who were seen at a pediatric trauma center. Interestingly, 7 of the 100 children who reportedly fell less than 4 feet died of their injuries, whereas no deaths occurred in 65 children who fell between 5 and 9 feet, and only one child died who fell between 10 and 45 feet. Further analysis of the data showed that the seven children who died from short falls were victims of abuse whose caretakers falsified their history.

Williams (1991) studied 106 children younger than 3 years of age who sustained free falls and whose history was corroborated by a person other than the caregiver. Other than three children who sustained depressed skull fractures from falls less than 10 feet, no life-threatening or other serious injuries (intracranial hemorrhage, cerebral edema or contusion, ruptured organ, or compound or comminuted fracture) occurred from falls from this height. Severe injuries occurred in 11 patients who fell between 10 and 40 feet. One child died from a fall of 70 feet. These data again show that *falls of less than 10 feet are unlikely to produce life-threatening injury or death.*

A History of No Trauma With Evidence of Injury (Magical Injury)

In most cases of accidental injury, the history of trauma can be explained by a caregiver or a verbal child. Minor injuries, such as small bruises, minor scrapes, or lacerations, are often unexplained. The trauma associated with these injuries is often minimal and not remembered. It is important to distinguish between unwitnessed and inflicted trauma because not all accidental trauma is witnessed. Children may sustain injuries when they are out of sight of their caregivers. In cases of significant unwitnessed injury to preverbal children, the health care provider obtains historical details related to specific events surrounding the time of the injury. For unwitnessed trauma, determine the child's condition before and after the event. It is important to determine the position in which the child was found and to describe any changes in behavior after the incident, such as refusal to walk. The history also includes the sequence of events from the time of the injury until the child was taken for medical care. For example, a toddler fracture (spiral tibial fracture in a young child) may result from a simple fall (Mellick & Reesor, 1990). The caregiver states that the child ran into the next room, and the child soon screamed. He was found sitting on the floor, crying. After being held, he refused to bear weight on his leg. The caregiver sat him on the couch and gave him juice to calm him down. After an hour, he still refused to bear weight on his leg and was brought for medical evaluation. This scenario is consistent with the finding of a toddler's fracture.

Caregivers describe various scenarios to explain identified injuries. They may provide a false history or deny that the child sustained any trauma. It is the norm that children with significant injury have some history related to a traumatic event. Children with "magical injuries," that seemingly occur spontaneously, are likely to be victims of abuse. *In cases of unexplained injury, the suspicion of abuse generally increases as the age of the child decreases.* Infants in the first 6 months of life are not developmentally capable of self-inflicting significant trauma. Depending on the severity of injury and the age and developmental abilities of the patient, magical injuries may be either pathognomonic of abuse or just one factor to consider in evaluating for the possibility of maltreatment.

A History of Self-Inflicted Trauma Incompatible With the Development of the Child

The possibility of child abuse is considered when the history of trauma is discordant with the child's developmental abilities. Caregivers may claim that injuries to abused children are self-inflicted (or inflicted by peers or siblings). In some cases, the child is developmentally incapable of injuring him- or herself in the manner described. Therefore, knowledge of infant and child development is essential to the evaluation of pediatric injuries.

Children develop increasingly complex motor abilities during the first years of life. Although the acquisition of new skills follows a predictable sequence, the rate and, to some extent, the order in which children reach new developmental milestones vary (see Table 2.2). As infants and young children gain new motor skills, the risk of self-inflicted injury increases as they explore their environment.

Whenever there is a report of a child with a self-inflicted injury, the health care provider considers the compatibility of the child's development and the history of the injury provided. A history of self-inflicted injury requires careful evaluation. Most self-inflicted injuries in young children are minor, although serious and life-threatening injuries can occur. Toddlers, for example, can pull hot liquids off of stove tops or counters and can crawl out of unprotected windows (Barlow, Niemirska, Ghandi, & Leblanc, 1983; Finkelstein, Schwartz, Madden, Marano, & Goodwin, 1992).

A careful and detailed history is obtained to determine whether a child's developmental ability conflicts with the history of trauma. Always ask open-ended, nonleading questions that do not put words or thoughts into the mind of the history giver. The caregiver's ability to provide precise descriptions may vary, causing an erroneous suspicion of abuse. For example, a 1-month-old infant brought for medical care because of irritability after "rolling off the couch" is found to have a linear parietal skull fracture. The history is suspicious because of the apparent discrepancy between the "rolling" and the motor abilities of most 1-month-old infants. Further history reveals that the baby actually squirmed off the couch when the mother left him to answer the phone on the other side of the room. The history is now more reasonable with regard to the child's development and the suspicion of an inflicted injury lessened.

Caregiver Blame for Serious Injuries on a Young Child

Caregivers may falsely ascribe an injury to an incident with a sibling or young child in an attempt to protect themselves. Verbal children are sometimes coerced into blaming a sibling for an injury out of fear of losing a parent or of further injury if the truth is discovered. On occasion, a child may seriously injure a sibling. Rosenthal and Doherty (1984) report 10 preschool children who either seriously injured siblings or attempted to do so. They described skull and leg fractures, extensive bruising, lacerations, and stab wounds. Although siblings do fight and injuries can result, serious or life-threatening injuries are not commonly attributable to young children. Children with multiple or serious injuries are not often injured by another young child, and the possibility of abuse should be raised in this situation.

In some cases, an injury inflicted by a child can be distinguished from that of an adult. For example, bite marks are sometimes abusive injuries that are blamed on young children. The size of the bite arc and the individual teeth can often differentiate adult and pediatric bites (Barsley & Landcaster, 1987). (See Chapter 8 for further discussion of bite marks.)

History of Injury Changes With Time

It is common for an abusive caregiver to provide a false history of injury or illness and to expand or change the history. *Documented histories that change over time increase the suspicion of abuse and support the diagnosis.* However, to obtain a complete and detailed history, the health care provider asks for detail and clarification of confusing statements. The caregiver of a seriously injured child initially may be overwhelmed and too upset to provide a coherent, detailed history. More detailed information obtained later during the evaluation may be misinterpreted as a changing history.

Delay in Seeking Treatment

Caregivers who have abused a child sometimes delay a medical visit until the injuries have partially resolved. Some children are brought for immediate medical care by either the abusive caregiver or an unrelated adult, whereas others are brought for care only when an adult uninvolved with the abuse recognizes the injury to the child. Some seriously injured children are never taken for medical care and may die of their injuries. The suspicion of abuse arises when there is a delay in seeking appropriate treatment.

There are a number of factors to consider in determining whether a delay in seeking care is reasonable. The more symptomatic the child is, the more of a concern a delay in seeking care becomes. For example, it is inappropriate to delay care in symptomatic children with life-threatening injuries such as severe closed head injury or abdominal visceral injury. Children with bone fractures may be symptomatic at the time of the injury, yet the seriousness of the injury may not always be recognized immediately. Some examples include clavicle fractures and "toddler's fractures," where the initial symptoms may be nonspecific. (See Chapter 4 for further discussion of fractures.)

In evaluating delayed treatment, it is important to ask about the child's behavior from the time of the injury. For example, a child with a broken tibia may refuse to walk on the leg or will limp and be in pain. It is suspicious when the history does not reflect these facts. Caregivers may delay seeking treatment when symptoms are nonspecific, as in young infants with closed head injury. In such cases, the history reflects a change in the behavior of the child and may help to date the injury.

A skull fracture may not be recognized for a number of days. The initial scalp hematoma associated with the fracture may expand so rapidly as to have a bony consistency. It is not until the hematoma softens that the caregiver feels the swelling and brings the child for care (Ludwig, 1993).

Caregivers may delay bringing a child for medical care until a home remedy fails to cure the patient. Burns that require medical attention are occasionally treated at home until they fail to heal or become infected. Not all of these burns are inflicted, although some professionals would categorize this type of care as neglectful. It must be noted that accidents due to neglect or lack of supervision are reportable as neglect on the part of the caregivers.

Finally, some caregivers do not bring an injured child for timely care because of true and/or perceived barriers to care. These include financial constraints, lack of transportation, work obligations, and child care problems (McCullock Melnyk, 1988). Although a delay in seeking care is often a flag for child abuse, each case is evaluated carefully with respect to all identified factors.

See Table 2.3 for an overview of the steps of the interview.

The Physical Examination

The purpose of the examination of the physically abused child is to identify trauma and injuries. It is important to maintain the child's modesty during the examination because it can be embarrassing for the child to be completely undressed. However, the whole body should be inspected with the child wearing an examining gown or by using appropriate draping. The examination proceeds from the least to most invasive procedure, saving the obviously injured areas for last. In severe injury, pediatric life support is instituted first and then followed by a systematic assessment of the trauma.

Table 2.3 The Interview Process at a Glance

I. Introductions
Determine how the caregiver is related to the child.
Obtain names, address, phone numbers of history givers and child
II. Narrative of the Child's Injury or Medical Problem (History is dependent on whether there is a history of trauma)
With history of trauma
Date and time of the injury
Who was with the child when the injury occurred?
Where did the injury occur?
What were the events leading up to the injury?
Did the caregiver witness the injury?
Did anyone else witness the injury?
What was the child's reaction to the injury?
What was the caregiver's response to the injury?
With no history of trauma
When was the last time the child appeared well?
When did the child become ill? How did the illness begin and progress?
Who was caring for the child when he or she first developed symptoms?
Who were the child's caregivers in the days (hours) before the child became ill?
What are the child's symptoms? How have the symptoms progressed?
Was the child given any treatment?
III. *Clarify* Any Confusing Statements/*Fill in* Missing Details
Upset or confused caregiver may add to or change details of the history.
Note any discrepancies in the history.
IV. Note Time Between Onset of Symptoms and Arrival for Evaluation
With excessive delay, note amount of time that reportedly has elapsed.
Reasons for the delay.
Caregiver treatment for the child prior to being seen.
Child's behavior since the injury (or onset of symptoms).
Reasons for bringing the child for care at this time.
V. Past Medical History
Child's general health, including prenatal and birth history.
Child's doctor.
Previous hospitalizations.
Previous injuries.
Treatment sites for previous injuries.
Immunization status
VI. Developmental History
Present developmental level.
Age of developmental milestones.
History of behavior problems.
School history, need for special education.
VII. Family/Social History
Family composition.
Health of family members.
Child's caregivers. Include those living both in and outside of the home.
Evidence of family stress.
Financial supports of the family.
Emotional supports for the caregivers.
History of domestic violence.
Screen for caregiver drug and alcohol use.
Previous involvement with social services.

Documentation of the physical examination includes a general description of the child, followed by plotted growth parameters. Record the location of each injury, and describe each in detail. Even minor injuries are important. Include in the description any appropriate negatives such as "abdomen was not tender," rather than using the phrase "within normal limits." Likewise, do not use the descriptor *normal* when more specific words or terms can be used. Document the color, size and shape of each bruise. Burn descriptions include location, size, patterns, lines of demarcation, and the approximate thickness of the burn. Use accurate terms such as *abrasions, lacerations, ecchymoses, hematomas,* and *scars*. Carefully drawn diagrams are a useful adjunct to written description. Standard forms that contain anterior and posterior line drawings of the body are helpful in documenting injuries (see Appendix 2.1).

The abuse evaluation emphasizes the following areas:

1. *Growth.* Measure the child's weight, height or length, and head circumference (when indicated) and record on a standard pediatric growth chart. If available, old growth points are plotted to evaluate the child's growth over time (see Chapter 7 for more detailed discussion).

2. *Skin.* Note bruises, burns, scars, or rashes and describe the injury in detail. Record the following characteristics of bruises: the measured size, location, pattern (if applicable), and color. Note the precise location of burns, including small splash marks, lines of demarcation, or patterns identified.

3. *Head.* Palpate for areas of swelling, bogginess, or cephalhematomas. Note step-offs or depressions overlying fractures. Observe for avulsed hair and bruises. Feel the fontanel to assess for increased intracranial pressure. It is often difficult to see scalp bruising because of the overlying hair. The scalp can be examined further during hair shampooing if the patient is admitted to the hospital.

4. *Ears.* Note bruises to the outer ear, and check behind the ear for Battle's sign (bleeding in the subcutaneous tissue of the mastoid area due to a basilar skull fracture). Note the presence of foreign bodies and the condition of tympanic membranes. Examine the middle ear for blood (hemotympanum) or infection.

5. *Eyes.* Note evidence of direct trauma such as edema, scleral hemorrhage, hyphema, or bruises. Assess scleral color, because blue sclera is associated with osteogenesis imperfecta (see Chapter 4). A fundoscopic examination is an essential part of the workup of an infant or young toddler who has sustained a shaking or impact injury, because up to 80% of these patients have retinal hemorrhages (Levin, 1990). It is not always possible to see the fundus well. A complete examination by an ophthalmologist is essential. Indirect ophthalmoscopy by an ophthalmologist is indicated as soon as possible in children

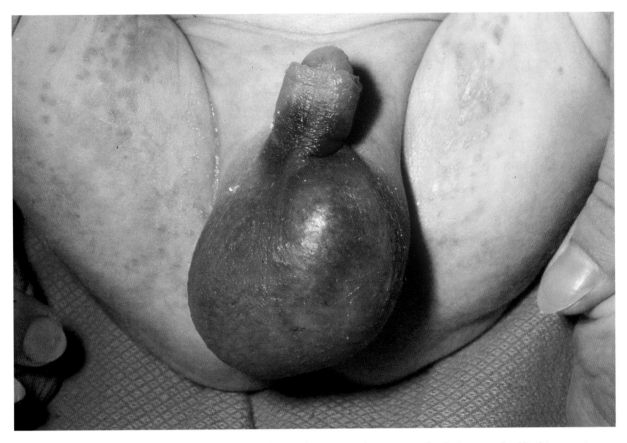

Photo 2.1. Thirteen-month-old child with a swollen, ecchymotic right scrotum after being punched by his caregiver.
Note: Photo courtesy of Dr. Howard Snyder.

suspected of a shaking injury, and unexplained changes in CNS status as hemorrhages may result in 24 to 72 hours.

6. *Nose.* Examine for edema, nasal bleeding, septal deviation, foreign bodies, and CSF rhinorrhea.

7. *Mouth/pharynx.* Examine for evidence of trauma. Labial or lingular frenulum lacerations (tears of the tissue that connects the gums to the midline of the upper or lower lips or the tongue to the base of the mouth) are pathognomonic of child abuse in young infants. Older infants and young toddlers can sustain these injuries accidentally by falling and hitting their mouth. The patient's teeth should be examined for trauma and caries (see Chapter 8).

8. *Chest/cardiac/lungs.* Feel for signs of healing rib fractures. Assess for tachycardia, murmurs, flow murmurs secondary to anemia, and signs of cardiac instability.

9. *Abdomen.* Listen for bowel sounds. Assess for indications of abdominal trauma, including abdominal tenderness, guarding, and rebound tenderness. Look for bruises, burns, or patterned marks.

10. *Back.* Look for bruises and unusual midline masses (which may represent vertebral injuries).

11. *Genitals/anus/rectum.* Assess for signs of trauma, including erythema, bleeding, bruising, bite marks, lacerations, abnormal anal tone,

and signs of infection. Retract labia majora and minora and assess external structures. Note Tanner Stage of development. (See Photo 2.1.)

12. *Extremities.* Assess for soft tissue swelling, point tenderness, and function.

13. *Neurologic.* For patients with significant trauma, the Glasgow Coma Scale provides a quick assessment of neurologic impairment (modifications in the scale are made to account for the abilities of infants and children). A neurologic exam to evaluate for focal deficits and to assess for cerebral or spinal injury is indicated in all children with possible head trauma.

14. *Development.* A developmental screening examination is done if the child is clinically stable.

See Table 2.4 for an overview of the physical examination.

Indicated Laboratory/ Diagnostic Evaluation

The historical and examination findings of the physically abused child guide the laboratory evaluation. *Laboratory and diagnostic tests help support or confirm the diagnosis of abuse and evaluate medical problems that can imitate abuse.* In cases of multiple system trauma resulting from abuse, laboratory data provide further evidence against alternative medical diagnoses. Cases of serious physical abuse sometimes will result in criminal prosecution. It is the responsibility of the medical caregivers to rule out illnesses that a jury or judge may believe would result in the injuries. This can be done by considering all of the medical findings and explaining why traumatic injury is the only reasonable explanation. Specific tests to rule out other causes may add credibility to the testimony. In addition, there are medical diagnoses that imitate child abuse, and part of the thorough evaluation of a child who presents with trauma is to evaluate for alternative medical explanations when clinically indicated.

The laboratory and diagnostic evaluation of the abused child varies depending on the age of the patient and the presenting injuries, and it is tailored to the clinical situation. The following tests are commonly performed when indicated in the evaluation of abuse.

Radiographic Skeletal Survey

A skeletal survey is a series of X-rays taken of the injured child to detect occult or healing fractures. Some fractures identified by skeletal survey in infants and young toddlers are specific enough to diagnose child abuse even without a clinical history. *A skeletal survey is indicated in all infants and children less than 2 years of age who are suspected of being physically abused.* Occult or clinically silent fractures are unusual in the older abused child, and therefore the skeletal survey generally is not a useful screening tool for chil-

Table 2.4 The Physical Examination at a Glance

Life support for children with life-threatening injury.
Growth (plotted on standard pediatric growth charts)
    Weight
    Length (height)
    Head circumference (infant, toddler—up to 2 years old)
Skin
    Describe injuries:
        Size (as measured with a millimeter ruler)
        Location
        Color
        Pattern
    Note signs of malnutrition and/or dehydration.
Head
    Look for bruises.
    Feel fontanelle.
    Search for avulsed hair.
    Palpate for signs of injury.
Ears
    Look for bruising.
    Check for Battle's sign.
    With otoscope, look for hemotympanum.
Eyes
    Assess scleral color.
    Examine for external eye trauma.
    Fundoscopic examination.
    Ophthalmology consultation for children with suspected shaking impact
      syndrome.
Nose
    Examine for trauma and CSF rhinorrhea.
Mouth
    Examine for injuries:
        Lips
        Frenula
        Teeth
        Palate and pharynx
Neck
    Look for bruising, strangulation marks.
    Feel for tenderness.
    Assess range of motion.
Chest/lungs
    Look for bruises.
    Auscultate heart and lungs.
    Palpate for rib fractures.
Abdomen
    Look for bruising.
    Auscultate for bowel sounds.
    Palpate for masses, hepatosplenomegaly, tenderness.
    Rectal examination when indicated.
Back
    Look for bruises.
    Look and palpate for midline masses.
Genitals/anus/rectum
    Look for erythema, bruising, lacerations, bleeding, discharge.
    Assess for abnormal anal tone, internal injuries (when indicated).

(continued)

Table 2.4 Continued

Extremities
    Look for bruises.
    Feel for tenderness, fractures, joint pain.
    Assess function.
Neurologic
    Glascow Coma Scale.
    Neurological examination.
Development
    Assessment done if child is stable.

Table 2.5 The Skeletal Survey

A full skeletal survey includes the following radiographs:
    Anteroposterior (AP) view of:
        Humeri
        Forearms
        Hands
        Femurs
        Lower legs
        Feet
        Chest/ribs
        Pelvis
    Lateral view of the axial skeleton (in infants)
    AP and lateral views of the skull
The radiographs must be monitored for technical adequacy.
Additional films, such as oblique views, may be needed.

Source: The American Academy of Pediatrics (1991).

dren over the age of 5. For toddlers between the ages of 2 and 5, the decision to do a skeletal survey is based on the clinical findings and suspicion of bony injury.

A skeletal survey is the method of choice for imaging the bones in cases of suspected physical abuse. The American Academy of Pediatrics Section on Radiology issued guidelines for skeletal surveys in 1991 (The American Academy of Pediatrics, 1991) (see Table 2.5). All skeletal surveys should consist of a series of X-rays, including anteroposterior views of the arms, forearms, hands, femurs, lower legs and feet, and lateral and anteroposterior views of the axial skeleton and skull, all on separate exposures. The skeletal survey should not consist of a single image of the patient's skeleton (babygram) because the detail is not sufficient to recognize subtle injuries. It is essential that the X-rays are read by a physician trained to recognize skeletal manifestations of child abuse. Some of the subtle but specific findings of abuse are missed easily by the untrained eye.

Radionuclide Bone Scan

The skeletal survey is the method of choice for imaging the bones in cases of suspected abuse. The bone scan is sometimes used as an adjunct to plain films. A bone scan is most often used in cases of suspected abuse of infants in which the skeletal survey is negative and more sensitive evaluation may diagnose the abuse with more certainty. A bone scan uses radioisotopes to identify areas of rapid bone turnover. It is more invasive and costly than a skeletal survey but more sensitive for detecting new (less than 7 to 10 days old) rib fractures, subtle diaphyseal fractures, and early periosteal elevation. A bone scan is not specific for fractures because a positive scan may indicate bone infection or tumor. Bone scans cannot be used to date fractures and do not identify skull or metaphyseal fractures reliably.

Computed Tomography (CT) Scan

CT scans are often an essential part of the child abuse evaluation. They are a series of radiologic images that provide sliced views through the area of the body scanned. CT scans of the head can identify manifestations of shaking impact syndrome, such as subarachnoid hemorrhage, most subdural hemorrhages, and cerebral edema and infarcts. A CT scan of the head is indicated in any infant or child that may have sustained significant head trauma. Unlike plain X-rays of the skull, CT scans provide images of the brain. Plain X-rays are more sensitive indicators of skull fractures and are the test of choice for evaluating such. CT scans of the chest and abdomen are the most sensitive and effective way to document injuries of the lungs and solid abdominal organs, such as the liver. CT scans are done under sedation because movement will cause artifact and potentially destroy the usefulness of the test.

Magnetic Resonance Imaging (MRI)

MRI scans provide sliced views through the body using interactions of hydrogen atoms with a magnetic field to provide an image of the scanned body in any plane desired. MRI generally is more sensitive than a CT scan and has the added advantage of being better able to identify subdural blood of different ages (Sato et al., 1989). MRI can be used instead of CT scans or as an adjunct to the CT scan. MRI is not universally available, is an expensive study, and takes longer to perform than does a CT scan. Presently, CT scan is typically the first method of imaging used in the acute setting, followed by MRI to further delineate injury or to evaluate injury that is highly suspected but not identified by CT.

Bleeding Evaluation

Some children who present with excessive bruising, in whom a hematologic condition is suspected based on history and physical examination, are screened for a bleeding diathesis. Both congenital and acquired bleeding disorders can present with excessive bleeding or bruising that may mimic child abuse (see Chapter 3). The standard screen done on the child with excessive bruising includes a complete blood count (CBC) with platelet count, a prothrombin time (PT), and a partial thromboplastin time (PTT). In the majority of cases, a thorough history and physical examination, along with normal screening blood work, will rule out medical problems that would cause bruising, including hemophilia, leukemia, idiopathic thrombocytopenic purpura, and others. If Von Willebrand's disease is suspected, a bleeding time is indicated. The CBC also evaluates for anemia, which may be due to blood loss, toxins such as lead, or nutritional abnormalities such as iron deficiency.

Toxicology Screens

Childhood ingestion of both legal and illegal substances is a common pediatric problem. Ingestion can be intentional, as with an adolescent drug overdose, or accidental, such as the toddler who ingests iron pills. At times, caregivers poison children knowingly, as in cases of Munchausen syndrome by proxy (Rosenberg, 1987), or somewhat less overtly, such as infants who passively inhale crack cocaine.

An infant or child with unexplained neurologic symptoms, such as seizures, lethargy, change in mental status, or coma, is evaluated with toxicologic screens and blood alcohol level. Urine, blood, and gastric content are available for screening. Variability exists among laboratories related to the drugs tested for on the standard toxicologic screen. See Chapter 8 for further discussion.

Tests for Abdominal Trauma

Recent studies have shown that abdominal injury as the result of abuse is underrecognized (Coant, Kornberg, Brody, & Edward-Holmes, 1992). Physically abused infants, toddlers, and children who are too ill to give a history of their injuries should be screened for possible abdominal trauma. Elevations in the hepatic transaminases (AST, ALT) suggest liver injury, and an elevated amylase and lipase suggest pancreatic injury. The screen for renal injuries includes a urinalysis to identify hematuria by dipstick and RBCs by microscopy. Occasionally, a dipstick will identify children with hematuria, but no RBCs are seen on microscopy. These children have either myoglobinuria or hemoglobinuria, which have both been reported as a result of abuse (Mukerji & Siegel, 1987; Rimer & Roy, 1977). Myoglobinuria indicates significant muscle injury. When measured in the acute setting, an elevated serum myoglobin, creatine phosphokinase (CPK), or urine myoglobin confirms the diagnosis (Schwengel & Ludwig, 1985). It is essential to order these screening tests immediately in the acute setting because these levels all rapidly return to normal. The tests described serve as a noninvasive, rapid way of identifying possible intra-abdominal injury. More extensive testing will be needed to characterize the extent and type of injuries identified by screening.

The above list represents common screening tests used in the evaluation of the abused child. Of course, each case is evaluated individually, and not all tests are necessary in every case. For some children, the history and physical examination are all that is

Table 2.6 Laboratory/Diagnostic Evaluation of the Physically Abused Child

Radiographic skeletal survey
    Method of choice for screening abused children for bony injury.
    For all children less than 2 years old with suspected physical abuse.
    Of limited use in children older than 5.
    For children 2 to 5 years old, use clinical findings.
Radionuclide bone scan
    Adjunct to skeletal survey.
    Most useful if there is high suspicion of bony injury and skeletal survey is negative.
Computed tomography (CT) scan
    Provides sliced views through internal organs, such as brain and abdominal organs.
    Essential part of the evaluation of seriously injured children.
    Initial test used for children with suspected shaking impact syndrome.
    Abdominal trauma.
Magnetic resonance imaging (MRI)
    More sensitive than CT for many injuries.
    Can provide images in multiple planes.
    Generally used as an adjunct to CT in the acute setting.
Blood tests for easy bruising/bleeding
    Complete blood count (CBC)
    Prothrombin time (PT)
    Partial thromboplastin time (PTT)
    +/- bleeding time
Screening tests for evidence of abdominal trauma
    Liver
        Alanine aminotransferase (ALT, SGPT)
        Aspartate aminotransferase (AST, SGOT)
    Pancreas
        Amylase
        Lipase
    Kidney
        Urinalysis
Toxicology screens
    For children with unexplained neurological symptoms or symptoms compatible with ingestion.
    Drugs tested for in "tox screen" vary among laboratories.
    Urine *and* blood and/or gastric contents are sent for screening.
    Consider blood alcohol levels for children with altered mental status.

needed to diagnose abuse (see Figure 2.1b). Critically ill or injured children will require extensive testing. The above serves as an introduction to the tests that are often used in the evaluation of suspected inflicted injury. Further information regarding laboratory testing is found in the chapters describing specific patterns of injury. See Table 2.6 for an overview of the laboratory/diagnostic evaluation.

Photographic Documentation

Photographic documentation of findings of abuse is part of the comprehensive evaluation and serves as an accurate record of a child's injuries (Ricci, 1991). Photographs are the only way to preserve physical findings that will undoubtably disappear as healing occurs. The diagnostic and treatment guidelines of the American Medical Association (AMA) recommend the photographing of all visible lesions. The benefits of photography in evaluation and description of abuse are multifold. Photographs facilitate review of the findings by multiple people, provide a standard for comparison during other evaluations, and are a valuable tool used in court to describe abusive findings and condition of the abused child (Ricci, 1991; Smistek, 1992).

Although photographs are an important documentation tool for injuries, they cannot be used exclusively and cannot replace the written and diagrammed description of the injuries. Cameras and photographers are not foolproof, and the techniques used to photograph the child, including the camera, film, lighting, and background, will affect the quality of the photograph. Some hospitals have a medical photography department whose employees can take photographs. Law enforcement agencies also have photographers adept at photographing injuries, crime scenes, and so on. However, many medical care facilities rely on the primary health care provider to obtain photographs.

The 35 mm camera is standard for photographic documentation. There are a wide variety of 35 mm cameras available, from "point-and-shoot" models, which tend to be the least expensive but offer limited close-up photograph capability, to expensive single lens reflex (SLR) cameras with multiple interchanging lenses and internal or ring flashes. The lens is the most important aspect of obtaining quality pictures. It is ideal to have macro or close-up capability (up to 0.25x) and medium telephotofocal length for minimal distortion (85-105 mm) (Ricci, 1991; Smistek, 1992).

Instant-processing photographs are available, but the resolution and the color of the photograph are poorer than with 35 mm cameras and may not provide useful documentation. Instant-processing cameras are used only if photographs are needed immediately, and 35 mm photographs should be taken along with the instant-processing photographs (Ricci, 1991; Smistek, 1992).

It is important that the photographer know how to use the camera and to have basic knowledge regarding photographing injuries, no matter which camera is used. Ricci (1991) identified errors made in the photographing of abused children and common reasons for the errors. These include blurry images (due to improper focusing or movement of the subject or camera), film that is not exposed (camera is loaded incorrectly), film that is overexposed or underexposed (incorrect setting of the aperture, film speed, shutter speed, or flash), and distorted photograph color (flash not properly used indoors).

Table 2.7 Photographic Documentation of the Abused Child

Equipment
    35 mm camera
        Single lens reflex (SLR)
        "Point and shoot"
        Avoid instant-processing cameras
    Electronic flashes are ideal
    Color film
    Color chart
    Ruler (to indicate injury size)
    ID of patient (by photograph and written record)
Technique
    Afar (indicates location of injury)
    Close-up (details of injury)
    Keep surface photographed parallel to the camera
    Multiple views of the injury
    Multiple exposures of each view

Source: Ricci (1991).

Proper lighting is most important in producing an accurate medical photograph because improper lighting can shadow or wash out bruises and misrepresent the child's injury. Electronic flashes are used routinely for medical photography to ensure proper illumination of the injury. Ring flashes are especially useful for uniform, shadowless illumination.

Thirty-five millimeter color slide film with ISO 100 or 200 is standard for medical use. Black and white film will not adequately document details of the injury. The injury is photographed both from afar and close up. The distant photograph shows the location of the injury on the patient's body, and close-up views show details of the injury. Photograph the surface of the injury parallel to the camera so that the injury does not appear distorted. Take multiple photographs to provide for proper representation of the injury. Identify the size of the injury on the photograph with a measuring device such as a ruler included in the photograph. Place a color chart in the field to ensure that the photograph accurately reflects the proper color of the injury.

Verification of identification for each photograph is accomplished by placing an identifying sign (e.g., child's name or medical record number) in the frame for each picture or using a camera databack to imprint time, date, and identifying mark (APSAC, 1995; Ricci, 1991). A photograph of the child's face is always included to establish the photographic record and identity link (Smistek, 1992). Finally, ensure identification of the patient by photograph and written record. Document in the medical record that photographs were taken and by whom. The photographs should be developed by a reliable laboratory and stored in a safe and retrievable location (see Table 2.7).

In Brief

- The medical evaluation of the abused child includes a history, physical examination, indicated laboratory and diagnostic studies, and observation of the caregiver-child interaction.
- A history of minor trauma that results in serious or life-threatening injury to a child should be suspect, and an evaluation for possible abuse should be performed.
- The recognition of abuse stems from the "building-block" approach, which synthesizes data from each part of the clinical evaluation to develop and confirm a suspicion of abuse.
- Knowledge of child development, mechanisms of injury, and the epidemiology of trauma is needed for proper diagnosis of child abuse.
- The diagnosis of physical abuse rests with the professional's ability to obtain a thorough history from the patient or family and to recognize discrepancies between the history and physical findings.
- The physical examination of the injured child should pay careful attention to subtle signs of trauma.
- Laboratory data and radiologic studies are important tools used to support the diagnosis of abuse and evaluate for medical conditions that may mimic abuse.
- Meticulous documentation of the history, physical examination, and laboratory data is an integral part of the evaluation of the abused child.
- If taken properly, photographs serve as an accurate record of a child's injuries.

Appendix 2.1

Forms Used by the Child Abuse Program at Children's Hospital in Columbus, Ohio (courtesy of Charles Felzen Johnson, MD, Director)

(See following pages)

Children's Hospital

700 Children's Drive
Columbus, Ohio

REPORT OF SUSPECTED PHYSICAL ABUSE

Children's
HOSPITAL
CHILD ABUSE PROGRAM

PATIENT IDENTIFICATION

Complete in Black Ink

DEMOGRAPHIC

CONFIDENTIAL
For Professional Use Only

ASSESSED IN:
❑ Emergency Department
❑ Family Development Clinic
❑ Teen-Age Clinic
❑ Inpatient Unit (specify)_____
❑ Other _____

Date of Exam: _____

Time of Exam: (military time)_____

Patient's Birthdate: _____

Patient's Name _____ Medical Record # _____
　　　　　　　　FIRST　　　　　MI　　　　　LAST

Address_____ Phone # (_____) _____
　　　　　　　STREET　　　　　　　　　　APT #

_____
CITY　　　　　　　　COUNTY　　　　　　　　STATE　　　　　　　　ZIP
Race:　❑ White　❑ Black　❑ Oriental　❑ Hispanic　❑ Combination　❑ Other _____　Sex: ❑ M　❑ F
Referral Source: ❑ private physician ❑ Children's Hospital, Columbus, OH ❑ child protection agency ❑ babysitter ❑ other medical facility
❑ police ❑ parent ❑ school/day care ❑ other _____
Regular Health Care Provided By: _____ Copy to Private Physician? ❑ Y　❑ N
Address _____ Phone _____

PRESENTING PROBLEM

History Provided by: : ❑ mother ❑ father ❑ stepmother ❑ stepfather ❑ social service worker ❑ other (specify)_____
Child being seen at request of: ❑ private physician ❑ Children's Hospital, Columbus, Ohio ❑ child protection agency ❑ babysitter
❑ other medical facility ❑ police ❑ parent ❑ school/day care ❑ other _____

History obtained by:

Print Name/Title_____ Signature_____

Print Name/Title_____ Signature_____

Child's Name _____ . _____

Medical Record Number_____ . _____

Complete in Black Ink.

PATIENT IDENTIFICATION

PHYSICAL EXAMINATION AND DOCUMENTATION OF INJURIES

Review of Systems   Normal _____

_____

_____

_____

Comments _____

_____

_____

_____

_____

T _____ P _____ R _____ BP _____ / _____

Weight _____ pounds/kgm ____ % Length _____ inches/cm _____ % H.C. _____ cm _____ %

General: _____

_____

_____

Behavior: _____

_____

_____

Norm.	Abn.	Not Exam.	COMMENTS	
❑	❑	❑	Head/Face/Hair	_____
❑	❑	❑	Eyes	_____
❑	❑	❑	Ears	_____
❑	❑	❑	Nose	_____
❑	❑	❑	Mouth/Throat	_____
❑	❑	❑	Teeth	_____
❑	❑	❑	Neck/Nodes	_____
❑	❑	❑	Chest/Lungs	_____
❑	❑	❑	Heart	_____
❑	❑	❑	Abdomen	_____
❑	❑	❑	Genitalia	_____
❑	❑	❑	Skin	_____
❑	❑	❑	Neurological	_____
❑	❑	❑	Extremities	_____
❑	❑	❑	Speech	_____
❑	❑	❑	Development	_____

Comments _____

_____

_____

FD-1 Report of Suspected Physical Abuse 2/94   RSpA 3/92 3/12

Evaluation of Abuse and Neglect

A. INJURY SHEET

Confidential: For Professional Use Only

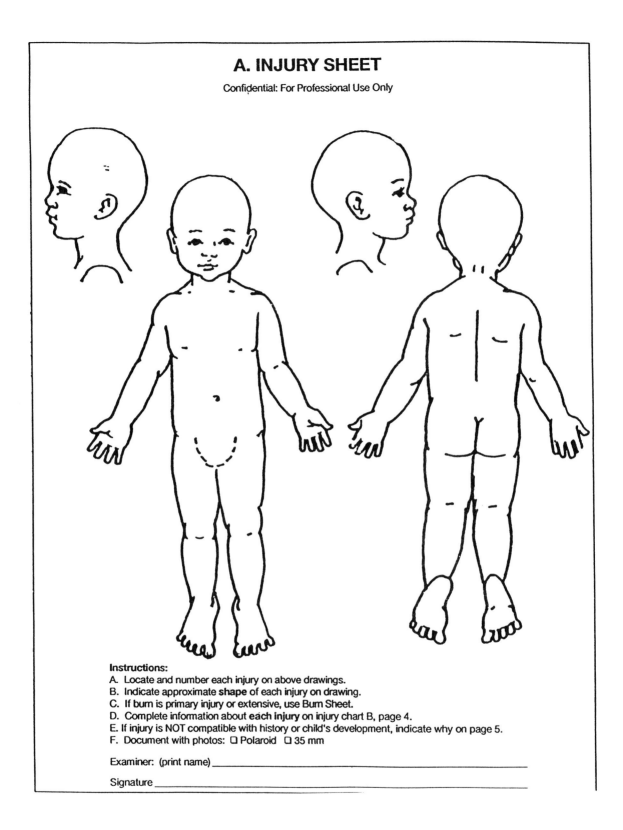

Instructions:

A. Locate and number each injury on above drawings.

B. Indicate approximate **shape** of each injury on drawing.

C. If burn is primary injury or extensive, use Burn Sheet.

D. Complete information about **each injury** on injury chart B, page 4.

E. If injury is NOT compatible with history or child's development, indicate why on page 5.

F. Document with photos: ☐ Polaroid ☐ 35 mm

Examiner: (print name) _____

Signature _____

Child's Name _____

Medical Record Number_____

Complete in Black Ink.

B. INJURY SHEET

PATIENT IDENTIFICATION

INJURY NUMBER	TYPE OF INJURY 1	SIZE	SHAPE	OBJECT 2	COLOR	OBSERVED AGE OF INJURY 3	STATED AGE OF INJURY 3	EXPLANATION BY: a) mother; b) father; c) child; d) other	IS INJURY COMPATIBLE WITH HISTORY?		
									Yes	No*	Uncertain

*If not compatible, why? (Comment by injury number. See page 6).
FD-1 Report of Suspected Physical Abuse 12/92

RSpA 3/92 5/12

C. COMPATIBILITY COMMENTARY

Injury Number	Comment: If injury **NOT** compatible, why?

1   Consider: abrasion, bruise, burn, erythema, fracture, laceration, puncture, swelling, bite, retinal hemorrhage, hemorrhage

2   Consider: belt, switch, electrical cord, rope, hand, fist, sharp object (knife), blunt object, burn (grid, liquid, caustic).

3   Determining the age* of a bruise or contusion:

DAY	1	2	3	4	5	6	7	8	9	10	13	21	28
	red/		blue					yellow-					
	blue		purple			green		brown			resolved		

Variables:

• Bleeding may be localized or diffuse. Loose tissue with poorly supported blood vessels, as is present in children especially in periorbital areas and external genitalia, is subject to extensive bruising.

• Contusion may not always appear at the site of impact. The arrangement of facial planes may prevent blood from reaching the skin surface at the precise point of the blow.

• A deep contusion may not come to the surface for hours or days after the injury.

• A particularly large or deep contusion may remain red or purple for days to weeks following the injury.

*Reference: Wilson, E.R.: Pediatrics, 60:

Child's Name _____

Medical Record Number_____

Complete in Black Ink.

PATIENT IDENTIFICATION

LABORATORY TESTS		Normal	Other
	_____ CBC*	_____	_____
	_____ Urinalysis	_____	_____
	_____ Platelet Count*	_____	_____
	_____ PT*	_____	_____
	_____ PTT*	_____	_____
	_____ Transaminase, LDH**	_____	_____
	_____ CPK***	_____	_____
	_____ X-rays (type)	_____	_____
	_____ Bone Survey	_____	_____
	_____ MRI	_____	_____
	_____ CT Scan	_____	_____
	_____ Other _____	_____	_____

*Ordered to rule out blood dyscrasia   **Ordered to rule out liver laceration. ***Muscle or brain damage.

MEDICAL TREATMENT AND PLAN

OTHER DIAGNOSES:

TREATMENT/RECOMMENDATIONS:

Consults to: _____ Orthopedics _____ Neurosurgery _____ Neurology _____ Surgery
 _____ Pedondontics _____ Ophthalmology _____ Other _____

Admitted to the Hospital? ❑ Y ❑ N If yes, which unit _____

Medical Follow-up: ❑ Y ❑ N Where _____When _____
 Where _____When _____

Psychological Follow-up: ❑ Y ❑ N Where _____When _____

D.O.A. Time_____ Coroner notified? ❑ Y ❑ N Autopsy? ❑ Y ❑ N

If autopsy performed, where: ❑ Children's Hospital ❑ Franklin County coroner
 ❑ Other (indicate)_____

Forms Attached: ❑ Nutrition ❑ Nursing ❑ Developmental ❑ Discharge ❑ Consultations

This form must be signed by licensed attending staff or PL2 or 3.

Physician's Signature _____

Print Name_____Phone_____

Child's Name _____ _____

Medical Record Number_____

Complete in Black Ink.

PSYCHOSOCIAL ASSESSMENT

I. Family Members In Home (at time of suspected abuse)

NAME FIRST	LAST	DOB/AGE	RELATIONSHIP TO CHILD	EDUCATION	EMPLOYMENT OCCUPATION
1.					
2.					
3.					
4.					
5.					
6.					
7.					

Child lives with: ❑ mother ❑ father ❑ step mother ❑ step father ❑ foster parent ❑ other _____

II. Significant Others

NAME FIRST	LAST	DOB/AGE	RELATIONSHIP TO CHILD	PHONE	ADDRESS
1.					
2.					
3.					
4.					

*Place asterisk beside the name(s) of those accompanying child to the hospital for assessment.

III. Suspected Perpetrator: Name _____DOB/Age _____

Info from: ❑ Child ❑ Mother ❑ Father ❑ Other_____. Info is reliable: ❑ Yes ❑ No

Relationship to child: _____ Caretaker of child?: ❑ Yes ❑ No

Sex: ❑ M ❑ F Race: ❑ B ❑ W ❑ Or ❑ Hisp ❑ Combo (specify)_____ ❑ Other _____

Employed: ❑ Yes ❑ No ❑ ? Occupation: _____

IV. Married Status of Biological Parents

Father: ❑ single ❑ married ❑ separated ❑ divorced ❑ remarried ❑ widowed ❑ unknown

Mother: ❑ single ❑ married ❑ separated ❑ divorced ❑ remarried ❑ widowed ❑ unknown

V. Name of Child's Legal Guardian: _____

VI. Child's School System: ❑ Columbus Public ❑ Other _____

Name of School_____ Grade _____

Teacher _____

Performance _____

_____

_____

_____

_____

_____

PATIENT IDENTIFICATION

IX. Identified Stress Factors: employment, illness, relationships'

X. Family Support Systems: include church affiliations, parents, friends, relatives

FD-1 Report of Suspected Physical Abuse 2/94

RSpA 3/92 11/12

VII. Pertinent Information: Circumstances of suspect abuse, how perpetrator had access to the child (if not apparent), disclosure, referral and previous interviews.

IX. Behavioral Observations: Parent-child interaction, parent affect, child's behavior while in the hospital

FD-1 Report of Suspected Physical Abuse 2/94

RSpA 3/92 10/12

XI. Community Referrals

*1. Child Protection Agency _____ Code # _____

Address_____ Contact Person _____

_____

Currently serviced: ☐ Yes ☐ No _____ Previous contact: ☐ Yes ☐ No

*2. Law Enforcement Agency_____

Address_____ Contact Person _____

_____

3. Other Agency Contacted _____

Address_____ Contact Person _____

_____

4. Private Physician _____

Address _____

_____

5. Family Support Program _____

XII. Recommended discharge planning:

Recommendations:

☐ Separate alleged perpetrator from child

☐ Emergency Court Order

☐ Protective Day Care

☐ Homemaker

☐ Public Health Nurse

☐ Counseling for child

☐ Counseling for parent

☐ Psychological or developmental evaluation of child

☐ Psychological evaluation of parent

☐ Other (specify) _____

Comments_____

_____

_____

_____

_____

_____

_____

_____

_____

_____

_____

XIII. Child discharged to:_____

Social worker's signature _____ Date _____

Print name _____ Phone _____

*Under Ohio Law (O.R.C. Section 2151.42) suspected child abuse/neglect (which includes non-organic F.T.T.) cases must be reported to the protective

agency and police (in county where abuse/neglect occurred).

FD-1 Report of Suspected Physical Abuse 2/94   RSpA 3/92 12/12

3 Skin: Bruises and Burns

Careful examination of the child's skin is an essential component of the abuse evaluation. Injuries to the skin are common findings in maltreated children and may include (a) contusions (bruises), abrasions, lacerations; (b) burns from scalding, direct contact with flame or hot objects, and electricity; (c) frostbite (O'Neill, Meacham, Griffin, & Sawyers, 1973); and (d) scars resulting from these injuries (Richardson, 1994). In one study examining the injuries of 616 children suspected of having been abused, at least 80% of the 775 primary injuries involved the skin, including (a) bruises/ecchymoses/hematomas (56%); (b) erythema/marks (9%); (c) burns (8%); and (d) abrasions/scratches (7%) (Johnson & Showers, 1985). Ellerstein (1979, 1981) noted the importance of cutaneous findings in maltreated children, because the recognition of these easily observed injuries by the child's relatives, neighbors, and schoolteachers may trigger contact with the health care provider. Health care providers evaluating children with suspicious skin findings need to consider physical abuse and/or neglect as a potential etiology and pursue a thorough evaluation.

O'Neill (1979) documented that soft tissue trauma, essentially skin injuries, are frequently the earliest and most common manifestation of physical maltreatment. He found that many seriously injured children had been evaluated previously for soft tissue injuries such as bruises and burns. Early recognition of minor injuries that may be inflicted may result in intervention and prediction of many serious injuries (O'Neill, 1979). In an epidemiologic study of injury variables, Johnson and Showers (1985) suggest that children with evidence of chronic maltreatment, such as nonhealed injuries of different ages, were at a 50% risk for further abuse and at a 10% risk for fatal injury.

This chapter focuses on the skin findings most commonly seen in both abused and nonabused children, namely, bruises and burns. Specific attention will be placed on the characteristics of these soft tissue injuries that suggest abuse and/or neglect. As in all cases of suspected maltreatment, the evaluation consists of a comprehensive history of the injury, a thorough physical examination, directed laboratory assessment, psychosocial assessment, and meticulous documentation.

Bruises

Overview   Bruises are common injuries in childhood, with all children from time to time having minor accidental bruising. Clinicians expect toddlers and young children to sustain minor bruising owing to the rough and tumble play that occurs during normal exploration and activity. A typical accidental bruise involves the skin overlying bony prominences such as the anterior tibia (shins), knees, elbows, forehead, and dorsum of the hands. Caregivers typically provide a history of noting the child's bruise after a bump or fall or of noting the bruise incidently during bathing or dressing the child. The child's physical examination may reveal other minor bruises in expected areas and no other injuries. Deviation from the typical childhood pattern of accidental bruising raises the health care provider's suspicion of possible child maltreatment.

Inflicted injuries to the child's skin also may cause bruising. However, patterns of abusive bruising overlap with "expected" patterns found in accidental bruising. Although inflicted bruises may be differentiated from accidental bruises by their location, age, shape, number, and severity, few bruising patterns are pathognomonic for child abuse (Sussman, 1968). Pascoe, Hildebrandt, Tarrier, and Murphy (1979) found that some lacerations were more likely accidental, whereas bruises to the relatively

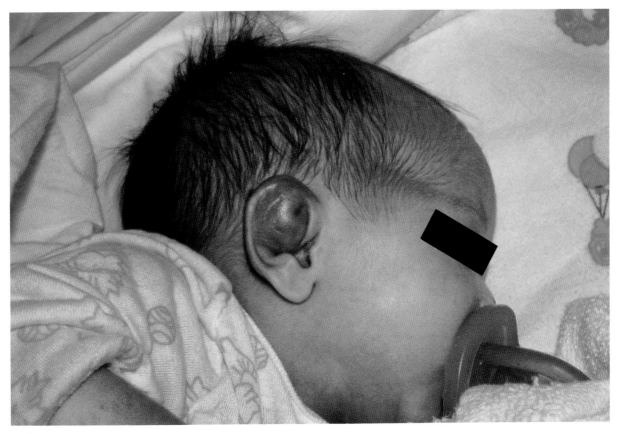

Photo 3.1.

Five-week-old with 1-week history of cough, vomiting, and recent ear swelling. Physical examination reveals large hematoma of the left pinna. This may lead to the later formation of a cauliflower, or boxer's, ear. Physical examination also revealed a torn labial frenulum and multiple healing rib fractures.

protected skin sites on the cheeks, neck, trunk, genitals, and upper legs were more frequently abusive in origin. Other bruising patterns that may raise concern for maltreatment include bruises in the young infant, multiple bruises of different ages, bruises and marks that have geometric shapes, and/or severe bruising that is not explained by the history provided.

Pathophysiology   A bruise or black-and-blue mark generally results from the application of a blunt force to the skin surface that results in the disruption of capillaries (and possibly larger blood vessels, depending on the force applied). As the bruise forms, subcutaneous blood leaks from the disrupted capillaries into the unbroken overlying skin (Wilson, 1977). A multitude of factors account for the size and depth of a bruise. These factors include (a) force of impact, (b) size of the disrupted blood vessels, (c) vascularity and connective tissue density of the injured tissue, and (d) fragility of the blood vessels involved (Ellerstein, 1979; Kornberg, 1992; Richardson, 1994). For example, the periorbital area is a well-vascularized tissue with relatively loosely supported blood vessels that may bruise extensively if subjected to blunt force.

The depth and location of the vessels and the arrangement of fascial planes in the surrounding tissue are also a consideration when assessing the extent and age of a bruise. Injury depth is a factor when the bruise appears. Relatively deep injuries may not be apparent for hours to days (Johnson, 1990; Langlois & Gresham, 1991). For example, a powerful blow applied to the thigh may result in injury to deep structures and may not be apparent for a day or two until bleeding from the deep vessels tracks toward the more superficial areas and becomes visible through the overlying unbroken skin.

Evaluation for Abuse

History   The evaluation of suspicious bruises begins with a history that includes the explanation of the injury, evaluation for medical conditions associated with easy bruisability or those that mimic bruising, and a history of prior allegations of maltreatment.

A. History of Injury
1. How and when was the bruising noted? By whom?
2. What is the explanation for the bruise(s)?
3. If age appropriate, what is child's explanation of the bruise?
4. Was the injury witnessed?
5. Was the bruise attributed to the child's self-injury or due to the actions of a sibling or playmate?
6. Is the explanation for the bruising implausible because of the age or developmental ability of the child?
7. Do explanations change over time, or are disparate accounts rendered by different caregivers?
8. If the injury is serious, is there a delay in seeking treatment after the injury? If so, why?
9. With a significant injury or suspicious bruising pattern, is there a lack of appropriate concern over the seriousness of the child's condition?

B. Medical and Family History
1. Does the child have a medical condition associated with easy bruisability or that mimics bruising? Is the child receiving any medications that might interfere with clotting?
2. Is there a history of unusual bleeding or bruising, such as extensive bleeding with circumcision, deep muscle bleeds

with immunizations, recurrent nosebleeds, or excessive gum bleeding with dental care?
   3. Is there a family history of any of the above?
C. History of Prior Maltreatment
   1. Is there a prior history of maltreatment or frequent visits for injury?
   2. Is the family known to social services for previous concerns of maltreatment?

An implausible history to explain the bruising should immediately alert the health care provider to the possibility of abuse. Basic knowledge of child development is essential in determining the plausibility of a history. For example, 6-month-old children are not developmentally able to climb onto furniture, raising the suspicion of abuse when the caregiver explains this as the cause of a baby's bruised back or neck (Kornberg, 1992).

Physical Examination
The physical examination of the bruised child includes a detailed description of each injury, identification of bruising patterns that are suggestive of abuse, and a search for other injuries. Bruises are potentially a subtle manifestation of more severe internal injury, especially in the infant or young toddler.

A. Describe Each Bruise Carefully
   1. Size of the bruise as measured with a millimeter ruler
   2. Location of the bruise
   3. Shape of the bruise (see below)
   4. Color of the bruise (see below for dating of bruises)
B. Bruising Patterns (note characteristics of the bruises identified)
   1. Do the bruises appear to be of different ages?
   2. Are the bruises in centrally located or protected areas?
   3. Do the bruises appear to be older or younger than disclosed in the history?
   4. Does the pattern of bruising differ from the history provided?
   5. Does the pattern of bruising suggest an inflicted mechanism (e.g., handprints, geometric shapes, loop marks)?
   6. Are multiple body surfaces bruised from a single episode of trauma?
C. Identification of Other Signs of Inflicted Injury
   1. Examine for underlying bone or internal organ injury.
   2. Assess for signs of physical neglect.

Shape

The shape of the bruise may help distinguish accidental from nonaccidental injury. A bruise may assume the shape of the

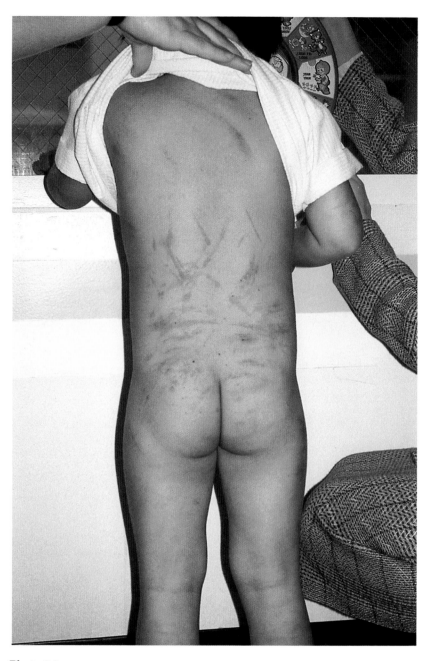

Photo 3.2.
Three-year-old girl beaten with a switch for not flushing the toilet.

object used to injure the child (Johnson, 1990) (see Figure 3.1). Identifiable marks may be left from corporal punishment using instruments such as a belt, cord, or paddle depending on how the instrument is held as it is used against the child's skin (Kornberg, 1992). A cord folded over and used to strike a child will customarily leave ecchymotic loop marks essentially pathognomonic for physical abuse. Restraint of a child's limbs during

CHILD PHYSICAL ABUSE AND NEGLECT

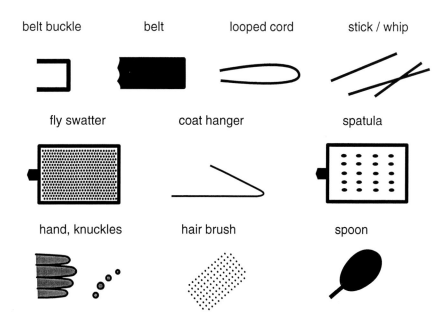

Figure 3.1. Marks left by objects on child's skin.

Common objects used to strike children that may leave identifiable shapes and patterns (Johnson, 1990). Used with permission.

abuse may cause circumferential wounds around the ankles and wrists (Kornberg, 1992). The perpetrator's hand may leave an impression upon the child's skin when sufficient force is used to either grab or slap the child (Kessler & Hyden, 1991). Bruises taking on the shape of objects are rarely accidental and require thorough investigation and protection of the child from further harm (Johnson, 1990; Kornberg, 1992; Richardson, 1994).

Dating of Bruises

Bruises undergo visible color changes as they heal. Although clinicians are frequently asked to "date" injuries based on the progression of color changes seen in bruised skin, current literature cautions the accuracy of the dating criteria (Schwartz & Ricci, 1996). Knowledge of bruise pathology and the basis for color changes helps practitioners understand the pathophysiologic process and provides reason for caution in trying to date the age of a bruise. Detailed color changes occur as a bruise progresses through various stages of healing (Richardson, 1994; Wilson, 1977). However, there may be no clearly predictable order or chronology of color progression in the healing process even though certain patterns seem to emerge (Schwartz & Ricci, 1996). However, after impact and until resolution, the bruise is a deep red, blue, or purple (Langlois & Gresham, 1991). Swelling is common for approximately 2 days until the serum is reabsorbed

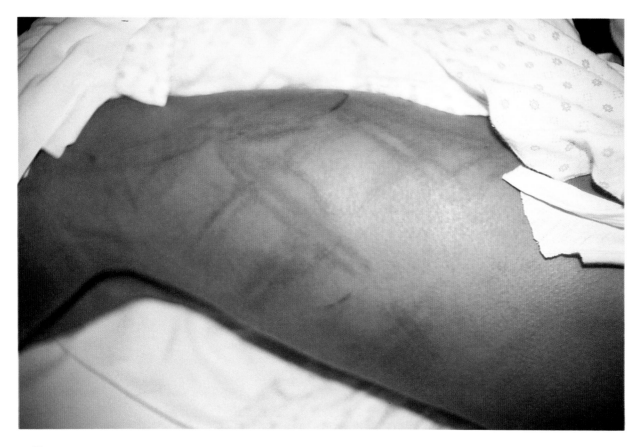

Photo 3.3.

Fourteen-year-old adolescent beaten by his father because of disciplinary problems in school. Child reported having his arms tied behind his back with an electric cord, being struck with a broom handle and cable, and being kicked multiple times. The child had extensive soft tissue injuries, including these cord marks. The CPK was greatly elevated, indicating underlying muscle injury.

(Richardson, 1994). With time, the blood collection separates into serum and a fibrin mass clot, and swelling decreases with the resorption of the serum from the injured area. Pigmented breakdown products of free hemoglobin, deoxygenated hemoglobin, biliverdin, and bilirubin are believed to account for the "play of colors" that the bruise undergoes over the next 2 to 4 weeks, as hemoglobin in the clot degenerates and is reabsorbed (Cotran, Kumar, & Robbins, 1989). The bruise may progress from a deep reddish purple to a more bluish color and then develop a greenish coloring that fades into a yellowish brown coloring prior to full resolution.[1] Bruises with yellow coloring are generally older than 18 hours (Langlois & Gresham, 1991), although yellow coloration may appear "earlier than most forensic charts indicate" (Schwartz & Ricci, 1996, p. 255). The amount of time for each color change to occur depends on the amount of blood involved, distance of the bruise from the skin, and baseline skin pigmentation of the individual (see Table 3.1). All combine to create the colors seen at the surface.

CHILD PHYSICAL ABUSE AND NEGLECT

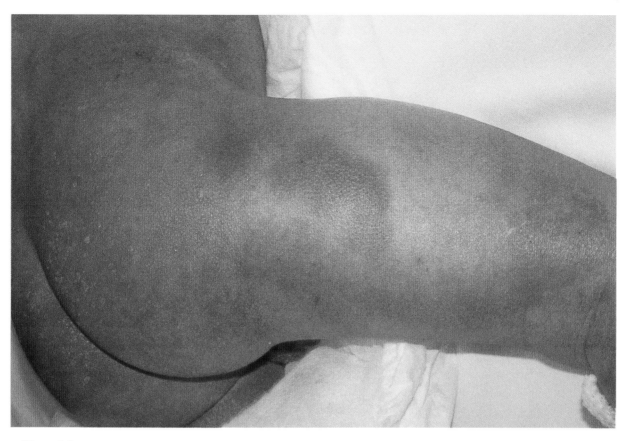

Photo 3.4.

Twenty-three-month-old with multiple injuries due to repeated abuse (see Photos 3.8 and 5.1). The child was brought for medical care by his mother for evaluation of "blisters on his legs." Shown here is a large, acute bruise to the right thigh.

Table 3.1 Color Changes for Bruises[a]

Skin color	Age in days (approximate)
Red-blue	1-2
Blue-purple	3-5
Green	6-7
Yellow-brown	8-10
Resolved	11-21

Source. Adapted from Wilson (1977) and Johnson (1990).

a. Please note that color changes are based on conflicting data and colors may not progress as stated because of variations such as force of impact, underlying tissues, and inherent differences in bruise pathology (Schwartz & Ricci, 1996).

Because of inherent limitation of efforts to estimate the age or date of injuries, Wilson (1977) suggests that clinicians document that the appearance of a bruise is *consistent with a given estimated age* rather than stating an exact age. Schwartz and Ricci (1996) caution that bruise literature does not support any certainty in determining the age of a bruise because of the varied factors in bruise development and the healing process.

Laboratory Evaluation

The clinician interprets the plausibility of the injury in conjunction with the past medical history, noted bruises, developmental factors, and laboratory data (Richardson, 1994). A child with bruising may not automatically require laboratory evaluation to assess for a hematologic disorder. However, it is important to focus on a screening history and physical examination for such disorders that guide the selection of indicated laboratory studies (Rapaport, 1983). After eliciting a thorough history and performing a complete physical examination, the health care provider may conclude that (a) the screening information is complete and consistent with normal clotting; no further workup is necessary; (b) the screening information is incomplete (or insufficient); further workup is necessary to ensure normal clotting; or (c) the screening information suggests a medical condition that is associated with easy bruisability or bleeding; further workup is necessary (Casella, 1990). Disorders of coagulation span a wide range of possible defects in hemostatic function, including (a) congenital and acquired abnormalities of platelet function, such as thrombocytopenia absent radius syndrome (TAR) and idiopathic thrombocytopenia purpura (ITP); (b) congenital and acquired abnormalities of coagulation factors, such as hemophilia (factor VIII deficiency) and vitamin K deficiency; and (c) congenital and acquired vascular abnormalities, such as hereditary hemorrhagic telangiectasia and a variety of vasculitides.

Screening for bleeding problems includes platelet count, prothrombin time (PT), partial thromboplastin time (PTT), and bleeding time. Additional tests are indicated for abnormal screens and are best obtained through consultation with a qualified pediatric hematologist. Regardless of how complex the workup becomes, tests are ordered based upon what the history and physical suggest rather than a random effort to exclude unlikely possibilities.

The Differential Diagnosis of Bruising

The differential diagnosis of a child who appears bruised includes accidental trauma; inflicted trauma (physical abuse); and a variety of dermatologic, hematologic, vasculitic, and infectious conditions, as well as congenital defects in collagen synthesis (Bays, 1994b; Coffman, Boyce, & Hansen, 1985; Davis & Carrasco, 1992; Ellerstein, 1979; Johnson, 1990; Kornberg, 1992; Richardson, 1994; Saulsbury & Hayden, 1985; Wissow, 1990a). In addition, folk-healing practices such as coining and others may cause bruising and raise the concern of possible abuse.

Table 3.2 Differential Diagnosis of Bruising

Dermatologic

Mongolian spots	—Slate blue patches of skin commonly seen in pigmented skin —Approximately 90% of African Americans have such spots —Congenital, commonly found on the lower back and buttocks (may occur anywhere) —Fade early in life (in most cases, completely faded by age 5 years) —Do not progress through the 2-week color sequence described for bruise healing (Tunnessen, 1990)
Hemangioma	—Visible vascular malformations —Capillary hemangiomas (strawberry marks), composed of capillaries —Congenital —Characteristic growth pattern: (a) rapid growth for approximately the first 6 months, (b) slowed growth paralleling the child's somatic growth until about age 3 years, and (c) involution with at least partial regression by age 6 years in more than 85% of cases (Pokorny, 1990)
Eczema	—Atopic skin condition —Reddened, dry areas on the child's skin —Pruritic, frequently associated with a family history for other atopic conditions such as asthma and hayfever, and occur episodically in "flares" —Responsive to topical steroids such as hydrocortisone

Erythema multiforme (EM)	—Acute hypersensitivity skin condition whose hallmark is red, targetlike lesions
	—Occurs in response to a number of drugs, foods, immunizations, and infections with both bacteria and viral agents (Cohen, 1993)
	—Severity of EM ranges from
	  —a minor form that is self-limited
	    to
	  —a major form, Stevens-Johnson syndrome, which has serious systemic consequences, involves mucous membranes, and manifests large areas of epidermal necrosis and sloughing
	—Variable in appearance, classically symmetric, may involve the palms and soles, and has variable lesions that typically progress from dusky red to a targetlike character occurring in crops and resolving in 1 to 3 weeks (Cohen, 1993)

Phytophoto-dermatitis	—Skin reaction to psoralens, chemical compounds found in citrus fruits such as limes —Skin in contact with psoralens upon exposure to sunlight manifests red marks that appear as bruises and, if severe, as burns —History contains information related to contact with psoralens followed by exposure to the sun (Coffman, Boyce, & Hansen, 1985)
"Tattooing"	—Dye from fabric such as denim discolors the child's skin, giving the appearance of a bruise; lightens or fades with rigorous washing —History should reveal contact with dyed fabric that became wet and "ran" (Tunnessen, 1985)

(continued)

As in all differential diagnoses, the history, physical examination, and laboratory assessment are crucial to the inclusion and exclusion of diagnoses and guide the assessment and workup. Bays (1994b) made a comprehensive review of the medical literature on conditions reportedly mistaken for child abuse. Note that children with medical conditions that cause easy bruisability tend

Table 3.2 Continued

Hematologic Disorders of hemostasis, congenital and acquired	
Hemophilia (Factor VIII & IX deficiency)	—A plasma coagulation disorder —In the neonatal period, cord separation or circumcision may result in prolonged bleeding (hemophilia; approximately 50% of affected males having such a bleeding history) —Bruising may become more pronounced as the child begins to cruise and walk, owing to falls and bumps —Bruising may have a nodular or firm consistency secondary to the deep bleeding into soft tissues seen in hemophilia —Hemophilia suggested by prolonged PTT —Consultation with a qualified pediatric hematologist necessary (Casella, 1990)
von Willebrand's disease	—Heterogenous group of disorders that results in decreased platelet adhesiveness, impaired agglutination of platelets in presence of ristocetin, and prolonged bleeding time —Patients have mild to moderate bleeding tendency typically involving mucous membranes —Easy bruising, nosebleeds, and prolonged bleeding after dental procedures are hallmarks (Casella, 1990)
Vitamin K deficiency	—May be secondary to malabsorption (e.g., cystic fibrosis) —Hemorrhagic disease of the newborn might be expected in an infant who failed to receive prophylactic Vitamin K at birth (Pearson, 1983). Breast-fed children born at home are most at risk. Presentation is typically in the first few days of life, and a high percentage occurs with a catastrophic intracerebral bleed (Bays, 1994b; Wetzel, Slater, & Dover, 1995).
Idiopathic thrombocytopenic purpura (ITP)	—Acute, usually self-limited —Platelets are peripherally consumed via an immunologic mechanism (Pearson, 1983) —Follows a viral illness in approximately 70% of cases —Petechiae and bruising are noted approximately 2 to 4 weeks after the minor illness resolves —Physical examination reveals petechiae or bruising, and normal lymph node, spleen, and liver size —CBC reveals a low platelet count —Resolution typically occurs in 8 to 12 weeks in more than 75% of cases
Leukemia	—Bone marrow becomes progressively infiltrated with neoplastic cells —Systemic signs and symptoms are typically present —CBC is markedly abnormal —Coagulation studies may also be aberrant depending on the stage of the illness
Anticoagulant ingestion	—Children may ingest anticoagulants from either medications in the household or those contained in commercial rat poison (Bays, 1994b; Johnson & Coury, 1988) —May be seen in MSBP (see Chapter 8)

to bruise most in common locations. Furthermore, children with hematologic or other medical conditions associated with bruising and bleeding are not immune to maltreatment (Johnson & Coury, 1988). Careful consideration of the possible conditions

Table 3.2 Continued

Vasculitis	
Henoch-Schönlein purpura (HSP)	—Palpable purpura and petechiae
	—Notable for (a) a variable purpuric rash that often involves the buttocks and lower extremities; (b) arthralgia/arthritis; (c) abdominal pain; (d) renal disease; and (e) occasionally subcutaneous, scrotal, or periorbital edema (Martin & Walker, 1990)
	—Tends to develop acutely, is usually self-limited, and runs its course over a 6-week period of time
	—Most common in children less than 7 years but older than 1 year
	—Up to 50% of affected children may have recurrences; these tend to be in older children.
	—Purpura without a low platelet count is essential for the diagnosis
Infections	—May be associated with the appearance of petechia and/or purpura (e.g., rickettsial disease)
	—Severe infections may result in complications such as disseminated intravascular coagulation (DIC) and purpura fulminans
	—History, physical examination, and laboratory evaluation confirmatory of serious infection
Collagen synthesis defects	
Ehlers-Danlos (ED) Syndrome	—Congenital defect in collagen synthesis, may lead to easy bruising
	—At least 10 forms are identified
	—Involves a variety of unique basic defects and inheritance patterns
	—Basic clinical triad that each variant shares to a greater or lesser extent: (a) skin hyperextensibility, (b) joint hypermobility, and (c) skin fragility
	—Consultation with an experienced clinical geneticist is recommended for children manifesting this triad (Zinn, 1994)
Osteogenesis imperfecta (OI)	—Congenital abnormality in quantity or quality of type I collagen synthesis
	—Heterogenous disorder with four subtypes
	—OI type I associated with easy bruising. Hallmarks include blue sclera, hearing impairment (35% of children after first decade), osteopenia, fractures, bony deformities, and excessive laxity of joints (Silence, 1983)
	—Punch biopsy of skin for analysis of collagen synthesis in children with repeat fractures when other s/s are not consistent with abuse (Bays, 1994b)
	—Consultation with metabolic specialist and geneticist required
Folk-healing practices	
Coining	—Described in Asian cultures as healing method
	—In coining, warmed oil is applied to the child's skin, which is then rubbed with the edge of a coin or a spoon in a linear fashion, usually on the chest or back
	—The repetitive rubbing leads to linear bruises and welts (Yeatman & Dang, 1980)
Cupping	—Described in Asian and Mexican cultures
	—In cupping, a cup is warmed and placed on the skin. A vacuum is created between the cup and the child's skin as the cup cools, which leads to a bruise (Sandler & Haynes, 1978)
	Coining and cupping are not done to injure the child but to comply with cultural beliefs that view them as necessary to help the child heal or recover from minor illnesses. Parental education is needed to assist the parent in understanding the injurious nature of these practices.

that mimic abuse serves the child's interests and prevents the misdiagnosis of abuse (see Table 3.2).

Burns

Overview

Burns represent a major public health problem for children. Each year, approximately 30,000 children are hospitalized for serious burns, and a significant number suffer disability, permanent disfigurement, and death (Ahlgren, 1990; Meagher, 1990). The mortality rate for burns ranks second behind automobile deaths and accounts for approximately 3,000 pediatric deaths each year in the United States. For burns involving more than 40% of body surface area, the mortality rate is close to 90% (Hathaway, Hay, Groothuis, & Paisley, 1993). Eighty percent of burn injuries occur in the child's own home, and approximately 10% to 25% of pediatric burns are a result of abuse (O'Neill, 1979; Purdue, Hunt, & Prescott, 1988). Mortality for accidental burns is approximately 2%, compared to a mortality rate near 30% for abusive burn injuries (Purdue et al., 1988). The number of children who suffer serious disability from burn injuries is approximately three times higher than the number of those who die from such injuries (O'Neill, 1979).

Burns, whether accidental or inflicted, occur more frequently in children under 5 years of age, with the highest incidence occurring in infants and toddlers under 3 years of age (Feldman, 1987; Johnson & Showers, 1985; Showers & Garrison, 1988). Burn injuries are classified as scalds (hot liquid), flame, contact (hot solid object), electrical, and chemical (Meagher, 1990). Scalding accounts for the majority of childhood burns, including both accidental and inflicted burn injuries, and accounts for 45% of all pediatric burn admissions (Ahlgren, 1990).

Pathophysiology

Human skin sustains injury from contact with heat. Human skin is composed of three layers: epidermis, dermis, and subcutaneous tissue. The deepest cells in the dermis are called the basal layer, and they serve to replenish the skin cells as they are sloughed or injured (see Figure 3.2). Cells that make up the skin contain protein and enzymes that function within limited temperature ranges. Permanent damage to the skin occurs when the proteins are subjected to temperature extremes that cause denaturation and an inability of the cellular mechanism to function.

At the cellular level, burn injuries consist of three concentric zones of affected tissue (Jackson, 1953; Robson & Heggers, 1988) (see Figure 3.3). The first zone consists of skin that has the most direct contact with the heat source. This area, known as the zone of coagulation, undergoes immediate coagulation necrosis with denaturation of proteins and no potential for cellular repair. Cells in the second zone, the zone of stasis, are exposed to direct injury from the heat source but retain some ability to repair themselves. Tissue in this zone is ischemic, and cells usually necrose in 1 to 2 days after the injury unless the burn is treated properly. Finally, cells in the third zone, called the zone of hyperemia, have sustained minimal direct injury and usually recover from insult over a 7- to 10-day period.

As cells die in the various zones, they release inflammatory mediators that may lead to further progression of injury. Furthermore, necrotic tissue that accumulates within the wound provides an excellent growth medium for microorganisms that have an adverse effect on the healing process.

Burn injuries are classified by the depth of the skin injured. The size of a burn is calculated as a percentage of body surface area involved. The depth of burns has historically been described as first-, second-, third-, and fourth-degree burns. Currently, the terms *superficial, partial,* or *full thickness* are used to describe the depth of the burn. Partial thickness burns are further classified as either superficial partial thickness (not to be confused with the simple "superficial" burn described above) or deep partial thickness.

A superficial burn, analogous to a first-degree burn, is the least severe. A common example is sunburn. The burned area involves only the uppermost layers of the epidermis and presents as reddened, painful skin without blister. Within a few days, the superficial layers of injured skin slough and heal as healthy cells are produced from the underlying skin cells. No scarring is expected from a superficial or first-degree burn.

A partial thickness burn, analogous to the second degree burn, causes blistering of the skin and is painful because nerve endings are exposed. Partial thickness burns are deeper than the simple superficial burn and extend past the epidermis into the dermis. Because of blood vessel disruption, these burns have a beefy red appearance. Depending on the depth of dermis involved, the partial thickness burn may be categorized further as either a superficial partial thickness or deep partial thickness burn. The superficial partial thickness burn extends just past the epidermis and minimally involves the dermis. The deep partial thickness burn is more extensive and goes deeper into the dermis. Healing in partial thickness burns progresses as healthy cells deep in the dermis replenish injured cells. Superficial partial thickness burns usually heal completely in approximately 2 weeks if infection does not occur. The deep partial thickness burn may heal in 3 to 4 weeks. Healing of partial thickness burns may result in scarring and hypertrophic changes, especially with deeper injury. Deep partial thickness burns may compromise the dermis's basal layer of cells and progress to a full thickness burn injury if not treated

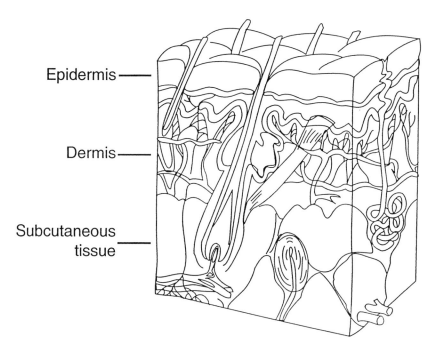

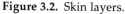

Figure 3.2. Skin layers.

The skin is divided into layers. The uppermost or most superficial layer is the epidermis. The dermis is deeper, is composed mainly of structural proteins, and contains skin appendages such as hair follicles, sweat glands, and nerve endings. These appendages contain reserves of skin cells that serve to aid in the healing process after injury. Finally, the subcutaneous tissue layer serves as an underlying support structure composed of fibrous bands and fat.

properly. Thus, observation over several days is necessary prior to final classification of burn depth.

A full thickness burn (analogous to third and/or fourth degree depending on depth of involvement) is the most severe and extends through the entire skin surface, past epidermis and dermis to underlying tissues such as subcutaneous tissue (third degree) or muscle and bone (fourth degree). The entirety of the overlying skin has been destroyed, including the basal layer of the dermis. Full thickness burns present as white and anesthetic because of complete destruction of blood vessels and nerve endings. Such a profoundly injured area cannot regenerate its own skin cells. Healing occurs through inward growth of skin from tissues surrounding the wound or surgically by way of skin grafting from nonburned areas of the body. Significant scarring and disfigurement occur as the full thickness burn heals.

Burns and Abuse

Inflicted burns have been recognized since the early years of professional inquiry into child maltreatment (Gillespie, 1965).

CHILD PHYSICAL ABUSE AND NEGLECT

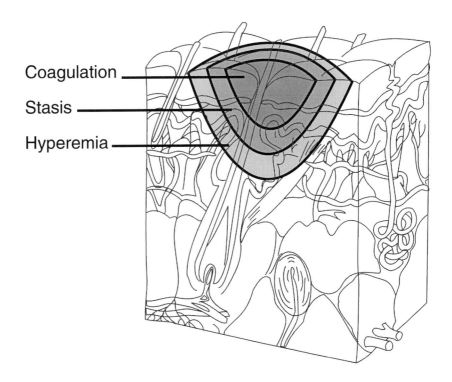

Figure 3.3. Concentric zones of thermal injury.
The zone of coagulation is the area in most direct contact with the heat source and sustains irreparable damage. Extending outward is the zone of stasis, which, although injured, retains some ability for cellular repair. Finally, the zone of hyperemia is the least injured area and has the greatest likelihood of repair and healing. (Adapted from Robson & Heggers, 1988.)

Although estimates vary depending on the population studied, approximately 10% of children hospitalized for burns are believed to have sustained inflicted injury (Feldman, 1987; Meagher, 1990; Purdue et al., 1988). These children tend to be young and have a higher mortality than do comparable children who were accidentally burned. Although few burn mechanisms are pathognomonic for abuse, certain patterns have a higher association with abuse than do others. For example, tap water scalds are more commonly seen in abusive burns than in accidental burns.

Investigators have studied specific historical and physical patterns associated with inflicted burns (Ayoub & Pfeiffer, 1979; Hammond, Perez-Stable, & Ward, 1991; Hight, Bakalar, & Lloyd, 1979; Keen, Lendrum, & Wolman, 1975; Lenoski & Hunter, 1977; Stone, Rinaldo, Humphrey, & Brown, 1970) and have developed criteria that raise the suspicion of abusive burns. These criteria include

1. Implausible history to account for burn based on child's development, age of burn, and/or pattern of burn identified on examination

2. No history for burn provided by caregivers because child was "found" with the burn (magical injury)
3. Caregiver responsible for child at time of burn not present with child during medical evaluation
4. Burn attributed to sibling or playmate
5. Patterns of burns that imply restraint during burn injury
6. Unexplained delay in seeking treatment
7. Other suspicious injuries, such as bruises and scars of varying age and at different stages of healing
8. Evidence of neglect, such as poor hygiene or malnutrition
9. History of prior injury

Scalds

Scalding is the most common mechanism of burn injury for abused children who are admitted to the hospital (Showers & Garrison, 1988). Scalding occurs when a hot liquid comes in contact with the child's skin. Some hot liquids responsible for scalds are (a) boiling water; (b) tap water; (c) waterlike liquids, such as tea or coffee; and (d) thicker liquids, such as soups or grease. Scald burns are classified as (a) splash/spill (hot liquid falls, is poured on, or is thrown at child); (b) immersion (child falls into or is submerged in hot liquid); and (c) forced immersion (pattern of burn suggests that restraint was used to plunge and hold child in the hot liquid).

Splash/spill burns may occur either in an accidental or in an inflicted manner. Overlap exists in the physical findings for both mechanisms of injury. Accidental scalds often occur in kitchen accidents as a child explores his or her environment and reaches unknowingly for containers of hot liquid that have been left within reach. Pots of boiling water and cups of hot beverages are likely culprits in such accidents. An accidental mechanism of injury is expected to give rise to a typical burn pattern. For example, if the child is looking up and reaching for a container, the hot liquid will fall first upon the child's cheek, neck, shoulder, upper arm, and upper chest. This area will be most severely burned, and as the spilled liquid runs down the body, it cools and leaves a less severe injury going outward from the points of initial contact (see Figure 3.4). Clothing holds the hot liquid in close contact to the skin, which makes the burn more severe. As the liquid falls on the child, splash marks may also appear as droplets of the hot liquid fall upon the child in other areas separate from the point of maximal contact.

Splash/spill burns also may occur in an abusive manner. Hot liquids may be poured or thrown at the child. Depending on the circumstances, the injury pattern of the burn may help differentiate an inflicted burn from an accidental spill/splash burn. For example, if a child is running from a perpetrator, the liquid may be thrown at his or her back and give rise to a burn pattern that is inconsistent with a history of the child looking up and pulling a pot of boiling water on top of him- or herself. However, if the

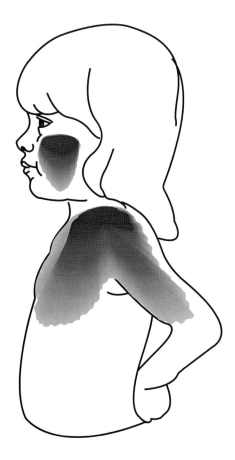

Figure 3.4. Typical spill burn pattern.

The typical pattern for a spill burn where a child reaches up and pulls a container of hot liquid on top of him- or herself. The hot fluid usually falls onto the child's face and shoulder first, causing the most severe burn at the point of initial contact (expressed by the darkest shading). As the liquid runs down the body and cools, the burn becomes narrower and less severe at the perimeter (expressed by lighter shading).

perpetrator pours the hot liquid on top of the child, the injury pattern may be similar to that described for the accidental burn and may not be useful in identifying the abusive origin of the injury. Other aspects of the medical evaluation will be necessary to diagnose abuse in such a case where burn patterns overlap.

Immersion burns occur when parts of the child's body become submerged in a hot liquid, and the burns may be accidental or inflicted. Such burns are commonly seen in abusive burning. Abusive immersion burns may occur at any age but are more common in infants and toddlers. For example, a typical immersion burn occurs when the child is held vertically by the arms or upper torso and then immersed in the hot water. In this scenario, the toes and feet come in contact with the hot water first. The child reflexively withdraws his or her lower limbs by flexing the knees and hips and assuming a cannonball-like position. The caregiver then immerses the genitals and buttocks.

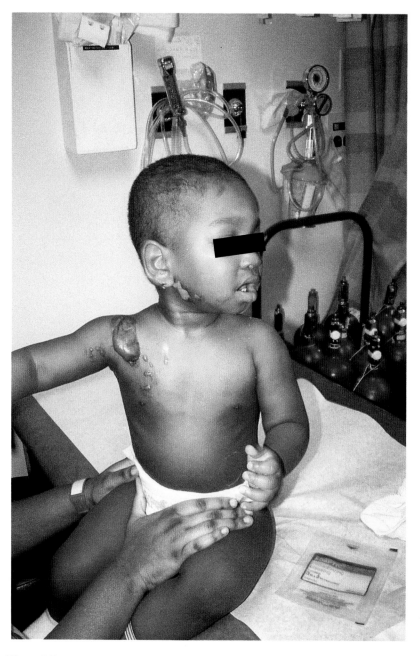

Photo 3.5.

Two-year-old with accidental second-degree burns to the neck, shoulder, and chest. Chicken noodle soup spilled on the child when he bumped into his older sister, who was carrying the soup.

Depending on the size of the child and the depth of the water in the container, the child's feet and lower legs are burned, the flexed knees may be spared of burn, and the buttocks and genital area are also burned. Distinct lines of demarcation will separate

CHILD PHYSICAL ABUSE AND NEGLECT

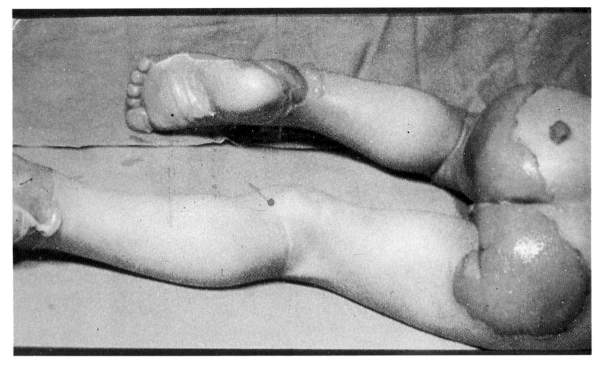

Photo 3.6a.
Two-and-a-half-year-old with acute, 2° immersion burns to the buttocks and feet. Note that the soles of the feet appear less severely involved. This is due, in part, to the thickness of the skin in that area.

the burned from nonburned areas, and splash marks may be limited. Such inflicted immersion burns are often related to toileting accidents or other activities that dirty a child and require that the caregiver clean the child. The pattern of burn injury described above would be inconsistent with an accidental injury, such as would occur if the child wandered over to and fell into a tub of water, or if the child was playing in an empty tub and turned on the hot water faucet.

A forced immersion burn has a pattern of injury that is consistent with the child being restrained by the perpetrator while submerged in the hot liquid. Forced immersion burns are among the most severe and extensive burns seen in abused children. A forced immersion pattern of injury occurs when the caregiver holds the child in such a way that certain areas of the skin are forced against the relatively cooler surface of the container or tub and are protected from the more extensive burn sustained by the skin that is in full contact with the hot liquid (see Figure 3.5). For example, this pattern results when a child is plunged into scalding hot water and is held in such a way that his or her buttocks are forcibly held against the relatively cooler tub bottom. In this scenario, the scalding water surrounds the

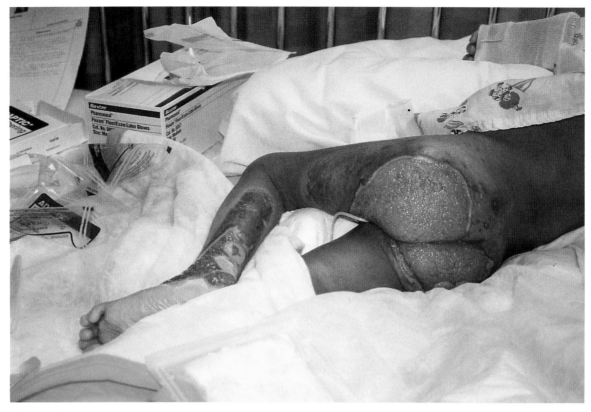

Photo 3.6b.

Two-and-a-half-year-old with severe immersion burns to buttocks and feet. Note evidence of previous, healed immersion burns to the same areas. The child was not taken for medical care until she presented with severe brain injury. Skeletal survey revealed a healing supracondylar fracture of the right humerus.

submerged skin while the buttocks skin in contact with the bottom of the tub is somewhat spared. Therefore, the resulting burn that is less severe on the buttocks manifests as the so-called hole in doughnut sparing pattern. In addition, as the child is forcibly held in the water, areas of skin that are held tightly opposed, such as in the femoral areas, may be spared as well because the hot water may be unable to seep into this space to burn the skin. The resulting burn shows thermal injury where the water was in contact with the skin and relative sparing where the hot water was unable to come in contact with the skin.

Stocking and glove burns are circumferential burns of lower and upper limbs that are another pattern of immersion burns pathognomonic of abuse. An extremity submerged in hot liquid causes a burn of the distal aspect of the extremity that has a clear line of demarcation separating the uniformly burned area from the nonburned area. Symmetric stocking and glove burns are highly suspicious for inflicted burn injury because few plausible histories could explain why a child would submerge both extremities equally into a hot liquid.

CHILD PHYSICAL ABUSE AND NEGLECT

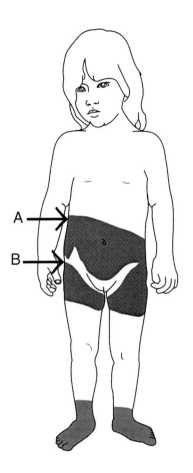

Figure 3.5a. Forced immersion burn.

As the child's buttocks are plunged into the hot liquid and held against the porcelain tub, the child instinctively flexes the hips. The burn is well demarcated (A). The crease between the thigh and abdomen is spared (B).

Tap Water: A Special Case

Tap water burns are associated with accidental, neglectful, and inflicted injuries. Injury prevention literature discusses the danger to children as well as to debilitated adults that is posed by hot tap water, depending on the temperature of the water and the duration of exposure (Baptiste & Feck, 1980). Early research done in the 1940s outlined the temperatures and duration of exposure at which adult skin suffers burns (Moritz & Henriques, 1947). The adult's thicker skin and the child's thinner skin are at significant risk for scalding injuries from a variety of common household sources. Home water heaters are set at temperatures that deliver water to the faucet that is between 120°F (49°C) and 150°F (65°C) (Erdman, Feldman, Rivara, Heimbach, & Wall, 1991). Comfortable water temperature for bathing occurs at approximately 101°F, and hot tubs are typically set at 106 to 108°F (Feldman, 1987). Water becomes painfully hot at 109 to 118°F. Adult skin can tolerate being

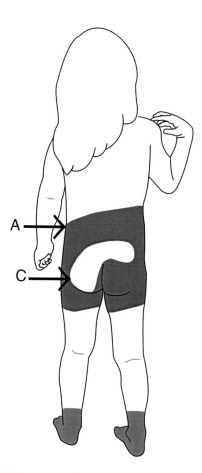

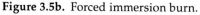

Figure 3.5b. Forced immersion burn.

The area of the buttocks that is held against the relatively cooler tub is less severely burned and gives rise to the "hole-in-a-doughnut" pattern (C). The child's heels may come in contact with the hot liquid, and the burn is well demarcated (A).

in water at a temperature of 113°F for approximately 6 hours prior to sustaining a partial thickness burn (Feldman, 1983). Higher temperatures produce burns in shorter time periods. Adult skin placed in water that is at 127°F would suffer a full thickness burn in approximately 1 minute. At three degrees higher, 130°F, only 30 seconds of exposure causes a full thickness burn, and a full thickness burn occurs in only 2 seconds at 150°F (Feldman, 1987; Moritz & Henriques, 1947) (see Table 3.3 and Figure 3.6). Feldman (1987) notes that a child's thinner skin would suffer similar burns in a shorter period of time. It is recommended that home water heaters be set at 120°F to reduce the frequency, morbidity, and mortality of tap water burns in children (Erdman et al., 1991).

Contact Burns   Contact (or dry) burns are another type of burn seen in physical abuse cases (Feldman, 1987). A dry burn occurs when the child's skin is placed in contact with a hot object, such as an

Table 3.3 Effects of Water Temperature

Water temperature	Effect
101° F	Comfortable for bathing
106-108° F	Typical hot tub temperature
109-118° F	Pain threshold for adult
113° F	Partial thickness burn in 6 hours
127° F	Full thickness burn in 1 minute
130° F	Full thickness burn in 30 seconds
150° F	Full thickness burn in 2 seconds

Source: Adapted from Moritz and Henriques (1947) and Feldman (1987).

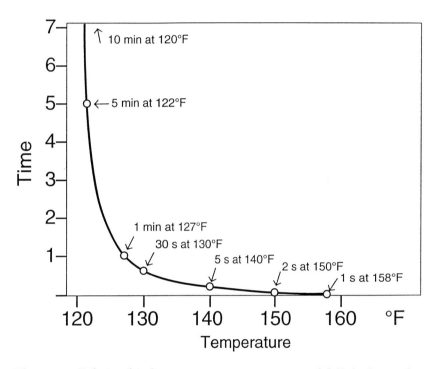

Figure 3.6. Relationship between water temperature and full thickness skin burns.

Graphic representation demonstrating the relationship between water temperature and the amount of skin contact time needed to result in a full thickness burn. (Adapted from Moritz & Henriques, 1947 [with permission]; Katcher, 1981; Richardson, 1994.)

iron or heating grate (Feldman, 1987; Lenoski & Hunter, 1977). The resulting burn frequently forms in the shape of the hot object being touched (see Figures 3.7 and 3.8). Whereas inflicted contact burns are often geometric, accidental burns tend to be less geometric in shape because of the more glancing, brief contact between the exposed body part and the hot object (Feldman, 1987). For example, cigarette burns have different charac-

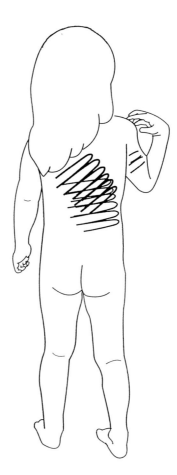

Figure 3.7. Contact burn.
The child is held against a hot object such as a heating grate, which leaves a characteristic pattern.

teristics depending on whether or not they are accidental or inflicted. Accidental cigarette burns occur when the child brushes up against a lit cigarette. This causes a glancing contact, with the child quickly retracting from the cigarette as his or her skin senses the heat, and it results in an irregularly shaped, superficial burn. Inflicted cigarette burns occur as the lit cigarette is forcibly held in contact with the child's skin. This gives rise to a uniform depth and a diameter of approximately 8 to 10 mm. Impetigo, a common bacterial skin infection, may be confused with cigarette burns. Impetigenous lesions are frequently of different sizes, are associated with crusting, and, if necessary, can be cultured for bacteria. Electrical, flame, microwave, and chemical burns also may be inflicted upon a child. Although these are less common modes of injury, any child sustaining such injury requires careful evaluation.

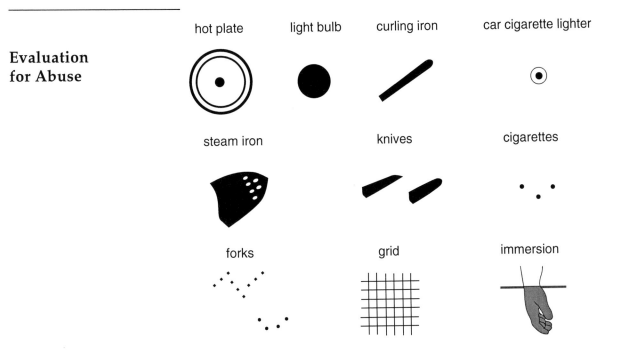

Figure 3.8. Hot objects that may brand a child.
Common hot objects that may leave identifiable shapes and patterns (Johnson, 1990). Used with permission.

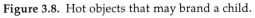

The history and physical examination are important in determining if abuse or neglect is the cause of the child's burn. The child's developmental ability, plausibility of the explanation, rapidity of seeking treatment, and extent and characteristics of the burn are important aspects of the evaluation of the child.

History

In all possible abuse cases, the history elicited from the caregiver, and from the child if verbal, is vital to the evaluation for maltreatment. The responses of the caregiver(s) to the health care provider's questions are noted and considered in the diagnostic process. Table 3.4 lists questions that are asked when a child has been burned.

*Physical
Examination*

The physical examination may offer clues in addition to the presenting burn to suggest the possibility of abuse. Table 3.5 lists the areas assessed in the physical examination.

*Indicated Laboratory
Assessment*

The diagnosis of a burn is essentially a clinical diagnosis. No specific laboratory or diagnostic study is indicated to diagnose a burn. Specific laboratory or diagnostic tests may be indicated depending on the severity of the burn or other diagnostic possibilities suggested by the history or physical examination.

Table 3.4 Evaluation of History of Burned Child

History of injury
    How did the burn occur?
    How did child come in contact with burning agent?
    Who noted the burn?
    For how long was child in contact with burning agent?
    Was skin covered or uncovered?
    Was the child taken for medical care immediately?
    What is the reason given for any delays in seeking treatment?
    Was the child taken for care by an adult other than the one supervising the child at the time of the burn?
        Why?
    Was the burn "magical"? (Child was discovered burned and no one saw the actual situation.)
    What was the child's reaction to being burned? (cried, etc.)
    Was the burn attributed to the actions of a sibling, playmate, or the child him- or herself?
    Is explanation of the burn implausible because of the age or developmental ability of the child, the age of
        the burn, or the pattern of the burn?
    Do the explanations change over time, or do different caregivers render differing accounts?
    What is the caregiver's reaction to the situation? (Is there a lack of appropriate concern over the
        seriousness of the injury?)
    What is the temperature of tap water in the house?
    Was the water standing or running?
Medical history and examination
    Does the child have a medical condition that mimics burning?
    What is the location and configuration of the burn?
    How deep is the burn?
    Are there other signs of abuse?
History of prior maltreatment
    Is there a prior history of maltreatment or frequent visits for injury?
    Is the family known to social services for previous concerns of maltreatment?

Table 3.5 Physical Examination for Burns

A. Description of each burn
    1. Type of burn(s): superficial, partial (either superficial or deep), full thickness
    2. Amount of body surface area (BSA) involved (Use Figure 3.9 for this estimation in the pediatric
       patient)
B. Burn characteristics and pattern
    1. Do burns appear older than disclosed in history?
    2. Is the distribution of the burn consistent with the history provided?
       a. Burn incompatible with the events as described (e.g., cigarette burn in normally clothed area, burn
          on area different from what would be expected to burn, isolated perineal and genital burns)
    3. Note signs of restraint
       a. During immersion in hot fluid (stocking and glove demarcation on extremities, sparing of flexure
          areas)
       b. Implausible splash marks or lack of them
       c. "Hole-in-doughnut" pattern
C. Identification of other signs of inflicted injury
    1. Presence of injuries such as bruises, fractures, or other burns of differing ages
    2. Evidence of maltreatment such as scars or malnourishment
    3. Injuries related to restraint such as multiple bruises mimicking fingers and hands on upper
       extremities (Ayoub & Pfeiffer, 1979)

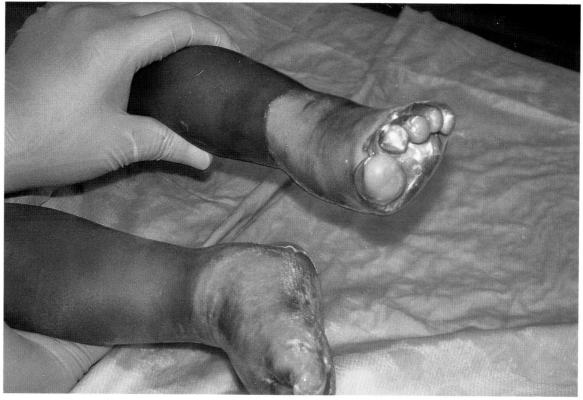

Photo 3.7.
Twenty-month-old child whose feet got dirty and reportedly was left to soak her feet in a basin of warm water. Stocking burns of the feet to both ankles are due to submersion in scalding water.

Differential Diagnosis of Burns

The differential diagnosis of a burned child includes accidental injury, inflicted injury, a variety of dermatologic and infectious disorders, and folk-healing practices (Bays, 1994b; Davis & Carrasco, 1992; Ellerstein, 1979; Johnson, 1990; Kornberg, 1992; Richardson, 1994; Wissow, 1990a) (see Table 3.6).

The history, physical examination, and, to a lesser extent, laboratory assessment guide the assessment and workup and are crucial to the inclusion and exclusion of possible diagnoses. Comprehensive reviews of the medical literature exist on conditions reportedly mimicking burning (Bays, 1994b; Saulsbury & Hayden, 1985). It is uncommon for children to have such medical conditions. Furthermore, children with disorders that may be confused with burns are not immune to maltreatment (Bays, 1994b; Johnson & Coury, 1988). Careful consideration of the possibility of conditions that mimic abuse serves the child's interests and avoids the misdiagnosis of abuse (see Table 3.6).

Table 3.6 Differential Diagnosis of Burns

Condition	Comments
Accidental burns	—May be difficult to differentiate from abusive burns —In one report, children were accidentally placed in contact with hot automobile upholstery, which subsequently burned their skin (Schmitt, Gray, & Britton, 1978). History and physical examination should support the caregiver's explanation of what took place prior to and at the time of the burn.
Dermatologic 　Epidermolysis bullosa (EB)	—Group of blistering skin conditions that vary in terms of inheritance pattern, presentation, histopathology, and biochemical markers and may mimic burns (Cohen, 1993) —Characteristic feature is the development of blisters and erosions in response to mechanical trauma —Congenital presentation for some of the milder forms may be later in onset, and discovery of some may not be until later childhood or even in adulthood (Tunnessen, 1990)
Dermatitis herpetiformis	—Chronic, recurrent papular skin condition that is generally symmetric in distribution —May be mistaken for cigarette burns if the lesions are excoriated and become hemorrhagic (Fitzpatrick, Polano, & Suurmond, 1983) —Lesions tend to be small, clustered in groups, and intensely pruritic, and they are frequently found symmetrically distributed on the extensor surfaces of the extremities, buttocks, back, and abdomen —Confirmed by biopsy and response to dapsone (Cohen, 1993)
Miscellaneous	—Dermatitis, such as seen with a severe diaper rash mimicking the denuded skin seen in scald burns —Chemical burns from contact of the skin with irritating chemicals, such as analgesic creams —Drug eruptions may have the appearance of a burn —Phytophotodermatitis, in addition to the red, bruiselike lesions discussed above, may also give rise to a blistered appearance
Infections 　Impetigo	—Superficial bacterial infection of the skin typically caused by *staphylococcus aureus* or group A beta-hemolytic streptococcus —Lesions tend to begin as pustules and then form crusts —Lesions are of different sizes —Local adenopathy is common, lesions tend to spread locally and are pruritic, and other family members may be affected —Lesions respond to oral or topical antibiotics and heal without scarring —Differentiate cigarette burns from streptococcal impetigo; cigarette burns cause scarring (Richardson, 1994)
Folk-healing practices 　Coining	—The skin may be eroded, causing linear lesions resembling burns
Cupping	—The cup may be overheated, causing circular burns to the child's skin
Moxibustion	—A variant of acupuncture in which sticks of incense or other material are burned near or on the skin at specific therapeutic points —The skin may become reddened, or if the heat is too intense, actual burning may result (Feldman, 1984) Parental education is necessary in these cases to help engage parents in less injurious health care practices.

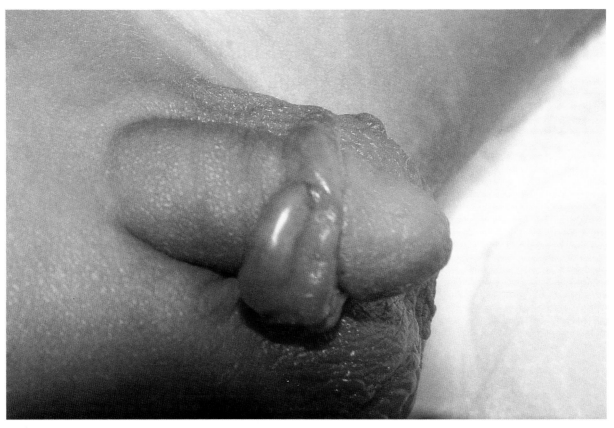

Photo 3.8.

Twenty-three-month-old with multiple injuries due to repeated abuse (see Photos 3.4 and 5.1). Shown here is an acute burn to the distal penile shaft. The child also had acute "stocking" burns to both feet and shins.

Treatment: Overview

The treatment and management of children who have burn injuries is complex. The reader is referred to medical texts that offer comprehensive discussion of such burn-related care (Fleisher & Ludwig, 1993; Purdue & Hunt, 1992).

When presented with any child who has a burn, whether or not in the context of maltreatment, the health care provider initially determines if the burn injury is (a) minor, (b) major, or (c) critical (Ahlgren, 1990). Initial treatment strategy depends on the extent and severity of the burn as well as the stability of the patient. The extent of the burn is based on an accurate assessment of the amount of the child's body surface area (BSA) that has been burned. Figure 3.9 offers one approach to calculating the BSA in children. Superficial burns (first degree) are not included in the BSA calculation.

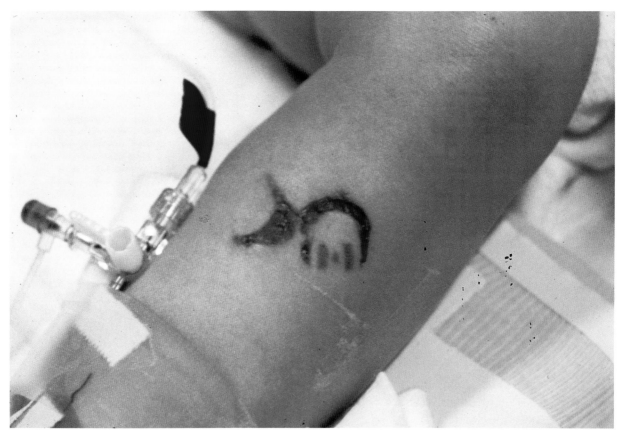

Photo 3.9a.

Child brought to hospital with seizures. Patterned burn to the leg is due to a disposable lighter (Photo 3.9b). Seizures were due to severe head injury.

Critical Burn   A critical burn is the most severe and, in general, involves more than 30% of the child's BSA and/or has an associated inhalation injury. The ABCs of cardiopulmonary life support may be required. This is a life-threatening situation, and the skills of a trained burn specialist/trauma surgeon are required. Referral to a regional burn center is recommended.

Major Burn   A major burn involves more than 10% of BSA or is at least 2% full thickness. Children with major burns require hospitalization after initial treatment. Initial management includes (a) attention to ABCs, (b) fluid management, (c) analgesia, (d) wound debridement and dressing, and (e) tetanus prophylaxis. Antibiotics are used to treat infection; prophylactic antibiotics are generally discouraged.

Hospitalization may be indicated in children with less than major burns if they are under 2 years of age and/or have burns involving face, hands, perineum, or feet (Meagher, 1990). Of

CHILD PHYSICAL ABUSE AND NEGLECT

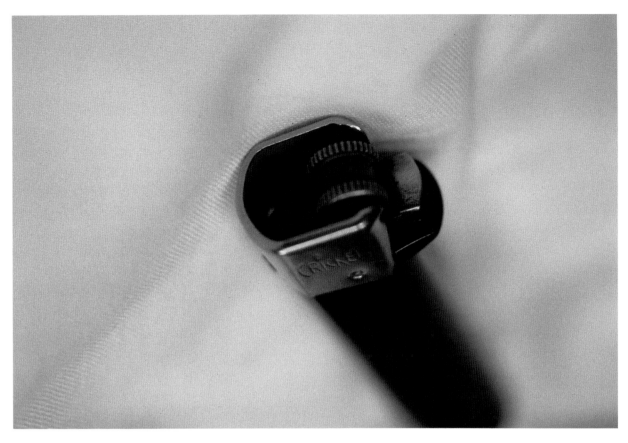

Photo 3.9b.
Child brought to hospital with seizures. Patterned burn to the leg is due to a disposable lighter. Seizures were due to severe head injury.

particular concern are circumferential burns of the extremities and chest, which may require emergency escharotomies.

Minor Burns   Finally, minor burns are those that involve less than 10% of the BSA and are less than 2% full thickness. After evaluation and initial management, minor burns may be treated in the outpatient setting with exceptions for the following situations: (a) children under 2 years; (b) burns on the face, hands, feet, and/or perineum; and (c) if abuse is the cause. Initial management includes (a) cooling the burn with water or ice; (b) careful cleansing of the wound with sterile saline, leaving blisters intact; (c) wound dressing with silver sulfadiazine; (d) tetanus prophylaxis; (e) no routine antibiotics; and (f) close follow-up with scheduled revisit in 24 to 48 hours. At the revisit, dressing supplies may be prescribed if the burn appears to be healing and no signs of infection are present. Periodic reassessment by the clinician is suggested to adequately monitor compliance.

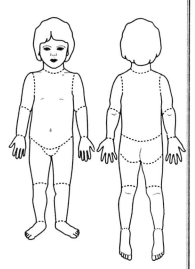

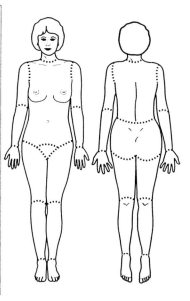

Patient information

Name _____

Date of Birth _____

_____

_____

_____

_____

Burn Record

Date _____

Height _____ Weight _____

2° _____ + 3° _____ = _____ %

Percent surface area burned (Berkow)

▨ Partial thickness ■ Full thickness

AREA	1 YR	1-4 YRS.	5-9 YRS.	10-14 YRS.	15 YRS.	ADULT	2°	3°
Head	19	17	13	11	9	7		
Neck	2	2	2	2	2	2		
Ant. trunk	13	13	13	13	13	13		
Post. trunk	13	13	13	13	13	13		
R. buttock	$2\frac{1}{2}$	$2\frac{1}{2}$	$2\frac{1}{2}$	$2\frac{1}{2}$	$2\frac{1}{2}$	$2\frac{1}{2}$		
L. buttock	$2\frac{1}{2}$	$2\frac{1}{2}$	$2\frac{1}{2}$	$2\frac{1}{2}$	$2\frac{1}{2}$	$2\frac{1}{2}$		
Genitalia	1	1	1	1	1	1		
R.U. arm	4	4	4	4	4	4		
L.U. arm	4	4	4	4	4	4		
R.L. arm	3	3	3	3	3	3		
L.L. arm	3	3	3	3	3	3		
R. hand	$2\frac{1}{2}$	$2\frac{1}{2}$	$2\frac{1}{2}$	$2\frac{1}{2}$	$2\frac{1}{2}$	$2\frac{1}{2}$		
L. hand	$2\frac{1}{2}$	$2\frac{1}{2}$	$2\frac{1}{2}$	$2\frac{1}{2}$	$2\frac{1}{2}$	$2\frac{1}{2}$		
R. thigh	$5\frac{1}{2}$	$6\frac{1}{2}$	8	$8\frac{1}{2}$	9	$9\frac{1}{2}$		
L. thigh	$5\frac{1}{2}$	$6\frac{1}{2}$	8	$8\frac{1}{2}$	9	$9\frac{1}{2}$		
R. leg	5	5	$5\frac{1}{2}$	6	$6\frac{1}{2}$	7		
L. leg	5	5	$5\frac{1}{2}$	6	$6\frac{1}{2}$	7		
R. foot	$3\frac{1}{2}$	$3\frac{1}{2}$	$3\frac{1}{2}$	$3\frac{1}{2}$	$3\frac{1}{2}$	$3\frac{1}{2}$		
L. foot	$3\frac{1}{2}$	$3\frac{1}{2}$	$3\frac{1}{2}$	$3\frac{1}{2}$	$3\frac{1}{2}$	$3\frac{1}{2}$		
TOTAL								

Figure 3.9. Pediatric burn body surface area (BSA) calculation.

As the child grows, the relative percentage of certain body parts changes. In calculating the body surface area that is burned, it is important to correct for these changes. This chart assists in determining an accurate calculation based on the child's age. (Courtesy of Gary F. Purdue, MD, Co-Director, Burn Center, University of Texas, Southwestern Medical School)

In Brief

- Examination of the child's skin is among the most important components of the suspected physical abuse and neglect evaluation.

- The history, physical examination, and laboratory assessment guide the assessment and workup of bruises and burns.

- The most common soft tissue injuries associated with physical abuse and neglect are bruises and burns.

- The differential diagnosis of a bruised child includes accidental trauma; inflicted trauma (physical abuse); a variety of dermatologic, hematologic, vasculitic, and infectious conditions; and congenital defects in collagen synthesis (Bays, 1994b; Davis & Carrasco, 1992; Ellerstein, 1979; Johnson, 1990; Kornberg, 1992; Richardson, 1994; Wissow, 1990b).

- Injuries to relatively protected areas such as the genitals, buttocks, proximal extremities (thighs, upper arms), neck, and back are suspicious of abuse (Richardson, 1994).

- A bruise may take on the shape of the object used to injure and then heal with a scar that preserves the shape of the object (Johnson, 1990).

- The history of a child who presents with bruising is an important part of the clinician's attempt to differentiate accidental from nonaccidental trauma.

- Attention to the pattern of injury helps the health care professional differentiate bruises caused by abuse from those that occurred accidentally.

- The differential diagnosis of a burned child includes accidental or inflicted injury, dermatologic and infectious conditions, and folk-healing practices (Bays, 1994b; Davis & Carrasco, 1992; Ellerstein, 1979; Johnson, 1990; Kornberg, 1992; Richardson, 1994; Wissow, 1990b).

- Scalds are the most common mechanism of burn injury found in children hospitalized for maltreatment.

- Mortality from burns ranks second behind automobile deaths and accounts for approximately 3,000 deaths each year in the United States (Ahlgren, 1990; Meagher, 1990).

- Approximately 4% to 10% of children hospitalized for burns are believed to have sustained abusive injury (Feldman, 1987; Meagher, 1990).

4 Evaluation of Fractures and Skeletal Injuries

General Principles

The identification of a skeletal injury may be the first indication of abuse. Estimates of the frequency of fractures in abused children vary from approximately 10% to 50% depending on the population studied, the type of diagnostic imaging used to detect fractures, and the age of the patients seen (Ebbin, Gollub, Stein, & Wilson, 1969; Herndon, 1983). Infants and young children sustain significantly more abusive skeletal injuries than do older children (Akbarnia, Torg, Kirkpatrick, & Sussman, 1974), with the majority of fractures occurring to children under 3 years of age. Six percent of 775 primary injuries were fractures or dislocations in a study of 616 children reported for suspected child abuse (Johnson & Showers, 1985).

The anatomic and physiologic characteristics of the immature skeleton affect the frequency, type, location, and healing of pediatric fractures. Developing bone is more porous than mature bone, affecting both the extent and type of fractures seen in children.

Table 4.1 Anatomy of the Long Bone

Bone	Characteristics
Condyle	The rounded articular (joint) surface at the end of a bone
Diaphysis	The shaft of a long bone
Epiphysis	The part of the long bone developed from a center of ossification —Separate from the shaft and separated from it by a layer of cartilage (the epiphyseal plate) —In infants and young children, not often visualized by X ray because it is not ossified
Metaphysis	Growth zone between epiphysis and diaphysis; radiographically identified by the flaring portion of the long bone
Periosteum	Thick, fibrous membrane covering surface of a bone and consisting of two layers: inner osteogenic (bone forming) and outer connective tissue layer containing blood vessels and nerves that supply the bone

Less dense, porous bone helps to stop the propagation of a fracture line, but this quality also makes the bone more vulnerable to compression, represented by bending or buckling of the bone. This is manifested clinically as greenstick and torus fractures, both of which are characteristically pediatric injuries. The periosteum, the fibrous membrane that covers the surface of a bone, is thicker, stronger, and more easily elevated off the diaphysis in a child. In addition, the periosteum of the child is more osteogenic, or bone forming. Bone healing is much more rapid in children than in adults and more rapid in infants than in older children. For example, the healing of a midshaft femur fracture may take only 3 weeks in an infant, but 20 weeks in a teenager (Ogden, 1990). This difference is mostly due to the contribution of the periosteum in the healing of young bones. A child's joint capsules and ligaments are strong and more resistant to stress than are the adjacent bone and cartilage. Therefore, joint dislocations and ligament injuries are less common in young children than in adults.

Bone Anatomy and Fracture Description

The description of a fracture includes the bone involved, the location of the fracture within the bone, and the type of fracture sustained. The mechanism of the injury is also noted in the fracture assessment. Table 4.1 describes the anatomy of the bone, and Table 4.2 describes different types of fractures (see Figures 4.1 and 4.2).

The history of the injury is important in identifying abusive fractures because historical information should be compatible with the type and location of fracture sustained. Fractures resulting from abuse are varied in their presentation. Clinically,

CHILD PHYSICAL ABUSE AND NEGLECT

Table 4.2 Types of Fracture

Type of fracture	Characteristics
Comminuted	Bone broken into multiple pieces
Compound	Open fracture (i.e., through the skin)
Depressed	Skull fractures in which a part of the skull is inwardly displaced (toward the brain)
Diastatic	Fracture with significant separation of bone fragments; often used in relation to skull fractures
Distal	Fracture located away from center of body (near the feet or hands when describing fractures of the extremities)
Greenstick	An incomplete fracture—the compressed side of the bone is bowed, but not completely fractured. Young bones are more malleable, porous, and less brittle than an adult's, and may bend and only partially break when injured.
Hairline	Fracture without separation of the fragments (similar to a thin crack of a vase)
Impacted	A compression fracture
Linear	Resembling a line; often used to describe skull fractures
Oblique	Fracture line angled across long axis of bone (from approximately 30 to 45 degrees)
Occult	—Condition in which there is clinical, but not radiographic, evidence of a fracture. X rays repeated in a few weeks show evidence of fracture healing. —May also indicate a fracture seen radiographically but without clinical manifestations (e.g., rib fractures and metaphyseal fractures)
Pathologic	Fracture that occurs in area of bone weakened by an underlying disease
Proximal	Fractures located toward trunk of body (for fractures of the extremities, near the hips or shoulders)
Spiral	Fracture line oblique and encircles a portion of the bone (resembles twist of a candy cane)
Stellate	Fracture lines of break radiate from central point; seen in some skull fractures
Supracondylar	Fracture to area above condyle, typically of the humerus
Torus	Impacted injury specific to children; bone buckles, rather than fracturing completely, and usually involves the metaphysis of the bone
Transverse	Fracture line perpendicular to the long axis of the bone

the preverbal child may present with signs and symptoms indicative of pain such as irritability, crying with movement of the affected area, and decreased use of a broken limb. Single injuries are most common. The identification of multiple fractures and/or fractures in different stages of healing should raise the possibility of child abuse.

The identification by a health care professional of an inflicted fracture is dependent on multiple factors. They include the ability to obtain a complete and detailed history of the trauma causing the fracture, knowledge regarding fracture mechanisms in child-

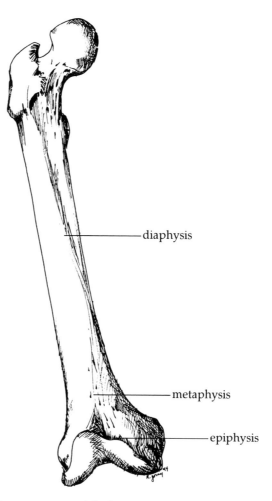

Figure 4.1. Gross anatomy of the bone.

hood, an understanding of pediatric development, and a complete and thorough evaluation of children who may have skeletal injuries that are the result of abuse. There are certain pediatric fractures that, in isolation, are so highly suspicious for child abuse that they raise concern of abuse in the absence of clinical history. These include metaphyseal and rib fractures in infants. Although diaphyseal fractures are the most common fractures that result from abuse, they are not specific for abusive injuries.

Imaging Techniques

Skeletal Survey

The diagnosis of skeletal injuries is made by history and physical examination, and confirmed by radiographic imaging.

CHILD PHYSICAL ABUSE AND NEGLECT

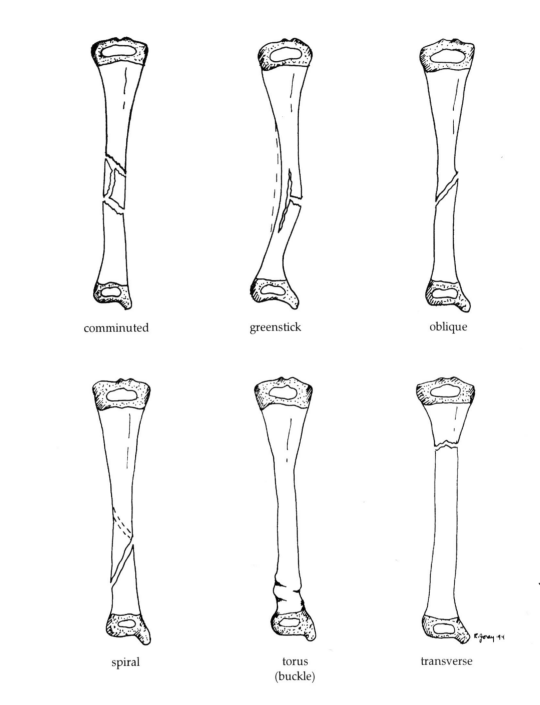

comminuted   greenstick   oblique

spiral   torus   transverse
(buckle)

Figure 4.2. Types of fractures.
Source. Adapted from Ogden (1990).

Some skeletal injuries may not be apparent by clinical examination. A radiographic skeletal survey is part of the workup in infants and young children suspected of abuse. A skeletal survey is a series of X rays taken of the child's skeleton to look for indications of new or old injury. The skeletal survey is mandatory in cases of suspected physical abuse for all infants and children under 2 years of age. It is not generally used in patients over 5 years of age. Clinical judgment is used to determine whether a screening survey is indicated for children between the ages of 2 and 5. The X rays must include restricted views of the areas radiographed in order to obtain proper quality and resolution of the bones (American Academy of Pediatrics, 1991). The skeletal survey includes additional radiographs, such as lateral and/ or oblique views when clinically or radiographically indicated. The following films are included as part of the skeletal survey:

1. Anteroposterior view of the arms, forearms, hands, femurs, lower legs, and feet, on separate exposures
2. Lateral and anterior views of the axial skeleton to evaluate for vertebral, sternal, rib, and pelvic fractures
3. Anteroposterior and lateral views of the skull to evaluate for skull fractures ("babygram," i.e., a single full body image is not acceptable) (see Chapter 2)

Radionuclide Bone Scan

The radionuclide bone scan is a sensitive test for detecting new (less than 7 to 10 days old) rib fractures, subtle diaphyseal fractures, and early periosteal elevation. It is sometimes used as an adjunct to plain films. Most fractures can be identified by bone scan within the first 48 hours after an injury. Bone scan does not allow for the dating of injuries. It is most often used in cases of suspected abuse of infants and young children in which the skeletal survey is negative and a more sensitive (but less specific) test is needed (see Chapter 2). A bone scan is used occasionally as a method of initial screening.

Dating of Skeletal Injuries

The dating of fractures estimates the age of injury and can identify multiple episodes of trauma. It is based on the radiographic appearance of periosteum, soft tissues, callus formation, and fracture line (Merten, Cooperman, & Thompson, 1994; O'Connor & Cohen, 1987). The healing of fractures in infants and young children is more rapid than in the older child. The appearance of periosteal reaction is sooner in infants (between 7 and 14 days) than in older children (between 10 and 14 days) because of anatomic and physiological differences between young and mature bone, and elaboration of the callus and remodeling occur more rapidly (O'Connor & Cohen, 1987). Other factors that affect the healing process include severity of injury, degree of fracture displacement, degree of immobilization of the injured body part, metabolic bone diseases that influence the healing process, and repetitive trauma.

It is possible to differentiate new from old injuries and, in some cases, estimate the age of a fracture in days, weeks, or months. The radiographic appearance of fracture repair is used in conjunction with historical information and physical findings to approximate the dating of injuries when possible (Chapman, 1992; Merten et al., 1994).

Stages of Fracture Healing

Fracture healing is divided into four stages that overlap radiographically. A number of abusive fractures, such as metaphyseal and skull fractures, do not follow these stages and are difficult to date. Additional factors that date bony injuries, such as fracture line definition, may aid in determining the age of an injury, because the edges of the fracture become less well defined with time. The estimate of fracture line sharpness, as with other parameters, is subjective and can provide only an estimate of age.

Stage 1: Initial Healing

The radiologic appearance of fractured long bones corresponds to the anatomic and histologic changes that occur with bone healing. Radiographically, soft tissue swelling around the injured bone represents the initial change and may be the only indication of the fracture. An injury to a bone and the soft tissues around the bone results in immediate hemorrhage and subsequent inflammation. This is clinically represented by swelling and tenderness. Many broken bones are not accompanied by external bruising over the fracture site (Rivara, Parrish, & Mueller, 1986). Radiographically evident soft tissue swelling with obliteration of normal fat and fascial planes may persist for a few days or may last longer if the injury is severe (Merten et al., 1994). In general, soft tissue swelling resolves as formation of the callus develops (O'Connor & Cohen, 1987).

Stage 2: Soft Callus

Callus formation begins with the laying down of periosteal new bone. This occurs approximately 10 to 14 days after an injury and may be earlier in young infants (7 to 10 days) (Merten et al., 1994). One week after the fracture, the callus consists of new blood vessels, fibrous tissue, cartilage, and new bone. Calcium deposition begins within a few days of healing but does not peak for several weeks. Both the laying down of new bone and the calcification of new cartilage account for the radiographic appearance of callus formation. Periosteal new bone is not specific for fractures and is laid down in response to a number of different injuries, including burns, frostbite, and infection (O'Connor & Cohen, 1987). In addition, both repetitive injury or continued mobilization of the injured bone will result in an increase in the quantity, thickness, and extent of the periosteal changes seen on X ray. The stage of soft callus ends with the bridging together of bony fragments at approximately 3 to 4 weeks. This occurs clinically when the fracture is stable and begins radiographically when the fracture line begins to resolve (O'Connor & Cohen, 1987).

Stage 3: Stage of Hard Callus

The stage of hard callus begins when lamellar bone bridges the healing fracture. This occurs approximately 1 week after the formation of the soft callus, or at approximately 2 to 3 weeks after the fracture occurs. The radiologic appearance at this stage is defined by a solidly united fracture with resolution of the fracture line (O'Connor & Cohen, 1987).

Stage 4: Remodeling

During remodeling, the original configuration of the bone is restored as the callus is smoothed circumferentially. The ability of a child's bone to remodel is great, and remodeling may occur over a number of years. This process begins at 3 months and may peak at 1 to 2 years of age (Merten et al., 1994). Some pediatric fractures are unrecognizable by X ray within months after they occur. The ability to detect an old fracture depends on multiple factors, including the bone injured, the type and extent of the injury, and the care the child received.

Long Bone Fractures

Fractures of the bones of the arms and legs are common childhood injuries (Rivara et al., 1986). Accidental trauma accounts for the majority of long bone fractures, and abuse accounts for only a minority. The likelihood that a long bone fracture is due to abuse is greatest in infants. The type of fracture sustained depends on the mechanical forces applied to the bone during the trauma. Correlating the history with the fracture type is often useful in identifying cases of nonaccidental injury, although it is important to realize that accidental fractures may be unwitnessed, and the exact mechanism of trauma may not be recounted. Each case requires careful evaluation to determine if an injury is suspicious for abuse. For example, spiral fractures of the femur or tibia are more suspicious for abuse in the nonambulatory infant than in the ambulating toddler. Careful evaluation is needed to uncover indicators of abuse for each case.

Diaphyseal Fractures   Diaphyseal fractures are injuries to the midshaft of the long bones. They are generally described by the bone injured (femur, humerus, ulna, radius, tibia, fibula), the location of the fracture within the bone (distal, proximal, midshaft), and type of fracture as defined by radiograph (transverse, spiral, torus, etc.). In infants, a diaphyseal fracture of the femur is often due to abuse, regardless of the fracture type. It requires substantial force to break the femur (although precise forces needed have not been elucidated), and healthy, nonambulatory infants do not take part in activities that generate the forces needed to sustain these fractures. Thomas, Rosenfield, Leventhal, and Markowitz (1991) reported the frequency of abuse found in infants with femur fractures and found that abuse was the cause of 60% of femur fractures in children less than 1 year of age. The study also found that 30% of femur fractures were thought to be accidental (10% were of uncertain mechanism). The accidental femur fractures occurred when infants were dropped. These findings underlie the need for an objective, thorough evaluation of femur fractures in infants.

Humerus fractures are reported for between 12% and 57% of abused infants and children (Merten et al., 1994) and are highly suspicious for abuse. Other than supracondylar humerus fractures of older children, which occur when children fall on the elbow or outstretched hand, humerus fractures in children under the age of 3 are often due to abuse (Kleinman, 1987b; Merten et al., 1994). As with femur fractures, the type of fracture (transverse, spiral, etc.) does not necessarily predict whether an injury is due to abuse or accident. Some authors estimate that as many as 88% of humerus fractures are due to abuse (Thomas et al., 1991), although others suggest a less significant association (Strait, Siegel, & Shapiro, 1995). There is no support for the notion that simple motor activities such as rolling over generate the forces needed to break the arm of an otherwise healthy baby. Table 4.3 describes the common types of diaphyseal fractures seen in childhood.

Treatment of diaphyseal fractures depends on patient age, fracture age when identified, and type and location of the fracture. In general, diaphyseal fractures impede the normal functioning of the involved bone. Treatment requires immobilization and limitation of weight bearing for lower extremity fractures.

Metaphyseal Fractures   Metaphyseal fractures of the long bones are highly specific for child abuse and are potentially pathognomonic of abusive injuries (Kleinman, 1987d). Until recently, metaphyseal fractures were thought to represent "chip fractures" of the metaphyses. Caffey (1957) postulated that these lesions were due to small avulsions of the metaphyseal cartilage and bone at the point of insertion of the periosteum. Recent findings in which histologic correlations to radiographic findings were done show that meta-

Table 4.3 Common Types of Diaphyseal Fractures Seen in Childhood

Type	Characteristics	Causes
Transverse	Fracture line perpendicular to long axis of the bone Force applied to bone is perpendicular to length of the bone	Direct trauma Associated with accidental and inflicted injury
Spiral	An oblique fracture where fracture line encircles a portion of the bone	Indirect torsional forces to the bone Often associated with abusive injuries Seen with accidental injury (in ambulatory children) and child abuse (primarily in infants and young toddlers)
Oblique	Fracture line angled across long axis of the bone (from approximately 30 to 45 degrees)	Indirect torsional (twisting) forces, similar to spiral fractures Seen in accidental and abusive injury
Toddler's fracture	A nondisplaced spiral fracture of the tibia Manifested by limp. There may be a delay in seeking medical care because the injury does not initially appear to be significant. May be occult: nondisplaced, little swelling, initial radiographs may fail to identify the fracture Diagnosed by bone scan at time of presentation or plain films repeated in approximately 2 weeks if clinical scenario indicates toddler's fracture but there is no fracture identified on initial radiographs	Common accidental injury in children between the ages of 1 and 3 Often occurs with routine play activities May result from running and slipping, jumping and falling, and even sliding with a difficult landing Uncommonly results from abuse History of trauma given may seem incomplete or insignificant (Mellick & Reesor, 1990)
Greenstick fracture	An incomplete fracture Compressed side of bone is bowed, but not completely fractured.	Occurs secondary to plasticity of a child's bone Commonly accidental and not commonly reported in the abused child
Torus (buckle) fracture	Localized buckling of the cortex of the bone Injuries located toward metaphysis of the bone Due to anatomy of the developing bone	Results from forces applied parallel to long axis of the bone
Impacted fracture	Involves entire bone	Both commonly accidental and not common in child abuse

Note: No type of diaphyseal fracture is diagnostic of abuse.

physeal fractures represent microfractures through the most immature portion of the metaphysis (Kleinman, Marks, & Blackbourne, 1986). Depending on the radiologic projection, metaphyseal fractures may appear as linear lucencies or densities across the metaphysis, "bucket-handle" fractures, or corner fractures. All of these lesions are subtle and are recognized by a skeletal survey or incidental X ray.

Metaphyseal fractures are injuries generally found in infants and young toddlers. The mechanism of injury is related to either acceleration-deceleration forces associated with the shaking impact syndrome or torsional and tractional forces applied to the

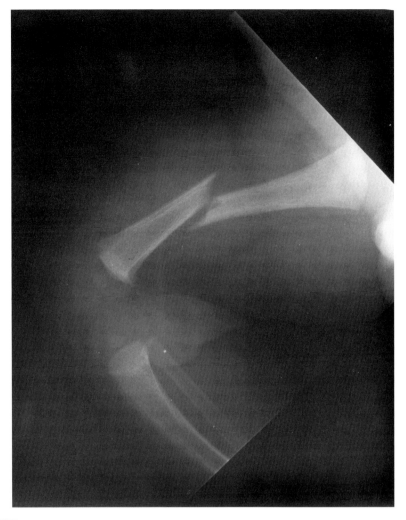

X Ray 4.1.

Ten-week-old infant with a mildly angulated oblique fracture of the right femur. Mother eventually admitted to twisting the baby's leg while changing his diaper. No other injuries were identified.

bone when an infant is twisted or pulled by an extremity (Kleinman, 1987d). Multiple metaphyseal fractures are usually associated with shaking impact injuries and most commonly occur in the proximal humerus, distal ulna and/or radius, the distal femur, and proximal and distal tibia and fibula. The number of bones involved varies from case to case, and fractures isolated to one or only a few bones are not uncommon. Metaphyseal fractures do not typically result in significant soft tissue swelling or external bruising and are not usually identified clinically by either a parent or the physician during the physical examination. In addition, most of these fractures heal without specific treatment or the need for immobilization.

The metaphysis is an area of rapid bone turnover due to normal growth of the infant skeleton. Because metaphyseal frac-

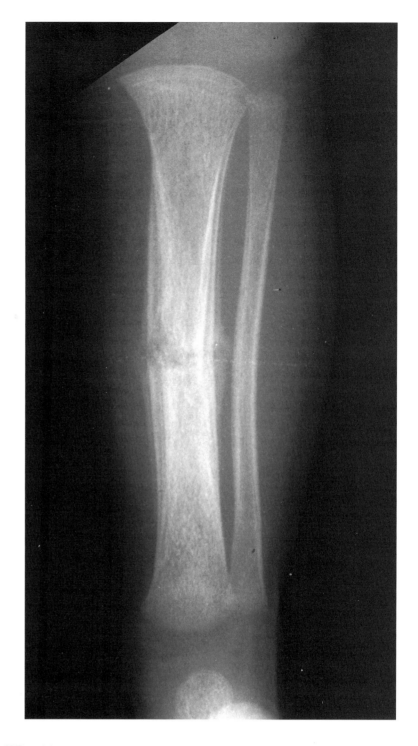

X Ray 4.2.

Two-month-old infant with irritability and decreased movement of the left leg. X rays show a healing transverse fracture of the left tibia, with a plastic bowing deformity of the fibula. The multiple layers of periosteal reaction (arrow) suggest repetitive trauma.

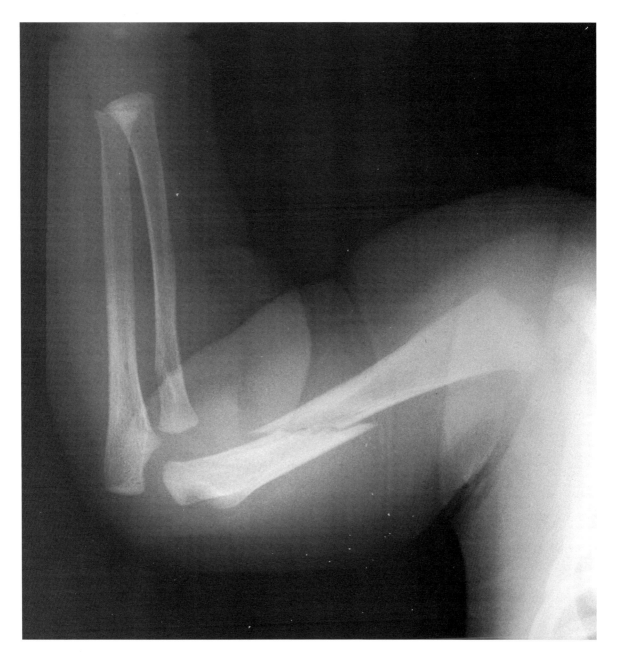

X Ray 4.3.

Ten-month-old infant noted one morning not to be using her right arm. The baby was reportedly well the previous night and the parents denied any trauma to the baby. X ray reveals an acute oblique fracture of the right humerus. No other injuries were identified.

tures are subtle and usually clinically silent, the skeletal survey remains the identification method of choice. A pediatrician or radiologist familiar with the skeletal manifestations of child abuse is often required to identify metaphyseal fractures. A bone scan, which identifies areas of rapid bone turnover, may not be

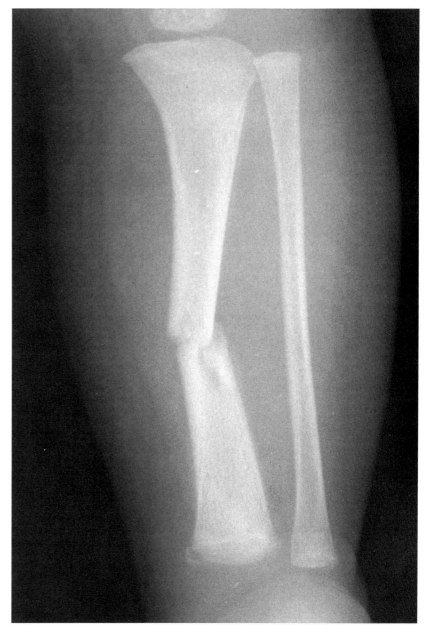

X Ray 4.4.

Fourteen-week-old infant presented for medical care with apnea. Evaluation revealed subdural and retinal hemorrhage, extensive bruising, and fractures of different ages. Shown here is an acute transverse fracture of the midshaft of the left tibia and metaphyseal fracture of the distal tibia and fibula.

helpful in identifying metaphyseal fractures because the metaphysis is normally an area of bone growth and turnover.

Metaphyseal fractures are difficult to date radiographically because the periosteum is often left undisrupted at the time of the injury. As a result, the fracture may not show signs of periosteal reaction, or the reaction may be only moderate. Massive periosteal reaction usually indicates a displaced fracture or a shearing injury to the periosteum itself (Kleinman et al., 1986). Metaphyseal fractures also may be dated by evaluating the sharpness of the fracture margins. As the injury heals, the margin becomes more poorly defined. Unfortunately, this is a subjective measure and one that has not been studied systematically. It is thought that future studies using magnetic resonance imaging (MRI) may help to date metaphyseal injuries more precisely.

Growth Arrest Lines

Growth arrest lines are radiopaque transverse lines across the metaphyses seen occasionally in abused or neglected children. They are not specific for maltreatment and may occur in children with illness, injury, starvation, or other stress that affects growth. Growth arrest lines represent periods of slowed growth and are most evident in bones that normally grow rapidly. They form because the usual orientation of the trabeculae of fast-growing bones is longitudinal (parallel to the long axis of the bone), as opposed to transverse (seen in the trabeculae of normally slow-growing bones) (Ogden, 1990). During periods of slow growth, the trabeculae become oriented transversely, causing a thicker appearance to the affected bone. When the stress is removed and the bone begins to grow at a normal rate, the normal longitudinal orientation of the bone resumes, and the thickened area appears as a discrete transverse line. Many children have evidence of multiple growth arrest lines in a single bone, representing prolonged periods of physiological stress. With time, the transverse orientation of the bone resolves, and growth arrest lines break down so that they are no longer visible.

Skull Fractures

Skull fractures are due to a direct impact to the head with a solid object. A description of the fracture includes the location identifying the skull bone involved and the type of fracture. Table 4.4 describes common types of skull fractures.

The skull consists of cranial and facial bones. The eight intramembranous cranial bones—frontal, occipital, sphenoid, ethmoid, and left and right parietal and temporal bones—develop directly within a membrane and not from cartilage, as with the long bones. The cranium is composed of a number of separate bones joined by immobile joints called sutures. Skull fractures related to child abuse generally refer to the cranial bones, although facial fractures occur (see Chapter 8). The growth and repair of the skull bones are distinct from that of the long bones, making dating of skull fractures more difficult. Additionally, bone scans do not identify skull fractures with any sensitivity. Plain skull films are more sensitive than even CT scans and are the method of choice for identifying abusive and accidental skull fractures.

Table 4.4 Common Types of Skull Fractures

Type	Characteristics
Basilar	Fracture of base of skull Difficult to identify radiologically CT scan is a more sensitive test than plain films Usually diagnosed by clinical criteria: CSF otorrhea, rhinorrhea, raccoon eyes (periorbital blood), or Battle's sign (ecchymoses over the mastoid area)
Comminuted	Complex fracture results in separate piece(s) of bone
Complex	Comprised of more than one line May be branched or stellate, or consist of more than one distinct fracture
Depressed	Occurs when bony fragment is displaced inward toward the brain Often a comminuted fracture and may be associated with neurologic deficits, usually due to underlying brain involvement
Diastatic	Fracture margins significantly separated Injuries to the sutures can result in diastasis, either in association with a fracture or as an isolated injury Diastasis of multiple sutures may occur with increased intracranial pressure or occasionally with rapid brain growth
Linear	A single, unbranched line that can be straight, curved, or angled
Ping-pong	Bone indented, but without a distinct fracture
Stellate	A type of complex fracture Fracture lines radiate from central point

Skull Fractures and Abuse

Skull fractures are the second most common form of skeletal injury in abuse (Merten et al., 1994). As isolated injuries, they are usually benign. Although no type of fracture is pathognomonic for abuse, some fractures are more commonly associated with abuse. Linear skull fractures and parietal fractures are the most common fractures found in both accidental and abusive injuries (Leventhal, Thomas, Rosenfield, & Markowitz, 1993). In young children, accidental linear fractures may occur from falls of less than 4 feet (such as off a bed, couch, or changing table), falls of greater distances (down stairs), or walker injuries (Duhaime et al., 1992). Likewise, linear fractures may result from abuse and are indicative of a direct impact to the head. Some report complex skull fractures, depressed fractures, and diastatic fractures as characteristic of intentional trauma (Hobbs, 1984). Others feel that multiple fractures, bilateral fractures, and fractures crossing sutures are more strongly associated with abuse (Meservy, Towbin, McLaurin, Myers, & Ball, 1987).

Duhaime et al. (1992) report accidental depressed fractures from falls greater than 4 feet, falls down stairs, or from an impact with a moving object. Accidental basilar or bilateral fractures involved falls of greater than 4 feet or down stairs. Bilateral

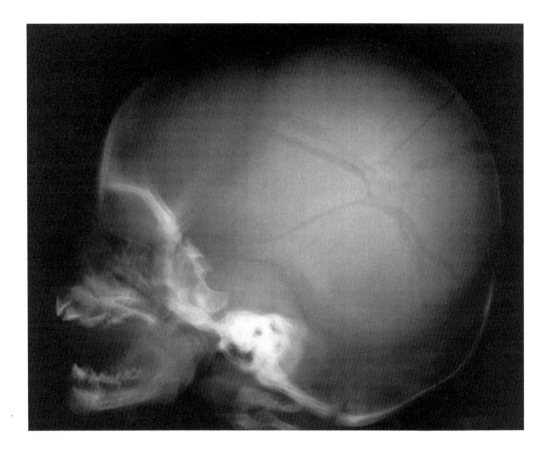

X Ray 4.5.

Eight-week-old abused infant with multiple skeletal injuries. Physical examination revealed soft tissue swelling of face and scalp with extensive facial bruising. Skull X ray shows a compound stellate parietal fracture with areas of mild diastasis. Computed tomography (CT) scan of head was normal.

fractures may result from crushing injuries (Hiss & Kahana, 1995). Young infants may sustain linear, depressed ping-pong fractures from simple falls because of the relative ease with which the skull can be deformed at this young age.

A delay of a few days between the time of injury and diagnosis occasionally occurs because an overlying subgaleal hematoma liquifies and becomes more noticeable, bringing the child to medical attention (Ludwig, 1993). Although no fracture type is pathognomonic for abuse, abuse is suspected when a history of minor injury results in a complex fracture.

Cranial fracture does not predict cerebral injury. Although most intracranial injuries in childhood are not associated with skull fractures, the absence of a skull fracture does not preclude the possibility of significant cerebral injury. For example, the majority of infants who are victims of shaken impact injuries do not have skull fractures. Yet in some cases, the cerebral injury may be so severe as to result in death. Controversy regarding the exact mechanism and biomechanics of shaking injuries relates to whether an impact is required to produce intracranial injury. Infants whose injuries are credited to shaking may have a skull fracture documented by skull films. As indicated by the fracture, these children have sustained a direct impact to the head in addition to shaking (see Chapter 6 for "Shaking Impact Syndrome").

Dating Skull Fractures

Skull fractures are more difficult to date than long bone fractures, both clinically and radiographically. Soft tissue swelling may not be apparent clinically in the acute period and may become noticeable only a week after the injury, when the associated scalp hematoma begins to degrade (Ludwig, 1993). Soft tissue swelling in the first 24 hours after a skull fracture should be evident by computed tomography (CT) scan. Kleinman and Spevak (1992) evaluated soft tissue swelling associated with acute (less than 24 hours old) accidental skull fractures in children. All fractures were associated with soft tissue swelling overlying the fracture of at least 4 mm, as seen by CT scan. Skull fractures do not heal with exuberant callus formation. Recognition of older injuries rests on the subjective determination of fracture line definition, and is therefore imprecise. Like those in other types of fractures, infant skull fractures heal relatively rapidly compared with older children and adults. In most cases, isolated skull fractures require no specific therapy. Rarely, a diastatic or large fracture that is associated with a dural tear may result in the later formation of a leptomeningeal cyst, so that infants and children with skull fractures are followed closely in the months following the injury.

Rib Fractures

Rib fractures are unusual pediatric injuries that commonly result from major trauma (such as motor vehicle accidents [MVAs] or child abuse). An evaluation for child abuse is performed when an infant or young child presents with unexplained rib fractures. Studies have confirmed the association between abuse and rib fractures (Cameron & Rae, 1975; Leventhal et al., 1993; Schweich & Fleisher, 1985) with estimates that they constitute between 5% and 27% of all skeletal injuries (Merten et al., 1994). Rib fractures secondary to abuse are most common in infants and young toddlers and are usually associated with shaking injuries. Direct blows to the chest can result in rib fractures and probably represent the mechanism of injury in older children with broken ribs. Re-

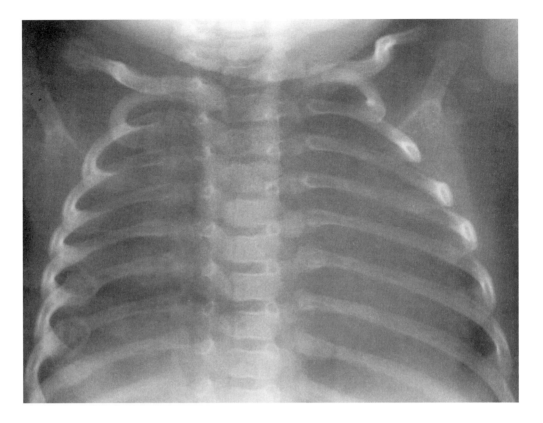

X Ray 4.6.
Eight-week-old infant brought to the hospital for evaluation of breathing difficulty. Chest X ray shows healing fractures of the right clavicle and right 6th and 7th ribs. The child had many additional fractures of varying ages. Mother confessed to beating the crying baby on multiple occasions.

cent histologic studies support anteroposterior thoracic compression in association with shaking as a cause of most abusive rib fractures (Kleinman, 1987a; Kleinman, Marks, Spevak, & Richmond, 1992). Kleinman et al. (1992) studied postmortem changes of fractured ribs in infants who died of abuse. The location (near the costotransverse process articulation) and the healing patterns (on the ventral, or internal, surface of the rib) of the fractures studied suggest that rib fractures occur as the rib is levered over the transverse process of the adjacent vertebra during violent chest compression. Rib fractures usually involve multiple ribs and are often bilateral, which supports a squeezing mechanism. Lateral and anterior fractures may occur by this same mechanism, although most fractures are located posteriorly.

Cardiopulmonary Resuscitation and Rib Fractures

In adults, rib fractures frequently occur in association with cardiopulmonary resuscitation (CPR) (Krischer, Fine, Davis, &

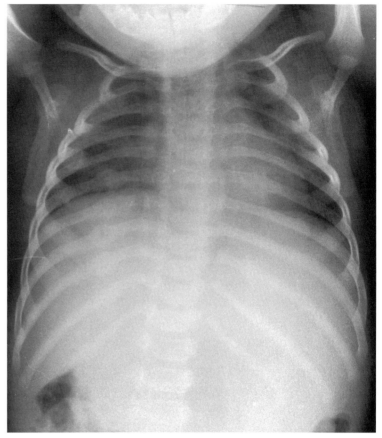

X Ray 4.7a.

Infant with rib fractures. Follow-up shows healing of rib fractures in Figure 4.7b.

Nagel, 1987). In infants and young children, rib fractures do not appear to be a clinically significant complication of CPR. The pliancy of a child's rib cage seems to protect against fractures associated with CPR. A study of 50 children who underwent CPR found that none had rib fractures attributed to CPR (Feldman & Brewer, 1984). Half of the children with rib fractures were abused, and the rest had fractures due to severe accidental trauma (MVAs), surgery, or metabolic bone disease. A review of autopsies and radiographs of infants who had undergone CPR and subsequently died found that none had rib fractures identified by autopsy or radiograph (Spevak, Kleinman, Belanger, Primack, & Richmond, 1994). Infants known to be abused were not included in the review.

Radiographic Findings of Rib Fractures

Rib fractures due to abuse are almost always occult and not recognized either by an unsuspecting caregiver or during rou-

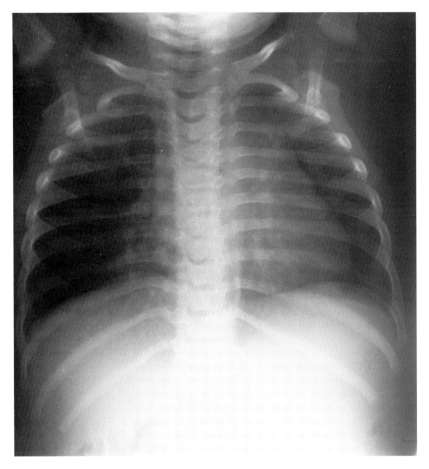

X Ray 4.7b.
Infant with rib fractures. Follow-up shows healing of rib fractures.

tine physical examination. Occasionally, healing fractures with exuberant callus can be palpated, but this usually occurs only after the fractures have been diagnosed radiographically. Acute (new) rib fractures are difficult to identify by plain X ray and are generally recognized only after callus formation and periosteal reaction are evident. Oblique views of the ribs are sometimes helpful in identifying fractures.

Bone scan best identifies acute rib fractures and is significantly more sensitive in identifying new (less than 7 to 10 days old) rib fractures than are plain films. In suspected abuse with negative skeletal survey, a bone scan may identify acute fractures, including those of the ribs. An infant who presents without a history of trauma but with intracranial bleeding should have a skeletal survey done as part of the evaluation. Infants who have manifestations of shaking impact syndrome may not have visible skeletal injuries at the time of presentation.

In the majority of cases, rib fractures are not associated with clinical pulmonary or liver injuries and do not interfere with normal respiration. These fractures typically heal rapidly and without specific therapy.

Other Fractures Associated With Child Abuse

Child abuse can result in injury to virtually any bone in the body, although the most common injuries are fractures of the extremities, ribs, and skull. Many fractures are clinically unrecognized, which emphasizes the need for careful radiologic assessment of all bones. The following sections review injuries occasionally seen in the abused child, although none is pathognomonic for maltreatment.

Vertebral Fractures

Injuries to the vertebral bodies or the spinous processes are probably more common than recognized, because they are often subtle and without clinical symptoms (Kleinman, 1987e). These skeletal manifestations of abuse are most common in infants and young toddlers and often result from severe hyperflexion/hyperextension of the torso or with torsional injuries. Most vertebral injuries are occult, although a few children present with spinal cord compression. Vertebral injuries are usually diagnosed by plain X rays of the vertebral column. MRI may be used to further assess significant vertebral and spinal cord injuries. Vertebral injuries, if stable, do not require specific therapy. Children with cord compression, however, require surgical intervention and often have permanent neurologic disability.

Pelvic Fractures

Fractures of the pelvic bones are uncommon injuries in abused children (Ablin, Greenspan, & Reinhart, 1992). Injuries to the pelvis that occur in infants and young children are often unrecognized prior to radiologic discovery. Most of the reported injuries are unilateral. The ischiopubic ramus is most commonly fractured. Although the precise mechanism of inflicted pelvic trauma is not described in the literature, accidental pelvic injuries in children are due to direct trauma in association with falls, MVAs, and crush injuries (Quinby, 1966). Associated soft tissue injury of the pelvis has been described in an abused child with radiographic pelvic injury (Ablin et al., 1992). Although accidental pelvic injuries may be life threatening, inflicted pelvic fractures are generally stable injuries that do not require surgical intervention.

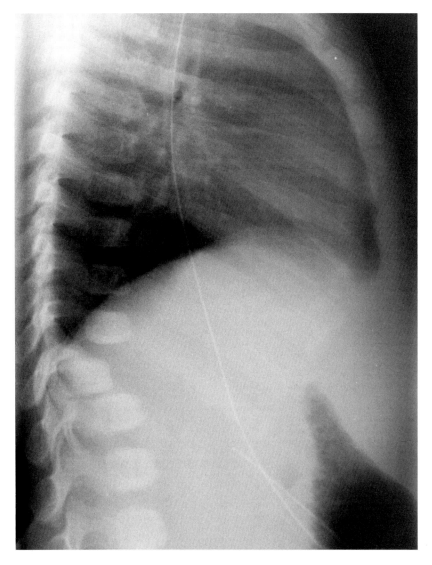

X Ray 4.8.

Ten-month-old infant who suddenly became unable to crawl 2 days after falling out of a crib. Lateral vertebral X rays reveal a fracture of vertebra T11 with posterior displacement of the T11 vertebral body into the spinal canal. These injuries are the result of severe hyperflexion. The child had also sustained a spiral femur fracture at 3 weeks of age.

Clavicle Fractures

Clavicle fractures are common accidental pediatric injuries and are occasionally associated with abuse (Ogden, 1990). Accidental clavicular fractures generally occur in the midshaft of the bone, and are associated with birth trauma, direct injury, or falling on an outstretched arm. Midshaft fractures are most common with both inflicted injury and accidental trauma. Clavicular fractures involving the acromioclavicular joint are associated with violent traction of the arms and shaking injuries (Kogutt, Swischuk, & Fagan, 1974). Inflicted clavicular fractures are typically associated with other skeletal injuries and are an uncommon isolated finding (Merten, Radkowski, & Leonidas, 1983). Clavicle fractures in older children are usually treated with a clavicle strap or figure-8 sling, primarily to ease discomfort. These injuries in young children and infants often heal well without immobilization.

Fractures of the Hands and Feet

Fractures of the hands and feet are suspicious injuries in infants and young toddlers but are often accidental injuries in older children. Fractures of the fingers may present with swelling, whereas fractures to the metatarsals, metacarpals, and phalanges are frequently asymptomatic and only incidentally discovered by skeletal survey. These fractures are often caused by direct trauma. For example, fractures to the small bones in the hands have been reported from a "knuckle beating" as a method of punishment (Kleinman, 1987b). Specific treatment depends on the extent and location of the fracture.

The Differential Diagnosis of Inflicted Fractures

Metabolic and physiological processes may lead to pathological fractures, or they may simulate fractures. Although some of these conditions are readily apparent and easily diagnosed, others can be confused with and misdiagnosed as abuse. The presence of a metabolic bone disease does not preclude abuse. The following sections describe some of the more common conditions included in the differential diagnosis of inflicted fractures.

Birth Trauma

Difficult or emergency deliveries, large infants, or breech presentations may cause diaphyseal or epiphyseal fractures of the clavicle, humerus, or femur. Multiple fractures in the newborn suggest an underlying neuromuscular or metabolic bone disease (Ogden, 1990).

Clavicle fractures are most common and may not be recognized in the days after delivery. They are often asymptomatic and may be detected initially by a parent who palpates the callus when the infant is a few weeks old.

Diaphyseal femur and humerus fractures may be noted at the time of delivery. These injuries typically cause a pseudoparalysis (the infant does not move the extremity in order to avoid pain and discomfort; to the observer, it appears "paralyzed") or asymmetry in the use of the extremities. Treatment generally requires splinting of the involved extremity for a few weeks during rapid healing.

Epiphyseal fractures most commonly involve the proximal humerus and are associated with difficult deliveries. The diagnosis may be made clinically and may be difficult to detect radiographically.

Fractures of the distal extremities or ribs are extremely rare in association with birth trauma. Fractures due to the birth process heal rapidly. By 2 weeks of age, they should *all* show radiographic signs of healing. In most cases, birth trauma is easily distinguished from abuse, although the possibility that an injury was the result of birth trauma occasionally arises. Fractures that do not show the callus by 2 weeks of age are not consistent with birth trauma, and the injuries should be accounted for by another mechanism.

Normal Variations Mistaken for Abuse

A number of normal variations of the developing skeleton may be mistaken for fractures and may sometimes suggest abuse. The most common of these variations is the periosteal new bone formation of the long bones seen in young infants. Periosteal changes typically appear in the first 2 to 3 months of life, often involve multiple bones, and are generally symmetric (Glaser, 1949). The infant is asymptomatic, in contrast to infants with congenital syphilis.

Congenital Syphilis

The osteochondritis, epiphysitis, and periostitis (inflammation of the periosteum) of congenital syphilis may mimic the metaphyseal fractures and periosteal new bone formation associated with child abuse (Fiser, Kaplan, & Holder, 1972). Approximately 30% of syphilitic infants have clinical evidence of bony involvement, and more than 60% show radiographic evidence of the disease (Schulz, Murphy, Patamasucon, & Meheus, 1990). Clinical signs of skeletal involvement include pseudoparalysis of affected limbs and swelling and tenderness of the ends of involved bones. The radius is most commonly involved clinically, followed by the femur, humerus, and fibula.

Radiographic changes are often diagnostic and usually involve multiple symmetric bones. The lower extremities are involved more often than the upper extremities. Metaphyseal destruction and periosteal new bone formation are characteristic of the skeletal changes associated with syphilis. Epiphyseal changes are evident radiographically approximately 5 weeks after infection, whereas periosteal changes are first seen after 4 to 5 months of infection. Therefore, the radiographic manifestations of syphilis vary depending on the trimester in which the fetus was infected.

Affected infants may have other clinical manifestations of congenital syphilis, including hepatomegaly, splenomegaly, anemia, jaundice, rash, sniffles, and adenopathy. Diagnosis is based on serologic testing. A skeletal survey is recommended in the evaluation of congenital syphilis, because bony changes may be evident before the VDRL is positive (Schulz et al., 1990).

Rickets   The radiographic appearance of rickets is identical regardless of its etiology and reflects the undermineralization of growing bones. There are multiple causes of rickets, including vitamin D deficiency, renal and hepatic disease, medications (antacids, anticonvulsants, furosemide), and other rare diseases. Children at risk for rickets include small, ill, premature infants (related to nutritional compromise, high growth rates, medication use); urban, breast-fed infants who do not receive Vitamin D supplementation; adolescents with poor nutritional habits; and children with kidney or liver disease (Bergstrom, 1991). Radiographic findings include fraying of the costochondral junctions and metaphyses, widening of the distance from the epiphysis to the mineralized portion of the metaphysis, flaring of the metaphyses, and cortical thinning. The changes that occur in the metaphyses and ribs are not usually confused with abuse. During healing, bony changes may mimic abuse because dense mineralization occurs adjacent to radiolucent bone, which may resemble metaphyseal fractures. Periosteal new bone formation may mimic trauma. The diagnosis of rickets is dependent on clinical suspicion and laboratory screen for rickets. Measure serum calcium, phosphorus, and alkaline phosphatase levels. The results are suggestive of rickets when the calcium level remains normal (low normal), serum phosphorus is low, and/or alkaline phosphatase is elevated. Treatment of rickets is guided by the primary cause.

Osteogenesis Imperfecta   Osteogenesis imperfecta (OI) is a rare, inherited disorder of connective tissue that results from an abnormal quantity or quality of type I collagen. There are different variable expressions of the disease, which is classified into four major clinical types based on phenotype and radiologic features. Most forms of this disease are easily distinguished from child abuse, but only the rare case may pose difficulties. The following sections describe the major features of each type of OI. Table 4.5 shows common characteristics of the four types of OI.

Type I

The most common form of OI is type I, which accounts for 80% of all cases and has autosomal dominant inheritance. Although type I is a relatively mild form of OI, the bone fragility varies from mild to moderately severe. Fractures are occasionally present at birth but characteristically begin during pre-

Table 4.5 Common Characteristics of Osteogenesis Imperfecta Types I to IV

Type	Major characteristics	Comments	Confused with abuse
Type I	80% of all cases Bone fragility mild to moderately severe Fractures occasionally at birth Fractures common during preschool years (Silence, 1988) Blue sclera Hearing impairment or family history of hearing impairment Easy bruising Short stature Dentinogenesis	Most common form Autosomal dominant inheritance	Rarely
Type II	Death by 1 month of age Severe skeletal deformities Blue sclerae Intrauterine growth retardation Multiple fractures at birth	Perinatal lethal form	No (not confused)
Type III	Severe bone fragility and osteopenia Fractures at birth (2/3 cases) (Silence et al., 1986) Growth retardation Skeletal deformities Sclerae: normal but may be mild blue at birth Triangular facies (85% cases) Dentinogenesis imperfecta (50%) Ligamentous laxity (50%) Easy bruisability (25%) Occasional hearing impairment	Rare and more severe form	Easily distinguishable from abuse
Type IV	Bone fragility mild to moderate Birth fractures (> 1/3 cases) Osteopenia Wormian bones Dentinogenesis imperfecta may be present Normal sclerae Hearing impairment uncommon Easy bruising uncommon	Rare Autosomal dominant inheritance Mild form of disease Bones may appear normal at time of first fracture	Most difficult form to distinguish Most at risk for diagnosis of abuse (Ablin, Greenspan, Reinhart, & Grix, 1990)

school years (Silence, 1988). All children have blue sclerae. Common findings include hearing impairment or a family history of hearing loss, and easy bruisability because of abnormal collagen in blood vessels. Associated findings, such as joint hypermobility, occur with some frequency. Short stature is also characteristic of type I OI.

Type II

Type II is the perinatal lethal form of the disease and is not confused with child abuse. Affected neonates all have severe skeletal deformities, blue sclerae, intrauterine growth retardation, short bowed legs and arms, and multiple fractures at birth. Affected children generally die in early infancy.

Type III

Type III is a rare and more severe form of OI, with autosomal dominant or new dominant mutation as the mode of inheritance. Bone fragility and osteopenia are more severe than in types I and IV, and fractures at birth are present in two thirds of affected patients (Silence et al., 1986). Growth retardation and skeletal deformities such as scoliosis and bowed limbs are common. Sclerae are typically normal, but may be mildly blue at birth. Eighty-five percent of patients eventually manifest triangular facies because of soft craniofacial bones and temporal bossing (Silence, 1988). This is usually not apparent in early childhood. Dentinogenesis imperfecta and ligamentous laxity occur in about half the patients, and easy bruisability in 25%. Hearing impairment is found only occasionally.

Type IV

Type IV is a rare form of OI with autosomal dominant inheritance. It is generally a mild form of the disease and may be most difficult to distinguish from abuse (Ablin, Greenspan, Reinhart, & Grix, 1990). Bone fragility varies from mild to moderate, and fractures at birth are present in less than one third of patients. The bones may be normal in radiologic appearance at the time of the first fracture. The sclerae are typically normal, and hearing impairment and easy bruising are uncommon. Dentinogenesis imperfecta may be present. Taitzs (1987) estimates the probability of encountering sporadic cases of type IV OI to be between 1 per million and 1 per 3 million births. For large cities, this translates to one case every 100 to 300 years. There are a number of clinical findings that help to identify children with OI. Blue sclerae, hearing impairment, dental abnormalities, hypermobility of joints, easy bruisability, short stature, wormian skull bones, osteopenia, bowing tendency, angulation of healed fractures, and progressive scoliosis all suggest OI. The fractures seen in OI are generally diaphyseal, although metaphyseal fractures resembling those seen in abuse are described (Astley, 1979). A few children with type IV OI have a normal physical examination, no obvious radiographic evidence of OI, and a negative family history. These children are at risk for incorrect diagnosis of abuse. Children with OI usually have a history of minor trauma that accounts for the location but not the severity of the injury. Recurrent fractures often occur in different environments, helping to distinguish OI from abuse (Gahagan & Rimsza, 1991). Biochemical analysis of type 1 collagen in cultured skin fibroblasts can confirm the diagnosis after careful clinical evaluation. In patients with clinical manifestations of OI, biochemical alterations of type I collagen are identified in greater than 85% (Wenstrop, Willing, Starman, & Byers, 1990). These data do not include abused children or children without clinical features of OI and therefore cannot be generalized to the abused population. Published data do not exist for the specificity and sensitivity of these tests in children suspected of being abused. Skin fibroblast testing is an expensive, not readily available test that can take many months to complete. Children with multiple and repeated fractures with features of OI and whose clinical features are not characteristic of abuse are candidates for biochemical analysis. If there is any question about the correct diagnosis, the child is placed in a protected environment while awaiting test results. Finally, it is important to note that OI and child abuse can coexist.

In Brief

- Fractures are a common manifestation of abuse, particularly in infants and young children.
- Diaphyseal fractures are the most common type of fracture associated with abuse, but are not specific for inflicted injury.
- The history of injury, development of the child, and type of fracture are considered in determining the likelihood of abuse in children with diaphyseal fractures.
- Rib fractures and metaphyseal fractures are highly specific for child abuse and are associated with infants and young children who are victims of shaking impact syndrome.
- A skeletal survey should be done for all children less than 2 years of age who have injuries suspicious for abuse.
- The yield from the skeletal survey decreases with increasing age of the child and is not a useful test in children older than 5 years.

- Standards for performing skeletal surveys exist and should be followed (AAP Section on Radiology, 1991).
- Radionuclide bone scan may identify infants and young children with subtle injuries that are not detected by skeletal survey.
- Bone scans are excellent in detecting rib injury, do not consistently identify metaphyseal fractures, and generally are not useful in identifying skull fractures.
- Dating of injuries cannot be done with bone scan.
- A number of disease states predispose to fractures, and careful evaluation usually distinguishes children with pathological fractures from those who are abused.
- Trauma is the leading cause of bony injury to otherwise healthy bones.

5 Abdominal and Thoracic Trauma

Significant injuries to the abdomen and chest are not commonly seen in abused children, although abdominal and thoracic injuries seem to be underreported. Major blunt trauma to the abdomen is a relatively infrequent finding in abused children, accounting for less than 1% of all reported cases of abuse (Cooper et al., 1988). Trauma to the internal thoracic structures are even less common than abdominal injuries. Unfortunately, the mortality rates due to visceral injuries remain unacceptably high. Although major abdominal trauma occurs infrequently, it is the second leading cause of death due to physical abuse.

The relatively high mortality rate due to abdominal and thoracic injuries is likely due to a number of factors, including (a) severity of injuries sustained to vital organs, (b) delay in seeking appropriate medical care, (c) delay in correct diagnosis that occurs when misleading or incomplete histories are provided, (d) brisk hemorrhage associated with certain injuries, and (e) young age of the victims.

Affected children are best managed by personnel trained in the management of pediatric trauma. The medical prognosis for

127

children who sustain abusive visceral injury improves if the child survives acutely and is managed aggressively.

Abdominal Injuries—General Principles

The majority of children who sustain significant purposeful abdominal trauma are young, generally between 6 months and 3 years of age (Cobb, Vinocur, Wagner, & Weintraub, 1986; Cooper et al., 1988), and tend to be younger than those with accidental abdominal trauma (Ledbetter, Hatch, Feldman, Ligner, & Tapper, 1988). When compared to children who die of inflicted head trauma, those with fatal abdominal injuries tend to be slightly older (Cooper et al., 1988). Ledbetter et al. (1988) compared accidental and abusive injuries and found that 11% of all abdominal trauma was due to abuse. However, below 4 years of age, child abuse accounted for 44% of abdominal injuries seen.

The high mortality rate associated with abusive abdominal injury is related to severe blood loss and/or a delay in seeking treatment. Studies have found greater mortality with abusive abdominal trauma than with accidental injury (Ledbetter et al., 1988; McCort & Vaudagna, 1964). The majority of deaths are due to massive blood loss, usually in association with vascular injury. These children present with either profound hemorrhagic shock or are dead on arrival to the hospital. Children who exsanguinate and die before reaching the hospital are often found to have more than 50% estimated blood volume loss at autopsy (Cooper et al., 1988).

Peritonitis and sepsis account for most other deaths. Many children with inflicted abdominal injury do not manifest symptoms immediately, and the severity of the injuries may not be readily apparent. Caregivers may incorrectly assume that their actions did not result in severe injuries and may not bring the child for medical care. The severity of the peritonitis and the rapidity with which signs and symptoms develop depend on the location and severity of the initial injury, the type of bacterial contamination of the peritoneal cavity, and the child's preexisting health. In general, signs of peritonitis develop within hours of the injury, although death may be delayed by a few days in untreated cases.

The pattern of abdominal injury overlaps for both accidental and inflicted trauma. Isolated, single, solid organ injuries are most common with both accidental and inflicted mechanisms, whereas hollow visceral injuries are more commonly associated with abuse (Ledbetter et al., 1988; McCort & Vaudagna, 1964). The small size of the child's abdomen lends to multiple organ injury. In cases of abuse, it is not unusual for abdominal injury to go undetected (Coant, Kornberg, Brody, & Edward-Holmes, 1992).

Blunt trauma accounts for the majority of injuries to the abdomen in abuse cases. Although penetrating injuries do occur (such as stabs or gunshot wounds), they are relatively infrequent when compared to blunt trauma (Thomas & Cameron, 1977).

Three basic mechanisms of blunt trauma account for the abdominal injuries commonly found in abused children:

1. *Crushing* of solid organs (liver, spleen, pancreas) of the upper abdomen against the vertebral bodies or bony thorax as a result of a blow to the upper abdomen. Hepatic or splenic injuries may be mild, with small amounts of blood loss, or may result in exsanguination and death. The patient's presentation generally reflects the degree of blood loss, ranging from asymptomatic injuries to hemorrhagic shock or cardiac arrest. Children with pancreatic injury may present with symptoms of pancreatitis.

2. *Sudden compression* of hollow abdominal viscera (intestines, stomach, colon, bladder) against the vertebral column as a result of a blow to the abdomen. With delay in seeking treatment, most patients with hollow visceral injuries present for medical care with signs of peritonitis or sepsis. Vomiting and abdominal pain also may result from hematoma formation.

3. *Shearing* of the posterior attachments or vascular supply of the abdominal viscera (mesenteric tears, disruption of small intestines at sites of ligamental support) as the result of rapid deceleration, such as when a child is thrown against a wall. Shearing forces also may result in intestinal perforations (Kleinman, 1987f). Children generally present with hypotension, shock, or cardiac arrest, reflecting severe blood loss. Patients with intestinal perforations from shearing forces generally present with symptoms related to peritonitis or sepsis.

The symptoms and presentation of the child generally reflect the type and severity of the injuries sustained, the time elapsed prior to seeking medical care, and the rate of bleeding. Patients often present with nonspecific abdominal complaints and without a history of trauma. Common, nonspecific presenting symptoms of children with inflicted abdominal trauma include vomiting, which may be bilious (if an obstruction exists), fever, and abdominal pain. Physical examination may reveal fever, abdominal tenderness, abdominal distention, diminished bowel sounds, and other signs indicative of obstruction or peritonitis. Classic peritoneal signs are not always present in infants and young children. In one series, absent bowel sounds and nonlocalized tenderness were the only consistent physical findings in children with intestinal perforations (Cobb et al., 1986).

Evaluation of Inflicted Abdominal Trauma

The evaluation of the abused child's abdominal trauma includes a careful history, thorough physical examination, indicated laboratory studies, psychosocial assessment, and meticulous documentation. The approach to the evaluation is dependent on the severity of the injuries. Children with severe injuries presenting in shock or cardiac arrest require full resuscitation. In addition, transport to medical centers with medical teams trained in the management of pediatric emergencies and trauma may be necessary. Children with less severe injuries are evaluated according to their symptoms and examination findings.

History

Historical clues to child abuse are the same for abdominal trauma as with other forms of physical abuse (see Chapter 2). The history provided by the caregiver of the child may be incomplete and misleading and may not include a history of trauma. The history may be even more obscure if the child is brought to care by a nonoffending caregiver who has not witnessed the injury. If the history provided by the perpetrator includes trauma, the trauma is often reportedly trivial. Common chief complaints may be falls down the stairs, off the bed, or off the couch. If the child is critically ill and has a reported minor trauma, attention may be focused incorrectly on central nervous system injury. In addition, children who present with both abdominal and head trauma make the clinical examination of the abdomen more difficult, adding further delay to the diagnosis.

With inflicted abdominal injuries, the history focuses on the following:

1. Details of any injury history given
2. Details of when the child was last well, and when the child became symptomatic
3. Details of who was with the child at the time of injury or when symptoms initially began

Physical Examination

After ensuring clinical stability, the examiner completes a full physical examination, with attention to the identification of all injuries. Of note, many children with serious abdominal trauma have *no* soft tissue injury to the abdomen (Cooper et al., 1988). The internal organs, rather than the skin, absorb the force of the impact (see Figure 5.1). Lack of abdominal bruising never eliminates intra-abdominal trauma from diagnostic consideration in an abused or otherwise injured child. During the initial evaluation and over time, attention is paid to assessment of vital signs, observation, auscultation, and palpation of the child's abdomen. Vital signs include body temperature, heart rate, respiratory rate, and blood pressure. They are an important meas-

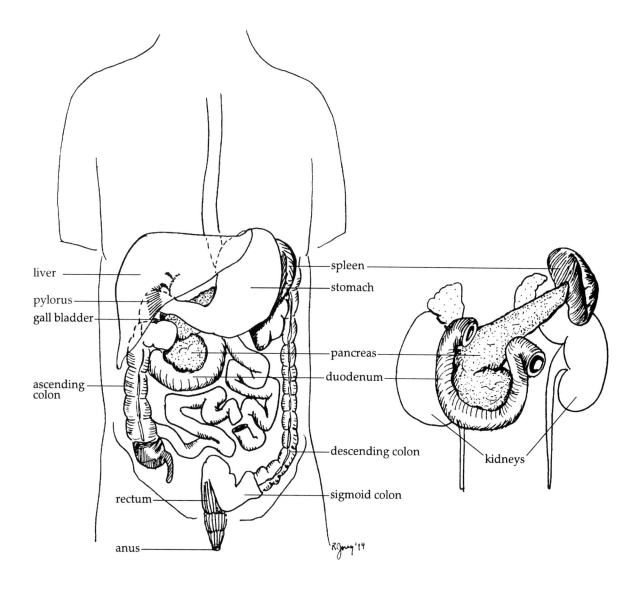

liver

pylorus

gall bladder

ascending colon

rectum

anus

spleen

stomach

pancreas

duodenum

descending colon

sigmoid colon

kidneys

Figure 5.1. On left, schematic of the abdominal anatomy showing the location of the vital organs with transverse colon not drawn. On right, relative organ position with stomach and intestines not drawn.

ure of hemodynamic stability and are serially monitored in all patients with suspected abdominal trauma. Serial measurements of the vital signs and hematocrit, especially in response to fluid resuscitation, may help to predict the type and severity of the injury (Cooper et al., 1988).

- Children with intestinal or pancreatic hematomas have mild blood loss into a confined space and present with mild anemia and stable vital signs.
- Children with intestinal perforations generally are not acutely anemic but have tachycardia and fever as the result of peritonitis.
- Children with minor solid organ injuries tend to present with low hematocrit, tachycardia, and hypotension but generally respond clinically to volume resuscitation.
- Children with major solid organ injury or vascular trauma typically present with low hematocrit and profound shock and do not respond clinically to fluid resuscitation.
- Children may maintain relatively normal blood pressure despite significant blood loss until late in the clinical course, at which time the child's condition can deteriorate rapidly.

Findings of the abdominal examination may suggest the etiology of the injury. In the comatose patient, the clinical examination of the abdomen is more limited and interpretation more difficult. The following suggests a systematic approach to the assessment.

1. Observation of the abdomen

   Look for signs of distention

   Abdominal distention can be due to gastric air. Distention that persists after the placement of a nasogastric tube may indicate solid visceral injury or peritonitis.

2. Auscultation (precedes palpation)

   Note bowel sounds

   Absent bowel sounds may indicate perforation and peritonitis. Peritonitis may be accompanied by fever, absent bowel sounds, bloody or bilious nasogastric aspirate, and marked abdominal tenderness with guarding.

3. Palpation

   Carefully palpate for liver, spleen size, and masses

   Note any voluntary or involuntary guarding or rebound tenderness.

Indicated Laboratory/Diagnostic Evaluation

Laboratory

The laboratory evaluation is an important part of the workup of abdominal trauma and may prove helpful in evaluating children with possible inflicted abdominal trauma (see Table 5.1):

1. *Complete blood count (CBC) with differential.* Identifies anemia (suggestive of blood loss in clinical setting of trauma) and infection (elevation of the white blood cell [WBC] count). Thrombocytopenia (low platelet count) may indicate dissemi-

CHILD PHYSICAL ABUSE AND NEGLECT

Table 5.1 At a Glance—Laboratory Tests

Laboratory study	Indications	Notes
CBC with differential, platelet count	Screen for anemia due to blood loss, nutritional deficiency Screen for infection Check platelet count	May need serial samples
Prothrombin time (PT), partial thromboplastin time (PTT)	Screen for coagulopathies and DIC	
Chemistry panel (electrolytes, BUN, creatinine, glucose, etc.)	Screens for metabolic abnormalities Helps assess ongoing fluid management	
Serum aspartate amino-transferase (AST, SGOT) and alanine aminotransferase (ALT, SGPT)	Screen for liver injury	Not specific for trauma
Urinalysis (U/A)	Screen for renal, bladder, genital injury, myoglobinuria or hemoglobinuria, UTI	
Serum amylase and lipase	Screen for pancreatic injury	Not specific for trauma

nated intravascular coagulopathy (DIC) or an underlying bleeding disorder.

2. *Prothrombin time (PT), and partial thromboplastin time (PTT).* Screens for coagulopathies or suspected DIC.

3. *Fluid and electrolyte assessment (chemistry panel).* Children with signs of intra-abdominal pathology frequently require fluid resuscitation and ongoing intravenous fluid management. A chemistry panel is often sent to the laboratory to assist in ongoing fluid management.

4. *Liver Function Tests (LFTs) (hepatic transaminases).* Elevations of the serum aspartate aminotransferase (AST) > 450 IU/L and the serum alanine aminotransferase (ALT) > 250 IU/L are sensitive predictors of liver injury associated with blunt abdominal trauma (Hennes et al., 1990). Coant et al. (1992) found that in abused children, milder elevations in these levels can identify patients with liver lacerations who are asymptomatic at presentation.

   Measure hepatic transaminases in all children with suspected abdominal trauma and in young victims of physical abuse as a screen for occult abdominal trauma. Serial measurements may be used to support the dating of an injury because enzyme levels return to normal rapidly after blunt trauma. Elevations of hepatic transaminases are not specific for trauma and, depending on the clinical situation, may necessitate evaluation for other etiologies, such as hepatitis.

5. *Amylase/lipase.* Elevations of the serum amylase and lipase are markers of pancreatic injury and is measured in all children with suspected abdominal trauma.

Table 5.2 At a Glance—Radiologic Evaluation

Study	*Detects*	*Limitations*
Plain abdominal radiographs	Intestinal obstruction, ascites, intra-abdominal foreign bodies, free air in abdomen, bone injuries surrounding abdomen	Difficult to detect solid organ injuries
Upper gastrointestinal (UGI) series, barium enema (BE)	Injuries to esophagus, stomach, duodenum, intestines, and colon	Requires contrast Patient must be stable
Ultrasonography (US)	Pancreatic, renal, liver, spleen, and pelvic injuries; free fluid within the abdominal cavity; intestinal hematomas; retroperitoneal injuries	Requires direct contact with abdominal wall
Abdominal CT scan	Solid organ injuries May detect hollow visceral injury, occasionally detects rib fractures	Requires contrast Patient needs to be hemo-dynamically stable
Radionuclide scans	Anatomy and function of specific organs	Length of time
Intravenous pyelography (IVP)	Abnormalities of urinary system Used as adjunct to other tests described	Requires contrast
Skeletal survey	New and healing fractures Other abnormalities of skeleton	Difficult to detect solid organ injuries

6. *Urinalysis (U/A).* Renal injury is usually indicated by the presence of gross blood in the urine, a positive urine dipstick for blood, or a microscopic urinalysis with greater than 20 RBCs per high power field. Occasionally, the urine is positive for blood by dipstick, but microscopy reveals no RBCs. Myoglobinuria, or occasionally hemoglobinuria, may be the cause. In the acute situation, elevation of the serum creatine phosphokinase (CPK) supports the diagnosis of myoglobinuria. Elevated CPK in this setting indicates deep contusions and muscle injury.

Radiological Evaluation

Children with abdominal injuries who are hemodynamically stable are approached differently from those with life-threatening injuries. The following are commonly used methods for imaging the abdomen in children (see Table 5.2).

1. *Plain abdominal radiographs.* Plain films are used for initial evaluation in all stable children with suspected intra-abdominal injury. Films are taken with the patient in the frontal view with the patient supine and erect. A cross-table lateral or left lateral decubitus film is used instead of an erect film for infants or children who cannot assume an erect posture. Hollow visceral perforations are sometimes, but not always, associated with pneumoperitoneum (free air in the abdominal cavity). Perforations of the stomach are most commonly associated with free peritoneal air. Retroperitoneal perforations (such as to the duodenum) are very difficult to detect on plain radiograph. Plain films can be used

to detect intestinal obstruction, ascites, intra-abdominal foreign bodies, and occasional injuries to the bony structures surrounding the abdomen.

2. *Upper Gastrointestinal (UGI) Series/Barium Enema (BE).* Contrast examinations of the GI tract define the location and extent of intestinal tract injuries. UGI is frequently used to evaluate esophageal, gastric, duodenal, and jejunal injuries. Small bowel follow-through is used in conjunction with the UGI to evaluate the small intestine. Contrast enemas visualize colonic abnormalities. Contrast examinations can localize the site of intestinal perforation and can be used for evaluating ulcers and hematomas. Water-soluble contrast media are recommended for patients with possible intestinal perforation.

3. *Ultrasonography (US).* Ultrasound of the abdomen is used as an adjunct to other tests described. Its use as a screening examination is limited because the transducer used to perform the examination requires direct contact with the abdomen, which may not be tolerated by a child with abdominal tenderness and pain. The bony thorax and the presence of air also limits the usefulness of this test. US identifies free fluid within the abdominal cavity, assesses pancreatic injuries (ruptures, pancreatitis, pseudocysts), and evaluates renal anatomy. Ultrasound identifies solid organ and intestinal hematomas and evaluates the retroperitoneum and pelvis.

4. *CT scan.* Abdominal CT scan is the radiographic method of choice for evaluating abdominal trauma. The following list describes conditions and situations where abdominal CT scan is recommended:

   1. Solid organ injuries (if hemodynamically stable)
   2. Intra-abdominal bleeding (if hemodynamically stable)
   3. Physical examination findings uninterpretable because of obtundation
   4. Child undergoing head CT scan because of neurologic signs of trauma.

   CT scan is the method of choice for detecting injuries to solid viscera such as the liver, spleen, or kidney and may detect hollow visceral injury. CT scan is contraindicated in children who have a history of anaphylaxis to contrast agents because abdominal CT scan is done with both IV and gastrointestinal contrast. CT scan is not recommended for patients who are hemodynamically unstable despite resuscitative efforts; these patients require emergency laparotomy in the operating room.

5. *Radionuclide scans (liver-spleen scan, radionuclide renal scan).* Radionuclide scans are occasionally used as an adjunct to the other studies described. They are used to evaluate specific organs for both anatomy and function.

6. *Skeletal survey.* Approximately two thirds of children with inflicted abdominal injuries have other manifestations of abuse by physical examination or skeletal survey (Ledbetter et al., 1988).

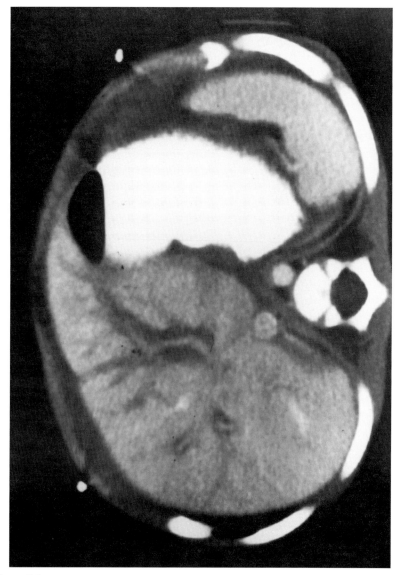

X-ray 5.1a.

Seven-month-old infant with 1-day history of lethargy, found pale and unresponsive by his mother. Examination revealed multiple bruises and a distended, tender abdomen. Abdominal CT shows periportal edema and contusion or laceration to the left lobe of the liver.

Therefore, it is extremely important to obtain a skeletal survey in children with inflicted abdominal trauma. Most victims of abusive abdominal injury are young, and approximately one third of patients with inflicted abdominal trauma will specifically have skeletal injuries (Cooper et al., 1988; Ledbetter et al., 1988). The skeletal survey is best performed when the patient is stable, but it should be done prior to discharge from the hospital (see Chapters 2 and 4).

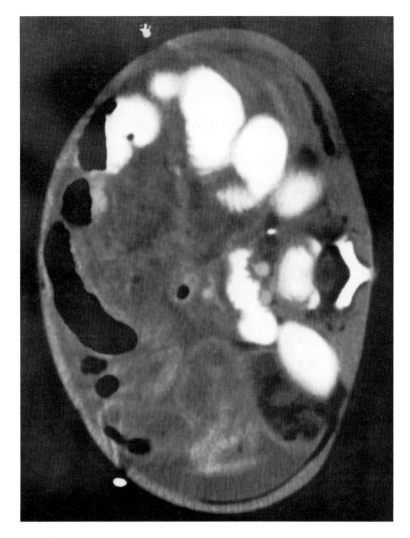

X-ray 5.1b.
Also present is a large amount of free intra-abdominal fluid with thickening of the bowel wall of the 4th portion of the duodenum. Surgical exploration revealed a mesenteric tear and jejunal perforation.

Specific Organ Injuries

Solid Organ Injuries   *Liver*

Liver injuries, such as lacerations and subcapsular hematomas, are among the most common abdominal injuries due to abuse. They are most often due to blows to the upper abdomen,

Table 5.3 At a Glance—Organ Injuries

Solid Organ Injuries

Liver	Commonly injured in abuse-related abdominal trauma	Lacerations Subcapsular hematomas
Spleen	Infrequently reported as abuse-related Protection from underlying the ribs	
Pancreas	Commonly injured in abuse related trauma	Crush injury Pancreatitis
Renal system	Infrequently reported as abuse-related Protection from surrounding tissues	

Hollow Visceral Injuries

Oropharynx/ Esophagus		Aspiration, traumatic perforations, burns resulting from caustic ingestion
Stomach	Infrequently reported as abuse related	
Duodenum	Commonly injured in abuse-related abdominal trauma Vulnerable because of fixed position near vertebral column	Hematomas Perforations
Jejunum/Ileum	Infrequently reported as abuse related	
Colon	Infrequently reported as abuse related	Penetrating rectal trauma of special concern, i.e., rule out sexual abuse

although penetrating injuries can result in liver laceration. The severity of liver injuries varies from asymptomatic to life threatening. (See Table 5.3 for an overview of organ injuries.)

Measurement of hepatic enzymes (ALT, AST) has been shown to be a sensitive (but nonspecific) marker of liver injury and is measured in all patients with suspected abdominal trauma and in infants and young children with other signs of physical abuse. CT scan is the method of choice for imaging the liver in cases of abdominal trauma and is done unless the child requires immediate surgical intervention. Small lacerations and many subcapsular hematomas are treated nonoperatively, although more extensive injuries require surgical repair.

Liver laceration is a reported complication of CPR in adults, usually in association with rib fractures. Liver lacerations also have been reported in association with CPR in young children (Krischer, Fine, Davis, & Nagel, 1987). The first reports date back to the early 1960s, prior to widespread acknowledgment of physical abuse. In these early case reports, abuse may not have been recognized. Although the children who died with liver lacerations were not identified as abused, the cause of death remained undetermined, and in one case, the child had previously suffered "traumatic brain injury" (Thaler & Krause, 1962). Liver lacerations resulting from CPR are extremely rare in children and should not be assumed to be the result of CPR, especially if the child dies and cause of death is undetermined.

Spleen

Splenic injury often is caused by accidental trauma. It is infrequently reported as the result of abuse (Caniano, Beaver, & Boles, 1986; Ledbetter et al., 1988). The reason for the protection of this organ from inflicted trauma is unclear but may relate to its position underlying the ribs (Cooper, 1992). Like liver injuries, the severity of splenic injuries ranges from minor to life threatening. Evaluation for splenic injuries is done by CT scan or liver spleen scan. Management is dependent on the extent of the injury, and surgical repair may be required.

Pancreas

Pancreatic injury resulting from blunt trauma to the upper abdomen occurs with some frequency. The body of the pancreas overlies the spine and can be crushed with significant blows to the epigastrium. Injury to the pancreas typically results in pancreatitis because of the release and activation of pancreatic enzymes. Causes of pancreatitis in childhood include biliary tract disease, congenital anomalies, cystic fibrosis, infection, and medications (Ziegler, Long, Philippart, & Klein, 1988). Trauma is a leading cause of pancreatitis in children (Cooney & Grosfeld, 1975). Abuse is a leading cause of traumatic pancreatitis in children less than 4 years of age and is often associated with other manifestations of abuse (Ziegler et al., 1988). Pancreatic pseudocysts, which may develop after abuse (Pena & Medovy, 1973), form as resultant fluid collections become confined, beginning within a few days of the injury.

The development of pancreatitis after trauma may be insidious so that not all children present with it in the acute period. Most children with pancreatitis eventually develop abdominal pain, vomiting, fever, abdominal distention, or other nonspecific symptoms. Elevation of the serum amylase and/or lipase level in children with abdominal symptoms indicates pancreatic involvement. Plain radiographs and UGI studies may indicate findings suggestive of pancreatitis, but ultrasound and CT scan are most useful in identifying pancreatic injuries.

The management of pancreatitis is usually conservative and consists of bowel and bed rest, nasogastric decompression, and pain and nutritional therapy. Surgery is reserved for children with severe pancreatic injury and those who require drainage of pseudocysts.

Kidney, Bladder, Urinary Tract

Abuse may result in injuries to the kidneys, ureters, and bladder. Severe blows to the flank most commonly cause renal contusions or lacerations. Because the kidneys are well protected by their location and surrounding anatomy, trauma severe enough to cause renal injury is often associated with injuries to other abdominal organs. Although children may present with flank pain and tenderness, these symptoms are not universally present. Hematuria (gross hematuria, or greater than 20 RBCs per high power field) generally indicates renal involvement in children with abdominal trauma. The severity of the renal injury is not reflected by the degree of hematuria, so that all children with hematuria require renal imaging by CT scan or other methods. Both myoglobinuria (secondary to rhabdomyolysis and muscle injury) and hemoglobinuria may result from abuse and can be mistaken for hematuria (Mukerji & Siegel, 1987; Rimer & Roy, 1977). Unlike hematuria, neither will show microscopic evidence of urinary RBCs.

Bladder injuries from abuse are unusual but have been reported (Halsted & Shapiro, 1979). Myoglobinuria and hemoglobinuria may result in renal failure. Most renal injuries are managed conservatively and do not require surgery. Myoglobinuria and hemoglobinuria require aggressive medical treatment.

Hollow Visceral Injuries

Injuries to the hollow viscera of the abdominal cavity may occur from abuse. The hollow viscera is more commonly injured in abused children when compared to children who sustain accidental abdominal trauma (Ledbetter et al., 1988). Hollow visceral injury is generally due to either direct blows to the abdomen or shearing forces associated with rapid deceleration. Children (particularly infants and toddlers) with perforations or hematomas to the intestinal tract, without a history of significant accidental trauma, require a full evaluation for child abuse.

Oropharynx/Esophagus

Injuries to the pharynx and esophagus are reported occasionally in the child abuse literature. Reported injuries include foreign body aspirations, traumatic perforations, and burns resulting from caustic ingestion (Friedman, 1987; McDowell & Fielding, 1984). Children with esophageal foreign bodies typically present with respiratory symptoms from either direct compression of the membranous tracheal wall by the object or infection that develops in surrounding tissues. Patients with significant injury to the posterior oropharynx, hypopharynx, esophagus, or trachea often present with fever, subcutaneous emphysema, erythematous swelling of the neck, hemoptysis, hematemesis, or pneumomediastinum. Finally, caustic ingestions manifest by drooling, respiratory distress, oral burns, and/or stridor.

Stomach

Gastric perforation is reported in the child abuse literature, although it is not a frequent injury (McCort & Vaudagna, 1964; Schechner & Ehrlich, 1974). Gastric perforation is more common if the child has a full stomach at the time of the trauma. Children with gastric perforation have rapid manifestations of the injury because of pain associated with gastric spasms and the noxious effects of gastric acid in the peritoneum. Gastric perforation is usually indicated by a distended, tense abdomen and pneumoperitoneum on plain radiograph. Gastric perforations require timely operative repair. Gastric perforation is reported as a complication of CPR, albeit rare (Krischer et al., 1987). Gastric distention can accompany duodenal hematomas secondary to the obstructive effect of the hematoma.

Duodenum

Duodenal hematomas and perforations are among the more frequent abdominal injuries that result from abuse (Ledbetter et al., 1988; McCort & Vaudagna, 1964; Woolley, Mahour, & Sloan, 1978). The duodenum is at risk for injury due to its relatively fixed position in the upper mid-abdomen, its proximity to the vertebral column, and its rich blood supply from the pancreaticoduodenal arteries. A crushing injury that forces the duodenum against the vertebral column typically results in rupture of the duodenal blood vessels. This results in a hematoma that develops between the mucosa and serosa. As the hematoma expands, the duodenal lumen narrows, leading to partial (or occasionally complete) obstruction. Duodenal hematoma can result from both accidental or inflicted trauma. Children with duodenal hematoma often have some delay in presentation, because the signs of obstruction develop with time. Children typically present with vomiting and abdominal pain and have abdominal tenderness on examination. Associated injuries may be found, especially to the pancreas.

Plain films may be normal but may show gastric dilatation and decreased bowel gas. The diagnosis of a duodenal hematoma can be made by UGI, CT, and ultrasound. Affected children may have significant anemia (Woolley et al., 1978). Children who present with unexplained duodenal hematoma should be screened for coagulopathies, and young victims should have a skeletal survey. Treatment of duodenal hematoma is conservative, with bowel rest and nasogastric suctioning. Surgery to evacuate the hematoma is occasionally required.

Transections, avulsions, and lacerations of the duodenum may also result from abuse (Tracy, O'Connor, & Weber, 1993; Woolley et al., 1978). Children with perforations of the duodenum present with vomiting, abdominal pain, and signs of sepsis. Classic signs of peritonitis may be absent because of the duodenum's location in the retroperitoneum. Plain films are often normal if the perforation is in the retroperitoneum. Radiographic diagnosis is best made by UGI with water-soluble contrast media. Treatment requires surgical repair.

Jejunum/Ileum

Perforations and hematomas of the small intestine may occur in abused children with abdominal trauma. They are infrequent in accidentally injured children (Ledbetter et al., 1988). The majority of intestinal perforations are located in the jejunum, near the ligament of Treitz, and are the result of either direct compression associated with blows to the abdomen or shearing forces. A delay in presentation is common. Peritoneal signs typically develop within 6 to 12 hours after perforation, but children are sometimes brought for medical treatment only after days have passed. Children may present with signs of peritonitis and sepsis, although classic peritoneal findings may not be present (Cobb et al., 1986). Plain radiographs may reveal free air. UGI may locate the perforation, although in many patients, the need for laparotomy precludes the usefulness of extensive radiographic evaluation. Surgical resection or repair constitutes definitive treatment.

Colon

Abused children sustain injuries to the colon infrequently. There are occasional reports of colonic injury from blunt abdominal trauma (Caniano et al., 1986). Injuries to the colon are also associated with penetrating rectal trauma that may be the result of physical or sexual abuse (Press, Grant, Thompson, & Milles, 1991). Signs related to peritonitis are often present. Rectal blood is usually present in children who present with injuries to the colon and/or rectum. Colonic perforations require surgical repair.

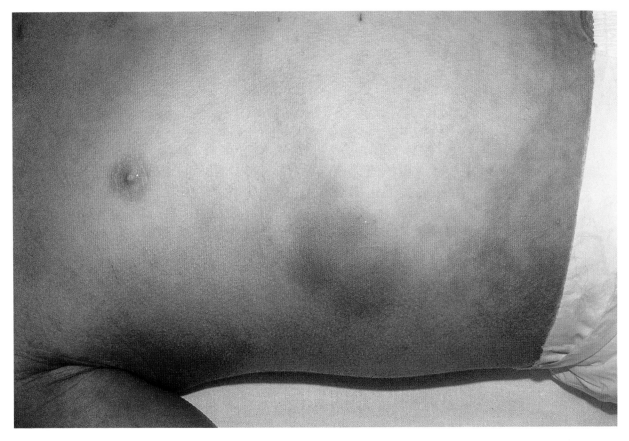

Photo 5.1.

Twenty-three-month-old with healing bruise to the lower chest. Physical examination revealed acute and healing bruises and acute burns to the legs and penis (see Photos 3.4 and 3.8). Laboratory evaluation revealed markedly elevated liver function enzymes, which rapidly returned to baseline. Skeletal survey revealed multiple healing rib fractures. Together, these findings are diagnostic of abuse.

Retroperitoneal Vascular Injuries   Severe deceleration injuries that result in shearing of the mesentery and retroperitoneal vascular supply to the abdomen are occasionally encountered (Cooper et al., 1988; Dworkind, McGowan, & Hyams, 1990). Shearing injuries result in retroperitoneal hemorrhage, which can be life threatening. Injuries to larger retroperitoneal vessels may result in hemorrhagic shock; emergency laparotomy is required to save the child's life. CT scan sometimes identifies smaller retroperitoneal hematomas. Children with less severe injuries may be managed conservatively, without operative repair.

Thoracic Injuries   Inflicted blunt trauma to the heart and lungs is less common than abdominal injuries, at least in part because of the protection afforded by the pliable, cartilaginous ribs of the young child. Underreporting of cardiac and pulmonary injuries is believed to occur as well.

Pulmonary Injuries

Contusions and lacerations of the lower lungs are occasionally identified by abdominal CT (Sivit, Taylor, & Eichelberger, 1989). Although rib fractures in abused infants are common (see Chapter 4), symptomatic pulmonary injury is unusual. As with significant abdominal trauma, external signs of trauma such as bruising over the chest wall may be absent despite serious intrathoracic injury.

McEniery, Hanson, Grigor, and Horowitz (1991) report a 6-week-old infant with pulmonary contusion, pulmonary edema, and a pneumomediastinum resulting from severe anteroposterior chest compression by his father. Patients with significant pulmonary contusions present with tachypnea and hypoxia. The contusions should be evident by chest X ray within hours of the injury. Management of most pulmonary injuries is supportive, and operative repair is not usually required for blunt force injuries.

Occasional penetrating injuries to the chest occur from child abuse. These injuries are best managed by pediatric surgeons trained in trauma.

Cardiac Injuries

Cardiac injuries as the result of abuse have been reported (Cumberland, Riddick, & McConnell, 1991; Marino & Langston, 1982; Rees, Symons, Joseph, & Lincoln, 1975). Rees et al. (1975) report a traumatic ventriculoseptal defect (VSD) that resulted from a kick to the chest of a 5-year-old girl. She presented in cardiac failure and was treated medically, with eventual surgical repair. This injury was felt to have occurred from the heart's being distorted and crushed against the vertebrae. Cumberland et al. (1991) report intimal tears of the right atrium found at autopsy of six children, three of whom were teenagers who died in motor vehicle accidents (MVAs) and three of whom were young victims of abuse. All six children had associated liver lacerations and other signs of abdominal trauma. The authors postulate that the cardiac injuries were the result of transmitted hydrostatic forces from the abdomen, through the inferior vena cava, and to the fixed right atrium.

Injuries to the heart can result in electrical conduction abnormalities. Children with suspected cardiac injuries may require chest X ray, electrocardiogram (EKG), and cardiac echography (ECHO). CPK MB fractions (evidence of cardiac muscle injury) have not been described in the evaluation of abused children with cardiac injuries but could potentially diagnose cardiac muscle damage that results from severe blunt thoracic injury.

In Brief

- Most victims of serious inflicted visceral injury are infants and toddlers.
- The vast majority of injuries are due to blunt trauma, not penetrating injury.
- The mechanism of injury is related to *crushing* of solid organs, *compression* of hollow viscera against the vertebrae or bony thorax, or *shearing* forces that result from sudden deceleration.
- The high mortality rate associated with abusive abdominal injury is related to severe blood loss or a delay in seeking treatment.
- Although solid organ injuries are the most common visceral injuries resulting from abuse, they are also seen with accidental trauma. Hollow visceral injury is more common with inflicted trauma than with accidental injury.
- Vital signs, serial hematocrit, and the response to fluids generally indicate the severity and probable type of abdominal injury present.
- CT scan has revolutionized the ability to detect visceral injury, although plain X ray, ultrasound, GI contrast studies, and radionuclide studies all contribute to the noninvasive evaluation of visceral trauma.
- Most solid organ injuries are treated conservatively, without the need for surgery. Intestinal perforations require laparotomy, as do significant mesenteric and vascular injuries.
- Children who survive the acute assault generally have good medical outcome.
- Infants and young children who are victims of physical abuse are screened for abdominal injuries with history, physical examination, and appropriate screening labs, including AST, ALT, and amylase.

6 Head Trauma

with A. C. Duhaime, MD

Head trauma is the leading cause of mortality in abused children and is second only to motor vehicle-related injuries as a cause of traumatic mortality in the pediatric population (Billmire & Myers, 1985; Duhaime et al., 1992; Gotschall, 1993). The exact incidence of inflicted head injuries is unknown because cases often go unrecognized by health care providers. Incidents may go unreported, and children with less severe injuries may not be brought for medical attention. It is estimated that nearly 25% of hospital admissions for head injury in infants and young children represent abused children. These children suffer disproportionately severe injuries (Duhaime et al., 1992). It has been suggested that there are cases of unexplained developmental delay and retardation related to previously inflicted head injuries sustained in infancy (Caffey, 1974). There is a potentially enormous cost for acute and chronic care and the loss of potential from brain damage suffered early in life. This

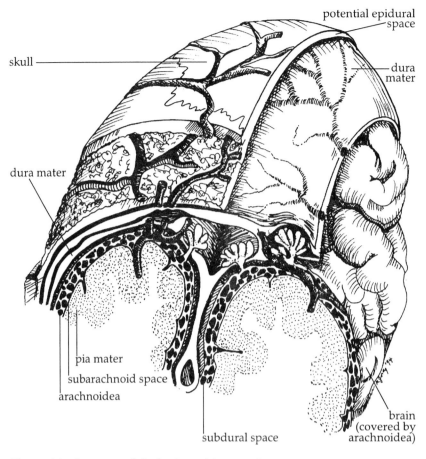

Figure 6.1. Anatomy of the brain and its covering.

Diagram of the various layers of tissue from the skull to the brain. Note the bridging veins that transverse through the subdural space.

chapter discusses the recognition and evaluation of the infant and older child with abusive head and spinal cord injuries.

Anatomy and General Principles

Head injuries sustained by abused children are in part described according to their anatomical location. Understanding the basic anatomy of the head and brain allows for better comprehension of the location and pathophysiology of the injury (see Figure 6.1). The following are definitions used to describe and locate injury. They are listed from most external to internal.

1. *Scalp.* The scalp consists of the skin and underlying tissues that cover the skull. Injuries to the scalp usually take the form of bruises, hematomas, and/or lacerations. Bruises on the scalp are often missed clinically because of the hair over-

lying the scalp. It is not uncommon for deep scalp injuries to be first identified during autopsy.

2. *Subgaleal hematoma.* Hemorrhage into the potential space between the fibrous layers of the scalp and the skull. Subgaleal hematomas are associated with blunt injury to the head but have also been reported from hair pulling (Hamlin, 1968). Subgaleal hematomas may be seen in association with an underlying skull fracture.

3. *Skull.* The skull consists of eight cranial and facial bones joined by immobile joints called sutures. The skull bones are named frontal, occipital, sphenoid, ethmoid, and left and right parietal and temporal bones. Most of the skull bones consist of an inner and outer cortex of bone separated by a spongy bone called the diploe. The thickness of the skull bones varies in different regions and is thinner in infants than in older children and adults. In infancy, prior to the complete fusing of the skull bones, fontanelles ("soft spots") are felt at the junction of the frontal and parietal bones and occasionally at the junction of the occipital and parietal bones. Fractures to the skull occur from both accidental and abusive trauma and may or may not be associated with more serious internal head injury (see Chapter 4).

4. *Skull fractures.* See Chapter 4.

5. *Intracranial hemorrhage.* A nonspecific term to describe bleeding inside the cranium, or skull.

6. *Meninges.* A series of three membranes that cover the surface of the brain and spinal cord. The outermost is the dura mater, the middle membrane is the arachnoid, and the inner membrane is the pia mater. Bleeding that occurs around the brain is designated according to its relation to these membranes.

7. *Epidural hematoma.* Bleeding into the space between the inner skull surface and the dura (i.e., the epidural space) is usually the result of accidental trauma. Epidural hematomas are not often the result of nonaccidental trauma but have been described in abused children (Merten & Osborne, 1984). Arterial epidural hematomas are due to a tear of the middle meningeal artery or one of its major branches, often in association with a skull fracture. Occasionally, small epidural hematomas are the result of venous bleeding from the skull and are not usually serious. Arterial epidural hematomas are surgical emergencies and can be life threatening. They can usually be distinguished from subdural hematomas by their appearance on CT scan, although small epidural bleeds may be difficult to distinguish from subdural hemorrhages.

8. *Subdural hemorrhage/hematoma.* Bleeding into the space that lies between the dura and the arachnoid membranes (i.e., subdural space) results from significant head trauma and is a hallmark of the shaking impact syndrome (see Figure 6.2b). Subdural hemorrhage most commonly results from tearing of the delicate bridging veins that join the surface of the brain to the dura during severe deceleration injury. The subdural hemor-

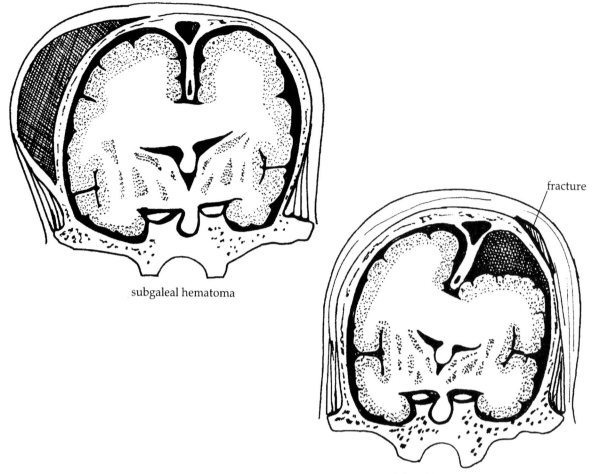

fracture

subgaleal hematoma

subdural hemorrhage

Figures 6.2a and 6.2b. Subgaleal and subdural hematoma.

Head injury may result in bleeding in a variety of locations. Subgaleal hemorrhage describes bleeding into soft tissues underlying the scalp, whereas subdural blood describes a collection of blood under the dura mater. In general, the prefix *sub* indicates "beneath" and *epi* indicates "upon" (e.g., epidural indicates bleeding upon or superficial to the dura, whereas subdural indicates bleeding beneath the dura).

rhage may be located in the posterior interhemispheric fissure and/or along the convexity of the brain. Motor vehicle accidents (including pedestrian and bicycle collisions with motor vehicles) account for most of the accidental trauma that results in subdural bleeds. On rare occasion, a minor focal impact will cause a subdural hemorrhage, but these children have a benign clinical course (Duhaime, in press). Infants and toddlers who sustain subdural hemorrhage are usually the victims of abuse. In this setting, a subdural bleed is a marker for severe head injury, and children are often critically ill. The child with such an injury presents for medical care with non-specific symptoms such as lethargy, apnea, irritability, poor feeding, seizures, or coma. Whereas the presence of subdural blood is a marker for severe injury, poor outcome in cases of

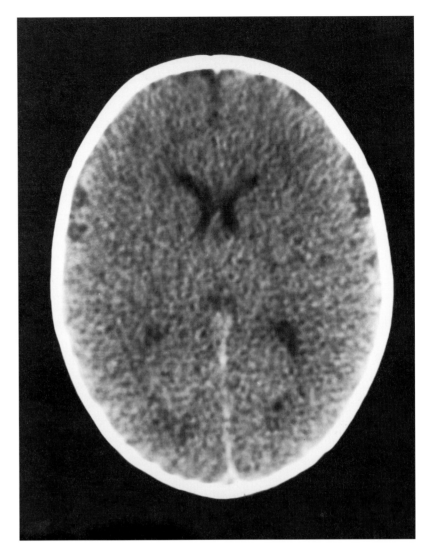

X Ray 6.1a.

Two-month-old infant with 2 days of vomiting. Baby developed seizures during evaluation. CT scan of head shows high density in the posterior interhemispheric fissure, which represents subdural hematoma.

inflicted cerebral trauma is due to a number of factors that ultimately result in cerebral swelling and diffuse brain infarction, such as local brain compression, apnea, hypoxia, mechanical trauma, and seizures. Cerebral swelling usually peaks at 48 to 72 hours after injury but may not maximize until 5 to 7 days posttrauma. Conversely, infants who do not appear critically ill at presentation often remain alert and promptly regain a normal level of consciousness despite acute subdural collections and do not progress to large delayed infarctions.

Brain swelling may be amenable to standard or even extraordinary medical management for increased intracranial

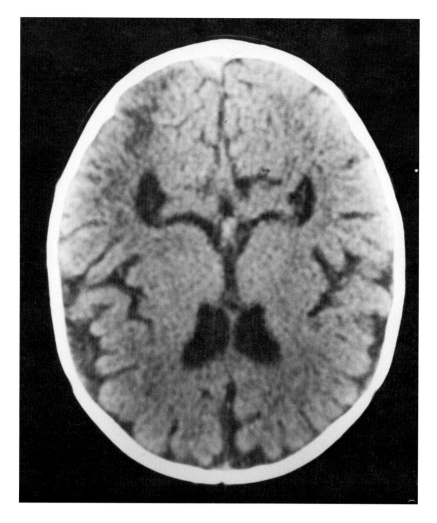

X Ray 6.1b.

Follow-up CT scan done 9 days later reveals a marked change in the appearance of the brain. The increase in the ventricle size and subarachnoid spaces is due to impaired reabsorption of CSF, with resultant hydrocephalus.

pressure in children in whom grey-white differentiation is lost. However, conventional therapy rarely, if ever, prevents the swollen brain from progressing to severe atrophy. In the first few months of life, brain swelling may not present a life-threatening problem because the skull simply expands to accommodate the swelling. These infants survive but in a neurologically devastated state. Consequently, the role of more aggressive measures in this population, including intracranial pressure monitoring, is controversial. It is hoped that newer treatments aimed at interfering with deleterious biochemical cascades initiated by the traumatic/hypoxic event but not yet completed may meet with more success (Bullock &

Fujisawa, 1992; Duhaime, 1994; McIntosh, 1992) (see Figure 6.2, Panel B).

9. *Chronic extra-axial fluid collections.* Large, bilateral, chronic extracerebral fluid collections composed of old blood and/or cerebrospinal fluid (CSF) are occasionally found in infants. These collections are often termed *chronic subdural hematoma,* although the content of the accumulation may vary from thin watery fluid resembling CSF to the consistency of thick motor oil, which is most characteristic of chronic subdural hematomas. Because the exact location and character of fluid may be difficult to discern, the term *chronic extracerebral fluid collections* is more accurate to describe these collections (Haines, Harkey, & Al-Mefty, 1993). These collections are usually discovered in early infancy, although they can be seen in young toddlers. The etiology of the fluid collection is not always clear. It may result from accidental trauma, coagulopathy, ventricular decompression from surgery, or from child abuse, and it has been described in association with osteogenesis imperfecta (Tokoro, Nakajima, & Yamataki, 1988).

Children with abnormal intracranial anatomy that includes an increase in the extra-axial space, such as children with ventricular shunts, are prone to subdural hemorrhage from relatively trivial trauma. It is not clear whether a similar mechanism is at work in infants with enlarged extracerebral spaces, such as those with so-called external hydrocephalus, or those with atrophy. Under these circumstances, tearing of bridging veins and arachnoid resulting from relatively mild trauma, as might occur accidentally, could theoretically result in a mixed collection of blood and CSF in both the subdural and subarachnoid spaces.

The frequency with which chronic extracerebral collections are due to abuse is unclear. In one series, 44% of the patients were known or suspected victims of child abuse (Parent, 1992). No specific etiology is found in most instances of chronic subdural collections. Although it is reasonable to assume that some degree of trauma preceded the development of the collections, it is not possible to presume child abuse in the absence of other supporting evidence. Until more is understood about the biomechanical mechanisms of chronic extracerebral collections, the diagnosis of child abuse as the etiology of chronic collections must rest on other findings indicative of child abuse. Such findings include unexplained long-bone fractures or characteristic soft-tissue injuries, because the presence of collections alone is insufficient to presume a deliberate violent traumatic event. Whether retinal hemorrhage alone, especially if minor, qualifies as corroborating evidence remains controversial, but at present, retinal hemorrhage probably should be considered supportive rather than diagnostic of inflicted injury.

Infants with chronic extra-axial collections present with signs of increased intracranial pressure: macrocephaly, fullness of the fontanelle, "sunsetting eyes," vomiting, irritability, lethargy, poor feeding, apnea, and/or seizures. Anemia may also accompany large fluid collections and probably arises from nutritional deficiency rather than blood loss into the extra cerebral spaces (McLaurin, Isaacs, & Lewis, 1971).

Diagnosis of chronic extra-axial fluid collections is by transfontanelle ultrasound, CT scan, or MRI examination of the head. MRI is the preferred study because it is able to distinguish high protein or bloody extra-axial collections from extra-axial CSF collections, which are commonly seen in asymptomatic infants. These may be termed *benign external hydrocephalus* and require no treatment.

Symptomatic infants require intermittent fontanelle taps to drain fluid and many need subdural-peritoneal shunts to provide for continual drainage of fluid. Infants with unexplained chronic subdural bleeds should have a skeletal survey and an evaluation for possible abuse.

The outcome of children with treated chronic extracerebral collections is highly variable. Approximately 50% may have normal development, but 30% will be moderately disabled, and 13% will be severely disabled (Aoki, 1990). Child abuse as the cause of the collection is a particularly poor prognostic factor because of underlying brain parenchymal damage that may have occurred at the time of the original injury. Series that included children with abuse probably included a certain number of children with brain atrophy as a contributing cause of delayed extracerebral collections, which would tend to increase the number of poorer outcomes.

10. *Subarachnoid hemorrhage (SAH).* Unlike subdural hemorrhage, isolated subarachnoid bleeding results from a variety of mechanisms and is not as highly associated with abuse. Arteriovenous malformations, cerebral aneurysms, coagulopathies, infection, and accidental trauma can cause subarachnoid bleeding (Broderick, Talbot, Prenger, Leach, & Brott, 1993; Meyer et al., 1989). SAH is associated with accidental trauma. When seen by itself, it is usually identified at the site of a focal impact and in association with depressed skull fractures or cortical contusions. SAH is also seen frequently in association with subdural hemorrhage as bridging veins rupture and bleed into both spaces. SAH related to accidental trauma usually indicates an increased severity of injury. Finally, SAH may be the result of abuse and is part of the spectrum of injuries that may result from shaking impact syndrome (Cohen, Kaufman, Myers, & Towbin, 1986; Merten & Osborne, 1984). It may be difficult to differentiate SAH from subdural hemorrhage or the normal falx in the posterior interhemispheric fissure (Cohen et al., 1986). CT scan is better than MRI at identifying SAH. Comparative findings between the two types of scans may be used to differentiate a small subdural from a subarachnoid hemorrhage, although this is not usually necessary. If the etiology of an acute SAH is unclear, skeletal survey, ophthalmology examination, and evaluation for other signs of trauma are warranted.

11. *Intracerebral hemorrhage.* Hemorrhagic contusions can result from both accidental or inflicted trauma and are often indicative of direct impact. The injuries are usually located along the cerebral convexities and in cases of abuse are often seen in association with other craniocerebral injuries (Kleinman, 1987c). Intracerebral hemorrhage can be identified by either CT or MRI. These injuries rarely require surgical management and will ultimately resolve, although encephalomalacia, porencephalic cysts, or subsequent seizures may develop.

12. *Diffuse axonal injury (DAI).* Diffuse microscopic tearing of axons in the white matter of the brain can be found on autopsy in some cases of child abuse (Vowles, Scholtz, & Cameron, 1987). DAI, which is due to movement of the brain within the skull (Gennarelli et al., 1982), requires extreme forces of angular deceleration and is responsible for prolonged coma in many patients after severe head injury. It may occur along with subdural hematoma. The diagnosis of DAI is made by MRI or after death by neuropathological evaluation.

13. *Intraventricular hemorrhage (IVH).* Outside of the newborn period, bleeding into the ventricles results from vascular malformations, coagulopathy, or trauma, or as a complication of surgery. IVH has been described in abused children (Kleinman, 1987c) but is rare; it may also result on occasion from accidental trauma.

14. *Hydrocephalus.* Hydrocephalus is a condition characterized by an increase in the amount of CSF, which is due to an imbalance of CSF production and absorption. The excess fluid causes dilatation of the ventricles, which may lead to increased intracranial pressure. There are many causes of hydrocephalus. Posttraumatic hydrocephalus may follow SAH or subdural hemorrhage that results in inflammation and adhesions of the meninges, blocking normal CSF absorption. Infants present with signs of increased intracranial pressure such as macrocephaly, vomiting, sunsetting of the eyes, irritability, or other changes in mental status. Infants and children with hydrocephalus may require a mechanical shunt that allows for CSF drainage.

15. *Cerebral atrophy/Ex-vacuo cerebrospinal fluid collections.* Brain tissue death results in cerebral atrophy and associated collections of extracerebral fluid (termed *hydrocephalus ex-vacuo*). The pathophysiology of this condition remains poorly understood, but large areas of low-density "black brain" will evolve to frank infarction in which large areas of brain parenchyma die (Duhaime, Sutton, & Schut, 1988; Whyte & Pascoe, 1989). Serial CT or MRI scans performed some months after the initial injury will show severe atrophy with a prominent sulcal pattern, loss of white matter, and massive extracerebral collections of slightly proteinaceous or cerebrospinal fluid density. These are the result of brain dissolution and shrinkage and are invariably accompanied by severe neurological damage. The head circumference may increase somewhat but tends to plateau over time. In general, surgical drainage of this sort of posttraumatic collection does not result in clinical improvement.

These definitions are meant to familiarize the reader with the common terms used in describing the head injuries associated with abuse. The remainder of the chapter will discuss the recognition, evaluation, and management of nonaccidental head trauma.

Shaking Impact Syndrome

The recognition that subdural hematoma and multiple long bone fractures were due to trauma was first made by John Caffey in 1946 (Caffey, 1946). The term *shaken baby syndrome* was later coined by Caffey in 1972 to describe infants with acute subdural and subarachnoid hemorrhage, retinal hemorrhages, and periosteal new bone formation at the metaphyseal regions of the long bones (Caffey, 1972). Although the diagnosis of the *shaken baby syndrome* rests on clinical and radiographic features, the name implies a specific mechanism of injury and was derived in part from the case of a nursemaid who admitted shaking several infants injured under her care in order to burp them (Caffey, 1972). Clinical and laboratory evidence for the damaging effects of angular acceleration on the brain was reported at about the same time that this syndrome was described (Ommaya, Faas, & Yarnell, 1968; Ommaya & Gennarelli, 1974; Ommaya & Yarnell, 1962). Thus, the mechanism of the injuries commonly found in abused infants was postulated to result from "whiplash-shaking" as a form of discipline, and the term *shaken baby syndrome* became widely accepted both as a diagnosis and as a description of how the injury occurred. This idea was strengthened by the observation that many infants with the intracranial findings of the syndrome had little, if any, evidence of blunt impact to the head seen on the initial physical examination. In addition, the infant's relatively large head, weak neck muscles, and high concentration of brain parenchymal water were thought to render them particularly vulnerable to severe injury from being shaken by the caretaker (Guthkelch, 1971). Central to the initial concept of the *shaken baby syndrome* was the idea that caretakers might inflict these injuries unwittingly in the course of a generally acceptable means of discipline, during choking, or even during play (Caffey, 1974). As will be discussed below, this is no longer believed to be the case.

Controversy as to the mechanism of these injuries exists because of the lack of reliable history typically available to the evaluating physician. When a history of trauma is offered, it is usually that of a relatively minor blunt impact rather than an unsolicited history of shaking. More recently, the term *shaken baby syndrome* has been questioned because clinical series, autopsies, and biomechanical and radiographic analyses suggest that many, if not most, of the infants do have evidence of blunt impact to the head, and that the deceleration forces generated by shaking alone are insignificant compared to those caused by impact, even when it is against a padded object (Duhaime et al., 1987; Duhaime et al., 1988; Hahn, Raimondi, McLone, & Yamanouchi, 1983). The frequent lack of dramatic scalp bruising can be explained by the dissipation of angular deceleration forces across a relatively wide and soft surface (Gennarelli & Thibault, 1985). It seems likely both from these studies and from careful questioning of perpetrators that although the infant may be shaken, the final thrust involves the head striking against a surface, causing the high deceleration forces required to cause subdural hemorrhage and frequently severe brain injury. Because of these newer findings, some authors prefer the term *shaking impact syndrome* to distinguish the mechanism in child abuse from less severe shaking during play, shaking to resuscitate, or other less forceful scenarios sometimes postulated as responsible for causing injury (Bruce & Zimmerman, 1989; Duhaime & Sutton, 1996). In addition, the frequent findings in these patients of skull fractures, subgaleal and subperiosteal hemorrhages, and focal contusions of the brain parenchyma suggest that impact has occurred. The forces necessary to cause the characteristic long bone injuries have not been analyzed sufficiently to determine the exact mechanism responsible for these findings. The question of whether shaking alone is ever sufficient to cause the brain injuries commonly seen in abused infants remains controversial. However, the syndrome of the battered child and that of the infant with the shaking impact syndrome probably represent different points on a continuum of child abuse with head injury (Alexander, Sato, Smith, & Bennett, 1990).

Regardless of the exact mechanism of injury, the clinical scenario in the shaking impact syndrome is often remarkably similar from one case to another. Children with this syndrome are nearly always 2 years of age or younger, and most are under 6 months. They are brought to medical attention because of irritability, poor feeding, or lethargy in mild cases, and because of seizures, apnea, or unresponsiveness in the more severely injured. The history is often vague, and in many cases, no history of trauma is offered. In other cases, a history of relatively trivial trauma is given. Sometimes, on questioning, a history of shaking to resuscitate is obtained. The diagnosis may come to light when a lumbar puncture done as part of a sepsis evaluation shows bloody spinal fluid (Duhaime et al., 1992). Infants and toddlers who are brought for medical care with either a history of minor trauma or no history of trauma and are discovered to have serious or life-threatening injuries are possible victims of child abuse and require a full evaluation for such.

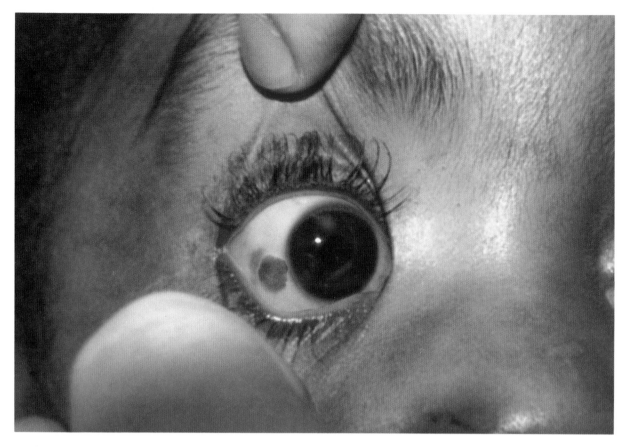

Photo 6.1.

Two-and-a-half-year-old battered and malnourished child with a scleral hemorrhage. Physical examination revealed multiple bruises, abrasions, and healing burns. Child also had multiple healing fractures. Scleral hemorrhages can result from direct trauma or the hemodynamic forces associated with chest compression.

The Physical Examination

The general and neurological examination of an infant with shaking impact syndrome can vary greatly (see Chapter 2 for details of the physical examination). The skin examination may reveal bruises of different ages. These bruises can be prominent or quite subtle. The back, chest, and neck should be examined for fingerprint-sized bruises, which can be critical in proving a traumatic etiology. The scalp should be examined and palpated for signs of trauma, although scalp bruises are often difficult to detect. External bruising is not necessary for making the diagnosis of shaking impact syndrome. In fact, infants with the most severe injuries may not have external markings on the body, so the lack of bruising does not eliminate the diagnostic consideration of abuse.

The retinal examination of the infant and young child may be technically difficult, but it is an essential component of the physical examination of the abused infant. Direct fundoscopic

CHILD PHYSICAL ABUSE AND NEGLECT

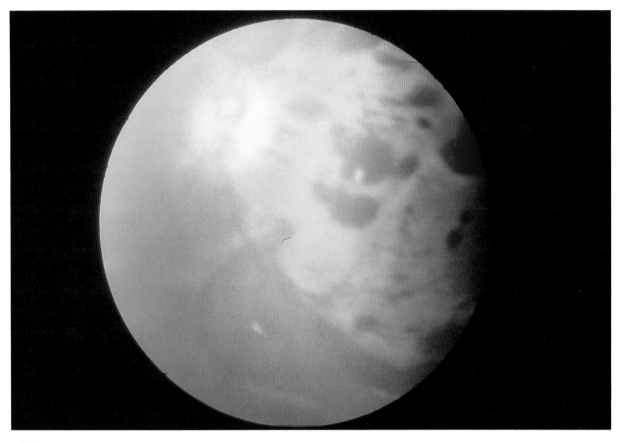

Photo 6.2.
Retinal hemorrhage (courtesy of Dr. Alex Levin).

examination may reveal retinal hemorrhages, but indirect ophthalmoscopy (done by an ophthalmologist) is required. Retinal hemorrhages are described by their location in the retinal layers. Preretinal or subhyaloid hemorrhages are found on the surface of the retina. Intraretinal hemorrhages are sometimes referred to as dot and blot hemorrhages. Hemorrhage into the superficial retinal nerve fiber layer results in flame-shaped hemorrhage. Finally, vitreous bleeding may result from extension of intraretinal or preretinal hemorrhages. Retinal hemorrhages occur in 50% to nearly 100% of victims of shaking impact syndrome (depending on definition and population studied) and often correlate with the severity of the child's acute neurologic presentation (Wilkinson, Han, Rappley, & Owings, 1989).

There are a number of causes of retinal hemorrhages. Newborns may have evidence of retinal hemorrhage, although the incidence reported varies greatly. Most neonatal retinal hemorrhages are mild and resolve within a few days (Baum & Bulpitt, 1970). Neonatal retinal hemorrhages have not been described after 6 weeks of age (Sezen, 1970). Retinal hemorrhages can result from severe accidental trauma, such as motor vehicle accidents or falls out of windows (Duhaime et al., 1992), or they may also occur from nontraumatic causes, including coagulopathy, meningitis, severe hypertension, endocarditis, vasculitis, sepsis, and carbon monoxide poisoning (Rosenberg, Singer, Bolte, Christian, & Selbst, 1994). Although there are reports of cardiopulmonary resuscitation (CPR) as a cause of retinal hemorrhage, it occurs infrequently and remains an area of controversy (Goetting & Sowa, 1990; Kanter, 1985). Retinal hemorrhages found in infants and children after CPR should not be presumptively attributed to the resuscitation, because they are more highly correlated with child abuse in this young population. Retinal hemorrhages may resolve spontaneously within weeks, although some last longer, require surgery, and lead to permanent visual problems. Retinal hemorrhages cannot be used to date an injury (Levin, 1990).

A range of neurologic abnormalities may be found in the infant, from mild irritability and lethargy to flaccid coma. Some children with seizures may show "bicycling" movements, which can be mistaken for normal spontaneous activity. Even severely injured young infants often show nonspecific withdrawal to noxious stimulation and even may have spontaneous eye openings. They can be distinguished from more normal infants by their paucity of normal spontaneous motor activity and by distinct lack of crying or vigorous grimacing to pain. The fontanelle may be full, and retinal hemorrhages are usually present.

The Glascow Coma Scale (GCS) is used in the acute setting to attempt to quantify the patient's level of consciousness and to follow the progression of the neurological examination. The scale was developed for use with adults and has been modified for use with infants and young children. The GCS rates the patient in three areas: eye opening, verbal response, and motor ability. The scale is difficult to apply to infants and young children, and care must be taken in interpreting the results of the GCS.

| **Laboratory Evaluation** | The laboratory evaluation of the patient includes a number of specific studies. The CBC may reveal anemia. The severity of the anemia varies depending on the chronicity of the abuse, other injuries sustained, and factors such as the age of the patient and nutritional status. The amount of blood lost into the subdural space is not usually great with an isolated, acute injury. A PT/PTT, bleeding time, and platelet count are used to evaluate bleeding diatheses. Coagulation defects are seen in patients with severe head injuries, including infants with shaking impact |

syndrome. This is thought to be caused by cerebral thromboplastin release (Mellion & Narayan, 1992). Patients who have persistently elevated PTT require evaluation for possible hemophilia. This is rarely required in practice.

Liver function enzymes, amylase, and urinalysis are used to screen for intra-abdominal injury. The abdominal examination of comatose patients is unreliable, and abused children with abdominal injuries may be asymptomatic (see Chapter 5).

Radiographic Evaluation

Skeletal survey is mandatory for children with shaking impact syndrome. The timing of the study is somewhat flexible. Children in critical condition can have the survey done when they are more stable. The study can also be done postmortem. Rib and metaphyseal fractures are highly associated with shaking impact syndrome but are not universally present. Metaphyseal fractures are found in a minority of patients but add convincing support to the diagnosis of abuse. Fractures to any bone may be found. The skeletal survey does not always reveal fractures. A bone scan should be done if the suspicion of abuse is high and the skeletal survey is negative. Bone scan is more sensitive in identifying acute rib fractures and subtle diaphyseal changes, although the rate of false positive scans is not known. If a skeletal survey completed acutely does not reveal fractures and a bone scan is negative, a skeletal survey repeated 2 weeks to 1 month later may reveal healing injuries that were not identified initially. (See Chapter 4 for more on the use of the skeletal survey and bone scan.)

Computerized tomography (CT) is the method of choice for the initial evaluation of the infant or child with suspected head trauma. CT scan images both parenchymal and bony pathology and is a relatively quick study to do. The scan can identify subdural hemorrhage, subarachnoid hemorrhage, cerebral edema, cortical contusions, and many fractures. Subdural hemorrhage may be unilateral or bilateral and has a particular propensity for the posterior interhemispheric space; this may result from impact to the back of the head, with bony displacement across the lambdoid sutures resulting in strains to the underlying venous sinuses and deep veins (Duhaime & Sutton, 1996; Zimmerman et al., 1979).

MRI is frequently superior to CT scan in demonstrating small subdural hemorrhages, parenchymal contusions, and diffuse axonal injury, and it can differentiate blood in different stages of resolution; this is particularly helpful when the diagnosis of a traumatic explanation for the child's symptoms is equivocal, such as when trauma is denied by the caretakers or the child has a chronic extra-axial fluid collection. MRI is a useful screening test

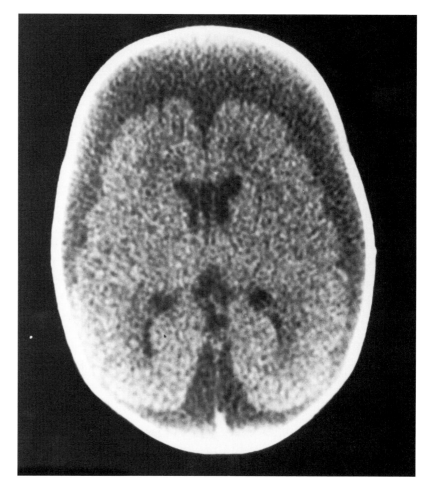

X Ray 6.2.

Four-month-old infant with a reported apneic event witnessed by her father. Apnea evaluation performed at a local hospital was normal. Baby presented 2 weeks later with lethargy and increasing head circumference. CT scan reveals large chronic subdural hemorrhage. Skeletal survey revealed healing rib fractures.

for arteriovenous malformation or other vascular anomalies that could cause subarachnoid hemorrhage, particularly when all other tests for associated injuries are unrevealing and the etiology of hemorrhage remains unclear. In rare cases, arteriography may be considered to rule out vascular abnormalities when there is no history or radiographic evidence clearly pointing to trauma and the child presents with an ictal intracranial hemorrhage.

In the more severe cases of shaking impact syndrome, the brain may lose its normal grey-white differentiation and have the appearance of a large unilateral or bilateral supratentorial infarction. This finding may be visible on the initial scan or may develop in the first 1 to 2 days after injury. Children with this finding are usually unresponsive on admission and have a dismal prognosis for neurologic recovery. The pathophysiology of the so-called black brain seen in these children is at present incompletely understood but may be due to the synergistic effects of hypoxia, mechanical trauma, and subdural hemorrhage (Whyte & Pascoe, 1989; Duhaime, Bilaniuk, & Zimmerman, 1993). In some children, evidence for a high spinal cord injury can be found, and this may contribute to the apnea and poor outcome seen in some cases (Hadley, Sonntag, Rekate, & Murphy, 1989).

The diagnosis of shaking impact syndrome is easier to make in cases in which there is no history of trauma but the infant has skull fractures and unexplained long bone trauma. However, in other cases, despite careful evaluation, the mechanism of injury remains obscure. An algorithm has been developed that matches the patient's injury type with associated findings and best history in an attempt to more objectively classify infant head injuries as accidental or inflicted (Duhaime et al., 1992). However, efforts to assign a definitive mechanism to every suspicious injury will remain incomplete until more is understood about the injury thresholds for children of different ages, the pathophysiology of retinal hemorrhages and the black brain, and the effects of chronic, repeated trauma on the immature nervous system.

Tin Ear Syndrome
The tin ear syndrome consists of the triad of unilateral external ear bruising, ipsilateral cerebral edema, and retinal hemorrhages (Hanigan, Peterson, & Njus, 1987). Blunt trauma to the ear resulting in significant rotational acceleration of the head causes the injuries. Hanigan et al. (1987) described three children between 2 and 3 years of age who presented for medical care within a day of a reported injury. All children died of cerebral herniation. Autopsy revealed ipsilateral subdural hemorrhage in all cases. Like shaking impact syndrome, the tin ear syndrome is specific for severe head injury and abuse.

Dating Head Injuries
The ability to date and time an injury is often of critical importance to the legal investigation of child abuse. On the basis of medical testing, physicians are often asked to precisely time an injury, especially if a child was left with multiple caretakers shortly before the onset of symptoms. The dating and timing of injuries is inexact and cannot be used to identify the time of injury and therefore the perpetrator. The history, physical examination findings, and interpretation of radiologic and labora-

tory studies used together offer the best chance of dating and timing an injury.

The history is important in establishing when the baby or child last appeared completely well. In general, the more severe the injury, the more quickly the child will be symptomatic. Children with mild injuries may not be brought for medical care acutely, and may present weeks to months later with chronic subdural hemorrhage and healing fractures. Although firm data are lacking in child abuse injuries, extrapolation from similar types of intracranial injuries from accidental head trauma suggests that children with life-threatening injuries are usually symptomatic immediately. Children whose injuries prove fatal, such as those with severe subdural hemorrhage, diffuse axonal injury, or hypoxia/ischemia, are symptomatic immediately. Symptoms can be nonspecific, and care must be taken before ascribing symptoms to inflicted trauma. In fact, some symptoms may be either the cause or the result of the abuse. For example, irritability and vomiting may be the result of a viral infection or head injury and increased intracranial pressure. A sick, irritable infant may cause caregiver frustration and abuse, in which case the onset of symptoms will not precisely coincide with the moment of injury. On the other hand, if multiple reliable individuals indicate that the baby appeared well and playful shortly before life-threatening or fatal injuries are discovered, it is highly unlikely that the baby had already been injured, and the possible timing of the injury can be narrowed.

The physical examination of a child with shaking impact syndrome may not reveal any external injuries. On occasion, bruises, burns, or bite marks can be helpful in timing the injury. Careful, sequential examinations may reveal skin injuries that are not apparent initially but develop over the first hours of admission. This would narrow the timing of injury to between 12 and 24 hours before admission. Injuries of different ages would indicate multiple episodes of trauma.

The appearance of CSF also can date an injury. Fresh blood is a reddish pink in color. As blood remains in the CSF, it undergoes biochemical changes that alter the appearance of the fluid. Xanthochromic CSF usually indicates that the CSF blood has been present for 12 to 24 hours, but it can be due to other factors. Chronic subdural hemorrhage results in CSF that is viscous and yellow in color. Some liken it to motor oil. Accumulated blood may organize and form membranous linings that originate from the dura and encapsulate the fluid. Parts of these linings are highly vascularized, which may predispose children with chronic subdurals to rebleeding into the same space. In this situation, imaging studies may show evidence of bleeds of various ages.

The interpretation of radiologic studies is of great value in dating injuries, especially if sequential studies are done. Both CT scan and MRI can date injuries to some extent, based on the appearance of blood, the presence of cerebral edema, and changes identified over the initial days to weeks after an injury. CT scan and MRI alone cannot determine the precise moment of injury. MRI has the advantage of being able to differentiate subdural blood of varying stages of resolution based on the breakdown of blood products in the fluid. The biochemical changes that predict the age of the blood can vary depending on the size and compartmentalization of the hematoma, so that caution is needed in assessing the age of injury by this method (Sato et al., 1989). Abused children with repeated injuries may be identified with MRI.

In summary, no one method can precisely time the moment of an unwitnessed injury. The most accurate method of determining the time of an injury is done using history, physical examination, and radiographic and laboratory data together. It must be recognized, however, that despite careful and complete evaluations, the ability to determine the timing of an injury to minutes or hours is sometimes impossible.

Physical Abuse in the Older Child

Most of the older children brought to medical attention suffer from soft tissue or visceral injuries from direct blows, although intracranial injuries do sometimes occur and can be serious or even fatal. The setting is usually that of a biological or foster family in which deviations from rigid codes of behavior are dealt with by physical punishment and beating.

Evaluation includes a careful history. The child should be questioned apart from the parent once some degree of trust is attained (if clinically possible). A general trauma evaluation is undertaken, including routine studies such as urinalysis for hematuria or myoglobinuria. Skeletal survey is usually of limited use in the older child because the typical occult injuries (e.g., metaphyseal and rib fractures) seen in infants do not occur in this age group, and remote skeletal injuries have usually healed to the point of being undetectable. A careful history of previous trauma, including fractures, and the physical exam are usually more helpful in detecting findings suspicious for child abuse in this age group.

Head injuries may include soft tissue trauma; linear, depressed, or basilar fractures; and the range of intracranial lesions seen in trauma in general. Management is guided by the specific injury.

Counseling is often in order, and a neuropsychological evaluation may be useful in the older child with acute or chronic brain involvement or behavioral disturbances in order to help with appropriate school placement.

Spine Injury Due to Child Abuse

Little attention has been paid to the spine in clinical and autopsy series. This is surprising in view of the commonly assumed "whiplash" pathophysiology of child abuse and the anatomy of the infant and childhood spine that renders it particularly vulnerable to damage due to flexion/extension forces. Devastating neurological injury can occur in children without vertebral bony fractures or other radiographic abnormalities, making diagnosis of spinal cord injury difficult to detect without sophisticated radiographic imaging procedures (Pang & Pollack, 1989). The incidence of spinal injury in the setting of child abuse is probably underappreciated, because overwhelming brain injury may mask clinical suspicion of an associated injury to the cervical spinal cord. Even at autopsy, the brain has often been removed at the cervicomedullary junction without examining the spinal cord.

There is evidence that a significant percentage of fatally injured, abused infants demonstrate autopsy findings of subdural and epidural hemorrhage and contusion of the high cervical cord, which may contribute to morbidity and mortality (Hadley et al., 1989). It is rare to have a clinically detected spinal cord injury in a child with a recoverable brain injury, so it may be that these injuries are usually fatal. Nevertheless, it is conceivable that apnea from transient spinal cord compression in association with a shaking impact injury might significantly contribute to the brain damage that is so prominent in child abuse cases.

Spine fracture and overt spinal instability appear to be uncommon aspects of nonaccidental trauma to infants but might be underrecognized (see X ray 6.3). Therefore, immobilization of the neck and screening spine radiographs as part of the evaluation of suspected child abuse is recommended. If MRI of the brain is performed, a screening study of the upper cervical region can also be obtained, although findings in survivors are unusual. Occasionally, overt spine injuries will be seen in battered children and appear to occur from extreme hyperflexion or hyperextension forces applied to the immature spine. More subtle vertebral body compression deformities are also described and are usually the result of hyperflexion injuries (Kleinman, 1987e).

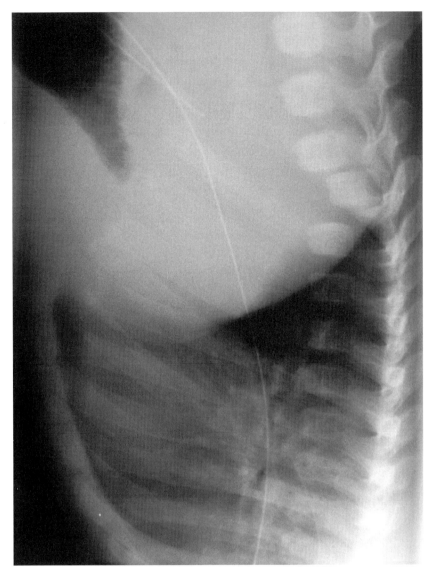

X Ray 6.3.

Lateral vertebral body fracture. Ten-month-old infant who suddenly became unable to crawl 2 days after falling out of a crib. Lateral vertebral X rays reveal a fracture of vertebra T11 with posterior displacement of the T11 vertebral body into the spinal canal. These injuries are the result of severe hyperflexion. The child also has sustained a spiral femur fracture at 3 weeks of age.

Outcome of Head Injuries From Child Abuse

Severely head-injured infants have a worse prognosis than do older children, which is possibly related to the preponderance of inflicted injuries in this age group (Kriel, Krach, & Panser, 1989; Levin et al., 1992). Mortality among abused children with head injuries ranges between 10% and 27% in various series, although exact figures are difficult to compile because of the differences in definitions of child abuse and referral populations (Duhaime et al., 1987; Duhaime et al., 1992; Hahn et al., 1983; Ludwig & Warman, 1984; McClelland, Rekate, Kaufman, & Persse, 1980). Nevertheless, it is clear that this etiology of head injury correlates with a high mortality.

Morbidity in survivors of inflicted injury is even more difficult to ascertain because long-term follow-up of patients injured in infancy is lacking. Children with widespread infarction and severe brain atrophy remain severely physically and cognitively disabled. Long-term deficits of children who are more mildly injured remain unknown.

With respect to visual problems, retinal hemorrhages resolve over time, but amblyopia may develop if the macula is obscured by hemorrhage for a prolonged period, and close follow-up is recommended. Retinal detachments frequently result in marked visual compromise and may require repair to optimize recovery. Retinal folds may also affect visual outcome adversely (Han & Wilkinson, 1990).

In Brief

- Head trauma is the leading cause of morbidity and mortality related to child physical abuse.
- Acute subdural hemorrhage in an infant or toddler should raise the suspicion of shaking impact syndrome unless a clear history of sufficient trauma is elicited.
- The etiology of chronic extra-axial fluid collections is not always clear. All infants and children with unexplained extra-axial collections should have an evaluation for possible abuse, along with a skeletal survey and social work evaluation.
- Infants and toddlers with shaking impact syndrome present for medical care with nonspecific symptoms, such as irritability, lethargy, vomiting, apnea, and seizures. The possibility of trauma is often not initially considered.
- CT scan is the preferred initial imaging study for children with acute injuries. MRI is more sensitive in identifying or clarifying many of the injuries seen in abused children.
- Skeletal survey and ophthalmology examination are mandatory for the evaluation of the abused infant and toddler with head injuries.

7 Neglect and Failure to Thrive

with Trude A. Haecker, MD, and

Martha M. Cockerill, MSN, CRNP

Neglect is the most commonly reported form of child maltreatment, representing 45% of the 2.936 million maltreatment reports made in the United States in 1992 (American Humane Association, 1993). It represents a situation in which the child's basic physical, supervisional, medical, emotional, and/or educational needs are not met (Gaudin, 1993a) (see Table 7.1 for categorization of different forms of neglect). Neglect is defined as

> a condition in which a [child's caregiver], either deliberately or by extraordinary inattentiveness, permits the child to experience avoidable suffering and/or fails to provide one or more

Table 7.1 Types of Neglect

Physical neglect	
Neglect of basic physical needs	Failure to provide clothing, food, shelter, and hygiene
Medical neglect	Failure to provide or a delay in providing needed care by a professional for a physical injury, illness, medical condition, or impairment
Supervisional neglect	
Abandonment/ Expulsion	Desertion of a child without arranging for reasonable care and supervision, including cases where (a) children are not claimed within 2 days, (b) children are left with no or false information given regarding caregiver's whereabouts, and (c) indefinite refusal of custody without adequate arrangement for care of child by others
Custody inattention	Apparent unwillingness to maintain custody by (a) repeated shuttling of child from household to household or (b) repeatedly leaving a child with others for days or weeks at a time
Safety	Inattention to the hazards in the child's physical environment and developmental capacity that place him or her at risk for injury
Emotional neglect	
Inattention to basic emotional needs/ nurturance/affection	Inattention to the child's needs for affection, emotional support, attention, and competence, including (a) markedly overprotective restrictions that foster immaturity or emotional overdependence; (b) chronically applying expectations clearly inappropriate in relation to the child's age or level of development; (c) domestic violence in the child's presence; (d) encouragement of or permitting drug or alcohol use by the child; (e) encouragement of or permitting other maladaptive behavior (e.g., severe assaultiveness, chronic delinquency)
Mental health care neglect	Failure to provide, or a delay in providing, needed care for a child's emotional or behavioral impairment or problem in accord with competent professional recommendation
Educational neglect	
Truancy	Permitted school absences averaging at least 5 days per month
Failure to enroll	Failure to enroll a school-age child, causing the child to miss at least one month of school, or a pattern of keeping a school-age child home for nonlegitimate reasons (e.g., to work, to care for siblings, etc.) an average of at least 3 days a month
Inattention to special education needs	Inattention to recommended remedial education services for child's diagnosed learning disorder or other special education need

Source: Adapted from NIS-2 (NCAAN, 1988b).

of the [components] generally deemed essential for developing [the child's] physical, intellectual, and emotional capacities. (Polansky cited in Gaudin, 1993, p. 4)

Neglect of the child's physical needs, such as food, clothing, hygiene, and medical care, accounts for more than half of the neglect cases identified each year (National Center on Child Abuse and Neglect, 1988a). Despite its high incidence, neglect receives less attention than physical or sexual abuse, prompting Wolock and Horowitz (1984) to decry the "neglect of neglect." The most commonly cited reason for lack of attention is ambivalence and discomfort among health care professionals in passing judgment on parental choices regarding child-rearing style (Dubowitz, Black, Starr, & Zuravin, 1993; Ludwig, 1992b).

This chapter presents an overview of neglect with a focus on failure to thrive (FTT).

Conceptual Approaches	Health care providers have been aware since the turn of the century that inadequate caregiving has deleterious effects on a child's growth, development, and well-being (Chapin, 1908; Fontana, Donovan, & Wong, 1963; Kempe, Silverman, Steele, Droegmueller, & Silver, 1962; Spitz, 1945, 1949). Recently, Dubowitz et al. (1993) called for a perspective of shared responsibility in describing neglect. They focus attention on the child's unmet needs, looking at the shared failures of the caregivers, family, community, and society to meet the child's basic needs. This ecological approach encourages health care providers to pay more attention to the strengths and weaknesses of the child's care-giving environment. This perspective also enables health care providers to formulate treatment plans that incorporate all the resources available in the child's environment. An example is a child who fails to grow because of a lack of formula. An approach that does not solely blame the mother but instead identifies the mother's lack of resources as part of the problem may be more beneficial to the child and caregiver. The problem can be solved by helping the mother apply for the Supplemental Food Program for Women, Infants and Children (WIC) benefits and assisting her to obtain necessary resources to provide for her child.

There is debate as to what constitutes good parenting. Most professionals reach similar conclusions when caregiver behaviors and choices fall far from expected norms (Ludwig, 1992b). For example, starving a child represents a failure to meet basic food needs, and not changing a diaper for 24 hours represents failure to meet a child's basic hygienic needs. However, does leaving a child home alone at age 11 constitute neglect of the child's need for supervision? The answer to this question depends on (a) the child's maturity, (b) the proximity and availability of a responsible adult, and (c) the duration of the caregiver's absence. In such gray cases, the health care provider is forced to rely on subjective, personal judgments. It is crucial that the health care provider not impose his or her personal child-rearing style and beliefs on other families. Instead, the approach is to focus on the child's unmet needs and ensure the child's growth and developmental well-being.

Effects of Neglect

A range of physical, emotional, and cognitive effects on the developing child occur when basic needs are unmet. Each child's response to neglect is different and depends in part on the type of neglect, the developmental stage at which the neglect occurs, the severity of the unmet need, and the effectiveness of the intervention by caring adults to halt the neglect. Commonly reported effects are (a) withdrawn affect; (b) decreased social interactions; (c) disorganized, aggressive interactions with peers; and (d) fewer positive play behaviors such as offering, sharing, accepting, and following (Peterson & Urquiza, 1993). In addition, children who have experienced impaired or delayed growth on the basis of neglect may experience delayed language development and social, maturational, and behavioral difficulties. They also may be slower than expected in achieving developmental milestones (Schmitt & Mauro, 1989).

Evaluation

The general approach to the evaluation of neglect mirrors the evaluation suggested for other forms of maltreatment. It is ideally based on a multidisciplinary approach that includes (a) a comprehensive medical history; (b) a thorough physical examination; (c) specific, directed laboratory and diagnostic testing; (d) a formal psychosocial assessment of the family, including observation of the child-caregiver interactions, and (e) meticulous documentation of the evaluation's findings.

Neglect and Growth: Failure to Thrive (FTT)

FTT is a working diagnosis generally applied to children who are similar only in an observable deviation from an expected growth trajectory (Barbero & Shaheen, 1967; Frank & Zeisel, 1988; Goldbloom, 1982; Johnson & Coury, 1992; Kempe, Cutler, & Dean, 1980; Kempe & Goldbloom, 1987). There is not a single etiology that accounts for all cases of FTT, and some suggest replacing FTT with other terms thought to be more accurate, such as growth failure, growth retardation, and growth deficiency (Goldbloom, 1987; Kempe & Goldbloom, 1987). Although these arguments have merit, FTT is a term firmly rooted in clinical practice, and it remains the working diagnosis for children not growing as expected (Ludwig, 1992b).

Table 7.2 Mixed FTT Subcategories

Type 1	An abnormal environment leading to poor care of a child (e.g., homelessness)
Type 2	An abnormal environment and a medically ill child occurring simultaneously (e.g., homelessness and a child requiring gavage feedings)
Type 3	An affected child whose care requirements disrupt the family and cause environmental breakdown (e.g., technologically dependent child who is brought home from the hospital). The stress of the need for around-the-clock care of their child has led parents to divorce.

Note: Gordon and Vasquez (1986) divided "mixed" FTT into three categories based on interplay between organic and psychosocial characteristics.

FTT usually presents in infancy and early childhood when there are rapid periods of growth. With malnutrition, weight is the first growth parameter affected, followed by height and then head circumference (Barbero & Shaheen, 1967). In evaluating a child with FTT as the working diagnosis, the clinician carefully considers the age of presentation, the presence or absence of risk factors for growth failure (such as underlying medical condition), and psychosocial factors that might affect feeding and growth. The diagnosis is made when the evaluation is completed and information from each component of the evaluation carefully considered. Once a definite etiology for the problem is uncovered, the term FTT may be linked with the appropriate diagnosis.

For many years, FTT was thought to be either organic (physically based) or nonorganic (socially based). Health care professionals thought that the growth retardation seen in children labeled as FTT originated either from a medical condition or illness or from a psychosocial aberration in the child's caregiving environment. This dichotomous view has since been modified as clinicians realized that a third category, "mixed" FTT, accounts for the large number of cases in which a combination of both organic and psychosocial factors contributes to growth failure (Homer & Ludwig, 1981). (See Table 7.2 for types of mixed FTT and Table 7.7 for questions asked in the evaluation of FTT.)

Consequently, the differential diagnosis of FTT includes a wide range of possible etiologies for growth failure that is as broad as the index of a pediatric textbook (Tunnessen, 1988). Goldbloom (1987) states that the growth failure seen in FTT should be ascribed to neglect only on the basis of positive findings in the history, physical examination, or family assessment rather than after a "negative" workup that fails to identify an "organic" cause. Table 7.8 contains a differential diagnosis for FTT. Psychosocial FTT is used when the growth failure is primarily attributed to characteristics in the child's caregiving environment, namely social, environmental, psychological, or behavioral factors that affect the amount of nutrition that the child functionally receives. (See Table 7.9 for an overview of the evaluation of FTT.)

Alexander (1992) summarizes the basic nutritional issues that underlie the growth problems seen in all types of FTT: (a) not enough calories going into the child, (b) too many calories excreted by the child, or (c) too many calories expended internally. Organic causes may be seen in children with gastrointestinal anatomic abnormalities such as short-gut, malabsorption, or a hypermetabolic state related to chronic inflammation. However, these organic conditions may coexist with social, environmental, psychological, and/or behavioral issues that contribute to or exacerbate the nutritional problem, thus giving rise to "mixed" FTT. For example, feeding a child with a cleft lip and palate may so challenge the caregivers that efforts to feed the child become dysfunctional and ineffective. Thus, an initial organic problem may become mixed over time as the psychosocial component becomes established.

FTT Evaluation

The following is included in the medical evaluation of a child whose growth is below expectation:

1. Comprehensive medical history with feeding and dietary history
2. Complete physical examination, including measurement of growth parameters (weight, height/length, and head circumference) and review of prior measurements
3. Laboratory workup, specifically indicated by history and physical examination
4. Psychosocial assessment with observation of caregiver-child interactions, especially around feeding
5. Careful documentation of all findings

(See Table 7.9 for an overview of the evaluation for FTT.)

History

The evaluation of FTT includes the medical history (see Chapter 2) and specific information about nutritional status, diet, and feeding behaviors. The following are areas to highlight in the FTT history:

1. Any history of medical conditions that may affect the amount of calories ingested, excreted, or internally expended (Peterson, Rathbun, & Huerrera, 1985).
2. Adequacy of caloric intake. The Committee on Dietary Allowances (1980) of the National Research Council estimates that healthy infants on average require approximately 115 kcal/kg

Table 7.3 Recommended Daily Allowances

Age	Average energy allocation (kcal/day)	Range of energy needs (kcal/day) (10th-90th percentile)
Infants		
0-6 months (mo.)	(kg)[a] × 108	(kg) × 95 to (kg) × 145
≥ 6 mo.-1 yr.	(kg) × 98	(kg) × 80 to (kg) × 135
Children		
1-3 years (yr.)	(kg) × 102	900 to 1800
≥ 3-6 yr.	(kg) × 90	1300 to 2300
≥ 6-10 yr.	(kg) × 70	1650 to 3300
Older children/adolescents (weight at 50th percentile)		
Females		
≥ 10-14 yr.	2200	1500 to 3000
≥ 14-18 yr.	2100	1200 to 3000
Males		
≥ 10-14 yr.	2700	2000 to 3700
≥ 14-18 yr.	2800	2100 to 3900

a. Weight in kilograms.
Source: Committee on Dietary Allowances (1980); Subcommittee on 10th Edition of the RDAs (1989).

during their first 6 months of life and that this can vary from 95 to 145 kcal/kg (10th to 90th percentile, respectively). From 6 months to 1 year of age, the caloric requirement, on average, decreases to approximately 105 kcal/kg, ranging from 80 to 135 kcal/kg (10th to 90th percentile, respectively). Approximate targets exist for the amount of formula an infant should receive based on the standard caloric content of commercial formulas (20 kcal/oz). Table 7.3 includes ranges for caloric requirements for children.

3. History of weight gain. On average, healthy infants who receive adequate caloric intake are expected to gain weight at standard rates, although a range of normal growth exists. The weight targets are as follows:

0 to 3 months of age → 27 gm/day (0.9 oz)

≥ 3 to 6 months of age → 24 gm/day (0.8 oz)

≥ 6 to 9 months of age → 18 gm/day (0.6 oz)

≥ 9 to 12 months of age → 16 gm/day (0.4 oz)

≥ 12 to 24 months of age → 40 gm/week (1.5 oz/week)

(Hamill et al., 1979; Hobbs, Hanks, & Wynne, 1993b; Schmitt & Mauro, 1989)

4. Family growth history, including information on the size, growth patterns, and timing of puberty of the biological parents as well as those of other family members (Peterson et al., 1985). Methods exist to correct for genetic height expectations based on analysis of parental size using parent-specific corrections such

Table 7.4 Midparental Height Correction

How to Use the Method

1. Measure and record the height of both the mother and the father.

2. When one parent's height cannot be measured, an estimate by the other parent can be substituted for measured height, and midparental height can be calculated.

   Alternatively, a perception of the other parent's height category (short, medium, or tall) can be used to determine midparental height (Chart 7.5, at end of chapter).

3. Calculate midparental height by adding the mother's height and the father's height in centimeters and dividing by two.

$$\frac{\text{Height of mother (cm)} + \text{height of father (cm)}}{2}$$

4. Measure, record, and plot the child's length (birth to 36 months) or height (3 to 18 years) in centimeters on the appropriate NCHS growth chart.

5. Calculate the child's *adjusted* length or height by using the parent-specific adjustments from Charts 7.1 and 7.2 for length or from Charts 7.3 and 7.4 for height, choosing the table appropriate for the sex of the child.

   a. Locate the age *closest* to that of the child.
   b. For that age, locate the horizontal row that includes the child's length or height.
   c. Locate the vertical column closest to the midparental height for the child.
   d. The appropriate parent-specific adjustment (in centimeters) is at the row-column intersection.
   e. Add the parent-specific adjustment to the child's measured length or height if the adjustment has no sign; subtract the adjustment if it has a minus sign.

6. Determine the child's parent-specific adjusted percentile by plotting adjusted length or height on the NCHS growth chart. Clearly label plotted measurements as being actual or adjusted values.

   The steps in calculating a parent-specific adjustment for a hypothetical child are illustrated in Example 1.

   Example 1: Steps in Calculating Parent-Specific Adjustment for Hypothetical Boy

   Example: Boy aged 12 months, length 71.1 cm, mother's height 153.7 cm, father's height 165.7 cm.

   > Son's actual length is 71.1 cm
   > Son's actual percentile is below the 5th
   > Mother's height is 153.7 cm
   > Father's height is 165.7 cm
   > Midparental height is (153.7 + 165.7)/2 = 159.7 cm
   > Adjustment is 2 cm (from Chart 7.1)
   > Son's adjusted length is 71.1 + 2 = 73.1 cm
   > Son's adjusted percentile is between the 10th and 25th (NCHS)

   Interpretation: Probably genetically short. Consider additional contributing factors.

Source: Himes et al. (1985). Used with permission.

as midparental height (average of both biological parents' adult height) (Himes, Roche, Thissen, & Moore, 1985; Tanner, Goldstein, & Whitehouse, 1970). Table 7.4 details the method described by Himes et al. (1985) to determine child's growth based on parental height.

Physical Examination

A thorough physical examination focuses on findings suggestive of underlying disorders, growth parameters, and objective

CHILD PHYSICAL ABUSE AND NEGLECT

developmental assessment. The following are areas to highlight in the FTT physical examination.

1. *Findings indicative of underlying disease and/or physical signs of maltreatment.*

   Signs of wasting as evidenced by loss of subcutaneous tissue in the buttocks, thighs, temporal and paraspinal areas, and around the rib cage (disease or maltreatment)

   Nutritional deficiencies may reveal themselves through changes in the skin (e.g., dry, cracked), hair (e.g., sparse, fragile), teeth (e.g., caries, delayed eruption), and nails (e.g., dystrophic) (disease or maltreatment)

   Physiological aberrations as evidenced by decreases in pulse, core body temperature, and body fat (disease or maltreatment)

   Congenital syndromes with characteristic findings in the hands, feet, face, head, extremities, and body habitus (disease)

   Signs of neglectful caretaking, such as dirty, poorly maintained clothing; excessive diaper rash; bald patch on the back of the head; poor grooming; and a general lack of proper hygiene (Hobbs et al., 1993b)

2. *Growth measurements.* Standard growth parameters are plotted for weight, height/length, weight for height, and head circumference on NCHS growth charts (Hamill et al., 1979). Many suggest expressing the child's weight as a "weight age." This is done by plotting the child's current weight and determining at what age this weight would represent the 50th percentile (Goldbloom, 1987). For example, a 2-year-old child at 9 kilos has a "weight age" of 10 months based on the NCHS charts.

   Plotting and reviewing previous growth points is an important part of the growth assessment and assists in visualizing the growth pattern over time.

   Head circumference is measured for at least the first 2 years, and recumbent length is measured until age 2 and then followed by a standing height.

   Correction for prematurity is necessary when plotting growth parameters. This is done by subtracting the number of weeks that the baby is premature (based on a 40-week gestation) from the baby's chronological age and then plotting the measured growth parameter against the corrected age. Head circumference measurements are plotted against corrected age until a chronological age of 18 months. Weight is corrected in this fashion until 24 months of age, and height measurements are corrected up to 40 months (Brandt, 1979).

   Despite age correction, extremely premature infants and infants with severe intrauterine growth retardation (IUGR) may remain short throughout life. To evaluate the growth of IUGR infants, determine whether the IUGR was asymmetric or symmetric. Asymmetric IUGR exists when weight is lower than anticipated for gestational age but head circumference and length are spared. Symmetric IUGR exists when head circumference, length, and weight are all equally reduced for gestational age. Infants with symmetric IUGR have a relatively poor developmental prognosis and often fail to grow properly.

FTT is suspected with the following findings:

Growth parameters

a. weight and/or height/length measurements are less than the 5th percentile
b. weight for height is less than 5th percentile
c. weight measurement is less than 80% of the median weight for age

Growth pattern

a. measurements that follow a curve less than the 3rd percentile (keeping in mind that from a statistical perspective, 3% of healthy children will follow this pattern)
b. measurements that drop across at least two formal growth curves, namely 95th, 90th, 75th, 50th, 25th, 10th, 5th percentile curves
c. measurements that give rise to a fluctuating, "saw-toothed" pattern suggesting normal or near-normal growth punctuated by periods of poor growth

In addition to standard growth measurements, anthropometric growth assessments, such as mid-upper arm circumference and triceps skinfold thickness assessment may be assessed. This provides an objective assessment of fat and muscle mass (Frischiano, 1974).

3. *Assessment of developmental abilities.* Objective assessment of developmental abilities is also possible during the physical examination because components of standardized developmental screening tests are easily accomplished (Dworkin, 1989).

Specific, Directed Laboratory Evaluation

Laboratory tests and diagnostic procedures may be needed to evaluate FTT (Berwick, Levy, & Kleinerman, 1982; Homer & Ludwig, 1981; Sills, 1978). Laboratory tests confirm a diagnosis suggested by the clinical evaluation, but not all children evaluated for FTT need a laboratory evaluation. Specific laboratory tests are done during the workup. Random panels of tests rarely uncover etiologies not initially expected based on the history or physical.

Studies indicate that the usefulness of laboratory and radiologic tests alone in the diagnosis of neglect is low (Berwick et al., 1982; Sills, 1978). Berwick et al. (1982) retrospectively studied 122 children (between 1 and 25 months) admitted to a tertiary care center for FTT evaluation. An average of 40 laboratory and radiological procedures were performed per child, and only 0.8% were deemed helpful in making a diagnosis. Sills's (1978) retrospective study of 185 children hospitalized for FTT found similar results. Only 1.4% of all tests ordered were of positive diagnostic value, and no test was useful without a specific indication from the clinical evaluation.

The health care provider presented with a child who is failing to grow considers a wide range of possible etiologies. Basic laboratory screens that may be helpful are (a) CBC (e.g., anemia, infection); (b) erythrocyte sedimentation rate (e.g., infection, inflammation); (c) urinalysis (e.g., renal disease, infection); (d) urine culture (e.g., infection); (e) lead screen (e.g., anemia); and (f) electrolytes, including blood urea nitrogen (BUN) and serum creatinine (e.g., metabolic disorder, renal disease, renal tubular acidosis) (Fomon, 1974; Ludwig, 1992b). A bone age may be useful as well as thyroid function tests if history and/or physical suggest a chromosomal or endocrinological disorder. The bone age is determined through a radiograph of the child's hand. The child's X ray is then compared to "standards" by the radiologist, and a bone age is assigned (Graham, 1972). This bone age is then compared to the child's chronological age looking for variation. After review of other evaluation components, further laboratory or radiological tests may be indicated based on clinician judgment.

Psychosocial Assessment and Feeding Observations

The evaluation of FTT includes a thorough psychosocial assessment that begins at the initial assessment and continues throughout the entire evaluation (see Chapter 9). Growth failure may be one of many indicators of psychosocial disorganization and may be associated with major life events. The health care provider explores the caregiving environment and asks questions about marital or relationship problems, lack of prenatal and postpartum care for the mother, and lack of immunizations and other health maintenance for the child (Ludwig, 1992b). In addition, observation of interactions surrounding the child's feeding remains a critical component of this assessment. Areas that require specific attention include the following:

1. The caregiver's comfort with the child and his or her appreciation of the child's developmental accomplishments. Goldbloom (1987) suggests that the health care provider ask the caregivers a simple question: "Are you having fun with the baby?" Responses that include an instant smile or a cheerful affirmation are encouraging. Delayed, equivocal, or silent responses are concerning.
2. The child's feeding/dietary history along with observations of the caregiver/child interaction during feeding reveal whether mealtime is a healthy, pleasurable experience for the pair or if it is completed in anger or with force by a rejecting caregiver (Schmitt & Mauro, 1989). For example, a disturbed mother may

Table 7.5 Infant Feeding Stages

Stage 1	Homeostasis	0-2 months	The caregiver and child settle on a feeding schedule. The caregiver learns the child's cues for hunger, the child's tolerance for distractions, and his or her signals for satiety.
Stage 2	Attachment	2-6 months	The child develops socially, and caregiver and child together refine a repertoire of behaviors around the feeding that makes it mutually satisfying and pleasant or uncomfortable and difficult.
Stage 3	Separation/ Individuation	Over 6 months	The child becomes more independent and capable of feeding him- or herself during separation/individuation. The caregiver's task is to support the developing independence in a nurturing manner.

Source: Adapted from Chatoor and Egan (1983).

feed her infant with disinterest or with an obvious lack of awareness of the infant's minute-to-minute needs (Schmitt & Mauro, 1989).

The observer may uncover oral-motor difficulties with sucking, gagging, or swallowing, as well as ongoing struggles with feeding and food refusal. Chatoor and Egan (1983) describe three overlapping stages of feeding in the infant under 3 years of age that provide a framework for feeding observations (see Table 7.5). Each stage describes specific caregiver/child tasks accomplished through mutual interaction. In addition, Satler (1990) identified behaviors that support healthy progression through these stages. Table 7.5 guides the observer through feeding interactions.

Treatment

The design of the treatment plan for the child with FTT depends upon the results of the evaluation. If psychosocial concerns are prominent, a multidisciplinary treatment plan is ideal because it draws on the expertise of physician, nurse, social worker, and nutritionist. The treatment plan consists of standard therapy for the condition in the relatively uncommon situation in which FTT is caused purely by a medical condition with no psychosocial overlay. For example, if the child's FTT resulted from chronic diarrhea secondary to a bacterial infection, then the appropriate treatment is antibiotics and careful refeeding. This text does not detail specific treatment plans for the variety of medical conditions responsible for growth retardation. Treatment plans are available in standard pediatric texts (Oski, DeAngelis, Feigin, & Warshaw, 1990).

More commonly, medical conditions coexist with psychosocial problems. In this situation, complex management plans are

Table 7.6 Questions in the FTT Assessment

I. Peripartum
    Was this pregnancy planned?
    How was the pregnancy? Labor? Delivery?
    How did you feel physically? Emotionally?
    How did your partner handle things? Your family? Friends?
    When did you first see the baby? What did you think?
    Who helped the first few weeks? Who helps now?
    Did you want a (another) child? What about your partner?
II. Developmental
    Does the baby/child have a routine? What is it like?
    Is the baby/child active? Playful? Social?
    Does he or she smile for you?
    What games does the baby play? In what ways do you play with him or her?
    What are the favorite toys?
    What is the baby/child doing now? Is he or she like your other children?
    Is anything different about this baby/child?
    Do you think your child is developing appropriately?
III. Feeding/Dietary
    A. Intake
        Is the baby breast-fed or bottle-fed? How did you decide?
        Describe a typical feed.
        How long on each breast? How long until next feed?
        Problems?
        Who gives you advice when there is a problem with feeding/eating?
        How much does he or she take? At a feed? For the whole day?
        How do you prepare the formula?
        Any formula changes?
        Does the infant drink any beverages besides formula?
        How do you hold the baby? Does he or she seem to be comfortable?
        How do you know when he or she is done? Do you burp him or her? How often?
        When did the baby start solids? What kinds? Any favorites?
        Does the baby refuse feeds/foods?
    B. Output
        Does the baby spit up? When? How much?
        How often do you change the diaper? Is it usually urine or stool?
        Does the baby have diarrhea? Constipation?
        Does the baby have gas? A lot? Is he or she uncomfortable?
        How do you quiet him or her down?
    C. Experience
        What is it like to feed the baby? Difficult? Frustrating?
        Where does the child eat? High chair? Table?
        Are there other children to feed?
        Who helps you with the feeding? Advice?
        Does the baby dribble food during the feeds? Does he or she make a mess?
        How do you plan for this? Bib? Newspapers under high chair?
        Do you think the baby has a weight problem? Any ideas what the problem is?
        Were any other children like this?
        What do you think of the advice that the doctors and nurses have given you so far?

Source: Adapted from Bithoney, Dubowitz, and Egan (1992), Hobbs (1992), Kempe (1987), and Ludwig (1992b).

necessary. In addition to indicated treatment for specific medical conditions, one needs to address the following: (a) nutritional

Table 7.7 Guide to the Observation of Caregiver-Child Interactions

I. General
  A. Caregiver
    Is there caregiver-child physical contact? What kind?
    Is there cuddling?
    Does caregiver smile at child? Do they look at each other?
    Does caregiver appear aware of child? Child's needs? Child's comfort?
    Is there playful behavior? Does caregiver engage the child with toys?
    Is there verbal communication? Pleasant? Angry? Commanding?
  B. Child
    Is the baby/child verbal? Speech delayed?
    Is the child alert? Withdrawn? Apathetic? Sad? Apprehensive?
    Are there unusual body postures? Tone floppy? Rigid?
    Does child respond to separation from caregiver?
II. Feeding observation (Chatoor & Egan, 1983)
  Observations of feeding occur in a comfortable place that is quiet and relatively free from distractions and interruptions.
  A. Homeostasis/Attachment
    Does the caregiver
      Begin the feeding touching the nipple to the infant's cheek?
      Stimulate the infant's lips and allow the child to open his or her mouth prior to introducing the nipple into his or her mouth?
      Seem aware of the amount flowing in the nipple?
      Hold the bottle at a comfortable angle for the infant, and avoid jostling the child or bottle?
      Notice when the infant is hungry and initiate feed promptly?
      Avoid excessive burping and wiping?
      Permit the infant to set the pace of the feed?
      Allow the child to rest, interact, and return to the feed?
      Balance the infant's need for attention with the need to avoid overstimulation that could be distracting?
      Notice when the infant appears satisfied and halt the feed when the infant displays behaviors indicating satiety, such as turning away and closing his or her mouth?
  B. Separation and individuation
    Does the caregiver
      Comfortably position the child for feeding/eating?
      Position him- or herself in an easily seen location and place the eating utensils in the child's view?
      Talk in a soothing, reassuring manner that does not overstimulate and distract the child?
      Demonstrate patience and permit time for the child to acclimate to meal time?
      Allow the child to handle the food and, when ready, permit self-feeding?
      Demonstrate patience for the child's pace?
      Respect the child's likes and dislikes?

Source: Adapted from Kempe and Goldbloom (1987), Ludwig (1992), and Satler (1990).

requirements for catch-up growth and feeding behavior, (b) inpatient versus outpatient therapy, (c) comprehensive follow-up programs, and (d) whether a child protective services (CPS) report should be filed. Each component is discussed below.

1. *Nutrition and feeding.* Children with FTT require significantly more calories than the standard, recommended amount. To achieve "catch-up" growth, Prader and colleagues (1963) estimate that a child will need on average 50% above the recom-

Table 7.8 Differential Diagnosis for FTT

Normal growth variants	
Constitutional short stature	Well-nourished, with a height and weight at a similar percentile and a weight for height curve that is normal
Shifting linear growth	Normal downward shift across percentile lines of the growth curve that occurs in 60% of children between the ages of 6 and 12 months. Approximately 25% of children will shift two growth curves
Normal leanness	Healthy and adequately nourished and often has other family members demonstrating a tendency toward slender somatotypes
Prematurity	Need birth measurements and gestational age. Correct chronologic age for gestational age: Head circumference to 18 months, weight to 24 months, and length to 40 months
IUGR	
Symmetric IUGR	Includes prenatal exposure to opiates, alcohol, tobacco, anticonvulsants, etc., congenital viral infections, or chromosomal syndromes
Asymmetric IUGR	Weight < length or head circumference; best prognosis for later growth
Early feeding difficulties	Children born at normal weight may show signs of feeding difficulty during the first few weeks to months of life. Causes for early feeding problems include incorrect formula preparation, breast-feeding problems, difficulties with mother-infant attachment, metabolic disorders, chromosomal disorders, and anatomic problems of the airway/esophagus
Metabolic	
Galactosemia	Usually presents early in neonatal period after initiation of feeds containing galactose. Symptoms include vomiting, diarrhea, jaundice, poor feeding, abdominal distention, poor weight gain, and hypoglycemia. Examination may reveal hepatosplenomegaly, ascites, edema, aminoaciduria, hypoglycemia, and persistently elevated conjugated bilirubin levels. Cataracts may be present at birth. Testing of the urine for reducing substances is an initial screen, and red cell assay for enzymatic activity confirms the diagnosis
Inborn errors of metabolism	Variable presentation depending on amino acid, organic acid, or enzyme involved. Classically, the more serious disorders present with recurring episodes of lethargy, poor feeding, vomiting, and seizures. Laboratory evaluation varies depending on defect and acid/base status variable as well
Anatomic	
Cleft lip or palate	Midline craniofacial defect. More commonly occur together, although cleft lip and cleft palate may occur independently of each other. Other anomalies in the oral facial structures may be present, and consultation with a cleft palate team composed of a maxillofacial surgeon, audiologist, speech pathologist, dentist, pediatrician, otorhinolaryngologist, and geneticist is ideal. Nutritional intake is a major concern, and surgical repair is necessary to allow for an adequate seal for sucking. Middle ear infections are frequently seen
GE reflux	Defined as the movement of stomach contents into the esophagus. Believed to be present in some degree in almost all neonates. May occur with or without vomiting. May interfere with adequate caloric intake, however, and has been associated with recurrent wheezing, coughing, pneumonitis, and apneic episodes. Debate exists concerning the appropriate workup, which may include UGI, gastric emptying, and/or pH probe studies. Medical regimens are used to decrease amount of stomach contents that are able to move into the esophagus. Surgery occasionally required

(continued)

Table 7.8 Continued

Gastrointestinal	
Inflammatory bowel disease	Pattern of remitting-relapsing symptoms: cramping, abdominal pain, diarrhea with variable amounts of blood in stool, fever, anorexia, weight loss, and growth failure, as well as nonspecific symptoms such as joint pain and malaise. Severe growth retardation occurs more frequently in Crohn's diseases (15% to 30%) than in ulcerative colitis (5% to 10%) and often precedes the onset of gastrointestinal symptoms by years (Green, 1986).
Hirschprung's disease (aganglionic megacolon)	Segmental absence of parasympathetic ganglion cells in the myenteric plexus; usually involving the rectum but can involve all or parts of the colon. Symptoms of delayed stooling are frequently noted during first days and weeks of life, although they may present later as intermittent obstipation and/or poor growth
Malabsorption disorders	A wide variety of disorders including celiac disease (intolerance to wheat gluten), carbohydrate malabsorption (intolerance to lactose, sucrose, etc.), cow's milk allergy, soybean allergy, group a beta lipoproteinemia, and pancreatic enzyme deficiency (Schwachmann-Diamond syndrome) or cystic fibrosis (see respiratory). Presentations include intermittent diarrhea, weight loss, and/or poor growth with various constitutional symptoms based on the specific diagnosis
Endocrine	
Thyroid disorders	Hyperthyroidism: Although congenital hyperthyroidism can occur, in general, the child presents with Graves' disease (autoimmune thyroid disease), tachycardia, nervousness, and weight loss in the face of increased appetite
	Hypothyroidism: Congenital hypothyroidism usually diagnosed by newborn screening, presents with constellation of signs and symptoms including decreased tone, lethargy, poor feeding, and diminished growth. Acquired hypothyroidism in the child presents primarily as a slowing of linear growth with delayed bone age and often delayed puberty
Neurologic	
Hypoxic ischemic encephalopathy (HIE)	Occurs as a result of significant hypoxia of the brain due to any number of causes (birth trauma/perinatal asphyxia, near-drowning, etc.), leading to severe developmental disabilities and feeding disorders resulting in poor growth
Renal	
Renal tubular acidosis (RTA)	Biochemical syndrome with several types and numerous causes resulting in metabolic acidosis leading to poor growth. Urine pH is basic and serum shows low bicarbonate level
Bacterial urinary tract infection (UTI)	Although many children with bacterial UTIs are asymptomatic, clinical symptoms may include fever, decreased feeding, diarrhea, vomiting, and weight loss. Urinalysis may show white blood cells, leukocyte esterase activity, and the presence of nitrates. Urine culture is positive for a urinary pathogen (is gold standard). Chronic, untreated UTIs can lead to renal damage, which will affect growth.
Renal failure	Growth failure secondary to metabolic abnormalities, nutritional restrictions, and hormonal influences is a chronic, often difficult-to-treat consequence of renal failure; especially severe in children who develop failure before the first year of life
Cardiovascular	
Congenital heart disease (CHD)	Poor cardiovascular function provides inadequate oxygenation, leading to acidosis, polycythemia, inadequate nutrition, and increased caloric requirements
Congestive heart failure (CHF)	Poor pumping function impairs the delivery of adequate oxygen and substrate needed to maintain normal metabolic function. The exertion of feeding often increases caloric consumption. Often, the only finding of CHF may be growth failure

Table 7.8 Continued

Respiratory	
Cystic fibrosis	Multisystem exocrine dysfunction with end-organ damage. Respiratory manifestations include wheezing; recurrent pneumonia and sinusitis are usually respiratory in nature. Growth failure becomes evident secondary to malabsorption and pancreatic deficiency
Chronic lung disease	Chronic lung disease that leads to FTT because of hypoxia, frequent pneumonia, and increased caloric consumption as a result of increased work of breathing
Infectious/Immunologic	
Immunodeficiency	Congenital: Encompasses a wide variety of defects of the immune system. Patients develop growth difficulties due to associated underlying genetic dysmorphisms/anomalies (craniofacial, cardiac, etc.), associated endocrine abnormalities (hypoparathyroidism, etc.), recurrent infections (e.g., increased work of breathing with chronic pneumonia or painful swallowing with chronic oral candidiasis), or chronic diarrhea and malabsorption
	Acquired: The GI manifestations in children with HIV/AIDS can lead to growth difficulties and may include esophagitis, diarrhea with or without infection (parasitic, viral, or bacterial), or malabsorption due to the involvement of the intestinal wall. General malaise contributes to decreased appetite, and recurrent infections make weight loss a common problem. The multiorgan involvement can also increase caloric requirements
Tuberculosis (TB)	In older children, TB occurs as primary asymptomatic TB. In young infants and children, 50% to 60% have symptomatic disease. In these patients, primary pulmonary TB causes chronic respiratory symptoms including fever, night sweats, and weight loss
Collagen vascular diseases	More common in older children. Include disorders such as juvenile rheumatoid arthritis (JRA), systemic lupus erythematosus (SLE), and dermatomyositis. Most of these disorders have associated difficulties with growth and development because of chronic malaise, decreased appetite, chronic inflammatory process, weight loss, mucocutaneous involvement, gastrointestinal difficulties, the effects of chronic steroid therapy, and joint symptomatology
Miscellaneous	
Malignancies	Neoplastic disorders result in abnormal growth due to neoplastic infiltration; poor metabolic state; anorexia secondary to the disease or the treatment; recurrent infections due to immunosuppressed state; chronic diarrhea secondary to effects of chemotherapy/radiation; and CNS disorders secondary to the disease or the treatment that affect the hypothalamic-pituitary axis, causing diminished growth
Anemia	Although pallor is the most common presentation for anemia, irritability and anorexia are noted, along with difficulties with attention and learning
Lead poisoning	Patients present with irritability and anorexia along with abdominal pain. Developmental difficulties frequently occur, and abnormal growth can occur as a late manifestation

Source: Adapted from Ballard (1988), Green (1986), Oski et al. (1990), Schmitt and Mauro (1989), and Tunnessen (1988).

mended requirement. Thus, an infant with an average need for 105 kcal/kg/day would require approximately 160 kcal/kg/day to achieve catch-up growth. If a baby weighs 6 kg and drinks a standard 20 kcal/oz formula, then he or she needs 32 oz (640 kcal) for routine growth and an additional 16 oz (total of 48 oz, 980 kcal) to ensure catch-up growth.

Table 7.9 Overview of Evaluation of FTT

History	—Birth history (premature, IUGR, twin, birth weight)
	—Familial history (short stature)
	—Growth history (growth charts)
	—Diet history
	—Past medical history
	—Past surgical history
	—Psychosocial history (family dynamics and stressors)
Physical assessment	—Growth
	—Nutrition (e.g., signs of nutritional deficiencies)
	—Congenital anomalies
	—Evidence of neglect/abuse
Indicated laboratory studies	—CBC
	—Electrolytes
	—Urinalysis
	—Urine culture
	—Sedimentation rate
Clinical observation	—Child's interactions with caregiver
	—Weight gain under supervision/ hospitalization
	—Feeding behaviors
Documentation	—Frequent visits with accurate recordings on growth chart

The requirement for catch-up growth frequently proves to be too large a volume for the child drinking a standard 20 kcal/oz formula. The caregiver can reconstitute concentrated or powdered formula using less water and achieve a higher caloric content. If the child is no longer on formula but on whole milk, the milk can be fortified with nonfat dry milk or instant breakfast preparations to increase its caloric content (see Table 7.10 for instructions). In addition, several high caloric beverages are commercially available that may be used for supplementation.

In older children, caloric intake is more difficult to measure because of solid foods in the diet that are more variable in nutritional content. Baby food jars of fruits and vegetables contain approximately 15 kcal/oz and those of meats and desserts are 25 to 30 kcal/oz (Schmitt & Mauro, 1989). In addition, the caloric value of the child's foods can be enhanced by adding high-calorie food fortifiers such as (a) butter (40 kcal/tsp), (b) cheese (100 kcal/oz), (c) peanut butter (100 kcal/tsp), and (d) sour cream (30 kcal/tsp) (Tougas, cited in Bithoney, Dubowitz, & Egan, 1992).

Adequate management by a primary care provider of mild to moderate malnutrition is possible if he or she has experience with such cases. Nutritional consultation is recommended for more severe malnutrition in order to provide appropriate nutrients and calories and to guard against refeeding syndrome.[1]

Table 7.10 Instructions for Increasing Caloric Content of Standard Formulas (Formula Preparation Discharge Instructions)

Calories/ounce	Liquid concentrate—Amount used	Powdered formula—Amount used
20 cal./oz.	13 oz. can liquid concentrate + 13 oz. water	1 cup (8 oz.) _____ powder + 29 oz. water
24 cal./oz.	13 oz. can liquid concentrate + 9 oz. water	1 cup (8 oz.) _____ powder + 24 oz. water
27 cal./oz.	13 oz. can liquid concentrate + 6 oz. water	1 cup (8 oz.) _____ powder + 21 oz. water
30 cal./oz.	13 oz. can liquid concentrate + 4 oz. water	1 cup (8 oz.) _____ powder + 18 oz. water

For powdered formula: The powder is packed in the measuring cup and leveled off with a knife

Please note: Formula preparations should be done only under physician supervision.

Source. Nursing staff at The Children's Hospital of Philadelphia, Philadelphia, Pennsylvania.

If feeding behaviors are poorly developed or dysfunctional, the caregiver requires (re)training that addresses general parenting skills, feeding routines, mealtime behaviors, and modeling of positive caregiver-child interactions. Videotaping of the caregiver-child interaction around feeding may provide the caregivers with insight into what some of these problems are.

2. *Inpatient versus outpatient therapy.* In the past, virtually all children who presented with FTT were admitted to the hospital for long lengths of stay to observe feeding and weight gain patterns. The changing health care environment discourages hospitalizations for children with FTT and, increasingly, shifts from inpatient care to outpatient care. However, clinical indications exist for both inpatient and outpatient care.

Inpatient stays offer the opportunity to provide close supervision and control over the amount and frequency of feeding. They are criticized as being artificial and potentially confusing to the caregiver if weight gain does not occur. In addition, requiring hospitalization to get a child to feed and gain weight may reinforce a sense of helplessness in the caregiver. Wissow (1990a) and Ludwig (1992b) suggest immediate hospitalization of infants with FTT if any of the following situations are present:

- Nonaccidental trauma
- Risk for nonaccidental trauma
- Sibling previously abused
- Caregiver appears angry, violent, or volatile
- Severe malnutrition, marasmus, kwashiorkor, or emaciation
- Weight less than birth weight at 2 months of age or older or no weight gain in more than 2 months
- Severe hygiene neglect, such as filthy, unwashed skin or severe diaper rash
- Severely disturbed caregiver
- Negative caregiver-child interaction
- Outpatient treatment failure: no weight gain with 1-month trial of increased caloric feedings

- Caregiver refuses assistance with child's problem

Each case must be handled individually viewing the above criteria as clinical practice guidelines.

Outpatient trials have the advantage of being more natural and replicating what is possible at home. However, there is less control and supervision in the outpatient setting. Outpatient trials are recommended for less severe cases when there is no immediate danger to the child's health. Schmitt and Mauro (1989) suggest outpatient management for children with FTT under the following conditions:

- Child over 12 months of age
- State of malnutrition is in the mild to moderate range
- The caregiver-child interaction has some positive aspects
- The caregivers are accepting of help
- Absent risk factors for nonaccidental injuries

3. *Follow-up.* Active, ongoing, and continuous involvement by the health care provider with the child and caregiver (and CPS worker, if involved) is essential to ensure that the treatment plan is working. Medical appointments, in-home services, and psychological services for the caregiver(s) are frequently necessary over a period of months to years, depending on the family and how successful the original regimen was in fostering growth. (See Chapter 9 for further discussion of CPS and maltreatment follow-up.)

4. *Whether a CPS report should be filed.* Whether to report a case of FTT to CPS remains a primary management decision in the treatment of FTT. Laws guiding the reporting of neglect and FTT are intentionally vague to allow for clinical judgment (Bithoney et al., 1992; Ludwig, 1992b; Wissow, 1990a). Cases where clear-cut parental misinstruction is the cause of the problem are best handled through education and close follow-up. For example, a case in which the caregiver misunderstood formula preparation instructions and mixed one part of formula with two parts of water may best be solved with caregiver education and careful follow-up in the health care provider's office (Schmitt & Mauro, 1989).

Wissow (1990a) suggests CPS reporting in cases where

1. Physical abuse is present
2. Pervasive patterns of neglect or cruelty are uncovered
3. The caregivers appear incapable of adequately caring for the child (e.g., caregivers who are seriously mentally ill, substance abusers, severely cognitively impaired, homeless, or resistant to accepting assistance with their child's problem)

CPS may recommend foster placement as being in the child's best interest. In general, foster placement is considered in FTT cases if the caregiver:

1. Rarely visits the child if hospitalized
2. Demonstrates a negative, punitive, or indifferent attitude toward the child
3. Remains uncooperative in the treatment protocol
4. Is an active substance abuser
5. Suffers from severe psychiatric illness
6. Is found to be severely cognitively impaired
7. Holds to dietary beliefs that are dangerous to the child's well-being (e.g., believes that child should feed only on fruits) (Kempe & Goldbloom, 1987)

Medical Neglect

Caregivers may be deemed neglectful by refusing or delaying to meet the health care needs of their child. Such health care needs include

- Routine preventive medical and dental care
- Timely access to acute care for illness or injury
- Meeting the ongoing care demands of a given condition (e.g., the chronically ill child) (Snyder, Hampton, and Newberger, 1983)

Medical neglect may present to the health care provider in a number of ways. Typical presentations include

- Delay in seeking care for an injury or illness
- Failure to administer prescribed medications
- Administration of recommended medications in a manner or schedule that impairs appropriate care
- Noncompliance with routine preventive care needs (such as immunization schedules, lead and anemia screening, dental checkups)
- Noncompliance with the treatment needs for both acute and chronic conditions (such as failure to suction a tracheostomy according to the neonatologist's instructions)

Variability in the range of presentations exists. For example, reported cases of medical neglect in asthmatic patients include parents who fail to administer medicines properly as well as those who refuse to remove or separate the child from household pets that are known triggers of the child's asthma exacerbations (Boxer, Carson, & Miller, 1988; Franklin & Klein, 1987).

A distinction exists between noncompliance and medical neglect (Ludwig, 1993). Noncompliance occurs when the caregiver fails to carry through on the recommendations of the treating health care provider. This may or may not have negative

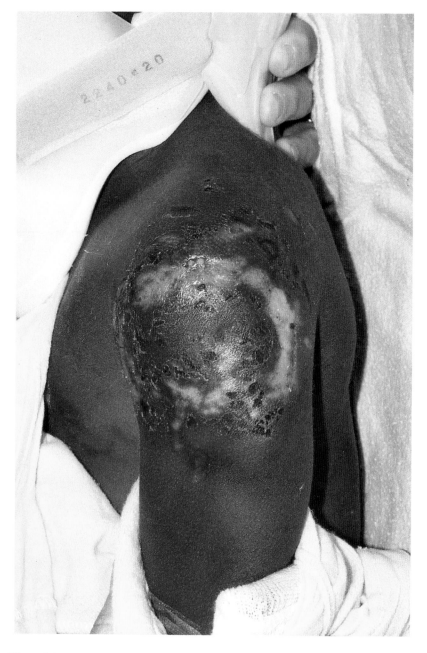

Photo 7.1.

Three-year-old battered child with injuries of different ages to the shoulder. The exact mechanism of these injuries is not known. Repeated delays in seeking treatment led to poor probability for full healing.

consequences for the child. Medical neglect, on the other hand, occurs when the noncompliance or delay in seeking care results in further illness or worsening injury (Ludwig, 1993). The distinction rests on the presence or absence of identifiable harm.

The treatment of medical neglect is tailored to each case depending on the child and caregiver. The evaluated level of risk

Photo 7.2.

Seven-month-old with life-threatening malnutrition and dehydration. The baby weighed less than his birth weight at the time of hospital admission (7 months old). Note the sunken eyes and scaphoid appearance of the abdomen.

or injury to the child will determine whether reporting medical neglect cases to CPS may be indicated. Hospitalization and/or removal from the home and placement in foster care may also be necessary if the child is at risk for injury or illness. Appropriate follow-up plans are essential to ensure compliance and assess adequacy of ongoing care.

A complete discussion of medical neglect includes a brief overview of the Baby Doe case and the legislation that was enacted in its aftermath. Baby Doe was a child born in 1982 with Down's syndrome and esophageal atresia. She died shortly after her parents opted not to have the esophageal malformation repaired and not to allow intravenous nutrition. The case generated a large amount of publicity because the child died from a life-threatening but surgically correctable condition. In 1984, Congress passed an amendment to the Child Abuse Prevention and Treatment Act that defined as neglectful the withholding of appropriate nutrition, hydration, medication, or other treatment that would be effective in ameliorating or correcting a life-threatening condition. This federal

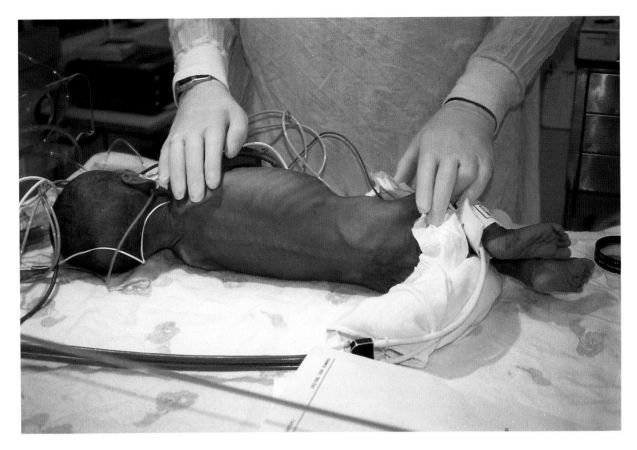

Photo 7.3.
Posterior view of previous baby. Note the severe wasting. Marks on the lower back represent Mongolian spots. The baby had no evidence of physical injury.

law defined as neglect the withholding of medically indicated treatment from disabled children with life-threatening conditions. The law states that quality of life is not to be used in the decision-making process, and food and water are always to be administered. Exceptions to the law include (a) infants who are irreversibly comatose; and (b) instances where the treatment would only prolong dying or be ineffective or futile in terms of the infant's survival (Gaudin, 1993b; Pless, 1983).

Other Forms of Neglect

The health care provider faces children with other forms of neglect that include the following:

- *Supervisional.* Children who are abandoned may be brought to an emergency department for evaluation after a neighbor or relative

CHILD PHYSICAL ABUSE AND NEGLECT

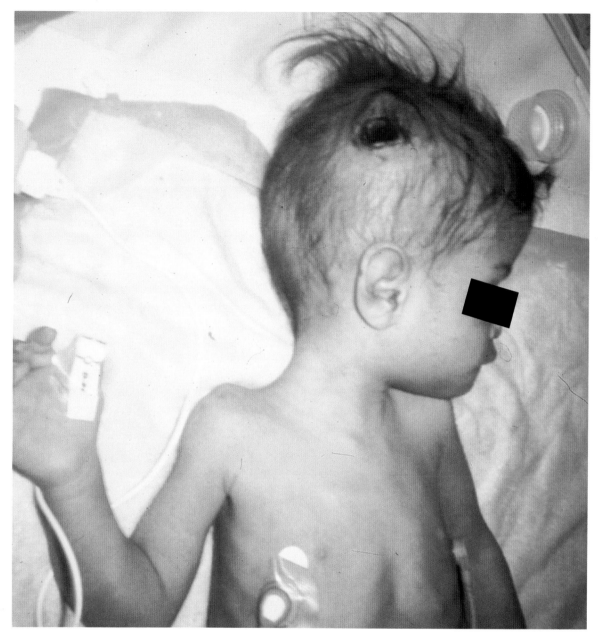

Photo 7.4.

Eighteen-month-old with life-threatening neglect. Pictured here is a decubitus ulcer on the scalp.

alerts authorities to the possibility of supervisory neglect. Children may also sustain injuries due to inadequate supervision and require medical intervention. Abandonment is supported by a physical examination that reveals (a) poor hygiene, (b) hoarse cry, (c) excessive hunger, or (d) dehydration (Ludwig, 1993). Appropriate management requires reporting the case to CPS and placing the child in a safe, properly supervised environment with either a family member or a foster parent. Another area that relates to supervisional neglect are children who sustain accidental injuries due to inadequate supervision.

- *Emotional.* Emotional (psychological) neglect is a form of maltreatment that involves caregiving that fails to provide a nurturing, development-promoting environment for the child's psychological and emotional well-being. The impact on the child is impaired psychological and emotional functioning. Many consider emotional neglect and emotional abuse synonymous because the damage inflicted upon the child's mental health by either is similar and often pervasive. Believed to be the most common form of maltreatment, emotional neglect is the least well defined, the least diagnosed, and the least understood. The caregiving to which the child is exposed creates an environment in which he or she is at

  1. A disadvantage in accomplishing developmental, peer, school, and community tasks
  2. Risk for experiencing chronic and severe anxiety, agitation, depression, social withdrawal, or unreasonable fears about his or her life
  3. Risk for failing to receive proper therapy for psychological or emotional problems (Ludwig, 1993)

  The caregiving that the child receives is characterized by repetitive episodes that include belittling, neglect, humiliation, and verbal attacks on the child's value and worth. The child's self-image is destroyed, and a myriad of dysfunctional behaviors, attitudes, and perspectives ensue (see Figure 7.1). Diagnosis of this form of maltreatment requires careful observation and documentation of the caregiver's interactions with the child, both verbal and nonverbal. Management and treatment for the emotionally maltreated child will require the skills of mental health professionals, and close follow-up is essential (Peterson & Urquiza, 1993).

- *Educational.* Educational neglect is a manifestation of a caregiving environment that fails to provide adequately for a child's school attendance and performance. This situation may be due to a wide variety of reasons, ranging from a caregiver who is overwhelmed by life circumstances to a caregiver-child dynamic where the child's absences are encouraged through excessive dependency. Psychosocial assessment is essential, and the root causes for the failure to comply with the needs for formal schooling need to be addressed. Management and treatment require attention to the underlying causes and an approach that supports the child and caregiver in complying with educational obligations.

In Brief

- Neglect is the most commonly reported form of child maltreatment representing 45% of the 2.936 million maltreatment reports made in the United States in 1992 (AHA3, 1993).

CHILD PHYSICAL ABUSE AND NEGLECT

- A child's response to neglect depends on the type of neglect, the developmental stage at which the neglect occurred, the severity of the unmet need, and the effectiveness of the intervention by caring adults to halt the neglect.
- FTT is a term rooted firmly in clinical practice, and it remains the working diagnosis for children not growing as expected (Ludwig, 1992b).
- The evaluation of FTT includes the medical history (see Chapter 2) and specific information about nutritional status, diet, and feeding behaviors.
- The physical evaluation of FTT focuses on findings suggestive of underlying disorders, growth parameters, and objective developmental assessment.
- Observation of the child's feeding interactions is a critical component of the FTT assessment.
- The design of the treatment plan for the child with FTT depends on the cause of the growth failure.
- Reporting a case of FTT to child protective services (CPS) remains a primary management decision in treatment of FTT.
- Laws guiding the reporting of neglect and FTT are intentionally vague to allow for the clinician's judgment (Bithoney et al., 1992; Ludwig, 1992b; Wissow, 1990a).
- The changing health care environment discourages hospitalizations for children with FTT and increasingly shifts care from inpatient to outpatient evaluation.
- Noncompliance occurs when the caregiver fails to carry through on the recommendations of the treating health care provider.
- Medical neglect occurs when the noncompliance or delay in seeking care results in further illness or worsening injury (Ludwig, 1993).
- Emotional (psychological) neglect is caregiving that fails to provide a nurturing, development-promoting environment for the child's psychological and emotional well-being.
- Educational neglect is a manifestation of a caregiving environment that fails to adequately provide for a child's school attendance and performance.

Note

1. *Refeeding syndrome* initially described the severe metabolic complications observed when a severely malnourished person was given concentrated calories via total parenteral nutrition. The term is now used more broadly and refers to the physiological complications that occur when a severely malnourished person is reintroduced to "normal" foodstuffs in an uncontrolled manner. In addition to phosphorus depletion, shifts in humoral potassium, magnesium, and glucose may have serious, even fatal, cardiovascular and neurological consequences (Solomon & Kirby, 1990).

Case A

E.T. demonstrates that medical causes of FTT may co-exist with overwhelming social causes.

E.T. is a former 6 lb. 1 oz. term infant born to a teenage mother with an uncomplicated pregnancy and delivery. The baby was noted to be gaining weight appropriately until age 6 months. Between 6 and 9 months of age, the health care provider became increasingly concerned about the child's weight gain. Mother had difficulty keeping appointments, and the infant's weight began to drop off significantly (points C on growth chart in Figure 7.1). Evaluation revealed sketchy history of intermittent constipation, and physical examination notable for hypotonicity and significant developmental delay. Due to mother's noncompliance with scheduled health care, the health care provider consulted social work services and arranged for home nursing visits.

Psychosocial evaluation uncovered a chaotic household and an inadequate diet due to the mother's lack of funds to purchase the infant's food. The health care providers considered that the "constipation" might be related to the poor diet. Between 9 and 11 months (C to C on growth chart in Figure 7.1), weight gain was noted but still below the fifth percentile. (In retrospect, this appears to have been related to severe constipation/impaction.) At age 12 months, weight loss was again noted, and the child was admitted to the hospital for an inpatient evaluation. E.T.'s length leveled off between 6 and 12 months as well (see Figure 7.2).

Workup revealed Hirschsprung's disease. E.T. underwent surgical repair including placement of a colostomy (Point S on growth chart). On follow-up, E.T. began to gain weight, and his development improved. Social services remained involved to assist with the psychosocial issues uncovered during the evaluation.

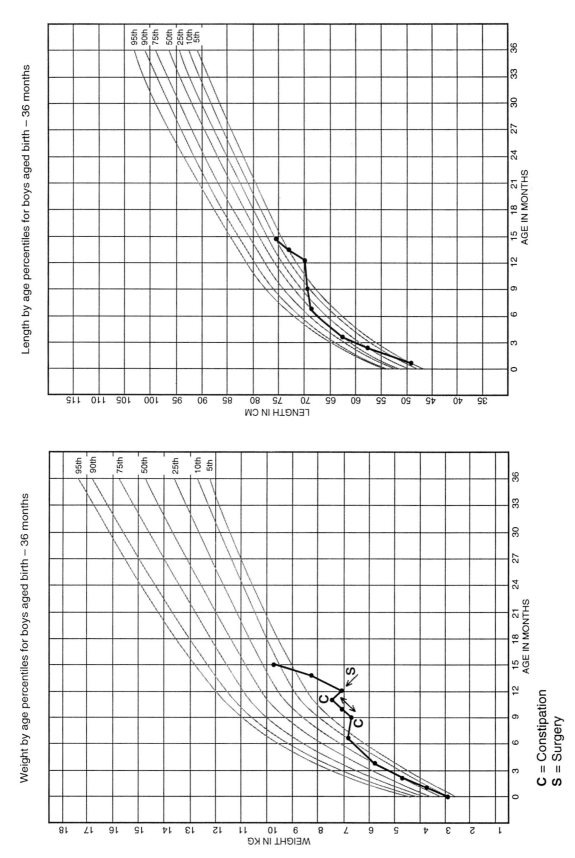

Length by age percentiles for boys aged birth – 36 months

Figure 7.2. Case A: E.T.'s length by age chart.

Weight by age percentiles for boys aged birth – 36 months

C = Constipation
S = Surgery

Figure 7.1. Case A: E.T.'s weight by age chart.

Case B

T.H. demonstrates that observation over time provides useful information that may clarify the etiology of the growth failure.

T.H. is a term infant born to a 23-year-old mother who had an uncomplicated prenatal course with no history of smoking or drug use. Infant was first seen in well-baby clinic at 2 weeks of age for routine care. She was breast-fed until 1 month of age, when mother stopped due to unsuccessful breast-feeding. Infant was initially placed on Isomil and then switched to Similac at 6 months of age. By 7 months of age, the baby's weight was noted to be dropping across percentiles (see Figures 7.3 and 7.4 for T.H.'s growth charts). This seemed to correlate with the introduction of solids. She continued to be closely followed and was referred to an early intervention feeding program.

Over the next 6 months, she was followed closely with frequent weight checks. Her weight gain continued to be poor (see Figure 7.3), and she was now below the fifth percentile. Length remained at approximately the 50th percentile (see Figure 7.4). Initial evaluation consisted of basic laboratory testing, and results were unremarkable. At 13 months of age, after no sustained improvement in weight gain, T.H. was hospitalized for an inpatient workup. She was able to demonstrate weight gain during the hospital stay.

Psychosocial evaluation noted that mother appeared depressed with sullen expression and flat affect. During ongoing care, the mother was noted to be losing weight herself. When questioned about her personal eating habits, she revealed a childhood history of multiple caregivers and foster care placement. She related being force-fed to vomiting for almost 1 year and appeared terrorized when recounting experience. Mother said she was afraid of making her daughter vomit. Mother also related how she can go a day or more without eating solids. "I sometimes don't feel hungry, so I don't eat."

The mother was unreceptive to the health care provider's suggestion that the mother seek psychological counseling, although she did agree that she was depressed. The child was referred to Child Protective Services for supportive services.

CHILD PHYSICAL ABUSE AND NEGLECT

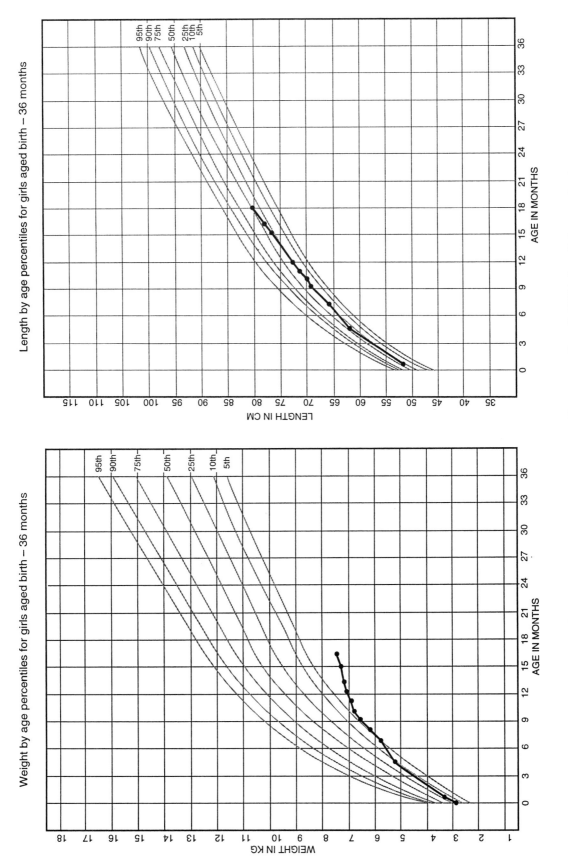

Figure 7.4. Case B: T.H.'s length by age chart.

Figure 7.3. Case B: T.H.'s weight by age chart.

Case C

S.S. demonstrates how careful assessment of the social environment and correlation to the growth pattern observed over time may uncover the cause of a child's growth failure.

S.S. is an SGA term infant born to a 17-year-old mother in 11th grade. S.S. is cared for by her mother during summer vacations (A on growth chart in Figure 7.5) and by her maternal grandmother during the school year (B on growth chart in Figure 7.5). Initially, her growth was consistent with an SGA infant whose mother was 5 feet, 2 inches tall. Her growth pattern over 18 months revealed intermittent periods of growth retardation (A on growth chart in Figure 7.5). Basic laboratory findings were unremarkable. Length seemed to follow a pattern consistent with an SGA infant (see Figure 7.6). At S.S.'s 18-month visit, the health care provider correlated the episodes of poor weight gain with the primary caregiver transition from grandmother to mother that occurred during summer vacations.

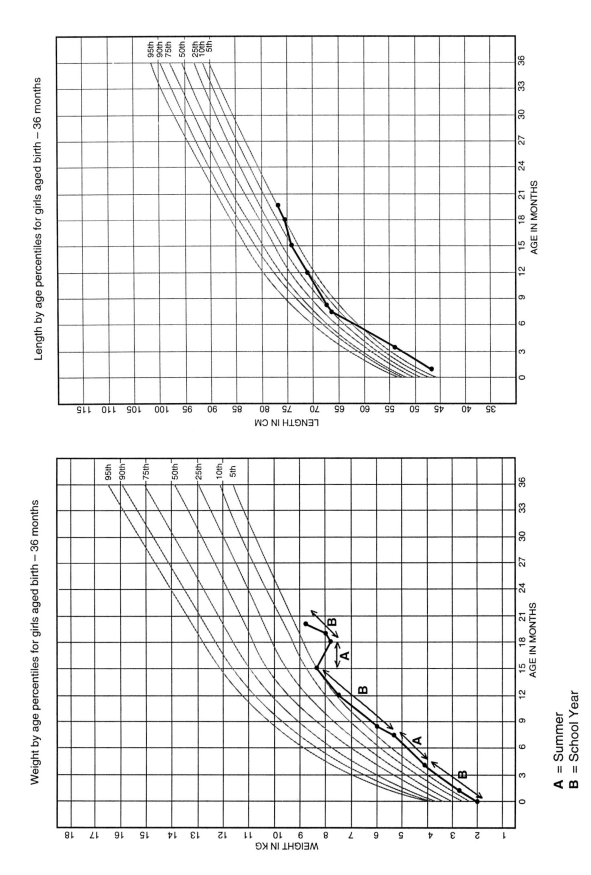

Length by age percentiles for girls aged birth – 36 months

Figure 7.6. Case C: S.S.'s length by age chart.

Weight by age percentiles for girls aged birth – 36 months

A = Summer
B = School Year

Figure 7.5. Case C: S.S.'s weight by age chart.

Neglect and Failure to Thrive

Chart 7.1 Parent-Specific Adjustments for Length of Boys from Birth to 36 Months*

Age (mo)	Length (cm)	Midparent Stature (cm)																	
		150	152	154	156	158	160	162	164	166	168	170	172	174	176	178	180	182	184
Birth	40.0-43.9	2	1	1	1	1	1	1	0	0	0	0	0	0	-1	-1	-1	-1	-1
	44.0-52.9	2	2	1	1	1	1	1	0	0	0	0	0	0	-1	-1	-1	-1	-1
	53.0-56.9	2	2	1	1	1	1	1	1	0	0	0	0	0	-1	-1	-1	-1	-1
1	40.0-44.9	2	2	1	1	1	1	1	0	0	0	0	-1	-1	-1	-1	-1	-2	-2
	45.0-48.9	2	2	2	1	1	1	1	0	0	0	0	0	-1	-1	-1	-1	-2	-2
	49.0-52.9	2	2	2	1	1	1	1	1	0	0	0	0	-1	-1	-1	-1	-2	-2
	53.0-56.9	2	2	2	2	1	1	1	1	0	0	0	0	-1	-1	-1	-1	-1	-2
	57.0-62.9	2	2	2	2	1	1	1	1	1	0	0	0	0	-1	-1	-1	-1	-2
3	52.0-56.9	3	2	2	2	1	1	1	1	0	0	0	-1	-1	-1	-1	-2	-2	-2
	57.0-60.9	3	2	2	2	2	1	1	1	0	0	0	0	-1	-1	-1	-2	-2	-2
	61.0-66.9	3	3	2	2	2	1	1	1	1	0	0	0	-1	-1	-1	-1	-2	-2
	67.0-68.9	3	3	2	2	2	2	1	1	1	0	0	0	0	-1	-1	-1	-2	-2
6	62.0-64.9	3	3	2	2	2	1	1	1	0	0	0	-1	-1	-1	-2	-2	-2	-3
	65.0-66.9	3	3	3	2	2	2	1	1	1	0	0	-1	-1	-1	-2	-2	-2	-3
	67.0-73.9	3	3	3	2	2	2	1	1	1	0	0	0	-1	-1	-1	-2	-2	-2
	74.0-76.9	4	3	3	3	2	2	2	1	1	1	0	0	0	-1	-1	-1	-2	-2
9	66.0-68.9	3	3	3	2	2	1	1	1	0	0	0	-1	-1	-2	-2	-2	-3	-3
	69.0-72.9	4	3	3	3	2	2	1	1	1	0	0	-1	-1	-1	-2	-2	-2	-3
	73.0-76.9	4	3	3	3	2	2	2	1	1	0	0	0	-1	-1	-1	-2	-2	-3
	77.0-80.9	4	4	3	3	3	2	2	1	1	1	0	0	0	-1	-1	-2	-2	-2
12	67.0-71.9	4	3	3	2	2	2	1	1	0	0	-1	-1	-1	-2	-2	-3	-3	-3
	72.0-74.9	4	4	3	3	2	2	1	1	1	0	0	-1	-1	-1	-2	-2	3	-3
	75.0-78.9	4	4	3	3	2	2	2	1	1	0	0	0	-1	-1	-2	-2	-3	-3
	79.0-82.9	4	4	3	3	3	2	2	1	1	1	0	0	-1	-1	-1	-2	-2	-3
	83.0-84.9	4	4	4	3	3	2	2	2	1	1	0	0	-1	-1	-1	-2	-2	-3
18	73.0-75.9	4	4	3	3	2	2	1	1	0	0	-1	-1	-2	-2	-2	-3	-3	-4
	76.0-80.9	4	4	3	3	2	2	2	1	1	0	0	-1	-1	-2	-2	-3	-3	-4
	81.0-84.9	5	4	4	3	3	2	2	1	1	0	0	-1	-1	-2	-2	-3	-3	-3
	85.0-88.9	5	4	4	3	3	2	2	1	1	1	0	0	-1	-1	-2	-2	-3	-3
	89.0-92.9	5	5	4	4	3	3	2	2	1	1	0	0	-1	-1	-2	-2	-2	-3
24	78.0-82.9	5	4	4	3	3	2	2	1	0	0	-1	-1	-2	-2	-3	-3	-4	-5
	83.0-86.9	5	5	4	4	3	2	2	1	1	0	0	-1	-2	-2	-3	-3	-4	-4
	87.0-92.9	6	5	5	4	3	3	3	2	2	1	1	0	-1	-1	-2	-3	-3	-4
	93.0-96.9	6	5	5	4	4	3	3	2	1	1	0	0	-1	-1	-2	-3	-3	-4
30	85.0-88.9	6	5	5	4	3	3	2	1	1	0	-1	-1	-2	-3	-3	-4	-4	-5
	89.0-92.0	6	5	5	4	4	3	2	2	1	0	0	-1	-2	-2	-3	-3	-4	-5
	93.0-96.9	6	6	5	4	4	3	3	2	1	1	0	-1	-1	-2	-3	-3	-4	-5
	97.0-100.9	7	6	5	5	4	3	3	2	2	1	0	0	-1	-2	-2	-3	-4	-4
36	88.0-90.9	6	6	5	4	3	3	2	1	1	0	-1	-1	-2	-3	-4	-4	-5	-6
	91.0-94.9	6	6	5	4	4	3	2	2	1	0	-1	-1	-2	-3	-3	-4	-5	-5
	95.0-98.9	7	6	5	5	4	3	3	2	1	1	0	-1	-1	-2	-3	-4	-4	-5
	99.0-102.9	7	6	6	5	4	4	3	2	1	1	0	-1	-1	-2	-3	-3	-4	-5
	103.0-106.9	7	7	6	5	5	4	3	2	2	1	0	0	-1	-2	-2	-3	-4	-4

*Adapted from Himes et al. (1985)[1] and reprinted with permission from Ross Laboratories, Columbus, OH.

Chart 7.2 Parent-Specific Adjustments for Length of Girls from Birth to 36 Months*

Age (mo)	Length (cm)	Midparent Stature (cm)																	
		150	152	154	156	158	160	162	164	166	168	170	172	174	176	178	180	182	184
Birth	40.0-42.9	1	1	0	0	0	0	0	0	0	0	0	0	0	0	0	0	0	-1
	43.0-50.9	1	1	1	0	0	0	0	0	0	0	0	0	0	0	0	0	0	-1
	51.0-54.9	1	1	1	0	0	0	0	0	0	0	0	0	0	0	0	0	0	0
1	46.0-56.9	1	1	1	1	1	1	0	0	0	0	0	0	0	0	-1	-1	-1	-1
	57.0-58.9	1	1	1	1	1	1	1	0	0	0	0	0	0	0	-1	-1	-1	-1
3	52.0-54.9	2	2	1	1	1	1	1	0	0	0	0	0	-1	-1	-1	-1	-2	-2
	55.0-60.9	2	2	2	1	1	1	1	1	0	0	0	0	-1	-1	-1	-1	-1	-2
	61.0-66.9	2	2	2	2	1	1	1	1	0	0	0	0	0	-1	-1	-1	-1	-1
6	58.0-60.9	3	2	2	2	1	1	1	1	0	0	0	-1	-1	-1	-2	-2	-2	-3
	61.0-63.9	3	3	2	2	2	1	1	1	0	0	0	-1	-1	-1	-2	-2	-2	-2
	64.0-68.9	3	3	2	2	2	1	1	1	1	0	0	0	-1	-1	-1	-2	-2	-2
	69.0-72.9	3	3	3	2	2	2	1	1	1	0	0	0	-1	-1	-1	-1	-2	-2
9	64.0-66.9	4	3	3	2	2	2	1	1	0	0	0	-1	-1	-2	-2	-3	-3	-3
	67.0-70.9	4	3	3	3	2	2	1	1	1	0	0	-1	-1	-1	-2	-2	-3	-3
	71.0-73.9	4	4	3	3	2	2	2	1	1	0	0	0	-1	-1	-2	-2	-2	-3
	74.0-76.9	4	4	3	3	3	2	2	1	1	1	0	0	-1	-1	-1	-2	-2	-3
12	66.0-68.9	4	4	3	3	2	2	1	1	0	0	-1	-1	-2	-2	-3	-3	-4	-4
	69.0-72.9	4	4	3	3	2	2	1	1	1	0	0	-1	-1	-2	-2	-3	-3	-4
	73.0-77.9	5	4	4	3	3	2	2	1	1	0	0	-1	-1	-2	-2	-3	-3	-4
	78.0-82.9	5	5	4	4	3	3	2	2	1	1	0	0	-1	-1	-2	-2	-3	-3
18	74.0-76.9	5	4	4	3	2	2	1	1	0	0	-1	-1	-2	-2	-3	-4	-4	-5
	77.0-80.9	5	4	4	3	3	2	2	1	1	0	0	-1	-2	-2	-3	-3	-4	-4
	81.0-84.9	5	5	4	4	3	3	2	2	1	0	0	-1	-1	-2	-2	-3	-3	-4
	85.0-88.9	6	5	5	4	4	3	2	2	1	1	0	0	-1	-1	-2	-2	-3	-4
24	77.0-80.9	5	4	4	3	3	2	1	1	0	0	-1	-2	-2	-3	-3	-4	-5	-5
	81.0-84.9	5	5	4	4	3	2	2	1	1	0	-1	-1	-2	-2	-3	-4	-4	-5
	85.0-88.9	6	5	5	4	3	3	2	2	1	0	0	-1	-1	-2	-3	-3	-4	-4
	89.0-93.9	6	6	5	4	4	3	3	2	1	1	0	0	-1	-2	-2	-3	-3	-4
	93.0-94.9	7	6	5	5	4	4	3	2	2	1	1	0	-1	-1	-2	-2	-3	-4
30	83.0-84.9	6	5	4	4	3	2	2	1	0	0	-1	-2	-2	-3	-4	-4	-5	-6
	85.0-89.9	6	5	5	4	3	3	2	1	1	0	-1	-1	-2	-3	-3	-4	-5	-5
	90.0-94.9	7	6	5	5	4	3	3	2	1	1	0	-1	-1	-2	-3	-3	-4	-5
	95.0-97.9	7	6	6	5	4	4	3	2	2	1	0	0	-1	-2	-2	-3	-4	-4
36	87.0-88.9	6	5	5	4	3	3	2	1	0	0	-1	-2	-2	-3	-4	-5	-5	-6
	89.0-92.9	6	6	5	4	4	3	2	1	1	0	-1	-2	-2	-3	-4	-4	-5	-6
	93.0-96.9	7	6	5	5	4	3	2	2	1	0	0	-1	-2	-3	-3	-4	-5	-5
	97.0-100.9	7	7	6	5	4	4	3	2	1	1	0	-1	-1	-2	-3	-4	-4	-5
	101.0-104.9	8	7	6	6	5	4	4	3	2	1	0	0	-1	-1	-2	-3	-4	-4

*Adapted from Himes et al. (1985)[1] and reprinted with permission from Ross Laboratories, Columbus, OH.

Chart 7.3 Parent-Specific Adjustments for Stature of Boys from 3 to 18 Years*

Age (yr)	Stature (cm)	Midparent Stature (cm)																	
		150	152	154	156	158	160	162	164	166	168	170	172	174	176	178	180	182	184
3	86.0-87.9	7	6	5	5	4	3	2	1	1	0	-1	-2	-3	-3	-4	-5	-6	-7
	88.0-97.9	8	7	6	5	4	4	3	2	1	0	-1	-1	-2	-3	-4	-5	-5	-6
	98.0-106.9	8	8	7	6	5	4	4	3	2	1	0	0	-1	-2	-3	-4	-4	-5
4	90.0-93.9	7	6	5	4	4	3	2	1	0	-1	-1	-2	-3	-4	-5	-5	-6	-7
	94.0-103.9	8	7	6	5	4	3	3	2	1	0	-1	-1	-2	-3	-4	-5	-6	-6
	104.0-112.9	8	8	7	6	5	4	3	3	2	1	0	-1	-1	-2	-3	-4	-5	-6
5	96.0-103.9	8	7	6	5	4	3	2	1	0	0	-1	-2	-3	-4	-5	-6	-7	-8
	104.0-113.9	9	8	7	6	5	4	3	2	1	0	0	-1	-2	-3	-4	-5	-6	-7
	114.0-122.9	9	9	8	7	6	5	4	3	2	1	0	0	-1	-2	-3	-4	-5	-6
6	102.0-111.9	8	7	7	6	5	4	3	2	1	0	-1	-2	-3	-4	-5	-6	-7	-8
	112.0-121.9	9	8	7	7	6	5	4	3	2	1	0	-1	-2	-3	-4	-5	-6	-7
	122.0-130.9	10	9	8	7	6	6	5	4	3	2	1	0	-1	-2	-3	-4	-5	-6
7	109.0-117.9	9	8	7	6	5	4	3	2	1	0	-1	-2	-3	-4	-5	-6	-7	-8
	118.0-127.9	10	9	8	7	6	5	4	3	2	1	0	-1	-2	-3	-4	-5	-6	-7
	128.0-136.9	12	10	9	8	7	6	5	4	3	2	1	0	-1	-2	-3	-4	-5	-6
8	114.0-115.9	10	9	8	6	5	4	3	2	1	-1	-2	-3	-4	-5	-6	-8	-9	-10
	116.0-125.9	11	9	8	7	6	5	4	2	1	0	-1	-2	-3	-5	-6	-7	-8	-9
	126.0-135.9	12	10	9	8	7	6	5	3	2	1	0	-1	-2	-4	-5	-6	-7	-8
	136.0-144.9	13	12	10	9	8	7	6	5	3	2	1	0	-1	-2	-4	-5	-6	-7
9	120.0-121.9	11	9	8	7	6	4	3	2	1	0	-2	-3	-4	-5	-7	-8	-9	-10
	122.0-131.9	11	10	9	8	6	5	4	3	1	0	-1	-2	-3	-5	-6	-7	-8	-10
	132.0-141.9	12	11	10	9	7	6	5	4	2	1	0	-1	-2	-4	-5	-6	-7	-9
	142.0-150.9	13	13	11	10	8	7	6	5	4	2	1	0	-1	-3	-4	-5	-6	-7
10	124.0-127.9	11	10	9	7	6	5	3	2	1	-1	-2	-3	-5	-6	-7	-9	-10	-11
	128.0-137.9	12	11	10	8	7	6	4	3	2	0	-1	-2	-4	-5	-6	-8	-9	-10
	138.0-147.9	13	12	11	9	8	7	5	4	3	1	0	-1	-3	-4	-5	-7	-8	-9
	148.0-158.9	14	13	12	11	9	8	7	5	4	3	1	0	-1	-3	-4	-5	-7	-8
11	128.0-133.9	12	10	9	8	6	5	4	2	1	0	-2	-3	-5	-6	-7	-9	-10	-11
	134.0-143.9	12	11	10	8	7	6	4	3	2	0	-1	-2	-4	-5	-6	-8	-9	-10
	144.0-153.9	14	12	11	10	8	7	5	4	3	1	0	-1	-3	-4	-5	-7	-8	-9
	154.0-162.9	15	13	12	11	9	8	7	5	4	3	1	0	-2	-3	-4	-6	-7	-8
12	132.0-141.9	12	10	9	8	6	5	4	2	1	0	-2	-3	-4	-6	-7	-8	-10	-11
	142.0-151.9	13	11	10	9	7	6	5	3	2	1	-1	-2	-3	-5	-6	-7	-9	-10
	152.0-161.9	13	12	11	9	8	7	5	4	3	1	0	-1	-2	-4	-5	-6	-8	-9
	162.0-170.9	14	13	12	10	9	8	6	5	4	2	1	0	-2	-3	-4	-6	-7	-8
13	136.0-139.9	12	10	9	8	6	5	4	2	1	-1	-2	-3	-5	-6	-7	-9	-10	-12
	140.0-149.9	12	11	10	8	7	6	4	3	1	0	-1	-3	-4	-6	-7	-8	-10	-11
	150.0-159.9	13	12	10	9	8	6	5	4	2	1	-1	-2	-3	-5	-6	-7	-9	-10
	160.0-169.9	14	13	11	10	8	7	6	4	3	2	0	-1	-3	-4	-5	-7	-8	-9
	170.0-178.9	15	13	12	11	9	8	6	5	4	2	1	0	-2	-3	-5	-6	-7	-9
14	142.0-145.9	13	11	10	8	7	5	4	2	1	-1	-2	-4	-5	-7	-8	-10	-11	-13
	146.0-155.9	14	12	11	9	8	6	5	3	1	0	-2	-3	-5	-6	-8	-9	-11	-12
	156.0-165.0	15	13	11	10	8	7	5	4	2	1	-1	-2	-4	-5	-7	-8	-10	-11
	166.0-175.9	15	14	12	11	9	8	6	5	3	2	0	-1	-3	-4	-6	-7	-9	-11
	176.0-184.9	16	15	13	12	10	9	7	6	4	3	1	-1	-2	-4	-5	-7	-8	-10
15	148.0-151.9	14	13	11	9	7	6	4	2	0	-1	-3	-5	-7	-8	-10	-12	-14	-15
	152.0-161.9	15	14	12	10	8	7	5	3	1	0	-2	-4	-6	-7	-9	-11	-13	-14
	162.0-171.9	17	15	13	11	10	8	6	4	3	1	-1	-3	-4	-6	1	9	6	8
	172.0-181.9	18	16	14	13	11	9	7	6	4	2	0	-1	-3	-5	-7	-8	-10	-12
	182.0-190.9	19	17	16	14	12	10	9	7	5	3	2	0	-2	-4	-5	-7	-9	-11

(continued)

Chart 7.3 Continued

Age (yr)	Stature (cm)	150	152	154	156	158	160	162	164	166	168	170	172	174	176	178	180	182	184
										Midparent Stature (cm)									
16	156.0-163.9	17	15	13	11	9	7	5	3	1	−1	−3	−5	−7	−9	−11	−13	−16	−18
	164.0-173.9	19	17	15	13	10	8	6	4	2	0	−2	−4	−6	−8	−10	−12	−14	−16
	174.0-183.9	21	19	17	15	12	10	8	6	4	2	0	−2	−4	−6	−8	−10	−12	−14
	184.0-192.0	23	21	19	17	14	12	10	8	6	4	2	0	−2	−4	−6	−8	−10	−12
17	162.0-165.9	17	15	13	11	9	7	4	2	0	−2	−4	−7	−9	−11	−13	−15	−17	−20
	166.0-175.9	20	17	15	13	11	9	6	4	2	0	−2	−4	−7	−9	−11	−13	−15	−18
	176.0-185.9	22	20	18	16	13	11	9	7	5	3	0	−2	−4	−6	−8	−11	−13	−15
	186.0-194.9	25	23	20	18	16	14	12	9	7	5	3	1	−1	−4	−6	−8	−10	−12
18	160.0-165.9	18	16	13	11	9	6	4	2	0	−3	−5	−7	−10	−12	−14	−17	−19	−21
	166.0-175.9	20	18	16	13	11	9	7	4	2	0	−3	−5	−7	−10	−12	−14	−17	−19
	176.0-185.9	23	21	19	16	14	12	9	7	5	3	0	−2	−4	−7	−9	−11	−14	−16
	186.0-194.9	26	24	22	19	17	15	12	10	8	6	3	1	−1	−4	−6	−8	−11	−13

*Adapted from Himes et al. (1985)[1] and reprinted with permission from Ross Laboratories, Columbus, OH.

Chart 7.4 Parent-Specific Adjustments for Stature of Girls from 3 to 18 Years*

Age (yr)	Stature (cm)	Midparent Stature (cm)																	
		150	152	154	156	158	160	162	164	166	168	170	172	174	176	178	180	182	184
3	82.0-83.9	6	5	4	4	3	2	1	1	0	-1	-1	-2	-3	-3	-4	-5	-6	-6
	84.0-93.9	6	6	5	4	3	3	2	1	1	0	-1	-1	-2	-3	-4	-4	-5	-6
	94.0-102.9	7	7	6	5	4	4	3	2	2	1	0	-1	-1	-2	-3	-3	-4	-5
4	92.0-93.9	6	6	5	4	3	3	2	1	0	0	-1	-2	-3	-3	-4	-5	-6	-7
	94.0-103.9	7	6	6	5	4	3	2	2	1	0	-1	-1	-2	-3	-4	-4	-5	-6
	104.0-112.9	8	7	7	6	5	4	3	3	2	1	0	0	-1	-2	-3	-3	-4	-5
5	100.0-101.9	8	7	6	5	4	3	2	1	1	0	-1	-2	-3	-4	-5	-5	-6	-7
	102.0-111.9	8	7	6	6	5	4	3	2	1	0	-1	-1	-2	-3	-4	-5	-6	-7
	112.0-120.9	9	8	7	7	6	5	4	3	2	1	1	0	-1	-2	-3	-4	-5	-6
6	106.9-109.9	9	8	7	6	5	4	3	2	1	0	-1	-2	-3	-4	-5	-6	-7	-8
	110.0-119.9	9	9	8	7	6	5	4	3	2	1	0	-1	-2	-3	-4	-5	-6	-7
	120.0-128.9	11	10	9	8	7	6	5	4	3	2	1	0	-1	-2	-3	-4	-5	-6
7	112.0-117.9	9	8	7	6	5	4	3	2	1	0	-1	-2	-3	-4	-5	-6	-7	-8
	118.0-127.9	10	9	8	7	6	5	4	3	2	1	0	-1	-2	-3	-4	-5	-6	-7
	128.0-136.9	11	10	9	8	7	6	5	4	3	2	1	0	-1	-2	-3	-4	-5	-6
8	116.0-123.9	9	8	7	6	5	4	3	2	1	0	-1	-2	-3	-4	-5	-6	-8	-9
	124.0-133.9	10	9	8	7	6	5	4	3	2	1	0	-1	-2	-3	-4	-5	-7	-8
	134.0-142.9	11	10	9	8	7	6	5	4	3	2	1	0	-1	-2	-3	-4	-6	-7
9	122.0-131.9	10	9	8	7	6	5	3	2	1	0	-1	-2	-3	-4	-5	-6	-7	-9
	132.0-141.9	11	10	9	8	7	6	4	3	2	1	0	-1	-2	-3	-4	-5	-7	-8
	142.0-150.9	12	11	10	9	8	6	5	4	3	2	1	0	-1	-2	-3	-5	-6	-7
10	126.0-127.9	10	9	8	6	5	4	3	2	1	0	-1	-2	-3	-5	-6	-7	-8	-9
	128.0-137.9	10	9	8	7	6	5	4	2	1	0	-1	-2	-3	-4	-5	-6	-7	-8
	138.0-147.9	11	10	9	8	6	5	4	3	2	1	0	-1	-2	-3	-4	-5	-7	-8
	148.0-156.9	12	10	9	8	7	6	5	4	3	2	1	0	-1	-3	-4	-5	-6	-7
11	130.0-133.9	10	9	8	6	5	4	3	2	1	0	-1	-2	-3	-4	-6	-7	-8	-9
	134.0-143.9	10	9	8	7	6	5	4	3	1	0	-1	-2	-3	-4	-5	-6	-7	-8
	144.0-153.9	11	10	9	7	6	5	4	3	2	1	0	-1	-2	-3	-5	-6	-7	-8
	154.0-162.9	11	10	9	8	7	6	5	4	3	1	0	-1	-2	-3	-4	-5	-6	-7
12	134.0-139.9	10	9	8	7	6	5	3	2	1	0	-1	-3	-4	-5	-6	-7	-8	-10
	140.0-149.9	11	10	9	7	6	5	4	3	2	1	-1	-2	-3	-4	-6	-7	-8	-9
	150.0-159.9	12	10	9	8	7	6	5	3	2	1	0	-1	-3	-4	-5	-6	-7	-8
	160.0-168.9	12	11	10	9	8	6	5	4	3	2	0	-1	-2	-3	-4	-5	-7	-8
13	140.0-145.9	10	9	8	7	6	4	3	2	1	0	-1	-3	-4	-5	-6	-7	-8	-10
	146.0-155.9	11	10	9	7	6	5	4	3	2	0	-1	-2	-3	-4	-6	-7	-8	-9
	156.0-165.9	12	10	9	8	7	6	5	3	2	1	0	-1	-3	-4	-5	-6	-7	-8
	166.0-174.9	12	11	10	9	8	6	5	4	3	2	1	-1	-2	-3	-4	-5	-7	-8
14	146.0-149.9	10	9	8	6	5	4	3	2	1	0	-1	-3	-4	-5	-6	-7	-8	-9
	150.0-159.9	11	9	8	7	6	5	44	3	1	0	-1	-2	-3	-4	-5	-7	-8	-9
	160.0-169.9	11	10	9	8	7	6	5	3	2	1	0	-1	-2	-3	-5	-6	-7	-8
	170.0-178.9	12	11	10	9	8	6	5	4	3	2	1	0	-2	-3	-4	-5	-6	-7
15	146.0-151.9	10	9	8	7	5	4	3	2	1	-1	-2	-3	-4	-5	-6	-8	-9	-10
	152.0-161.9	11	10	9	7	6	5	4	3	1	0	-1	-2	-3	-4	-6	-7	-8	-9
	162.0-171.9	12	11	10	8	7	6	5	4	2	1	0	-1	-2	-4	-5	-6	-7	-8
	172.0-180.9	13	12	11	9	8	7	6	5	3	2	1	0	-1	-3	-4	-5	-6	-7
16	146.0-151.9	11	10	8	7	6	5	3	2	1	-1	-2	-3	-4	-6	-7	-8	-10	-11
	152.0-161.9	12	10	9	8	7	5	4	3	2	0	-1	-2	-4	-5	-6	-7	-9	-10
	162.0-171.9	13	12	10	9	8	6	5	4	3	1	0	-1	-3	-4	-5	-6	-8	-9
	172.0-180.9	14	13	11	10	9	7	6	5	4	2	1	0	-2	-3	-4	-5	-7	-8

(continued)

Chart 7.4 Continued

Age (yr)	Stature (cm)	Midparent Stature (cm)																	
		150	152	154	156	158	160	162	164	166	168	170	172	174	176	178	180	182	184
17	148.0-153.9	11	10	9	7	6	5	3	2	1	0	-2	-3	-4	-6	-7	-8	-10	-11
	154.0-163.9	12	11	10	8	7	6	4	3	2	0	-1	-2	-4	-5	-6	-8	-9	-10
	164.0-173.9	13	12	11	9	8	7	5	4	3	1	0	-1	-3	-4	-5	-6	-8	-9
	174.0-182.9	14	13	12	10	9	8	6	5	4	2	1	0	-1	3	-4	-5	-7	-8
18	148.0-149.9	10	9	8	7	5	4	3	2	1	-1	-2	-3	-4	-6	-7	-8	-9	-10
	150.0-159.9	11	10	8	7	6	5	4	2	1	0	-1	-3	-4	-5	-6	-7	-9	-10
	160.0-169.9	12	11	9	8	7	6	4	3	2	1	0	-2	-3	-4	-5	-6	-8	-9
	170.0-178.9	13	11	10	9	8	7	5	4	3	2	1	-1	-2	-3	-4	-5	-7	-8

*Adapted from Himes et al. (1985)[1] and reprinted with permission from Ross Laboratories, Columbus, OH.

Chart 7.5 Values for Parental Statures Used in Calculation of Midparent Stature When One Parent's Stature Is Reported as Short, Medium, or Tall*

Parent	Values (cm) of Stature Categories		
	Short	*Medium*	*Tall*
Father	167.6	176.3	185.4
Mother	154.9	162.8	170.7

*Adapted from Himes et al. (1985)[1] and reprinted with permission from Ross Laboratories, Columbus, OH.

8 Other Patterns of Injury

There are multiple ways in which parents and caregivers harm their children. The knowledge accrued since the first modern descriptions of child abuse allows professionals to better recognize children at risk. Some injuries are diagnostic of abuse and identify affected children immediately. In many cases, children remain at high risk because injuries are not identified as resulting from abuse. Finally, there are children injured by such unusual methods that the diagnosis of abuse commonly and predictably escapes detection. This chapter discusses a range of injuries found in abused children. Some injuries are easily identified as inflicted, whereas others are uncommon and overlooked more easily.

The Battered Child Syndrome

Although child abuse is as old as recorded history, it has become an issue for pediatricians only in the mid-20th century. John Caffey first described the association between subdural hemorrhage and long bone fractures in 1946 (Caffey, 1946). He recognized that both were traumatic in origin but did not recognize the causal mechanism. Caffey thought that trauma leading to these injuries was either unobserved or denied because of negligence. In one reported case, Caffey (1946) raised the possibility of inflicted trauma but stated that the "evidence was inadequate to prove or disprove [intentional mistreatment]" (p. 172). In the early 1950s, Frederic Silverman (1953) emphasized the repeated, inflicted nature of the trauma, despite denial by caregivers. Subsequent medical literature contained numerous reports of abuse, but little attention was given to the issue. It was not until Kempe coined the term *battered child* in 1962 that the medical and legal communities took action (Kempe, Silverman, Steele, Droegemueller, & Silver, 1962).

Within a few years, most states had adopted abuse-reporting statutes (Heins, 1984). By 1967, all fifty states had some form of legislation regarding child maltreatment (Fontana & Besharov, 1979; Heins, 1984). Legislative efforts culminated in a 1974 federal statute called the Child Abuse Prevention and Treatment Act (PL 93-247). This law focused national concern on the prevention, diagnosis, and treatment of child abuse. Model legislation was part of this effort, and states were encouraged to evaluate their statutes and adequately address the issues of child abuse and neglect.

Kempe first used the term *battered child* in a 1961 address to the American Academy of Pediatrics to describe young children who were victims of serious physical abuse. Subsequently, he and his colleagues published a study by the same name in 1962 (Heins, 1984; Kempe et al., 1962). The first description was of children generally younger than 3 years old, often with evidence of malnutrition and multiple soft tissue injuries. Subdural hemorrhages and multiple fractures were commonly found. Kempe et al. (1962) also included children with less severe or isolated injuries in their description of the battered child. Although any child with an inflicted injury has been battered, the term *battered child* describes a child with repeated injuries to multiple organ systems. Physicians who treat children should be able to identify those who are severely abused and injured.

Fontana, Donovan, and Wong (1963) extended the early conceptualization of child abuse to include forms beyond physical injury by introducing the term *maltreatment syndrome*. Maltreatment included both battered children and children who were poorly fed and inadequately supervised. Fontana et al. (1963) added neglect to the evolving description of child abuse.

The original articles by Caffey (1946), Silverman (1953), Kempe et al. (1962), and Fontana et al. (1963) provide the modern medical history of child abuse. Their insight and persistence set the stage for the recognition of child abuse as a pediatric problem and resulted in an outpouring of medical, social, and psychological literature dealing with abuse and neglect (see Figure 8.1).

CHILD PHYSICAL ABUSE AND NEGLECT

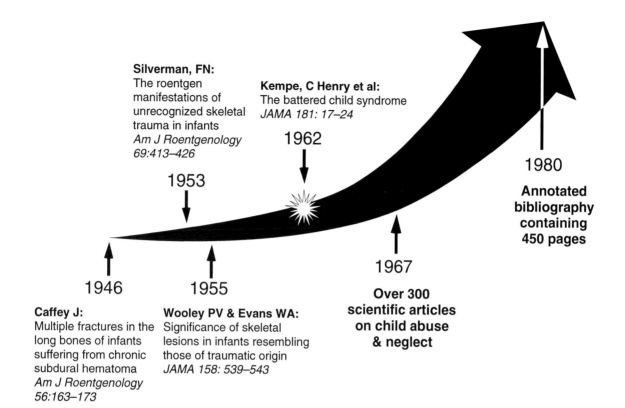

Figure 8.1. Rapid growth of the professional literature in child abuse and neglect.

Note. The two decades *before* the 1962 publication of Kempe and colleagues' seminal article are dotted with approximately three articles. The two decades *after* have seen an explosion of related articles numbering in the thousands, covering a wide range of topics involving child maltreatment (Heins, 1984).

Thirty years after the Kempe et al. (1962) article, Dr. Richard Krugman (1992), then the director of the C. Henry Kempe National Center for Prevention of Child Abuse and Neglect, observed how far the child protection movement had come in a short time. He compared the 1962 figure of 447 reported victims of battering to the 1991 estimate of 2.7 million reports of abuse (Krugman, 1992). Krugman stressed the staggering disparity between 447 cases and 2.7 million reports, even if not all reports of abuse result in a determination of maltreatment. In addition, Krugman (1992) observed that the 1991 estimate of 2.7 million reports of abuse did not account for the number of unreported cases that were either not suspected, misdiagnosed, or simply not reported.

Oral and Dental Trauma

Abused children often sustain injuries to the face and mouth because this easily targeted area has significant psychological importance. A child's crying may incite physical abuse and injury to the mouth. Some estimates show that up to 50% of physically abused children have injuries to the face or mouth (Becker, Needleman, & Kotelchuck, 1978). Facial injuries include contusions, abrasions, lacerations, burns, bites, and fractures. Injuries limited to the mouth include fractured, missing, and displaced teeth; contusions; abrasions; lacerations; and burns. There is a bimodal age distribution of affected children, with the majority of injuries occurring in the 0- to 4-year age group and another peak occurring during adolescence (da Fonesca, Feigal, & ten Bensel, 1992). Despite the high incidence of facial injuries in abused children, dentists infrequently report suspected abuse (Needleman, 1986). Likewise, physicians are not always thorough in their examination of the mouth, so that many injuries may go unrecognized.

Examination of the Mouth and Teeth

The face and mouth examination of the abused child is simple and quick if the child is cooperative and not in a great deal of pain. Important abnormalities are detected by a thorough mouth examination (see Figure 8.2).

Begin the physical by examining the face for symmetry and injuries. If possible, have the child open and close his or her mouth a few times and observe for asymmetry or difficulty; listen for any noises. Palpate along the mandibular borders, zygoma, nasal areas, and around the eyes, searching for areas of tenderness or evidence of fractures.

Examine the child's teeth and look for bleeding, missing or injured teeth, malocclusions, and caries. Have the child bite down and assess for pain. Reflect the lips back individually to examine for frenulum lacerations, scars, burns, and abrasions. Move the upper teeth back and forth between the fingers to check for maxillary fractures, loose teeth, and instability. Examine the molars for caries, and check the buccal mucosa for injuries. Finally, have the child stick out his or her tongue. Check for injuries and lift the tongue to examine the lingual frenulum[1] (Bernat, 1981) (see Figure 8.2).

Oral Injuries

A number of oral injuries result from physical abuse. Most injuries are nonspecific, and the diagnosis of abuse rests on the history or additional physical findings that indicate trauma.

Injuries to Teeth

Injuries to the teeth of children are very common accidental injuries; none is pathognomonic for abuse. Da Fonesca et al. (1992) report that of more than 1,200 cases of child maltreatment reviewed, only five tooth injuries were reported. It is not known

CHILD PHYSICAL ABUSE AND NEGLECT

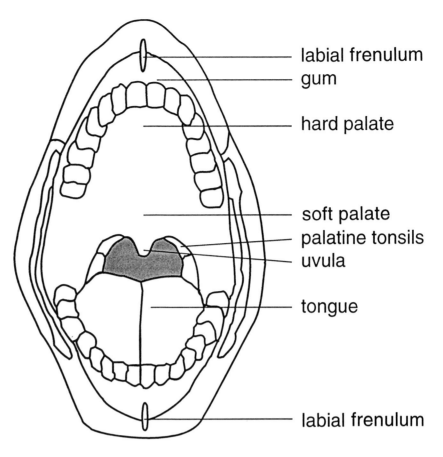

Figure 8.2. Diagram of the mouth.

Note. This is a diagram of intra-oral structures. Note that there is a lingular frenulum in addition to the two labial frenula located underneath the tongue. Although injuries to the upper labial frenulum are most commonly seen, any of these structures can be injured.

whether this is an underrepresentation of the actual number of inflicted tooth injuries. The management of loose teeth is dependent on the age of the child. Direct blows to the mouth may result in loosening of a tooth or teeth. Severe blows to the incisal edge of the teeth may cause tooth intrusion into the alveolar bone. Intruded teeth may appear shorter than the surrounding teeth, and those completely intruded may appear to be missing. In this case, radiographs identify the location of the tooth.

A severe blow to the mouth that results in avulsion, or removal, of the teeth more commonly occurs to the permanent teeth. Immediate dental referral is arranged when permanent teeth are avulsed because the tooth needs to be placed back in the socket as soon as possible to salvage it. Fractures to the anterior teeth occur from direct blows, commonly with falls. Finally, dental color changes resulting from previous pulpal injuries may be seen in accidental injury or abuse. All children with tooth injuries are referred to a dentist for definitive evaluation and treatment.

Mucosal Injuries

Mucosal injuries are rather common in abused children. Lip injuries include burns, contusions, and lacerations. Direct blows to the mouth that trap the lip between the teeth and the external object can result in abrasions, contusions, or lacerations. Lacerations may require suturing, which is best done by a plastic or oral surgeon. Labial or lingual frenulum tears may result from both accidental or inflicted trauma. Upper frenulum tears are common accidental injuries in older infants and young toddlers who are unsteady on their feet, because the child may fall and strike his or her mouth against the ground or other hard objects. Associated abrasions or contusions to the lip or philtrum may be found. Frenulum tears also occur during attempts to silence a crying infant or to feed a refusing child if hands, pacifiers, bottles, or eating utensils are forced into a child's mouth. A frenulum tear is usually indicative of abuse in young infants (see Photo 8.1).

In most cases, frenulum tears are managed conservatively but may require suturing if the injury is extensive or the alveolar bone is exposed (Needleman, 1986).

Facial Fractures

Facial fractures are relatively uncommon abusive injuries, representing less than 5% of facial injuries (Becker et al., 1978). The most commonly reported injury is to the mandible, although the nasal bone, mandible, zygoma, or maxilla may be fractured. Mandibular fractures are usually bilateral. They can be missed on skeletal survey and are better detected clinically. There may be contusions over the fracture. Palpation of the mandibular condyles will elicit pain, and jaw opening may be difficult. All children with mandibular fractures are referred to an oral surgeon for full evaluation (including radiographic evaluation) and treatment.

Bite Marks Bites are common pediatric injuries, and bite marks may be an indicator of abuse. Animal bites occur more frequently than human bites, although human bites are common. Human bites to children occur during fights, play, and sports, or as a result of maltreatment. Baker and Moore (1987) report one human bite per 615 visits in an emergency department. In this series, 1% of bites seen in the ED were the result of abuse. More common

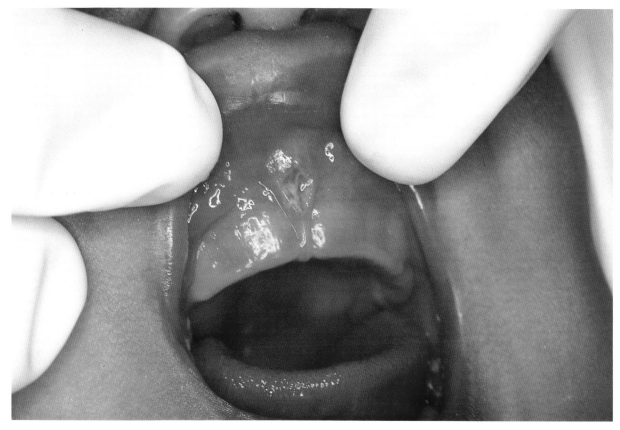

Photo 8.1.

Note. A 2-month-old awoke one morning with bleeding from the mouth. Physical examination revealed an acutely torn labial frenulum. The father was responsible for feeding the baby during the night but denied any trauma. Frenulum tears in young infants are often the result of forced feeding.

causes of human bites in children included fighting, playing, and sports-related activity.

Human bites are complex injuries produced by crushing pressure from the teeth, cutting from the incisors, and dragging the teeth over soft tissue (Whittaker, 1990). The mark left on the child is dependent on the biting forces applied, the duration of the bite, and the degree of movement between the tissues and the teeth (Sognnaes, 1977). Human bite marks may appear ovoid, arched, or round, or they may resemble paired parentheses. The pattern depends on the location of the injury and whether one or both arches leave marks. The size of an adult dental arch (the width from canine to canine) is approximately 2.5 to 4 cm (Barsley & Landcaster, 1987). The intercanine distance for children is smaller than it is for adults, although some overlap exists. Some bite marks contain suction petechiae, or a central area of ecchymosis possibly due to injury of the blood vessels trapped between the jaws of the biter (Barsley, 1993) (see Photo 8.2).

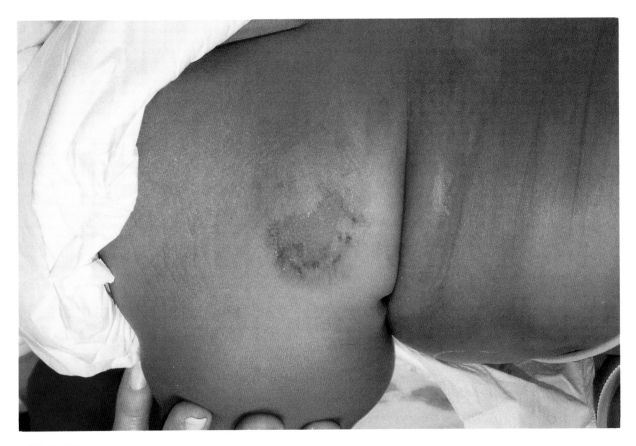

Photo 8.2.

Note. A 3-month-old infant reportedly rolled off a bed. The baby had subdural and retinal hemorrhages, a diastatic skull fracture, healing rib fractures, and this human bite to the buttocks. Note the imprints made by the upper incisors and the central ecchymosis, which is due to injury of the blood vessels trapped between the jaws of the biter.

Evaluation of Bite Marks

The first step in the evaluation of a bite is to identify whether the bite was made by a person or animal. Animal bites tend to puncture the skin, the cross-sectional size of individual teeth is small, the shape of teeth marks tends to be circular, and the incisor number may be greater than with human bites (Barsley, 1993).

Bites can occur anywhere on the body. In infants, bite marks tend to be found on the cheek, arm, shoulder, buttocks, or genitalia (Wagner, 1986). The timing of bite injuries is difficult and dependent on many factors. Bites that do not break the skin last from several minutes to 24 hours (Wagner, 1986). When skin is broken, the bite can last a number of days, depending on the thickness of the tissue (thinner areas retain bite marks longer). Abuse victims may have bite marks that are of different ages.

The recognition, proper evaluation, and documentation of a bite mark can be of great assistance in confirming the diagnosis of abuse and identifying the perpetrator of the bite. An initial procedure for preserving bite mark evidence is the collection of salivary samples from the wound. Health care professionals often overlook the collection of these data. A salivary sample can identify the ABO group of the perpetrator, because 80% of the population with type A and B blood groups secrete blood group antigens corresponding to their blood group in saliva (Mollison, 1993). Sampling is done prior to washing the bite mark, using a sterile cotton swab moistened in sterile saline and allowed to air dry. Control swabs taken from unaffected skin and a blood sample should also accompany the specimen. The samples should follow chain of evidence procedures to a forensic laboratory for analysis. In some areas, odontologists may be consulted to assist in bite mark evaluation.

Photographic evidence is usually the most valuable tool in assessing bite marks because it shows the location of the bite on the body as well as details of the wound. It is important to photograph multiple views of the bite. A reference scale such as a ruler to indicate size or length of the mark should be included in the photo. A number of separate photographs of each arch may be needed because bites can be found on curved areas of the body. In addition, photographs are taken over time because the clarity and appearance of the mark change as edema resolves and the wound heals (Whittaker, 1990). In some cases, a forensic odontologist may make impressions of the wound. Guidelines developed by the American Board of Forensic Odontology exist for the analysis of bite marks (American Board of Forensic Odontology, Inc., 1986).

Dental Neglect   The definition of dental neglect varies by state, institution, and individual, and is imprecise. There are numerous factors that contribute to the neglect of oral health, including parental ignorance, family isolation, financial restraints, and lack of perceived value of oral health (Committee on Early Childhood, Adoption and Dependent Care, 1986). Abused children are at high risk for dental neglect (Greene, Chisick, & Aaron, 1994). The health care professional educates the family regarding the effects of dental neglect. If attempts to improve oral health fail, or the child's oral health has been adversely affected, a report to the child welfare system is indicated.

Abuse by Poisoning

Poisoning is a health problem in childhood. The Poison Prevention Packaging Act passed in 1970 had a significant impact in reducing the morbidity and mortality associated with accidental ingestion of medications by children (Walton, 1982). However, poisoning as a pattern of abuse remains a poorly understood and underreported form of child maltreatment that is now receiving more attention in the medical literature (Dine & McGovern, 1982; Fazen, Lovejoy, & Crone, 1986; Rogers & Bentovim, 1981; Sibert & Murphy, 1980). Intentional or abusive poisoning is more deadly than accidental poisoning, with fatality estimates ranging from 17% to 33% compared to the mortality rate of 0.04% for accidental poisoning (Bays, 1994a). Poisoning may be associated with findings of other forms of abuse. Dine and McGovern (1982) and Bays (1994a) report that approximately 20% of their respective samples of abusive poisoning cases also had evidence of physical abuse.

Fischler (1983) organizes intentional poisoning into four types: (a) impulsive parental acts related to stress (e.g., use of sedatives, alcohol, antihistamines, or paregoric to quiet a child); (b) neglect (e.g., unsupervised child ingests medications or alcohol, or repeated ingestions); (c) bizarre parenting practices (e.g., using toxic doses of vitamins, minerals, or herbs, and water or salt intoxication); and (d) Munchausen syndrome by proxy (e.g., medication or chemical given to create a fictitious illness) (see next section).

The clinical presentation of inflicted and accidental poisoning overlaps. Common symptoms include altered states of consciousness, cardiorespiratory depression or excitation, gastrointestinal symptoms, seizures, and other challenging and unexplained symptom complexes (Wiley, 1991). Altered mental status is a common presentation. Fazen et al. (1986) examined 90 children admitted to the hospital for ingestion; 84% had an altered level of consciousness when first examined that varied from coma to agitation and seizure activity.

Historical factors that raise the concern for intentional poisoning include (a) previous poisoning in child or sibling, (b) implausible history, (c) changing history, (d) history discordant with child's development, (e) child or sibling blamed, (f) excessive delay in seeking treatment, and (g) unexplained symptoms that resolve when the child is not in the care of a suspected perpetrator. Physical examination findings in poisoning are variable and depend on the pharmacologic actions of the substances involved.

Laboratory assessment plays an important role in the evaluation of the poisoned child (Hepler, Sutheimer, & Sunshine, 1986; Wiley, 1991). However, the health care provider must be aware of the limitations of toxicology screens. Wiley (1991) reports wide variability in the accuracy of toxicological testing. Laboratories frequently receive inadequate specimens, mostly because of a common misperception that a blood sample alone is sufficient. Toxicologists are adamant that proper toxicological screening requires both blood and urine (Hepler et al., 1986). Gastric contents can be a useful addition if available. The urine sample allows for qualitative determinations of substances, whereas the blood sample allows for specific quantitative analysis. Sending one without the other hampers the evaluation. In addition, not all drugs and chemical compounds can be identified by standard laboratory processes used for toxicological screens. The most comprehensive screens available detect only about 90 compounds (Wiley, 1991). Substances such as ammonia, clonidine, chloral hydrate, cyanide, insulin, petroleum distillates, and sodium sulfate (found in shampoo) may not be detected in currently available toxicology screens (Fazen et al., 1986; Wiley, 1991). There are wide local and regional variations in which drugs and substances are screened. Therefore, the health care provider is encouraged to contact the reference laboratory used at his or her own institution and obtain a list of what the screen tests, which screens need a special request, and what is not available.

Commonly used poisons in reported cases of abuse include alcohol, caffeine, benzodiazepines, glutethimide, insulin, ipecac, laxatives, marijuana, oral hypoglycemics, pepper, salt, and a variety of other prescription and illicit substances. In addition, the health care provider must consider substances used in alternative medical practices.

Munchausen Syndrome by Proxy

Munchausen syndrome is a psychiatric disorder in which patients repeatedly offer false histories of illness and/or fabricate evidence of disease in order to gain medical attention (Asher, 1951; Zitelli, Seltman, & Shannon, 1987). It was first described in the adult medical literature by Asher in 1951. Meadow (1977) reported two children subjected to innumerable hospitalizations and medical tests because their mothers had either falsified the history of illness or induced illness in the child. Meadow (1977) coined the term *Munchausen syndrome by proxy* (MSBP) to describe this form of nonaccidental injury because of its reminiscence to the adult Munchausen syndrome. Although presentations of MSBP are numerous, there are common features (Rosenberg, 1987) that include the following:

1. The child's illness is either simulated and/or produced by a parent or primary caregiver of the child.
2. The child's persistent presentation for medical assessment and care usually results in multiple medical procedures.

3. The perpetrator denies any knowledge of the etiology of the child's illness.

4. Acute signs and symptoms of the illness abate when the child is separated from the perpetrator.

MSBP is often reported as an unusual manifestation of child abuse. Although the prevalence of the disorder is unknown, it is thought to be much more common than is reported in the medical literature (Schreier & Libow, 1993). Infants and young children are the most common victims of MSBP, but school-aged children, adolescents, and even adults are at risk (Smith & Ardern, 1989). In cases involving older children and adolescents, the child often gets drawn into the illness-fabricating behavior, either by validating the mother's claims or by colluding with the mother to produce illness. In addition, older children may independently display behavior more typical of the adult Munchausen patient (Abrol, Heck, Gleckel, & Rosner, 1990).

The majority of MSBP perpetrators are mothers, although fathers, grandmothers, nurses, foster care mothers, and day care workers are also reported perpetrators. A classic description of the "MSBP mother" is as follows: The mother often appears to be completely devoted to the child, attentive to the child's medical problems, and very knowledgeable about the child's medical condition. The mother is active in the child's medical care during hospitalization, often spending all her time at the child's bedside. She is commonly friendly and pleasant and develops a close relationship with hospital staff. The mother seems supportive of the doctors and nurses, regardless of the staff's inability to diagnose and cure the patient. Although MSBP mothers are often described as upper middle class, with a background in a health-related field, perpetrators have been described in all socioeconomic groups and may have no medical background. It is important to note that although a classic description of the MSBP perpetrator exists, there is great variation in the characteristics of the perpetrator.

A critical analysis of maternal attributes reveals important characteristics of the MSBP mother. Although seemingly devoted to the child, these mothers may show little emotional attachment to the child when left alone and can seem more interested in spending time with other parents and hospital personnel than with their ill child. Although most parents abhor the thought of having to put their child through medical testing, MSBP mothers welcome testing and can become angry when they do not get what they want (usually hospitalization and further testing). It is not uncommon for the child's symptoms to escalate shortly after hospitalization is denied or testing is completed. Between 10% and 25% of MSBP mothers are believed to suffer from Munchausen syndrome (Rosenberg, 1987), so that fabrications regarding the mother's past medical history are common.

An important clue to the diagnosis of MSBP sometimes lies in the inappropriateness of the mother's affect. At times when the child is critically ill, the mother may appear calm, disinterested, elated, or even excited (Schreier & Libow, 1993). The mothers can be quite brazen at times, signing releases of information or agreements of cooperation when most parents would not.

Fathers are often involved minimally in the child's medical care and in the family. In some cases, the father is unaware of the child's medical problems, despite the child's extensive involvement with the medical community (Guandolo, 1985).

The classic description of the MSBP parents should not be interpreted as the only parental presentation of MSBP. Perpetrators can be male or female, rich or poor, married or single, intelligent or intellectually slow, and friendly or abrasive. What all perpetrators share is a lack of empathy for the child. Indeed, Schreier and Libow (1993) postulate that the child means less to the parent as a person than as an object to be manipulated. Because the perpetrator's behavior in MSBP is so discordant with that of a caring parent, it is easy to assume that MSBP mothers are psychotic. Although a number of psychiatric disorders have been described in MSBP mothers, including personality disorders with hysterical, narcissistic, antisocial, and borderline traits (Bools, Neale, & Meadow, 1992), perpetrators of MSBP are not psychotic and are deliberate in their actions. Many perpetrators have normal findings on psychological tests.

The Medical Presentation of MSBP

There are generally two methods by which parents cause fictitious illness in their children. The first, simulated or apparent, describes those cases in which a parent fabricates a history or produces false evidence of illness but does not cause direct harm to the child. Alternatively, the perpetrator may induce actual illness through a variety of mechanisms referred to as produced or actual illness. Either mechanism can be employed in isolation, or both may be used to fabricate the illness. One method does not seem to be less harmful to the child than the other. The risk to the child regarding safety and future well-being is high, regardless of the methods used.

The creativity of MSBP parents in their attempts to deceive physicians is truly remarkable. There are numerous signs, symptoms, and diagnoses reported in the literature that are ultimately diagnosed as MSBP. Rosenberg (1987) reviewed the literature on MSBP and described the most common presentations. The presentations (in decreasing order) were bleeding, seizures, CNS depression, apnea, diarrhea, vomiting, fever, and rash (Rosenberg, 1987). Less common presenting diagnoses include cystic fibrosis, bacte-

Table 8.1 Suspicious Signs Associated with MSBP

A child who presents with medical problems that do not respond to treatment or follow an unusual course that is puzzling and unexplainable

Physical or laboratory findings that are extremely unusual, discrepant with the history, or clinically impossible

A caregiver (usually the mother) who seems medically knowledgeable and/or fascinated with medical information and seems to enjoy the hospital environment

A highly attentive caregiver who is reluctant to leave the child's side

A caregiver who appears unusually calm in the face of serious difficulties in the child's medical course while being highly supportive of physicians, or one who is angry, devalues staff, and demands further intervention and more procedures

A caregiver who works in the health care field or professes interest in a health-related job

Signs and symptoms of a child's illness that fail to occur in the parent's absence (hospitalization and careful monitoring may be needed to establish this causal relationship)

A family history of unusual or numerous medical ailments that is not substantiated

A family history of similar sibling illness or unexplained sibling illness or death

A caregiver with symptoms similar to the child's illness

A suspected caregiver with an emotionally distant relationship with her spouse; the spouse often has little or no contact with the hospital, even though the child is suffering from a serious illness

A caregiver who reports dramatic, negative events, such as house fires, burglaries, car accidents, and so on, that affect the family while the child is undergoing treatment

A caregiver who seems to have an insatiable need for adulation or who makes self-serving efforts at public acknowledgment of her abilities

---

Source. Adapted from Schreier and Libow (1993), p. 203. Used with permission.

rial sepsis, iron deficiency anemia, and even physical and sexual abuse (Ernst & Philip, 1986; Hodge, Schwartz, Sargent, Bodurtha, & Starr, 1982; Meadow, 1993; Orenstein & Wasserman, 1986). In the majority of cases, the child appears to have a chronic illness, although some mothers fabricate illness on a more intermittent basis. There is almost always a delay in diagnosing MSBP. Rosenberg (1987) reports a mean length of time to diagnosis of 14.9 months (+/- 14 months) from the onset of symptoms.

Some delay in diagnosis of MSBP is expected given the nature of the deception and staff assumption that caregivers are truthful in their reports. Unfortunately, MSBP is not often considered in the differential diagnosis until the child has suffered significant morbidity or has died.

Clues to the Diagnosis of MSBP

The detection of MSBP is a great challenge to the health care professional. The diagnosis is usually considered after a number of suspicious indicators become apparent. Table 8.1 describes commonly noted signs associated with MSBP that raise the suspicion of the diagnosis. It is important to note that not all factors are present in any one case, and that no one single factor should be used to make the diagnosis.

Management of MSBP

Confirmation of the diagnosis of MSBP is accomplished in a variety of ways, depending on the circumstances of the case.

Most children with MSBP require hospitalization for evaluation and surveillance, although cases have been handled in the outpatient setting (Guandolo, 1985). In reality, many cases are first suspected during hospitalization of the child for evaluation of reported symptoms. Social work and/or mental health providers are involved as early as possible when the diagnosis is suspected, and a team meeting with all professionals involved in the case should occur at that time. At the team meeting, staff review the medical history and discuss concerns regarding the diagnosis. It is important to discuss any doubts or concerns related to the diagnosis. MSBP mothers are notorious for manipulating and splitting staff, and it is common to have dissention regarding the diagnosis.

The next step in management entails careful surveillance of the mother and child and documentation of findings. For presentations where surveillance is thought to be of value, a number of methods are available. These include covert video surveillance, one-to-one nursing, and enforced separation of the parent and child (Epstein, Markowitz, Gallo, Holmes, & Gryboski, 1987; Malatack, Wiener, Gartner, Zitelli, & Brunetti, 1985). Video surveillance is not universally available, and consultation with the hospital's legal counsel is recommended prior to initiating covert videotaping. Surveillance of the caregiver is done in the least intrusive manner possible. This limits the invasion of the parent's privacy while attempting to diagnose the condition and protect the child (Wilde & Pedroni, 1993). The nursing staff is valuable in MSBP because they have frequent or continuous interactions with patients and their families and are able to observe parent and child interactions closely.

When staff suspect MSBP, they should move the child to a room where he or she can be monitored easily. The caregiver's involvement in the child's care should be limited, and he or she should not be allowed to give the child any medications. If the child develops acute symptoms, the staff critically evaluate the history of the presentation, including the identity of the adult with the child at the onset of symptoms. If the child is verbal, he or she is interviewed apart from the caregiver. Younger children often provide valuable information because they may not recognize the connection of their symptoms with the actions of their mother.

The collection of laboratory data follows chain of evidence collection if possible. Old medical records are reviewed to provide information regarding the child's medical history and the veracity of the parent's history. Staff should meet with other adult family members because they are often a source of useful information. In many cases, the mother prevents efforts to meet with other family members. Because such behavior is somewhat diagnostic, it may be necessary to arrange a family meeting without the caregiver's knowledge. Finally, careful and complete documentation of interactions is extremely important. All records are objective and professional in documenting observations and interactions of the staff and the parent and the parent and the child.

Once the team establishes a diagnosis of MSBP, another team meeting is called with representatives from the child protection agency and/or the police. Unlike the case with most forms of abuse, CPS and the police are usually informed prior to alerting the parent. At the time of the report, it is recommended that the CPS worker be invited to a meeting to discuss the diagnosis and its implications, because it is not uncommon for CPS workers to have little understanding or experience with MSBP (Kaufman, Coury, Pickrel, & McCleery, 1989).

Confronting the Perpetrator

As in all cases of suspected abuse, the caregiver(s) must be told of the diagnosis of MSBP. This is stated in a clear, simple, and nonaccusatory manner. The reactions of parents when told of the diagnosis vary, but they do not usually confess immediately. Some caregivers remain calm, whereas others become belligerent. In an effort to prove the diagnosis incorrect, the caregiver often attempts to focus attention either on the child's actual illness or on symptoms that cannot be explained. It is important to respond in a calm, professional manner but remain firm in the diagnosis. The caregiver is told that a report to CPS has been made. Because some mothers attempt to sign the child out of the hospital at this point, it is wise to be prepared to immediately protect the child legally. Finally, there may be reactions of disbelief from family members not previously involved in the case. For this reason, it is prudent to limit the number of family members present at the meeting if possible.

Prognosis of MSBP

According to published reports, the mortality rate associated with MSBP approaches 10% (Rosenberg, 1987). This high mortality rate may be inflated because of underrecognition of the syndrome and the tendency to report severe cases. Nevertheless, the mortality and morbidity associated with MSBP is substantial. There are little data regarding the long-term effects of MSBP. McGuire and Feldman (1989) report a range of psychological problems exhibited by MSBP victims, including infant feeding disorders, withdrawal, hyperactivity, hysteria, and adoption of Munchausen behavior in the child. Psychological evaluation of and therapy for both the mother and the child are required given the etiology of MSBP and the damaging effects it has on its victims. The therapist chosen to treat the mother must have knowledge about this disorder. The child must be separated from the perpetrator; in fact, many experts recommend that the child not be placed with a relative because of the risk that the offending parent will have continuing access to the child. The issue of family reunification in cases of MSBP must be evaluated with extreme caution because there are limited data on the outcome of psychotherapy and reunification.

Death of the Abused Child

The mortality rate for child abuse is difficult to determine precisely. Fatal maltreatment is underestimated because of both underidentification of child homicides and inaccurate classification of pediatric fatalities in official reports. Differentiating fatal abuse from natural causes of death may be difficult. Child homicides are often misclassified as accidents, drownings, falls, natural illness, or undetermined causes (Ewigman, Kivlahan, & Land, 1993). Distinguishing homicide from natural death is especially difficult if the victim is an infant (Kleinman, Blackbourne, Marks, Karellas, & Belanger, 1989). Differentiating SIDS, metabolic diseases, accidental suffocation, and other natural causes of death from homicide requires a careful, complete investigation.

Few jurisdictions in the United States have the resources—both money and properly trained personnel—to conduct a thorough investigation into each childhood death in the community (Committee on Child Abuse, 1993). In addition, needed collaboration between the agencies responsible for investigating a child's death and those previously involved with the family is lacking in most jurisdictions. Methods used to classify causes of death are not standardized, so that recognized child abuse fatalities may be labeled as child abuse and neglect, child battering, child homicide, or violent death (Ewigman et al., 1993). McClain, Sacks, Froehlke, and Ewigman (1993) estimate that between 15% and 30% of official death records are properly coded to identify the fatality as due to child abuse and neglect. Improved investigations, standardized definitions of child abuse fatalities by different agencies, and improved methods of recording abuse fatalities would provide a better understanding of the magnitude of the problem.

It is estimated that between 1,000 and 2,000 children in the United States are murdered by their caregivers each year (McClain et al., 1993). Approximately 40% of fatal abuse occurs among infants, and 90% occurs to children less than 5 years of age. Younger children are more vulnerable to fatal maltreatment because of their small size, their inability to communicate verbally, and because they live a relatively isolated existence, out of contact with adults other than their caregivers (Committee on

Child Abuse, 1993). The weapons used to murder children vary according to age (Division of Injury Control, 1990). At least half of the deaths to children ages 0 to 4 years are caused by direct blows, and less than 10% are due to firearms. Alternatively, firearms account for two thirds of adolescent homicides, and direct blows account for less than 5% of adolescent deaths. The frequency with which direct blows contribute to death in infants and young children primarily reflects injuries due to shaking impact syndrome and inflicted abdominal trauma. Finally, death rates due to abuse vary geographically, with the highest rates reported in the South and West and the lowest rates in the Northeast (McClain et al., 1994). Reasons for these geographic variations are not clear. Standardized data collection of all child deaths might provide information that would explain these regional variations and provide the foundations for prevention.

Child Death Review Teams

Many states and local jurisdictions have developed child death review teams to better identify and understand the causes of childhood deaths. Since the first team was started in Los Angeles in 1978, child fatality reviews have developed in 39 states (West & Yunghans, 1994). Teams function at the state or local level, with a trend toward establishment of both local and state teams. Child death review teams were initially established to review suspicious childhood deaths, although many jurisdictions now review all pediatric deaths. Members of the review team vary by jurisdiction but are generally composed of professionals from specific disciplines. Standard team members include coroners and/or medical examiners, law enforcement agents, prosecuting attorneys, CPS workers, pediatricians with child abuse expertise, and public health professionals. Additional representatives come from mental health agencies, fire departments, probation and parole departments, substance abuse treatment centers, education, and SIDS foundation and child advocacy centers (Durfee, Gellert, & Tilton-Durfee, 1992).

Child death review teams provide an important method for systematic review of the factors contributing to pediatric deaths. Multidisciplinary reviews are more complete than are single agency reviews, they can more easily identify suspicious deaths, and they provide the opportunity to review protocols within and among participating agencies (Durfee et al., 1992). Implementation of death review teams may also improve the quality of death investigations at the local level, identify barriers to death investigations, allow for better allocation of limited resources, and improve the understanding of the causes of child death (Committee on Child Abuse, 1993). Most child death review teams in the country have been developed during the past 5 years, and national outcome data are limited. Systematic review of deaths has been shown to identify child abuse homicides that would otherwise go undetected. Ewigman et al. (1993) retrospectively reviewed more than 350 pediatric injury deaths involving children less than 5 years old in Missouri from 1983 to 1986 using multiple data sources. Death certificates appropriately identified maltreatment deaths in less than 50% of cases, and the FBI crime reports database identified less than 40% of these deaths as homicides. Missouri now mandates review of all child deaths under the age of 15. It is hoped that death investigations will improve prevention strategies, hold more adults responsible for killing their children, and better protect siblings of murdered children from future harm.

Sudden Infant Death Syndrome

Sudden infant death syndrome (SIDS) is defined as the sudden and unexpected death of an infant that remains unexplained after a complete postmortem investigation, including autopsy, death scene evaluation, and review of the case history (Willinger, James, & Catz, 1991). SIDS accounts for more than 5,000 deaths in the United States each year and is the leading cause of infant death between 1 week and 1 year of age (Hunt & Brouillette, 1987). By definition, SIDS does not occur in children over 12 months of age. The peak incidence in SIDS occurs between 2 and 4 months of age, with more than 90% of SIDS deaths occurring by 6 months (Peterson, 1988). Epidemiological factors have been studied extensively to identify infants at risk for SIDS. Poverty, low birth weight, sleeping prone, prematurity, infants born small for gestational age, poor weight gain, and maternal smoking are among the factors reported to increase the risk of SIDS. None of these factors is proven to cause SIDS, and all are factors associated with infant deaths in general (Haas et al., 1993). It is presently impossible to predict which infants will ultimately die of SIDS.

The typical history of a SIDS death is as follows: A previously healthy infant is put down for a nap or for the night. Some infants have a history of recent upper respiratory infection but are otherwise healthy. Some time later, the baby is found dead. No struggle or crying was heard. At times, some pink, frothy discharge may be found at the nose, at the mouth, or on the sheets, and postmortem lividity may be present. The caregiver immediately calls for emergency help, and the infant is brought to the nearest hospital and pronounced dead.

Etiology of SIDS

There are numerous theories that attempt to explain the etiology of SIDS, but the cause (or causes) of SIDS remains unknown. Some of the characteristics of SIDS deaths suggest that most infants die from a similar mechanism involving the respiratory system. This is supported by seasonal variations in SIDS deaths, the frequent association of upper respiratory infection shortly before death, and the characteristic intrathoracic petechiae found on postmortem examination (Culbertson, Krous, & Bendell, 1988). No single theory can explain all SIDS deaths, despite extensive research into the association of SIDS and respiratory abnormalities. Central apnea, obstructive apnea, cardiac arrhythmias, and gastroesophageal reflux (GER) are postulated as possible mechanisms causing SIDS (Davidson Ward et al., 1986; Kahn et al., 1988; Oren, Kelly, & Shannon, 1986; Schwartz, 1987; Valdez-Dapena, Greene, Basavanand, Catherman, & Truex, 1973). The relationship between these disorders and SIDS is complex, but none is presently thought to adequately explain the etiology of SIDS.

The relationship between environmental factors and SIDS has recently been explored. Hyperthermia and overheating has been suggested as an etiological factor and may have a role in some deaths (Ponsonby et al., 1992; Stanton, Scott, & Downham, 1980). The relationship between infant sleeping position and SIDS is presently receiving much attention. Numerous studies suggest that the prone sleeping position increases the risk of SIDS, and that decreases in the rate of prone sleeping position results in a decrease in SIDS deaths (Willinger, Hoffman, & Hartford, 1994). This has prompted the American Academy of Pediatrics to recommend that healthy infants be put to sleep positioned on their back or side (AAP Task Force, 1992).

Approximately 15% of unexpected infant deaths are discovered to have a known cause by postmortem examination (Keens & Davidson Ward, 1993). Congenital and cardiac anomalies, metabolic diseases, infection, tumors, and accidental or inflicted trauma may all cause sudden and unexpected death that is not identified until autopsy (Emery, Chandra, & Gilbert-Barness, 1988). Death scene investigation may also identify environmental factors that contributed to death (Bass, Kravath, & Glass, 1986; Holton et al., 1991), although caution in interpretation is warranted. Most infants are quickly removed from the death scene when they are discovered, so the body is not usually examined at the death scene, and the existing environmental conditions at the time of the scene investigation may not reflect the conditions at the time of death.

SIDS and Child Abuse

The possibility of child abuse is often raised when a child dies suddenly and unexpectedly. Many of the risk factors reported for infant mortality overlap with risk factors for abuse, causing further concern. In reality, only a small percentage of SIDS deaths are attributable to fatal child abuse (Emery, 1985; Reece, 1993). If the infant is autopsied (as should be required in all cases of sudden, unexplained childhood death), a competent pathologist should recognize forms of violent assault such as shaking impact syndrome and abdominal trauma. Toxicological tests may identify poisoning, but the most common challenge is to identify infants who are intentionally suffocated.

The findings on postmortem examination in cases of SIDS and suffocation are indistinguishable (Smialek & Lambros, 1988). Infants have long been known to accidentally suffocate, especially if sleeping conditions are unsafe (Kemp & Thach, 1991; Smialek, Smialek, & Spitz, 1977). Autopsy findings cannot differentiate accidental suffocation from SIDS and cannot differentiate intentional suffocation from SIDS. Death scene investigation may identify infants and children who are victims of accidental suffocation but is less likely to identify intentionally suffocated infants. The past medical history may be helpful in identifying victims of fatal suffocation. Meadow (1990) reported 27 infants and children intentionally suffocated by their mothers and compared the features of the children suffocated with clinical features associated with SIDS. The study made the following comparisons:

1. Ninety percent of suffocated children had previous apnea, compared to < 10% of SIDS infants
2. Forty-four percent of the suffocated children had a previously unexplained medical problem, whereas > 95% of SIDS infants were previously healthy
3. Fifty-five percent of suffocated children were older than 6 months at the time of diagnosis
4. Forty-eight percent of the suffocated children had a sibling who had previously died, compared to 2% of SIDS deaths

Although differences may identify some children who are intentionally suffocated, differentiating fatal abuse by suffocation from SIDS remains extremely difficult.

In summary, SIDS is a term used to describe infants who die suddenly and unexpectedly and whose cause of death remains unknown after a full postmortem evaluation, including death scene investigation, and clinical review of all information. SIDS is a diagnosis of exclusion. For this reason, there must be a full investigation of the cause of death in all infants and children before the death is labeled SIDS. There are standards for the autopsy and investigation of SIDS deaths (Jones & Weston, 1976). A skeletal survey should also be a requirement because bony injuries not identified clinically or by autopsy may be identified that support the diagnosis of abuse (Kleinman et al., 1989). The cause of most sudden and unexpected infant deaths relates to natural causes that cannot be identified adequately by medical science; most are not due to fatal abuse. The health care provider's approach to families of SIDS fatalities is supportive and not accusatory throughout the investigation of the cause of death.

In Brief

- Child abuse has become an issue for pediatricians only in the mid-20th century.
- *Battered child* describes a child with repeated injuries to multiple organ systems.
- There is a high incidence of facial injuries in abused children that go unreported by dentists and physicians.
- Most oral injuries that result from physical abuse are nonspecific, and the diagnosis of abuse rests on the history or additional physical findings.
- Mucosal injuries are common in abused children.
- Infant frenulum tears occur when hands, pacifiers, bottles, or eating utensils are forced into a child's mouth in an attempt to silence a crying infant or feed a refusing child.
- The evaluation of a bite mark helps to confirm the diagnosis of abuse and identify the perpetrator of the bite.
- Poisoning as a pattern of abuse is poorly understood and frequently underreported.
- Munchausen syndrome by proxy (MSBP) is a psychiatric disorder in which a caregiver repeatedly offer false histories of a child's illness and fabricate evidence of disease in order to gain medical attention (Asher, 1951).
- MSBP is a manifestation of abuse that affects children of all ages. It may be more common than is reported in the medical literature (Schreier & Libow, 1993).
- The detection of MSBP is a great challenge because diagnosis is delayed and usually considered after a number of suspicious indicators become apparent.
- Fatal maltreatment is underestimated because of both under-identification of child homicides and inaccurate classification of pediatric fatalities in official reports.
- Between 1,000 and 2,000 children in the United States are murdered by their caregivers each year (McClain et al., 1993).
- Approximately 40% of fatal abuse occurs among infants, and 90% occurs to children less than 5 years of age (Committee on Child Abuse, 1993).
- Death review teams that review suspicious childhood deaths may also improve the quality of death investigations, identify barriers to death investigations, allow for better allocation of limited resources, and improve the understanding of the causes of child death (Committee on Child Abuse, 1993).
- A small percentage of SIDS deaths are attributable to fatal child abuse (Emery, 1985; Reece, 1993).
- Findings on postmortem examination in cases of SIDS and suffocation are indistinguishable (Smialek & Lambros, 1988).

9 Psychosocial Assessment

with Jennifer Diem Inglis, LSW

The psychosocial assessment is a critical component of the evaluation for suspected child abuse and neglect. It includes psychological, environmental, behavioral, and emotional components of the caregiving system and characterizes strengths and weaknesses of care provided to the child. The assessment is separate and distinct from the mandated investigation performed by the child protective services (CPS) agency that typically follows a report of suspected maltreatment.

In the context of interdisciplinary child abuse care, the clinical social worker is involved in a case of suspected abuse immediately. The social worker conducts or jointly contributes to the

The authors would like to acknowledge Toni Seidl, ACSW, RN, for conceptual advice and ongoing encouragement throughout the writing of this chapter.

psychosocial assessment of the child and his or her caregiver(s) during the maltreatment evaluation. There may not be a social worker or interdisciplinary child abuse team to oversee the complete evaluation of the child and family in smaller hospitals or clinic or practice settings. Therefore, it is essential that all health care providers who assess child and family systems be familiar with the psychosocial assessment and be able to obtain information necessary to determine if a referral to CPS is needed. This chapter uses the term *health care provider* in those situations where psychosocial information is gathered or provided. The term *social worker* is used where it is most likely a clinical social worker involved on an interdisciplinary team for child abuse evaluation.

This chapter addresses the components of the psychosocial assessment, interview process, and social work consultation, and how the health care professional interfaces with the CPS investigation.

The Psychosocial Assessment

The psychosocial assessment evaluates the child's family and home environment for risk factors associated with abuse. It contains details such as ages of caregiver, child, and household members; history of previous injuries in the child; caregiver substance abuse; history of intrafamilial violence; prior CPS involvement; economic pressures; inadequate or overcrowded housing; and other risk factors for abuse (Miller, 1987). Information from the psychosocial assessment may be shared with and used by CPS and law enforcement agencies (Schmitt, Grosz, & Carroll, 1976).

Preparation for Psychosocial Assessment

Prior to the interview with the child or caretakers, the health care professional familiarizes him- or herself with details of the case. This includes discussions with other health care professionals to determine what has been explained to the family, a review of the medical record for findings supportive of abuse, and any prior psychosocial assessments available.

Health care providers are obligated to provide information only to the child's legal caregivers, although information may be obtained from any other family or caregiver sources. It is important to identify the child's legal caregiver early in the process to avoid inappropriate sharing of information with visitors or relatives who do not have legal responsibility for the child.

In the initial meeting with caregivers, the interviewer introduces him- or herself, explains his or her role in the evaluation process and the purpose of meeting with the caregiver(s), and explains how he or she can be of help to them. The health care professional defines the problem, listens carefully to the family's concerns, respects privacy, and assesses family strengths and vulnerabilities. Protecting the family's privacy is a challenge in multipatient rooms or in clinical areas that offer little private meeting space. It is ideal to conduct in-depth interviews away from other patients and their families and away from the injured child, who may become upset or confused by the difficult issues that are discussed. At all times, the health care provider conveys concern for the caregiver and child.

Although interviews are confidential, legal mandates require that all information learned during the evaluation be shared with CPS and law enforcement authorities when there is suspicion of abuse. Explaining to the caregiver at the onset of the evaluation about possible disclosure of information with other professionals, CPS, and law enforcement agencies may help the family avoid feeling betrayed when information is shared.

Finally, the interviewer has the opportunity to observe nonverbal communication, such as the caregiver's affect, and interactions with the child and/or others in the family.

Caregiver Interview

The interview with the caregiver begins by collecting demographic information about the home and the family structure. Information such as who is living together, who is the primary caregiver for the child at home, what a "normal" day is like, and who is available to help with child rearing is essential in determining the caregiving environment (Franklin & Jordan, 1992). Table 9.1 contains questions asked of the caregiver in the psychosocial assessment. The age, intellectual capacity, and parenting experience of the caregiver are considered when structuring the interview and completing the assessment.

A central component of the psychosocial interview is the caregiver's description of the circumstances surrounding the child's injury. The interviewer assesses the caregiver description for consistency between the history of the injury and the child's development. Questions concerning the details of the child's injury are essential but may engender hostile reactions. However, such anger or hostility is not necessarily an indication of guilt. Realizing that the injury may be considered suspicious for abuse, the caregiver may be upset and perceive that he or she is being treated poorly by the health care professionals. Additional stressors on the caregiver's ability to cope may include fear of separation from the child, seeing one's child in pain, and lack of power to care for the child (Kelly, 1989).

There are cultural and ethnic factors to consider when assessing or interpreting behavior or interactions. The interviewer's open attitude to difference is more important than extensive

Table 9.1 Psychosocial Assessment: Caregiver Questions

Identifying information
    Names, ages, and address and phone number(s) of caregiver(s) and child
    Local or referring physician or health care professional
Presentation
    Caregiver behavior and appearance
    Caregiver mental status/developmental level
    Evidence of drug or alcohol use
    Ethnic/cultural background
Nature of problem
    How and when did child become injured/ill? (caregiver's description of problem)
    Has this happened before?
    Has your child been injured in the past? If so, when, how? Determine each injury.
    What made caregiver decide to seek medical care?
Family history
    A. Household composition
        Who lives at home?
        With whom does child spend most of his or her time?
        Where do other family members/caregiver(s) reside? (if child is cared for by others)
        Were there other living arrangements in the past (i.e., another caregiver)? If so, why?
    B. Caregiver information
        Who is the primary caregiver?
        With whom does the child spend time?
        Does the caregiver have other responsibilities? If so, what?
        Is there a history of substance abuse in caregiver(s)?
    C. Family structure
        Are biological parents, siblings, extended family involved in child's care? How?
        Who is legal guardian, if not natural parent or caregiver?
        Who cares for child when caregiver goes out?
        What is a regular day like for the child?
        What time does everyone in family get up?
        What do you do in the morning? in the afternoon? in the evenings?
Child's history
    When does child eat? Sleep?
    What does child like to do?
    Does he or she seem normal for age?
    Who does child play with?
    How would you describe your child? Describe behavior.
    What do you do when your child misbehaves?
    What developmental milestones has child achieved? (be specific)
    Does your child have any special needs concerning his or her care?
School
    Where does child go to school?
    Is child in the usual grade for age?
    What grades does the child get?
    Are there any problems at school with child, other children, and teachers? If so, how are they handled?
    Does the child get along with peers?
Environment
    Describe the housing situation.
    Is there a history of conflict or violence in the home?
    Describe employment/financial support.
    Is transportation available to family?
Social support
    Who helps the caregiver when needed: family, friends, community?
    Other social agencies: Has CPS been involved in the past or present? If so, why?

knowledge about specific ethnic, cultural, or racial groups (Kadushin & Kulys, 1983). Communication and parenting styles vary. The culturally sensitive practitioner understands his or her own feelings about child rearing and child abuse and is aware of the impact that ethnic and class backgrounds can have on interactions with the family as well as within the family (Devore & Schlesinger, 1987).

The use of an independent interpreter is essential in a family for whom English is a second language or where someone is hearing impaired. Interpreter services are used even if one caregiver speaks some English because it may be less stressful and more accurate for the caregiver to converse in his or her primary language. In an abuse or neglect evaluation, it is not appropriate to ask children to interpret for adults in the family.

Interview of the Child

The psychosocial assessment includes an evaluation of the verbal child with the child away from the caregiver. The interview is tailored to the child's age, developmental level, and cognitive abilities. The interviewer conveys a sensitive, caring manner that is flexible to the child's individual needs and creates a relaxed and comfortable setting for the interview. Encourage the child to relax by beginning the interview with some form of play in the younger child, or with casual conversation unrelated to injury concerns in the older child. Do not interview the child when he or she is under considerable stress or feeling unsafe (e.g., when in pain, when sleep deprived, or before an invasive procedure). The interviewer reassures the child and explains why difficult questions are asked. Regardless of attempts to make the interview easy for the child, he or she may still find the interview emotionally draining and distressing.

Interview Technique With Child

The ideal interview occurs when the child provides a narrative of events while the interviewer asks questions for clarification. A developmentally relevant approach to the interview distinguishes between "age-inappropriate language" and "developmentally sensitive language" (Saywitz, 1990). Age-inappropriate language fails to account for the child's developmental level and is potentially confusing. Inappropriate interviewer language includes the following: (a) long, complex, multiclause questions; (b) use of passive voice; (c) nonspecific pronouns; (d) double negatives; (e) multisyllabic words and complex verbs; and (f) hypothetical remarks. In contrast, developmentally sensitive language includes (a) simple, single-clause questions; (b) the use of active voice; (c) the use of names rather than pronouns; (d) single negatives; (e) short, understandable words that incorporate the child's terms when possible; and (f) the use of direct statements.

Leading questions are inappropriate to use in an interview because they suggest an anticipated answer from the child. For example, if a child is describing maltreatment during a violent interchange with his or her father, it is preferable to say "What happened next?" or "And then what happened?" rather than "Did your father hit you in the face with his fist?" (Faller, 1990; Garbarino & Stott, 1989).

Young children are often unable to give specific times and calendar dates for events. An effective technique is to ask the child to frame events around familiar dates and times such as a major holiday, the beginning of a vacation, or before or after school. Another method is to ask the child to draw a time line using crayon and paper. This also provides written documentation that may be included in the chart.

Success of the interview depends on sensitivity to the child's difficulty in communicating the details of his or her abuse and neglect. The interviewer praises the child periodically for his or her efforts during the questioning. Note that praise is given for the effort and not the content that is expressed (Saywitz, 1990). Comments such as "This stuff is hard to talk about" or "This seems like scary stuff to think about" may be useful to make the child feel more comfortable.

The interview deals with four areas of child competence. They are (a) psychological, (b) cognitive, (c) language, and (d) sociocultural communication (Garbarino & Stott, 1989). Psychological competence refers to the child's basic set of coping strategies and is at the root of the child's ability to handle stressful situations, such as the interview itself. Cognitive competence deals with the child's intellectual capacity and generally increases with age and schooling. Children at different developmental levels will process questions differently and respond in a manner that reflects their ability to track details and respond to requests for information. Language competence describes the child's abilities with speech and communication. The child's vocabulary and use of speech change and mature with growth. Finally, sociocultural communication refers to the child's appreciation for customs governing interpersonal communication (Garbarino & Stott, 1989). Children approach communication differently depending on unique cultural and social norms. For example, children raised in an environment that avoids sharing details about personal subjects such as intrafamilial violence may resist the questioning and change the topic.

Caregiver-Child Interaction

Observation of interactions between the child and caregiver provides valuable information about their relationship. Spending time at the bedside or in an examination room with the

Table 9.2 Observation Guide to Caregiver and Child Interactions

How do caregiver and child interact with each other?
What positive feelings or attachment is demonstrated?
Does the caregiver provide reassuring comments and comfort?
How does the caregiver respond to the child's responses, demands, or crying?
What physical contact do you observe?
What expectations does the caregiver have for the child's behavior in a medical setting? Are they age appropriate or reasonable?
Does the caregiver attempt to involve the child in conversation? in play?
What are the caregiver's comments to the child or about the child in his or her presence?

caregiver and child permits the observation of both verbal and nonverbal communication. Note how the caregiver and child speak to each other, what tone of voice is used, and how they position themselves in the room. This provides information about family dynamics that is not easily assessed through interviewing alone. Table 9.2 includes questions that guide the observation of caregiver and child interactions.

Documentation

The psychosocial assessment includes the interview, observations, and plan of care. The interview includes the family and social history, events leading up to the child's injury, past injuries, and emotional and environmental stressors experienced by the family. The identity of the source of the information is included. Example 9.1 demonstrates sample documentation in a high-risk situation that warrants reporting to CPS.

Example 9.1

This adolescent mother cannot provide a clear history of how her child was injured. She seems to be guessing at what might have happened when she left him alone in his bedroom. Given the vague history, her admitted drug use, and limited identified social supports as described above, a referral to CPS is indicated for further evaluation.

The psychosocial assessment may not reveal conclusively whether child abuse has occurred. Rather, it uncovers risk factors related to the child's injury and familial characteristics that may put the child at risk for injury. The documentation highlights concerns that necessitate supportive or preventive intervention even when the medical evaluation is benign or inconclusive (see Example 9.2).

Example 9.2

> It is extremely concerning that this 5-month-old has sustained two traumatic injuries over the past 9 weeks. Although the parent provides a clear history of two falls from a bed, and the medical evaluation indicates that the injuries could have beeen caused by a fall off of a bed, this child seems to be at risk because of questionable parental supervision and lack of knowledge about child development. A referral to CPS is recommended.

In addition, the psychosocial assessment may document low risk but defer final recommendations until more information is available (see Example 9.3).

Example 9.3

> The father has provided the same history of events leading up to his child's injury to several physicians and to this writer. There is no history of any previous illness or injury, and no indication of extraordinary social or emotional stress was identified. The father seems to be calm and demonstrates concern for his son by providing comfort and involving himself in his care. There are no indications of child abuse risk factors, and no concerns raised by psychosocial evaluation.

It is appropriate to describe the actual caregiver behaviors that are observed rather than to document broad generalizations about a caregiver's character or guilt. For example, document that the caregiver failed to visit the child during hospitalization rather than stating that the caregiver is neglectful and uncaring.

Child Protective Services

Once a report of suspected abuse is made, the CPS agency is obligated to investigate within a specified time frame. For most jurisdictions, the investigation must be initiated within 24 hours. Interaction with the police may also be indicated based on the nature and severity of the suspected maltreatment and the specific mandates of the jurisdiction. The CPS investigation generally proceeds as follows: (a) intake; (b) initial risk assessment; (c) family assessment; (d) case planning; (e) case management, including treatment/intervention and follow-up; and (f) case closure (Mulford, 1979; National Center on Child Abuse and Neglect, 1992a, 1992b) (see Figure 9.1). The CPS worker responsible for investigating the case may request details from the health care provider's psychosocial assessment.

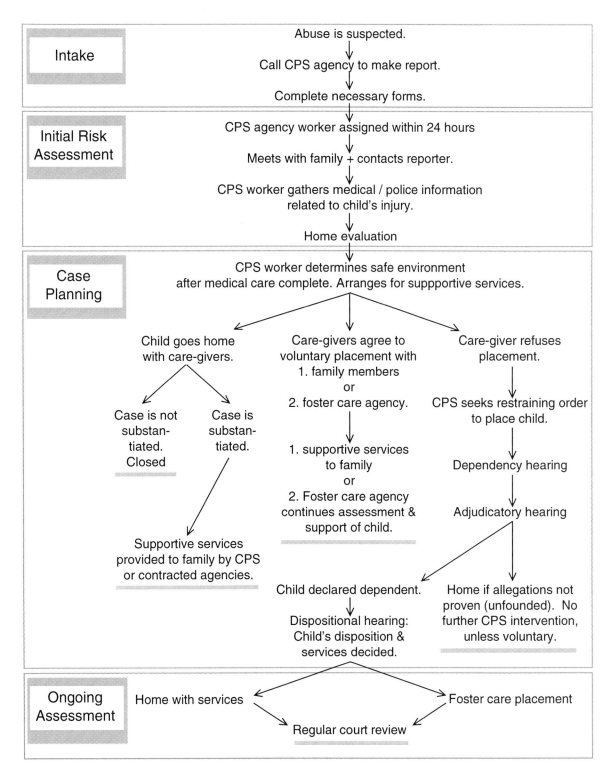

Intake

Abuse is suspected.
↓
Call CPS agency to make report.
↓
Complete necessary forms.

Initial Risk Assessment

CPS agency worker assigned within 24 hours
↓
Meets with family + contacts reporter.
↓
CPS worker gathers medical / police information related to child's injury.
↓
Home evaluation

Case Planning

CPS worker determines safe environment after medical care complete. Arranges for supportive services.

Child goes home with care-givers.

Care-givers agree to voluntary placement with
1. family members
or
2. foster care agency.

Care-giver refuses placement.

Case is not substantiated. Closed

Case is substantiated.

CPS seeks restraining order to place child.

1. supportive services to family
or
2. Foster care agency continues assessment & support of child.

Dependency hearing

Adjudicatory hearing

Supportive services provided to family by CPS or contracted agencies.

Child declared dependent.
↓
Dispositional hearing: Child's disposition & services decided.

Home if allegations not proven (unfounded). No further CPS intervention, unless voluntary.

Ongoing Assessment

Home with services

Foster care placement

Regular court review

Figure 9.1. Child Protective Services process.

Note. The CPS process for handling suspected child abuse and neglect occurs in four distinct phases: intake, initial risk assessment, case planning, and ongoing assessment. The solid bar indicates the end point for each arm of the algorithm (DePanfilis & Salus, 1992).

Ultimately, the CPS caseworker creates a plan for the safe care of the child. It is necessary to check protocols of CPS in specific areas or regions because responsibilities and approaches to care vary. CPS plan options include a range of supportive services to the family and possible removal of the child from the home to ensure the child's safety. In cases where placement is necessary, CPS caseworkers strive to obtain a voluntary agreement from the caregiver for out-of-home placement. If the caregiver refuses, the CPS agency brings the case before the court for legal action. In these cases, most state laws require a swift hearing to determine if the caregiver's actions or lack of actions fall within acceptable societal expectations of child rearing. If it is determined that child rearing is deficient and dangerous to the child, the child is labeled "dependent" and the court proceeds to a dispositional hearing where in-home services or out-of-home placement is determined (Rose & Schwartz, 1992).

The Interdisciplinary Team and the Social Work Consult

There are varied compositions of interdisciplinary child abuse teams in institutions and communities. They may include only two professionals, such as a physician or social worker, or may be composed of large, multidisciplinary groups. In either case, teams attempt to address the complex issues regarding evaluation and potential interventions in cases of child abuse or neglect (Krugman, 1987; Wilson, 1992). The social worker on an interdisciplinary team enhances the evaluation by adding a social-environmental perspective and knowledge of family systems, human behavior and development, and the helping process to the assessment and plan of care for the child (Abramson & Mizrahi, 1986). This section provides an overview of the role of a clinical social worker and the interdisciplinary team in the evaluation of child abuse and neglect.

During the evaluation, the social worker contributes in the following ways: (a) performs the psychosocial assessment; (b) provides initial therapeutic intervention with the family, especially those in crisis; (c) coordinates and collaborates with CPS, civil and criminal legal systems, and community agencies; (d) provides ongoing education and support to family and staff; (e) communicates with caregivers about the evaluation process; and (f) tracks care after the evaluation to ensure compliance with treatment plans (Schmitt et al., 1976). The social worker may also act as the coordinator of the team's activities, facilitating the evaluation process and coordinating team meetings. (See Table 9.3 for the role of the clinical social worker in the health care setting.)

Table 9.3 The Clinical Social Work Role in the Health Care Setting

Preparation	Gather information
	Discuss concerns for maltreatment with staff
	Review past social work records
	Field calls from CPS if prior report has been made (i.e., by referring physician or hospital)
Assessment	Meet family: introduction/explanation of role
	Conduct psychosocial evaluation:
	Interview caregiver
	Interview child, if possible
	Observe caregiver-child interaction
	Assess family/home environment
	Explain concerns about maltreatment
	Process of reporting/investigating
	Share assessment with team and collaborate in making decision to report to CPS
Intervention	Arrange family and team meeting to discuss concerns and evaluation with family
	Report to CPS
	Contact CPS agency
	Facilitate meeting between family and CPS worker
	Provide CPS with necessary medical/social evaluations
	Provide anticipatory guidance and crisis intervention to family
	Educate family about investigation and rights
	Advocate for child
	May include contact with CPS supervisor to resolve issues around planning appropriate disposition
	Discharge planning
	Assist with arranging transportation and follow-up appointments
	Contact insurance company for equipment and visiting nurse
	Facilitate rehab referrals
	Support medical staff: education, debriefing
Follow-up	Contact family to assess needs and coping after discharge
	Contact CPS about services provided to family
	Track follow-up appointments
	Inform CPS of missed appointments
	Re-report concerns if crucial care is missed
	Send follow-up letter to CPS outlining original concerns for maltreatment, assessment of family, and suggested plan
	Continue to support family by providing information about the investigative process and resources
	Provide referrals as needed:
	Legal
	Mental health
	Public health nursing
	Support groups
	Give feedback to rest of team

Families may associate a social worker with child removal and foster care. This perception may cause caregiver fears and hostility and create barriers that prevent positive engagement and interaction between the social worker and caregivers. Introducing the clinical social worker as a member of the health care team alleviates stereotypical concerns. When the family is upset about the investigation of suspected abuse and perceives that it is being "accused," the social worker is frequently asked to help the caregiver identify feelings and develop coping strategies that allow the caregiver to begin to problem solve with the team (Slakieu, 1990). Other efforts that may involve the social worker include explaining the process of the medical evaluation and explaining the health care professional's responsibility to evaluate suspicious injuries and report them to appropriate agencies.

Reporting to CPS

Because the social worker is knowledgeable about the legal requirements of reporting as well as the service provided by CPS, he or she may make initial contact with CPS (Howing & Wodarski, 1992). Furthermore, the social worker apprises the medical team of the investigation status and communicates necessary information to the agency. The social worker provides the CPS caseworker with information needed to conduct the evaluation and may facilitate meetings between the CPS caseworker and the family.

The social worker talks with the caregivers to explain the reasoning behind the decision to report to CPS and what they can expect from the CPS investigation. A family meeting involving the CPS caseworker and the interdisciplinary team may be beneficial to share information, clarify medical information, and explain special treatment or follow-up care required for the child. The social worker supports the caregiver in asking questions of both the medical team and the CPS worker.

Coordination and Follow-up

Health care professionals may disagree with the determination of the CPS agency, especially when a child is returned to a home believed to be potentially dangerous. The staff's impression may be communicated verbally and in writing to CPS to explain why an alternate discharge plan should be considered and to request the appointment of a child advocate such as an attorney to represent the child's interest. It is typically the social worker who communicates with CPS.

The social worker can assist the staff in their ability to cope with the outcome. A case discussion during or after discharge or disposition may be a therapeutic method of expressing strong feelings and discussing constructive ways to integrate the experience into their medical or nursing practice.

After the evaluation of the case, the social worker maintains contact with the family and agencies involved and is available to the family as long as care is sought at the hospital or medical facility. The social worker may assist with transportation to appointments, provide phone or personal counseling, and refer family members to a mental health agency or to local support groups for ongoing problems. There may also be nursing visits to assist in complicated medical care or to provide in-home safety education. The social worker may track follow-up appointments to ensure compliance and call caregivers if a child misses critical follow-up care. If necessary, the social worker may alert the team to noncompliance or further concerns about the child's safety, and he or she may make another report to CPS.

Staff Reaction to Abuse

Child maltreatment cases often evoke strong reactions among staff members. Emotional preparation among all staff involved in child abuse cases is important. It is possible to feel overwhelmed by identifying with the child's or family's situation and to become powerless to provide meaningful intervention. The social worker provides interventions for staff to address these issues and prepares the team emotionally for the stresses of working with cases of abuse (Germain, 1984).

In Brief

- A psychosocial assessment of the child's family is a critical component of the suspected child abuse and neglect evaluation.
- It is imperative to accurately identify the child's family and speak with the adult(s) who is (are) legally responsible and with those who were present when the child became ill or injured.
- It is essential to make the family aware of staff concerns and the legal mandate that requires reporting and sharing the results of the abuse evaluation.
- A thorough psychosocial assessment explores the structure of the family and the function of its members and includes social history and demographics.
- The psychosocial assessment uncovers information concerning the caregiver's understanding of the child's injury and how the injury occurred.
- The clinical social worker is involved early in the evaluation of suspected child abuse and/or neglect to optimize the evaluation.
- The social worker provides support to both the family and the staff.

10 Legal Issues and Documentation

with Susan Perlis Marx, JD

The investigation of suspected child abuse is a multidisciplinary effort; police officers, child protective services (CPS) workers, prosecutors, and health care professionals all have vital roles to play in the identification and protection of the abused child. There are tensions inherent in the multidisciplinary approach: Professionals must maintain their distinct roles and perform individual responsibilities while recognizing that their actions have a great impact on the efficacy of the investigative effort. Because physicians, nurses, hospital social workers, and paramedics are often the first professionals to have contact with the abused child and his or her family, health care providers become crucial participants in the gathering of information for the investigation and potential prosecution of the perpetrator. The safety of a child often depends on the health care provider's awareness of the information needed by law enforcement officials and prosecutors to identify and prosecute the perpetrator successfully.

This chapter provides a discussion of the legal aspects of the medical professional's evaluation of suspected physical abuse and neglect. It addresses (a) mandatory reporting requirements for the health care professional, (b) medical record documentation in cases of suspected abuse and neglect, (c) guidelines for preparation and presentation of testimony, and (d) hearsay evidence. The practices suggested in the following pages should be discussed by medical professionals, members of hospital child abuse teams and county multidisciplinary investigative teams, and local prosecutors. Health care professionals are encouraged to adapt these suggested procedures to the law and custom in each specific locality.

Reporting Suspected Child Abuse

The reporting of child abuse and neglect is a central responsibility for all health care providers. By 1967, every state had enacted some form of legislation seeking the accurate reporting of injuries inflicted upon children (Myers, 1992b). Many reporting laws do the following: (a) specify those professionals obligated to report suspicions of abuse, (b) include suspected neglect in reporting requirements, (c) prescribe procedures for investigation of abuse and neglect cases, (d) call for legal advocates or guardians ad litem for the child involved in abuse and neglect cases,[1] and (e) address issues such as confidentiality of records and public and professional educational programs directed at increasing awareness of child abuse (Myers, 1992b).

Medical professional communities vary in their responses to the enactment of mandatory reporting laws. Some smaller communities have no reporting guidelines, leaving health care professionals without guidance when faced with a case of suspected child abuse. Some health care professionals form multidisciplinary teams (see Chapter 9) staffed by nurses, doctors, clinical social workers, and others. Teams develop protocols for evaluating, reporting, and treating suspected child abuse victims. The clinical social worker on the team often serves as a liaison between hospital staff and local investigators and prosecutors. In some jurisdictions, health care professionals participate in community-based multidisciplinary teams (MDTs), which may include law enforcement officials, prosecutors, CPS workers, mental health professionals, school personnel, and other involved professionals. The local MDT may provide input for the medical professional in designing protocols for reporting procedures. Finally, some jurisdictions assemble a task force of health care professionals, prosecutors, law enforcement and CPS investigators, and other interested community members to draft protocols for reporting child abuse (Bross, Krugman, Lenherr, Rosenberg, & Schmitt, 1988; *Investigation and Prosecution of Child Abuse*, 1993).

State statutes dictate procedures that health care professionals must follow when they suspect child abuse or neglect. The American Medical Association strongly recommends that medical professionals become familiar with their state reporting laws (Council on Scientific Affairs, 1985; Warner & Hansen, 1994). Local protocols aid health care professionals in determining who must report abuse, when and to whom reports of suspected abuse and neglect should be made, which cases must be reported, and how reports are documented. Protocols should be clear, delineating step-by-step procedures for the medical professional to follow when evaluating and reporting a case of suspected abuse. Health professionals are encouraged to consult with local prosecutors or hospital attorneys to obtain copies of state reporting laws to comply with current reporting practices.

Mandated Reporting

Who Must Report Child Abuse?

Most state statutes delineate specific professionals who must report cases of suspected child abuse (Myers, 1992b). These professionals and institutions are often referred to as "mandated reporters." Mandated reporters include hospitals, clinics, health care professionals, teachers, social workers, child care providers, mental health professionals, and law enforcement officials. Some state statutes also define "mandated reporters" to include a broader set of individuals or institutions, such as those called upon to render aid or medical assistance to children or having responsibility for the care and treatment of children. Currently, physicians and nurses are mandated reporters in every state (Information on Civil Child Abuse and Neglect Statutes, 1993). In all of these cases, the patient-client privilege is superseded by the duty to report (Myers, 1992b).

Health care professionals who work in hospitals, multiphysician practices, or other organizations must check state law to determine who is responsible for reporting. Some states specifically allow professionals who work as a team and jointly have knowledge of abuse to designate one individual from their team to make the report (Information, 1993). State statutes may relieve the individual who discovered the abuse from the obligation to report when he or she informs an appropriate superior. The supervisor then takes on the responsibilities of the mandated reporter (Myers & Peters, 1987). State law may compel both the health care professional who uncovered the abuse and his or her superior to report (Myers & Peters, 1987).

Who Receives the Child Abuse Report?

State statutes and local protocols dictate to whom a health care professional reports when he or she suspects that a child has been abused or neglected. Generally, health care professionals are required to call a CPS agency, which investigates allegations of caregiver abuse, or a police department, which investigates all criminal allegations of child abuse. Some jurisdictions require health care providers to determine initially if the suspected perpetrator is a caregiver of the child. If the suspected perpetrator is a caregiver, health care professionals must contact the local CPS agency. In all other cases, law enforcement officials are notified. Some jurisdictions require that the medical professional contact both CPS and law enforcement agencies, regardless of the relationship of the suspected perpetrator to the child. Again, the clinical social worker of a hospital's multidisciplinary team, a team member of the community's multidisciplinary investigative team, or the local prosecutor may be most aware of step-by-step protocols and legal requirements and can provide assistance.

Medical professionals may use local or state telephone hotlines to make the initial phone report required by most states. It is important to carefully document the telephone call in the medical record, including the name of the agency, individual employee contacted, and the date and time of the report. A follow-up written report of the case is usually required. Hospital emergency departments or local CPS agencies often have a designated form for the reporter to complete.

Time Frame for Reporting Child Abuse

How Quickly Must a Report of Child Abuse Be Made?

State statutes require that a telephone report be made *immediately* upon suspicion of abuse (Information, 1993). How quickly a health care provider forms a "suspicion" that a child has been physically abused or neglected varies, depending upon the information available in any given case. After the telephone contact, state law usually specifies a time frame in which written documentation is to be submitted (Information on Mandatory Reporting Laws, 1993).

Cases of "Suspected" Child Abuse

When Is a Case "Suspected" Child Abuse?

State law defines such terms as *abuse, neglect, abused child,* and *neglected child.* In general, states mandate reporting when a child's physical or mental health or welfare is harmed, or threatened with harm, by the acts or omissions of a parent or any other person. *Harm,* or an equivalent term in the statute, is often broken into specific subject areas, including, but not limited to, nonaccidental physical injury; mental injury; sexual abuse and exploitation; abandonment; failure to supervise or to supply the child with basic food, clothing, shelter, or health care; and psychosocial (environmental) failure to thrive (Information, 1993). Some states mandate a report when a newborn is physically dependent upon certain drugs or when the mother used a controlled substance during her pregnancy (Warner & Hansen, 1994). Health care professionals must report suspected nonaccidental physical injury or neglect, even if it purportedly resulted from the caregiver's religious practices (Warner & Hansen, 1994).

Health care providers must report any *suspected* child abuse. A physician need not diagnose definitively that a condition is the result of abuse in order to trigger the duty to report (Warner & Hansen, 1994). Although the physician participates in the case, it is not his or her responsibility to prove that the case is one of abuse or who the abuser is. The juvenile or criminal court makes these determinations (Silver, Dublin, & Lourie, 1969).

When does a medical professional's concern about possible child abuse become a suspicion, triggering the duty to report? In essence, the health care provider must make a report when the provider has evidence that would lead a competent professional to believe abuse or neglect is reasonably likely to have occurred (Myers, 1992b; Warner & Hansen, 1994). CPS screens the reports to assess which are appropriate for agency intervention. A thorough investigation is conducted by CPS and law enforcement officials to determine if abuse has indeed occurred. CPS investigators then determine if the child's safety is in question and take appropriate steps to protect the child and provide supportive services to the child and the child's family. Law enforcement investigators will determine if a crime occurred and if there is probable cause to make an arrest. Figure 10.1 provides the health care provider with guidelines for reporting physical abuse when evaluating an injured child.

Liability of the
Reporting Health
Care Professionals

Will the Reporting Medical Care Professional
Be Immune From Liability?

Health care professionals voice concern about professional and personal liability if CPS investigators determine the report to be "unsubstantiated" or "not indicated," or if law enforcement officials do not arrest a perpetrator. (See Chapter 1 for further discussion of substantiation.) Should an angry parent file a lawsuit against the reporter, state statutes provide immunity

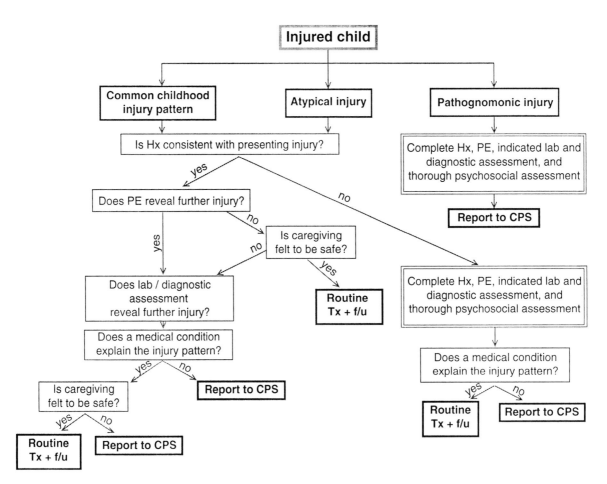

Figure 10.1. Injured child.

Note. Beginning with the injured child, the evaluation progresses differently depending on what is uncovered during the different phases in the clinical evaluation. The boxes in boldface indicated the end point for each arm of the algorithm.

from civil and criminal liability to all mandated reporters who report suspected abuse in "good faith." This is true even if the report is investigated and determined to be unsubstantiated or not indicated. Good faith does not include instances when a false report is knowingly made (i.e., the health care provider making the report knew that the report was false) (Myers, 1992b; Statutory Compilations on Immunity for Mandated Reporters, 1993).

Penalties for Failure to Report

Is There a Penalty for Failure to Report a Suspected Case of Child Abuse or Neglect?

It is a criminal violation in most states to *fail* to report suspected child abuse. Penalties include fines and prison sentences. Some statutes also provide that mandated reporters may be held liable for damages caused by a failure to report (Myers, 1992b; Statutory Compilations on Penalties for Failure to Report Child Abuse, 1993).

Summary   Health care providers fulfill a crucial child advocacy function as central participants in the identification, protection, and
treatment of abused and neglected children. Medical communities should be in full compliance with statutes that mandate
reporting of suspected child abuse and neglect. It is important
that health care providers be familiar with local protocols and
community resources, including institutional or local multidisciplinary teams. Should the community lack guidelines and
resources, health care professionals can take a lead role in developing protocols and beginning the process of multidisciplinary coordination.

Documentation of Findings

The best interests of abused and neglected children are served
when health care professionals provide clear and comprehensive documentation. Entries made in medical records can provide essential clues needed to evaluate the safety of the child's
environment. Accurate records that clearly reflect the child's
medical history, physical examination, and laboratory findings
are often pivotal in the investigation and prosecution of physical
abuse and neglect cases. Should the health care professional be
called upon to testify, nothing refreshes the provider's memory
better than clear, legible, and comprehensive documentation in
the medical record. Finally, medical records may be admitted
into evidence at trial.

Documentation   Statements made by the child, family members, and other
Guidelines   caregivers and given to medical professionals before the caregivers have information about the child's actual medical condi-
tion may be inconsistent with the degree or type of injury. In
addition, the abusing caregiver may give contradictory statements
to health care personnel during the initial evaluation and hospitalization, if admission occurs. These statements, coupled
with evidence that the child was in the "sole care" or "exclusive
custody" of the perpetrator at the time of the injuries, often
provide the fulcrum of the prosecution's case. The following
sections outline suggested guidelines for documentation of statements and other information relevant to the investigation and
prosecution of child neglect and physical abuse.

Documentation   *Who Should Document?*
of Care
     All health care professionals, including paramedics or emer-
gency medical technicians, triage nurses, emergency room personnel, attending and consulting medical staff, in-patient care

nurses, and social work staff, should document statements and actions of the child, the child's family, and other caregivers during the evaluation of children. Documentation begins as soon as the child arrives at the site of care or the paramedic arrives at the scene. Documentation continues throughout the evaluation, workup, and treatment of the child's injuries. The hospital's multidisciplinary team uses the documentary trail to analyze information, synthesize an impression, and develop an assessment and treatment plan for the particular case. Comprehensive, *ongoing* documentation allows investigators and prosecutors to evaluate the overall picture that emerges during the child's contact with medical professionals and aids in the identification and prosecution of a perpetrator.

General Documentation Guidelines

The medical record should reflect the statements and interactions of the child and family. The following are entries that should be included in the record:

1. Name of person making the statement or exhibiting the behavior and his or her relationship to the child
2. Date and time of the statement/behavior
3. Questions or actions of the health care professional that immediately preceded the statement/behavior
4. Exact words of the statement, using quotation marks where appropriate, and/or a detailed description of the behavior exhibited
5. Demeanor of the person making the statement or exhibiting the behavior
6. Names of those present at the time the statement was made or behavior was observed
7. Name and beeper number or extension of the person making the entry into the hospital chart

Health care providers should avoid documenting personal opinions regarding caregivers even though working with suspected abusive caregivers may elicit a wide range of negative emotional responses. Comments in the record such as "this mother is a flake" or "dad doesn't have a clue" signify a loss of objectivity and will certainly undermine the credibility of the medical professional, both in the hospital and in the courtroom. The health care professional should document only what was said or observed.

Members of the hospital or community multidisciplinary team may be helpful in determining the format of the written documentation. Some professionals prefer a question and answer format; others may choose to use a summary format. Either method is effective if accurate and complete (Heger, 1991). It is important that all entries are legible.

CHILD PHYSICAL ABUSE AND NEGLECT

Finally, preservation of all records is essential. Destruction or loss of documents may call into question the accuracy and impartiality of the health care provider's findings and subsequent testimony.

Interviewing the Child and Documentation Guidelines

The In-Depth Interview

Who Should Conduct the In-Depth Interview of the Child?

In the medical evaluation of possible child maltreatment, health care providers initially determine whether the child's age and/or medical condition will delay or bar an interview. Once a determination is made that a child can be interviewed, the health care professional most familiar with child development and most skilled in interviewing children conducts the in-depth interview of the child. In an emergency situation, however, the examining health care provider will often interview the child.

What Should the Health Care Professional Ask the Child in the In-Depth Interview?

The health care professional's interview of the child is often crucial to any subsequent CPS and criminal investigations. An in-depth interview of the child, rather than a cursory history-taking, is essential in cases of suspected abuse. Improper questioning when a child is first interviewed may taint the rest of the investigation. Health care providers should receive training regarding proper interviewing techniques to enhance the quality of child interviews and the information elicited. Guidelines for approaching this important interview are provided in Chapters 2 and 9.

If the child is verbal and medically stable, it is appropriate for the health care provider to discuss the physical injury with him or her. The following discussion directs the health care professional to subject areas that will provide information needed to distinguish between abusive and accidental injuries, aid investigators and prosecutors in successful identification and prosecution of the perpetrator, and allow all concerned professionals to accurately assess the safety of the child's environment (Investigation, 1993; Warner & Hansen, 1994). The "interview" continues during the entire evaluation. It begins by asking the child for a narrative about the incident. Direct questions are used to fill in gaps or clear up confusing statements. Questions should cover the following topics:

1. *Circumstances surrounding the most recent injury.* Ask the child how he or she got hurt, who did it, and any "reasons" the child perceived for the assault (i.e., the child dropped his or her peanut butter sandwich; parent was drunk again). Reassure the child that the injuries were not his or her fault.

2. *Instrument used.* Ask the child whether an instrument was used to hurt the child (e.g., shoe, cigarette, lighter, coat hanger, curling iron). If an instrument was used, ask the child to describe it. Have the child draw it if he or she is unable to describe or name the instrument. Date the picture, indicate who drew it, and include the drawing in the medical record.

3. *Current and prior injuries.* Ask the child about current and prior injuries found on examination. Establish who caused the injuries and how. Record each visible injury on a drawing, labeling each and describing in detail the size, color, and pattern of the injury. Make sure the child's name or chart number appears on each page of the medical record, including the page with the drawing.

Use of Photographs

Photograph all injuries if possible.

When photographing, include a card with the child's name or chart number to identify the child.

When photographing, include a centimeter ruler and color balance chart to allow judges and jurors to evaluate the size and color of the injury.

Photograph the child's injuries periodically throughout the child's hospital stay to show the healing process and to negate a claim that hospital treatment caused the injury.

Use a 35mm camera; Polaroid instant cameras produce inferior photographs.

Make sure to accompany all photographs with meticulous descriptive text and hand-drawn diagrams, because the quality of photographs cannot be guaranteed.

Make sure photographs and negatives are carefully stored and preserved. Loss of medical photographs could hinder an effective prosecution. See Chapter 2 for further discussion.

4. *Perpetrator's statements to child.* Ask the child if the suspected perpetrator said anything to him or her before, during, or after the assault. Statements such as "I'm going to kill you," made by the perpetrator during a violent assault, reported by the child during the evaluation, and documented by the health care provider, may enable the prosecutor to prove that the assault was not accidental.

5. *Report of assault or delay in seeking care.* Determine how the child ended up at the hospital. Did a caregiver bring the child in? Did a teacher notice bruising and report to a CPS worker, who brought the child in for an examination? Failure by the offender

to get prompt treatment for an ill child is admissible at trial to show the perpetrator's guilty knowledge and attempt to conceal the injuries.

6. *Injuries to other children.* Find out if the child knows whether any other children in the household were injured. Make sure that a CPS worker or police officer arranges for those children to have a medical evaluation. Document all of the children's statements and injuries. Injuries to other children may be admissible at trial to prove that the perpetrator intended to harm the children and that the injuries were not accidental.

7. *Child's relationship with caregiver(s).* Ask the child about his or her relationships at home. Who is home when he or she gets home from school? What does he or she do after school? With whom does he or she do things? Document the child's appearance: height and weight, developmental level, the condition of his or her clothing, his or her overall cleanliness, whether he or she is hungry, and so on. Carefully note the child's behavior with the caregiver(s) in the hospital throughout the stay. Does the child avoid physical contact with the caregiver(s)? Does the child look to the caregiver(s) for support? Does the child ask if the caregiver(s) will be coming to visit at the hospital? Include descriptions of the child's demeanor as he or she talks about the caregiver(s). Recognize, however, that there is no "textbook" response or demeanor that an abused child should have toward a perpetrator. Do not make conclusions as to the child's state of mind in the medical record (Investigation, 1993).

The medical professional documents the following: (a) the child's exact statement about the abuse, even if it is "nothing happened"; and (b) the actions and demeanor of the child (i.e., the child "cried throughout the questioning," "remained silent and stared at the examining table," etc.). The phrase "child denies abuse" should be avoided because it overstates the child's response and may not accurately reflect the medical facts uncovered during the evaluation (Heger, 1991). When appropriate, the medical professional notes that the child's assertion that "nothing happened" is inconsistent with the physical findings.

Interviewing the Caregivers and Documentation Guidelines

What Should the Health Care Provider Ask the Child's Caregiver(s)?

During any medical evaluation, health care providers discuss the child's condition with the child and the child's caregiver(s). Although initial, cursory questions may be asked with all parties present at the triage booth or by a receptionist at a doctor's office, the child and each caregiver should be interviewed separately as soon as a potential abuse situation surfaces. Privacy may encourage each individual to speak openly. Document the following in the medical record: (a) caregiver's answers to questions posed by the health care professional, (b) refusals to answer questions, (c) equivocal responses, and (d) silences when asked questions.

In addition to the formal interview that occurs during the history-taking phase of all medical evaluations, the health care provider should take note of more casual statements made in the emergency room, by the child's bedside, in the hallway, and throughout the child's evaluation and treatment. Documentation of all interactions paints a picture for health care professionals, investigators, and prosecutors that may, in turn, lead to the identification of the perpetrator and safe placement for the child.

Chapters 2 and 9 include detailed descriptions of the interview process. The discussion that follows highlights subject areas that should be included in the caregiver interview:

1. *Time of injury.* The health care provider asks the caregiver when the injury occurred. If the caregiver has difficulty remembering dates or times, some health care professionals encourage the caregiver to draw a timeline in an attempt to fix the time of injury. Have the caregiver sign and date the timeline. Should the caregiver refuse to sign the timeline or should the health care provider feel uncomfortable requesting a signature, the health care provider may sign the timeline. In this situation, indicate the date, time, and name of the person who drew the timeline. Keep any timelines or drawings in the medical record.

2. *Course of symptoms.* Ask the caregiver to describe the course of the child's symptoms, particularly if the caregiver claims no knowledge of the exact time of the injury. Health care professionals, investigators, and prosecutors can use the detailed description of the course of symptoms to approximate the time of injury or to determine if the caregiver's explanation of the injury makes sense. If needed, have the caregiver draw a timeline.

3. *Exclusive custody.* Ask the caregiver when the injury occurred without revealing the health care professional's estimation of the time of injury. Did the caregiver leave the child with anyone? When? Was the caregiver always watching the child? Was anyone else at home? Any siblings in the home? Ages? Were the siblings left alone with the child? What are the developmental capabilities of the siblings? Identification of the perpetrator becomes much easier should the caregiver admit to having exclusive custody of the child at the time that the injury happened.

4. *Explanations, lack of explanations, and changing explanations.* At the initial interview, ask the caregiver how the injury occurred.

Encourage the caregiver to tell all that he or she knows. Record all of the answers in detail. Ask the caregiver to demonstrate explanations using props, and document the demonstration in detail. If, for example, the caregiver admits to shaking the child, have the caregiver use a purse or other object to illustrate the amount of force used in the shaking episode.

The health care professional may not wish to present all that is known about the mechanism of the injury at the beginning of the interview. Later, the interviewer may reveal some information should the explanation prove highly implausible. Record what information was given and the caregiver's response. For example:

Q: "Tell me what you know about how the child was injured."

A: "Well, I was home alone with the baby. The baby was upstairs in his crib. I was downstairs watching TV. I heard a thud. I ran to the stairway, and the baby was lying at the bottom of the stairs, crying. I guess he fell down the steps."

Q: "Had anything happened to the baby before that?"

A: "No."

Q: "Had you noticed any injuries or odd symptoms before that?"

A: "No."

Q: "This baby has an injury to his abdomen." (Doctor points to the caregiver's abdomen.) "Do you know how he got that?"

A: "Oh yes. I forgot to tell you that he must have hit himself on the table at the bottom of the steps when he landed."

Q: "Can you describe where the table was?"

A: "Well, it's usually off to the side, away from the steps, but I had just moved it in front of the steps to polish it."

The health care professional, as part of a multidisciplinary team or with the investigator and prosecutor, will analyze caregivers' statements in conjunction with the medical findings, photographs of the scene, and other evidence. A caregiver's implausible explanation as to the mechanism of the injury may provide valuable clues as to the identity of the perpetrator.

5. *Self-inflicted injury.* Should the caregiver claim that the child accidentally injured him- or herself, get some details about the developmental capabilities of the child. Also, explore the plausibility of such an injury, given the specifics of the explanation. For example, the caregiver may assert that the child climbed into the bathtub and turned on the hot water spigot. Follow-up questions might include: Where is the bathtub located? Can you show me how tall the bathtub is? What was the water level in the bathtub? Is the child able to walk? How long has the child been walking? When you came into the room, where was the child? Still in the tub? In what position? What was the child doing?

6. *Initial response.* Determine what the caregiver did when he or she noticed injuries or symptoms. Was there a delay in seeking

medical care? Did the caregiver attempt home remedies rather than take the child to the hospital? Did the caregiver keep the child home from school for a few days?

7. *Past injuries and illnesses.* A comprehensive history of prior medical problems and treatment is crucial not only to the medical diagnosis but also to the investigation and prosecution of a child abuse case. For example, if the child had actually been examined by a pediatrician 2 days prior to the emergency room visit and was found free from visible injury, the timing of the presenting injury becomes much easier to determine. The identity and intent of the perpetrator may become clearer should the child's medical history reveal neglect by the caregiver, such as failure to obtain immunizations or to bring the child in for well-child care visits. Should a caregiver claim at the emergency room that the child is "accident prone," prior medical records may show old injuries that, in fact, were inconsistent with accidental injury and most likely inflicted. When a caregiver claims that the child falls frequently because of a lifelong problem with recurrent dizziness, the absence of prior complaints regarding that problem is highly significant.

   Have the caregiver describe the nature of any prior physical problems. What caused any prior injuries? Where was the child treated? Who treated the child? Any previous hospitalizations? Document the names, addresses, and phone numbers of all prior persons who treated the child, including any medical professionals who provided well-child care. A perpetrator may bring the child to a different doctor each time the child suffers an inflicted injury to avoid suspicion, knowledge, and documenting of repeated injuries by health care providers.

8. *Child's relationship with caregiver.* Have the caregiver describe his or her relationship with the child. Did the child have any disabilities? Special needs? Toilet training difficulties? Was the child on medication for hyperactivity or other condition? Did the caregiver only recently begin caring for the child? With an older child, were there recurrent disciplinary problems? Questions like these will uncover possible "triggers" for an abusive incident.

9. *Caregiver's concerns and demeanor.* Document in the medical chart the concerns voiced by the caregiver. Does the caregiver want to know how long the child will be in the hospital or if the child is in any real danger? Is the caregiver preoccupied with whether the doctor will contact CPS? Does the caregiver show any emotion when discussing the child's condition? Note the demeanor of the caregivers toward each other and toward the child throughout the hospital stay or course of treatment. Does one caregiver forbid another from talking to the medical staff? Does either caregiver visit the child in the hospital or comfort the child? Again, these clues, along with all of the evidence gathered from a myriad of sources during the investigation, add to the investigative picture (Investigation, 1993; Myers & Carter, 1988).

Documentation of Medical Conclusions

Health care professionals routinely record information that they elicit during the history-taking, physical examination, and laboratory assessment stages of clinical evaluation. After the completion of the clinical evaluation, the health care provider formulates a probable diagnosis. In cases of physical abuse, a completely "normal examination" is unlikely because the child's injury is typically what brings the child to the health care provider's attention. When injuries are pathognomonic of abuse, it is certainly appropriate to diagnose child abuse or battered child syndrome. In some cases of suspected physical abuse or neglect, however, the medical evaluation may not yield enough information to diagnose abuse definitively, although the clinician suspects that abuse occurred. In such cases, the most appropriate way to frame the conclusion section of the medical record is to summarize the clinical information from the history, physical examination, and laboratory assessment and state whether the injury is consistent with the history provided. In this way, the conclusion or impression documented at the end of a medical evaluation for physical injury is either injury consistent with history provided, or injury inconsistent with history provided.

Health care professionals may voice concern that CPS workers, law enforcement officers, and prosecutors want more definitive conclusions in the medical records than health care professionals are able to give. Assessment findings that state that there is "no evidence of abuse" or that "evidence confirms abuse" do not allow for the possibility that the CPS worker or police detective may uncover additional information that clearly supports the opposite conclusion.

In cases of suspected neglect with no physical findings on examination, describe the physical examination of each system. Detailed description of a lack of affirmative findings for each system examined can then be compared to prior and subsequent examinations of the child. Avoid use of global statements such as "no evidence of neglect." Investigators and prosecutors may uncover signs of neglect at the home or other locations of which the health care professional was unaware at the time of diagnosis.

Documentation of referrals to CPS and counseling is helpful to those reviewing the chart at a later date. Include the names of the health care professional who made the referral and the CPS intake worker or counselor who accepted the referral. (See Tables 10.1 and 10.2.)

Table 10.1 Information Documented in the Chart

Who brought child to hospital

Who lives with child

Statements by caregivers and child upon initial contact and throughout hospital stay (demeanor/ actions/statements)

Consent to treat form signed by caregivers (or refusal to sign)

Condition of child when admitted ("critical"; "intensive care")

Caregiver response to medical information/requests for admission or additional tests

Complete medical examination findings and lab/X ray results

Description of findings on review of systems

Impression and treatment

Action taken (report to CPS, referral to counseling, etc.)

Caregiver visitation restrictions and compliance

Delivery of child's specimens, clothes, and so on to law enforcement officials

Doctor's name, position, and office and beeper numbers (clearly written)

Table 10.2 Information Not Included in the Chart

Personal opinions about child, caregivers, and others

Phrases such as "no evidence of abuse" or "no evidence of neglect"

Health Care Providers in the Courtroom

Health care professionals who treat children, particularly physicians, may be subpoenaed to testify in child abuse cases. In a criminal case, a subpoena directs the health care professional to come to court and provide information to aid a jury or judge in determining the guilt or innocence of a defendant. In a noncriminal case, a subpoena directs the health care professional to come to court and provide information that will aid in a variety of determinations (i.e., whether a child should be removed from the home, offered court-ordered services, or awarded monetary damages for abuse suffered). Subpoenas sometimes order the production of records (subpoena *duces tecum*). Generally, a subpoena *duces tecum* directs that medical records be delivered to the court under seal for review or to the party issuing the subpoena. Upon receipt of a subpoena in a criminal case, the health care provider should clarify his or her obligations under that subpoena with the local prosecutor or hospital counsel.

In a criminal child abuse case, health care professionals may be subpoenaed by the prosecutor, the defense attorney, or the court. Generally, however, the examining and treating health care providers are subpoenaed by the prosecutor. The following discussion will assume that the health care provider has been subpoenaed by the prosecutor to testify in support of the prosecution's case.

The health care provider should establish protocols with the local prosecutor to facilitate the process of preparing for and appearing in court. For example, the name and phone number of the prosecutor handling the case and the name of the child/ patient should be included prominently on each subpoena.

When potentially privileged documents (i.e., psychiatric or psychological records) are included in the medical record, the medical facility and the prosecutor should develop procedures to ensure judicial scrutiny of the material before the records are released to the attorneys. The judge will balance the privacy rights of the child with any legal requirements for disclosure of records. Criminal cases are often postponed for reasons beyond the control of the prosecutor. Illness of a witness, unavailability of the judge or defense attorney, or failure of the defendant to appear for trial are some situations that may result in an unscheduled delay in the trial. Medical professionals often express understandable frustration with repeated postponements and multiple subpoenas. In some jurisdictions, the prosecutor keeps the health care provider "on call" during the trial; the medical professional remains at the hospital or clinic until the prosecutor notifies him or her to appear. It is the prosecutor's responsibility to apprise the health care provider as soon as possible that the case has been postponed.

Prior to testifying in court, the health care provider and the prosecutor should schedule a preparatory session. Defense attorneys may also wish to interview or depose the health care professional prior to trial. The health care provider may discuss with the prosecutor the rules that are followed in such a deposition and determine whether the prosecutor will accompany the health care provider to the interview or deposition scheduled by the defense attorney. Interviews or depositions should be held in a neutral, comfortable setting. Preparation prior to any interview, deposition, or trial appearance is essential, and health care providers should know the medical record thoroughly (see Appendix 10.1).

The Medical Professional on the Stand: Fact or Expert Witness?

A medical professional may be asked to testify as a "fact" witness, an "expert" witness, or both. A fact witness testifies as to what was observed; an expert witness, because of specialized training, experience, and knowledge, may testify not only to observations but to opinions based on those observations (Cleary, 1983). The prosecutor and the health care professional discuss the health care professional's level and areas of expertise to determine whether he or she will be called as a fact or expert witness. For example, a pediatric intern, although highly educated and well trained, may not feel him- or herself to be an "expert" in a particular area. On the other hand, many medical professionals underestimate their qualifications and can be readily qualified as experts in court.

Fact Witness

If the prosecutor determines that the health care professional will testify as a fact witness, there is the possibility that a medical expert will augment the testimony of the fact witness. Another physician may testify, for example, regarding causation and the timing of the child's injuries. Whether or not an expert witness will be called, the fact witness should review records during the preparatory session with the prosecutor, explain medical terminology, and review the subject areas for direct testimony. Testimony of the fact witness may include the following:

- Education and experience of witness
- Observations during contact with child (see Section 10.5)
  - Who brought child to the hospital or office
  - Child's demeanor, dress, level of cleanliness, and so on
  - Child's and caregivers' statements
  - Medical findings
  - Actions taken (reported to CPS hotline, ordered more X rays, etc.)

Expert Witness

A medical expert is often a vital witness in a prosecutor's case because there may be no eyewitnesses to a physical assault, many victims are too young to testify, and most judges and jurors lack knowledge regarding the medical aspects of child abuse. The expert witness and the prosecutor must have an in-depth preparatory session. The prosecutor should review an updated resumé or curriculum vitae of the expert witness. The preparatory session includes subject areas to be covered, limitations in the witness's expertise, and identification of any areas that need to be supplemented with the testimony of an additional expert. The expert witness and the prosecutor together review all of the medical documents that will be used at trial and determine if there are missing medical documents that are vital to the case, such as prior well-child care records, prenatal health care records of the child's mother, X ray and MRI results, and so on. The medical expert should review all police reports that give accounts of how, when, and where the injuries occurred and prior testimony given by experts in the case (preliminary hearing, grand jury, dependency, or other pretrial hearings). The more information the expert can review, the better grasp he or she will have of the overall picture. Review studies that both support and refute the opinion of the expert. Also discuss diagrams, charts, or models that will be necessary for the trial. Table 10.3 includes subject areas of expert testimony. See Appendix 10.1 for pointers for expert witnesses.

Testimony in the Courtroom

During testimony in a criminal proceeding, the prosecutor, defense attorney, and judge may ask questions of the witness.

Table 10.3 Possible Subject Areas for Expert Testimony

Education and experience (to qualify the witness as an expert)
Condition of child prior to injury
Lack of preexisting illness or condition to account for injury
Clinical course of injury
Timing of injuries
Implausibility of defendant's explanations for the injuries
Nature of paramedic, emergency room, and in-patient care
Implausibility of self-infliction of injury
Implausibility of injury by young sibling
Mechanism of injury
Force necessary to cause injury
Degree of injury
Degree of pain
Medical significance of omissions or misrepresentations made by caregiver
Prior injuries to child
Injuries to other children
Significance of delay in seeking treatment
New explanations for the child's injuries offered by the defense at trial

Source. Investigation (1993); Myers and Carter (1988).

In a civil dependency or family court proceeding, the judge and the attorneys for each of the parties, including the attorneys for the parents, the CPS agency, and the child, may ask questions of the witness. "Direct examination" consists of questions put to the witness by the attorney who has subpoenaed him or her to court. "Cross-examination" is questioning by the opposing attorney. Again, the following discussion assumes that the prosecutor subpoenaed the health care provider to court.

Direct Examination   Direct examination should hold no surprises if the witness is adequately prepared. Presumably, after the preparatory session with the prosecutor, the health care provider will know what will be asked of him or her. Consider the following tips:

- While on the witness stand, use medical records to refresh recollection as needed. However, do not rely on the records; be thoroughly familiar with their contents.
- If reference to the records is necessary during testimony, fasten notes ("stickees") or paper clips to salient pages *before you come to court.* Fumbling through the medical record while on the stand will create an unfavorable impression and undermine even the most powerful testimony. Prior to trial, consult the prosecutor regarding any obligation to provide the defense attorney with any additional notes made by you during preparation for testimony or any other materials brought to the courtroom.
- Listen carefully to the question. Answer honestly, succinctly, and without equivocation. Avoid "yes" or "no" answers if greater explanation is needed. If there is an objection by either the

prosecutor or the defense attorney, do not answer until the judge has indicated that you may do so.

- Use diagrams, tables, and charts to clarify technical points to the jury. Enlargements of photographs and critical pages of the medical record, timelines, medical illustrations with overlays, dolls, and mannequins can be useful.
- If possible, get off the witness stand during direct testimony and draw on a chalkboard or flip chart to better explain concepts. Prior to trial, make arrangements with the prosecutor for the necessary equipment.
- Explain all medical terms, using analogies and examples to clarify medical concepts. Avoid condescending language directed at the jurors or the judge.
- Prosecutors should ask questions on direct examination that elicit any problem areas in the testimony. For example, if there are limits on how exactly the expert witness can date the injuries, explain that limitation on direct examination.
- Acknowledge if there are several possible causes for the injury. Explain to the jury, however, that there is no evidence in the record to support the alternative causes and emphasize that the probability is low that anything other than the mechanism of injury described caused the injury. (Investigation, 1993)

The prosecutor may ask hypothetical questions of the medical expert during direct testimony. The content of the hypothetical question will vary depending upon the medical findings, other evidence gathered by investigators, and the law of the jurisdiction. Attorneys may vary hypothetical questions to include facts that are not part of the medical findings. The following is an example of a hypothetical question:

Q (Prosecutor): "Doctor, assume that Johnny, 10 months old, was watching TV on a sofa, fell asleep, rolled off the sofa onto the floor, and started to cry. Johnny's mother then brought him to the emergency room. At the emergency room, Johnny was found to have pain in his right arm, and an X ray was taken of the arm. The X ray revealed a spiral fracture to the upper portion of the arm. In your opinion, to a reasonable degree of medical certainty, is that injury consistent with the history described? Why or why not?"

Prior to trial, review all hypothetical questions with the prosecutor. See Appendix 10.1 for further information.

Cross-Examination

Cross-examination can be a stress-provoking experience. For the fact witness, cross-examination tends to be narrow in focus, emphasizing discrepancies in the records and the relative lack of experience of the witness. An expert witness may be cross-examined more extensively, first as to qualifications, then as to the opinions given and the bases for those opinions.

Defense attorneys usually cross-examine witnesses to uncover alleged bias. The expert witness should disclose, without any equivocation or apology, any payment received for testimony; in fact, the *prosecutor* may want to elicit information about any expert witness fee. Reasonable expert witness fees, particularly when a large percentage of the fee goes to the expert's hospital, should be understood by the judge and jurors.

Defense counsel may ask questions concerning the health care provider's role on a hospital or community multidisciplinary team. Explain the function of the team, and clarify that not every case consultation results in a finding of abuse or a prosecution. Emphasize that the medical professional's salary does not increase based on the number of cases found to involve abuse. If the defense attorney questions the health care provider about repeated court appearances on behalf of the prosecutor and few, if any, for defense attorneys, point out any prior consultations with defense attorneys on child abuse cases. Although such consultations may not have culminated in courtroom testimony, the willingness to discuss cases with either the prosecutor or defense attorney rebuts claims of bias. Discuss other factors that demonstrate objectivity; the prosecutor should elicit those factors on direct examination (Investigation, 1993).

Expert witnesses will be cross-examined regarding their opinions and the bases for their opinions. The witness should ask the prosecutor, prior to trial, about the defense attorney's demeanor, familiarity with the literature, questioning style, and other issues of concern. An expert witness should be familiar with the relevant literature because defense attorneys may cite studies without a complete understanding of a study's methodology. Always be patient and polite on the witness stand, even with the most confrontational defense attorney. The expert witness, however, should not allow the attorney to minimize his or her expertise or force opinions in an area outside of his or her expertise.

After testifying, the medical professional may want to discuss the experience with the prosecutor to find out what went well and what steps should be taken to make the testimony more effective in the future (see Appendix 10.1).

Hearsay Evidence

Statements made to health care professionals by children and their caregivers are essential to the investigation and prosecution of child abuse cases (see the section on documentation of medical conclusions). The health care provider may be subpoenaed to relate those statements to the jury. The admissibility of such statements at trial depends on the law of hearsay in specific jurisdictions.

Hearsay statements are statements (a) made outside of the courtroom, (b) recounted by the person to whom the statements were made, and (c) offered as evidence of the truth of the statements' contents. For example, a child may report to an examining physician that "My daddy burned me with an iron." The physician may then be called to the witness stand and asked to tell the judge or the jury what the child said in the hospital. If the testimony is offered as evidence that the father of the child did, in fact, burn the child with the iron, then it is hearsay.

A hearsay statement is inadmissible unless it fits an exception to the hearsay rule. In general, there are certain statements that may be admissible at trial, such as those made by a child, caregiver, or other person when startled or excited by an event ("excited utterances"); statements made by a caregiver against his or her own interest ("statements against interest"); and statements made by a child during the course of a physical examination ("statements made for purposes of medical diagnosis and treatment"). Other out-of-court statements that do not fit traditional hearsay exceptions may be admissible at trial for other reasons. Document all statements carefully, whether or not they appear to fit into a hearsay exception, and check with the local prosecutor regarding the particular nuances of your state's hearsay law. For general reading on the law of hearsay, see Myers (1992a).

In Brief

Do's

- Describe medical findings clearly and simply.
- Use diagrams and photographs to supplement written descriptions of injuries.
- Educate yourself regarding proper child interviewing techniques.
- Document thoroughly any statements given by the child or caregiver, using, if possible, the speaker's exact words.
- Document statements throughout contact with the child and the family. Urge the entire clinical staff to do likewise.
- Question caregivers separately from each other and from the child.
- Document speaker's demeanor and behaviors.
- Document caregiver's frequency of visitation and nature of contact with child.
- Note inconsistency of explanations with nature of injury.
- Consult with your local multidisciplinary investigative team and prosecutor.

CHILD PHYSICAL ABUSE AND NEGLECT

- Prepare with the prosecutor prior to testifying.
- Listen carefully to all questions put to you by attorneys and judges and answer clearly and truthfully.

Don'ts
- Don't rely on memory; compile a well-documented chart to use later to refresh your recollection.
- Don't include personal opinions about the patient or the patient's family in the medical record.
- Don't record preliminary conclusions; wait for all required test and examination results.
- Don't testify without adequate preparation.
- Don't destroy notes or other documentation.
- Don't guess; if you cannot answer with certainty, say so.
- Don't answer a question unless you are sure you understand it.

Appendix 10.1: Pointers for Expert Witnesses

1. Assume responsibility for ensuring that the lawyer calling you as an expert witness presents you in the best possible light. To accomplish this, you should:

   a. Be prepared. Always know the pertinent facts of the case better than anyone else in the courtroom.

   b. Demand a pre-trial conference with the attorney to learn what s/he wants from you and to educate her/him about the subject matter of your testimony. Review with him/her other cases where you have given similar testimony. Discuss which subjects you will not be permitted to testify about in court.

   c. Avoid using professional jargon. Review your testimony with the attorney and identify the difficult words. Use a thesaurus to find simple and clear alternative words that the judge/jury will understand.

   d. Provide the attorney calling you as a witness with a list of foundation questions. You will be more at ease knowing the questions you will be asked and the attorney will be grateful to you for making her/his job easier.

   e. Provide the lawyer calling you as an expert witness with an up-to-date resume of your professional credentials and educational background.

   f. Dress conservatively.

2. Maintain a ready file of literature pertaining to the specialty area in which you will be offering expert testimony, including monographs, articles and books. Make these available to the attorney calling you so that s/he will be more educated on your subject. Also, be sure that the attorney is aware of anything you have written pertaining to the subject of your testimony.

3. If you are going to be interviewed by opposing counsel, avoid doing so in your office. By meeting in your personal office you will give the attorney a chance to look around at the various reference books and texts and then challenge you in court with one of your own reference books. A neutral place like a restaurant, conference room, or even the attorney's office is a better place for your meeting.

    a. Avoid sitting for an interview with opposing counsel, or for a deposition, until you are fully prepared, know the facts of your case and the relevant references to the professional literature.

    b. Segregate your personal notes and work product from the case file. Do not disclose them to the opposing counsel without either permission of the attorney calling you as a witness or a court order.

    c. At an interview with opposing counsel or deposition, have a "game plan" to either:

        i. impress the other attorney with the facts supporting your position by "telling all" to encourage settlement, or

        ii. if litigation is expected, answer questions honestly but narrowly.

4. Always tell the truth, and maintain the appearance of being absolutely fair and objective.

5. If you anticipate the advocate for the other side will be calling an expert, suggest to the attorney calling you that you spend time preparing her/him to deal with the adverse expert. You can even sometimes sit with the attorney in court and suggest methods of cross-examination to her/him.

6. Remember, when approaching or inside the courthouse, anyone you pass may be a judge, juror, hostile witness, or opposing attorney. Always conduct yourself accordingly.

7. When you enter the courtroom, do not do anything immediately. Before sitting down, make brief eye contact with the judge and/or jury. Adjust the chair and microphone so that you don't have to lean forward to answer questions.

8. Be aware of spatial positioning and, if possible, use it to your advantage.

    a. Adversary position—Face to face, squarely in front of the person or group of people.

    b. Communication position—At an angle to the person or group.

    c. Cooperation position—Side by side.

9. Before answering each question, control the situation by consciously pausing. This allows the judge/jury to mentally shift from hearing the attorney's question to listening to your answer. For example:

Q: "State your name and occupation."
Three-count pause

A: "My name is _____. I am a social worker for the
_____."
Q: "How long have you been employed?"
Three-count pause
A: "I have been working there for _____ years."

10. Answer each question with a declarative statement rather than a word or phrase. The opposing attorney may only want the judge/jury to hear his or her question. By using the three-count pause, the declarative sentence, and spatial positioning you will take psychological control away from the attorney.

11. When answering questions, don't guess. If you don't know, say you don't know, but don't let the cross-examiner get you in the trap of answering question after question with "I don't know."

12. Understand the question before you attempt to give an answer. You can't possibly give a truthful and accurate answer unless you understand the question.

13. Listen and try to avoid asking the lawyer to repeat the question. Keep a sharp lookout for questions with a double meaning and questions that assume you have testified to a fact when you have not done so.

14. Answer the question that is asked and then stop, especially on cross-examination. Don't volunteer information not called for by the question you are asked.

15. Choice of words is very important. Develop your ability to use words that not only depict what happened but also convey the impression you intend.

Positive "Soft" Words	Negative "Hard" Words
mother	woman, respondent, abuser
father	subject, suspect ,defendant
child	juvenile, youth
cut	laceration, open wound
molest	rape, sexual assault
bruise	contusion

16. Talk loudly enough so everyone can hear you, yet softly enough so that you can suddenly raise your voice to emphasize a point.

17. Avoid distracting mannerisms such as eating mints, chewing gum, or fumbling through a file.

18. Give an audible answer so the court reporter can hear it. Don't nod your head yes or no. Remember that the court reporter is writing everything you say for appellate review.

19. Don't look at the lawyer who called you as a witness or at the judge for help when you are on the witness stand.

20. Beware of questions involving distances and time. If you make an estimate, make sure that everyone understands that you

are estimating. Think clearly about distances and intervals of time. Be sure your estimates are reasonable.

21. Don't be afraid to look the jurors in the eye. Jurors are naturally sympathetic to witnesses and want to hear what they have to say. Look at them most of the time and speak to them frankly and openly as you would to a friend or neighbor.

22. Don't argue with the lawyer cross-examining you. S/he has every right to question you and the lawyer who called you will object if s/he gets out of bounds. Don't answer a question with a question unless the question you are asked is not clear.

23. Don't lose your temper no matter how hard you are pressed. If you lose your temper, you have played right into the hands of the cross-examiner.

24. Be courteous. Being courteous is one of the best ways to make a good impression on the court and on the jury. Be sure to answer, "Yes, Sir," and "No, Sir," and to address the judge as "Your Honor."

25. If asked whether you have talked to the lawyer calling you as a witness or to an investigator, admit it freely. If you are being paid a fee, admit, without hesitation, that you are receiving compensation.

26. Avoid joking, wisecracks, and condescending comments or inflections. A trial is a serious matter.

27. Most people learn visually. Use blackboards, diagrams, charts, and so on liberally. At the blackboard or easel, turn around and talk to the jury. Almost inevitably, witnesses not following this instruction will get into an inaudible conversation with the blackboard. Remember spatial positioning.

28. Draw in proportion. Before drawing anything—think! Don't start with the old cliche, "Well, I'm not much of an artist." Draw in proportion and never refer to "here" and "there." A reviewing court will not understand what you mean. Describe what you draw orally and number each relevant representation.

29. Never read from notes unless absolutely necessary. If you must, announce the fact that you are doing so and state your reason (i.e., refreshing memory, need for specificity, etc.). The lawyer cross-examining you will most likely have a right to see the notes at that time.

30. Never give an opinion about things you are not trained in, and never give an opinion you cannot support.

31. An opposing attorney may cross-examine you with articles, books, other people's opinions, or things you have said previously. You may be confronted with something that appears contradictory in an effort to show that your opinion is inconsistent with these other sources. Ask to see the book or article the opposing attorney refers to. Read it, compare it, and almost every time you will find that something has been taken out of context or misinterpreted by the attorney. You can then demonstrate not only that you are right, but that the article or book agrees with you.

CHILD PHYSICAL ABUSE AND NEGLECT

32. Be familiar with the book *Coping with Psychiatric and Psychological Testimony*, 3rd ed., by J. Zisken, published by Law and Psychology Press, 202 South Rexford Drive, Beverly Hills, California 90212. You can be assured that the lawyer cross-examining you will probably have read this book. If you have not, no matter how competent you are in your field, you may be embarrassed.

33. When you finish testifying, nod to the judge/jury, and say thank you.

34. After each appearance as an expert witness, check with the attorney or others present for a critique of your performance. Use the critique to improve or modify the way you testify.

Copyright by American Prosecutors Research Institute.
Used with permission of APRI.

Note

1. A guardian ad litem is a special guardian, often an attorney, appointed by the court to represent the interests of a child in court proceedings.

References

AAP Task Force on Infant Positioning and SIDS. (1992). Positioning and SIDS. *Pediatrics, 89,* 1120-1126.

Ablin, D. S., Greenspan, A., & Reinhart, M. A. (1992). Pelvic injuries in child abuse. *Pediatric Radiology, 22,* 454-457.

Ablin, D. S., Greenspan, A., Reinhart, M. A., & Grix, A. (1990). Differentiation of child abuse from osteogenesis imperfecta. *American Journal of Radiology, 154,* 1035-1046.

Abramson, J., & Mizrahi, T. (1986). Strategies for enhancing collaboration between social workers and physicians. *Social Work in Health Care, 12*(1), 1-21.

Abrol, R. P., Heck, A., Gleckel, L., & Rosner, F. (1990). Self-induced hematuria. *Journal of the National Medical Association, 82,* 127-128.

Ahlgren, L. S. (1990). Burns. In S. S. Gellis & B. M. Kagan (Eds.), *Current pediatric therapy* (13th ed., pp. 682-683). Philadelphia: W. B. Saunders.

Akbarnia, B., Torg, J. S., Kirkpatrick, J., & Sussman, S. (1974). Manifestations of the battered-child syndrome. *Journal of Bone Joint Surgery, 56A,* 1159-1166.

Alexander, R. (1992). Failure to thrive. *The Advisor, 5*(4), 1, 11-12.

Alexander, R., Sato, Y., Smith, W., & Bennett, T. (1990). Incidence of impact trauma with cranial injuries ascribed to shaking. *American Journal of Diseases of Children, 144,* 724-726.

Allen, R. E., & Oliver, J. M. (1982). The effects of child maltreatment on language development. *Child Abuse & Neglect, 6,* 299-305.

American Academy of Pediatrics, Section on Radiology. (1991). Diagnostic imaging of child abuse. *Pediatrics, 87,* 262-264.

American Association for Protecting Children. (1989). *Highlights of official child neglect and abuse reporting 1987.* Denver: The American Human Society.

American Board of Forensic Odontology, Inc. (1986). Guidelines for bite mark analysis. *Journal of the American Dental Association, 112,* 383-386.

American Humane Association. (1993). *AHA fact sheet #3: Child abuse and neglect data.* Englewood, CO: Author.

American Humane Association. (1994). *AHA fact sheet #12: The use of physical discipline.* Englewood, CO: Author.

275

American Humane Association. (1995). *AHA fact sheet #1: Child abuse and neglect data.* Englewood, CO: Author.

Aoki, N. (1990). Chronic subdural hematoma in infancy: Clinical analysis of 30 cases in the CT era. *Journal of Neurosurgery, 73,* 201-205.

APSAC. (1995). *Practice guidelines: Photographic documentation of child abuse.* Chicago: Author.

Asher, R. (1951). Munchausen's syndrome. *Lancet, 1,* 339-341.

Astley, R. (1979). Metaphyseal fractures in osteogenesis imperfecta. *British Journal of Radiology, 52*(618), 441-443.

Augoustinos, M. (1987). Developmental effects of child abuse: Recent findings. *Child Abuse & Neglect, 11,* 15-27.

Avery, M. E., & First, L. R. (1989). *Pediatric medicine.* Baltimore: Williams & Wilkins.

Ayoub, C., & Pfeiffer, D. (1979). Burns as a manifestation of child abuse and neglect. *American Journal of Diseases of Children, 133,* 910-914.

Azar, S. T. (1991). Models of child abuse: A metatheoretical analysis. *Criminal Justice and Behavior, 18,* 30-46.

Baker, M. D., & Moore, S. E. (1987). Human bites in children. *American Journal of Diseases of Children, 141,* 1285-1290.

Ballard, R. A. (1988). *Pediatric care and the ICN graduate.* Philadelphia: W. B. Saunders.

Baptiste, M. S., & Feck, G. (1980). Preventing tap water burns. *American Journal of Public Health, 70,* 727-729.

Barbero, G. J., & Shaheen, E. (1967). Environmental failure to thrive: A clinical view. *Journal of Pediatrics, 71,* 639-644.

Barlow, B., Niemirska, M., Ghandi, R. P., & Leblanc, W. (1983). Ten years' experience of falls from a height in children. *Journal of Pediatric Surgery, 18,* 509-511.

Barsley, R. E. (1993). Forensic and legal issues in oral diagnosis. *Dental Clinics of North America, 37,* 133-156.

Barsley, R. E., & Landcaster, D. M. (1987). Measurement of arch widths in a human population: Relation of anticipated bite marks. *Journal of Forensic Science, 32,* 975-982.

Bass, M., Kravath, R. E., & Glass, L. (1986). Death-scene investigation in sudden infant death. *New England Journal of Medicine, 315,* 100-105.

Baum, J. D., & Bulpitt, C. J. (1970). Retinal and conjunctival hemorrhage in the newborn. *Archives of Diseases of Children, 45,* 344-349.

Bays, J. (1994a). Child abuse by poisoning. In R. M. Reece (Ed.), *Child abuse: Medical diagnosis and management* (pp. 69-106). Philadelphia: Lea & Febiger.

Bays, J. (1994b). Conditions mistaken for child abuse. In R. M. Reece (Ed.), *Child abuse: Medical diagnosis and management* (pp. 358-385). Philadelphia: Lea & Febiger.

Becker, D. B., Needleman, H. L., & Kotelchuck, M. (1978). Child abuse and dentistry: Orofacial trauma and its recognition by dentists. *Journal of the American Dental Association, 97,* 24-28.

Belsky, J. (1980). Child maltreatment: An ecological integration. *American Psychologist, 35,* 320-335.

Berger, A. M., Knutson, J. F., Mehm, J. G., & Perkins, K. A. (1988). *Child Abuse & Neglect, 12,* 251-262.

Bergstrom, W. H. (1991). Twenty ways to get rickets in the 1990s. *Contemporary Pediatrics, 8*(12), 88-106.

Bernat, J. E. (1981). Bite marks and oral manifestations of child abuse and neglect. In N. S. Ellerstein (Ed.), *Child abuse and neglect* (pp. 141-164). New York: Wiley.

Berwick, D. M., Levy, J. C., & Kleinerman, R. (1982). Failure to thrive: Diagnostic yield of hospitalization. *Archives of Diseases of Childhood, 57,* 347-351.

Billmire, M. E., & Myers, P. A. (1985). Serious head injury in infants: Accident or abuse? *Pediatrics, 75,* 340-342.

Bithoney, W. G., Dubowitz, H., & Egan, H. (1992). Failure to thrive/growth deficiency. *Pediatrics in Review, 13,* 453-459.

Bools, C., Neale, B., & Meadow, R. (1992). Co-morbidity associated with fabricated illness (Munchausen syndrome by proxy). *Archives of Disease in Childhood, 67,* 77-79.

Bourne, R. (1979). Child abuse and neglect: An overview. In R. Bourne & E. H. Newberger (Ed.), *Critical perspectives on child abuse.* Lexington, MA: Lexington Books.

Boxer, G. H., Carson, J., & Miller, B. D. (1988). Neglect contributing to tertiary hospitalization in childhood asthma. *Child Abuse & Neglect, 12,* 491-501.

Brandt, L. (1979). Growth dynamics of low birthweight infants with emphasis on the perinatal period. In F. Faulkner & J. Tanner (Eds.), *Human growth neurobiology and nutrition.* New York: Plenum.

Breslau, N., Staruch, K. S., & Mortimer, E. A. (1982). Psychological distress in mothers of disabled children. *American Journal of Disabilities of Children, 136,* 682-686.

Briere, J. N. (1992). *Child abuse trauma: Theory and treatment of the lasting effects.* Newbury Park, CA: Sage.

Broderick, J., Talbot, T., Prenger, E., Leach, A., & Brott, T. (1993). Stroke in children within a major metropolitan area: The surprising importance of intracerebral hemorrhage. *Journal of Child Neurology, 8,* 250-255.

Bronfenbrenner, U. (1977). Toward an experimental ecology of human development. *American Psychologist, 32,* 513-531.

Bross, D. C., Krugman, R. D., Lenherr, M. B., Rosenberg, D. A., & Schmitt, B. D. (1988). *The new child protection team handbook.* New York: Garland.

Bruce, D. A., & Zimmerman, R. A. (1989). Shaken impact syndrome. *Pediatric Annals, 18,* 482-489.

Bullock, R., & Fujisawa, H. (1992). The role of glutamate antagonists for the treatment of CNS injury. *Journal of Neurotrauma, 9*(Suppl. 2), S443-S473.

Caffey, J. (1946). Multiple fractures in the long bones of infants suffering from chronic subdural hematoma. *American Journal of Roentgenology, 56,* 163-173.

Caffey, J. (1957). Some traumatic lesions in growing bones other than fractures and dislocation: Clinical and radiological features. *British Journal of Radiology, 30,* 225-238.

Caffey, J. (1972). On the theory and practice of shaking infants: Its potential residual effects of permanent brain damage and mental retardation. *American Journal of Diseases of Children, 124,* 161-169.

Caffey, J. (1974). The whiplash shaken infant syndrome: Manual shaking by the extremities with whiplash-induced intracranial and intraocular bleedings, linked with residual permanent brain damage and mental retardation. *Pediatrics, 54,* 396-403.

Cameron, J. M., & Rae, L. J. (1975). The radiological diagnosis. *Atlas of the battered child syndrome* (pp. 20-50). London: Churchill Livingstone.

Caniano, D. A., Beaver, B. L., & Boles, E. T. (1986). Child abuse: An update on surgical management in 256 cases. *Annals of Surgery, 203,* 219-224.

Cappelleri, J. C., Eckenrode, J., & Powers, J. L. (1993). The epidemiology of child abuse: Findings from the second national incidence and prevalence study of child abuse and neglect. *American Journal of Public Health, 83,* 1622-1634.

Casella, J. F. (1990). Disorders of coagulation. In F. A. Oski, C. D. DeAngelis, R. D. Feigin, & J. B. Warshaw (Eds.), *Principles and practice of pediatrics* (pp. 1550-1563). Philadelphia: J. B. Lippincott.

Chadwick, D. L. (1991). In A. M. Rudolph, J. I. E. Hoffman, & C. D. Rudolph (Eds.), *Rudolph's pediatrics* (19th ed., pp. 838-850). Norwalk, CT: Appleton & Lange.

Chadwick, D. L., Chin, S., Salerno, C., Landsverk, S., & Kitchen, L. (1991). Deaths from falls in children: How far is fatal? *Journal of Trauma, 31,* 1353-1355.

Chapin, H. D. (1908). A plan for dealing with atrophic infants and children. *Archives of Pediatrics, 25,* 491-496.

Chapman, S. (1992). The radiological dating of injuries. *Archives of Diseases of Children, 67,* 1063-1065.

Chatoor, J., & Egan, J. (1983). Nonorganic failure to thrive and dwarfism due to food refusal: A separation disorder. *Journal of the American Academy of Child Psychiatry, 22,* 294.

Chiaviello, C. T., Christoph, R. A., & Bond, R. (1994). Stairway-related injuries in children. *Pediatrics, 94,* 679-681.

Christian, C. W. (1992). Etiology and prevention of abuse: Societal factors. In S. Ludwig & A. E. Kornberg (Eds.), *Child abuse: A medical reference* (2nd ed., pp. 25-37). New York: Churchill Livingstone.

Cleary, E. W. (1983). *McCormick's handbook of the law of evidence* (2nd ed.). St. Paul, MN: West.

Coant, P. N., Kornberg, A. E., Brody, A. S., & Edward-Holmes, K. (1992). Markers for occult liver injury in cases of physical abuse in children. *Pediatrics, 89,* 274-278.

Cobb, L. M., Vinocur, C. D., Wagner, C. W., & Weintraub, W. H. (1986). Intestinal perforation due to blunt trauma in children in an era of increased nonoperative treatment. *Journal of Trauma, 26,* 461-463.

Coffman, K., Boyce, W. T., & Hansen, R. C. (1985). Phytodermatitis simulating child abuse. *American Journal of Diseases of Children, 139,* 239-240.

Cohen, B. A. (1993). *Atlas of pediatric dermatology.* London: Wolfe.

Cohen, R. A., Kaufman, R. A., Myers, P. A., & Towbin, R. B. (1986). Cranial computed tomography in the abused child with head injury. *American Journal of Roentgenology, 146,* 97-102.

Committee on Child Abuse and Neglect and Committee on Community Health Services. (1993). Investigation and review of unexpected infant and child deaths. *Pediatrics, 92,* 734-735.

Committee on Dietary Allowances. (1980). *Recommended dietary allowances* (9th ed.). Washington, DC: National Academy of Sciences.

Committee on Early Childhood, Adoption and Dependent Care. (1986). Oral and dental aspects of child abuse and neglect. *Pediatrics, 78,* 537-539.

Cooney, D. R., & Grosfeld, J. L. (1975). Operative management of pancreatic pseudocysts in infants and children: A review of 75 cases. *Annals of Surgery, 182,* 590-596.

Cooper, A. (1992). Thoracoabdominal trauma. In S. Ludwig & A. E. Kornberg (Eds.), *Child abuse: A medical reference* (2nd ed., pp. 131-150). New York: Churchill Livingstone.

Cooper, A., Floyd, T., Barlow, B., Niemirska, M., Ludwig, S., Seidl, T., O'Neill, J., Ziegler, M., Ross, A., Gandhi, R., & Catherman, R. (1988). Major blunt trauma due to child abuse. *Journal of Trauma, 28,* 1483-1487.

Cotran, R. S., Kumar, V., & Robbins, S. (1989). Cellular injury and adaptation. In R. S. Cotran, V. Kumar, & S. Robbins (Eds.), *Robbins' pathologic basis of disease* (4th ed., pp. 25-26). Philadelphia: W. B. Saunders.

Council on Scientific Affairs. (1985). AMA diagnostic and treatment guidelines concerning child abuse and neglect. *Journal of the American Medical Association, 254,* 796-800.

Crittenden, P. M. (1992). Children's strategies for coping with adverse home environments: An interpretation using attachment theory. *Child Abuse & Neglect, 16,* 329-343.

Culbertson, J. L., Krous, H. F., & Bendell, R. D. (1988). *Sudden infant death syndrome: Medical aspects and psychological management.* Baltimore, MD: Johns Hopkins University Press.

Cumberland, G. D., Riddick, L., & McConnell, C. F. (1991). Intimal tears of the right atrium of the heart due to blunt force injuries to the abdomen. *American Journal of Forensic Medicine & Pathology, 12,* 102-104.

da Fonesca, M. A., Feigal, R. J., & ten Bensel, R. W. (1992). Dental aspects of 1248 cases of child maltreatment on file at a major county hospital. *Pediatric Dentistry, 14*(3), 152-157.

Davidson Ward, S. L., Keens, T. G., Chan, L. S., Chipps, B. E., Carson, S. H., Deming, D. D., Krishna, V., MacDonald, H. M., Martin, G. I., Meredith, K. S., Merrit, A., Nickerson, B. G., Stoddard, R. A., & vanderHal, A. L. (1986). Sudden infant death syndrome in infants evaluated by apnea programs in California. *Pediatrics, 77,* 451-455.

Davis, H. W., & Carrasco, M. (1992). Child abuse and neglect. In B. J. Zitelli & H. W. Davis (Eds.), *Atlas of pediatric physical diagnosis* (2nd ed., pp. 6.1-6.30). London: Wolfe.

Deley, W. W. (1988). Physical punishment of children: Sweden and the U.S.A. *Journal of Comparative Family Studies, 19,* 419-431.

DePanfilis, D., & Salus, M. K. (1992). *Child protective services: A guide for caseworkers* (The Circle, Inc. No. HHS-105-88-1702). Washington, DC: U.S. Department of Health & Human Services.

Devore, W., & Schlesinger, E. G. (1987). *Ethnic sensitive social work practice* (2nd ed.). Columbus, OH: Merrill.

Dine, M. S., & McGovern, M. E. (1982). Intentional poisoning of children—an overlooked category of child abuse: Report of seven cases and review of literature. *Pediatrics, 70,* 32-35.

Division of Injury Control, Center for Environmental Health and Injury Control, Centers for Disease Control. (1990). Childhood injuries in the United States. *American Journal of Diseases of Children, 144,* 627-646.

Drabman, R., & Spitalnik, R. (1973). Social isolation as a punishment procedure: A controlled study. *Journal of Experimental Child Psychology, 16,* 236-249.

Dubowitz, H., Black, M., Starr, R. H., & Zuravin, S. (1993). A conceptual definition of child neglect. *Criminal Justice and Behavior, 20,* 8-26.

Duhaime, A. C. (1994). Exciting your neurons to death: Can we prevent cell loss after brain injury? *Pediatric Neurosurgery, 21,* 117-123.

Duhaime, A. C., Alario, A. J., Lewander, W. J., Schut, L., Sutton, L. N., Seidl, T., Nudelman, S., Budenz, D., Hertle, R., Tsiaras, W., & Loporchio, S. (1992). Head injury in very young children: Mechanism, injury types, and ophthalmologic findings in 100 patients younger than 2 years of age. *Pediatrics, 90,* 179-185.

Duhaime, A. C., Bilaniuk, L., & Zimmerman, R. (1993). The "big black brain": Radiographic changes after severe inflicted head injury in infancy. *Journal of Neurotrauma, 10*(Suppl. 1): S59.

Duhaime, A. C., Gennarelli, T. G., Thibault, L. E., Bruce, D. A., Margulies, S. S., & Wiser, R. (1987). The shaken baby syndrome: A clinical, pathological, and biomechanical study. *Journal of Neurosurgery, 66,* 409-415.

Duhaime, A. C., & Sutton, L. N. (1996). Head injury problems peculiar to pediatrics. In G. T. Tindall, D. L. Barrow, & P. R. Cooper (Eds.), *The practice of neurosurgery.* Baltimore: Williams and Wilkins.

Duhaime, A. C., Sutton, L. N., & Schut, L. (1988). The "shaken baby syndrome": A misnomer? *Journal of Pediatric Neuroscience, 4,* 77-86.

Durfee, M. J., Gellert, G. A., & Tilton-Durfee, D. (1992). Origins and clinical relevance of child death review teams. *Journal of the American Medical Association, 267,* 3172-3175.

Dworkin, P. H. (1989). British and American recommendations for developmental monitoring: The role of surveillance. *Pediatrics, 84,* 1000-1010.

Dworkind, M., McGowan, G., & Hyams, J. (1990). Abdominal trauma—Child abuse. *Pediatrics, 85,* 892.

Ebbin, A. J., Gollub, M. H., Stein, A. M., & Wilson, M. G. (1969). Battered child syndrome at the Los Angeles County General Hospital. *American Journal of Diseases of Children, 118,* 660-667.

Egeland, B., Sroufe, A., & Erickson, M. A. (1983). The developmental consequences of different patterns of maltreatment. *Child Abuse & Neglect, 7,* 459-469.

Ellerstein, N. S. (1979). Cutaneous manifestations of child abuse and neglect. *American Journal of Diseases of Children, 133,* 906-909.

Ellerstein, N. S. (1981). Dermatologic manifestations of child abuse and neglect. In N. S. Ellerstein (Ed.), *Child abuse and neglect: A medical reference.* New York: Wiley.

Emery, J. L. (1985). Infanticide, filicide, and cot death. *Archives of Disease in Childhood, 60,* 505-507.

Emery, J. L., Chandra, S., & Gilbert-Barness, E. F. (1988). Findings in child deaths registered as sudden infant death syndrome (SIDS) in Madison, Wisconsin. *Pediatric Pathology, 8,* 171-178.

Epstein, M. A., Markowitz, R. L., Gallo, D. M., Holmes, J. W., & Gryboski, J. D. (1987). Munchausen syndrome by proxy: Considerations in diagnosis and confirmation by video surveillance. *Pediatrics, 80,* 220-224.

Erdman, T. C., Feldman, K. W., Rivara, F. P., Heimbach, D. M., & Wall, H. A. (1991). Tap water burn prevention: The effect of legislation. *Pediatrics, 88,* 572-577.

Ernst, T. N., & Philip, M. (1986). Severe iron deficiency anemia: An example of covert child abuse (Munchausen syndrome by proxy). *Western Journal of Medicine, 144,* 358-359.

Ewigman, B., Kivlahan, C., & Land, G. (1993). The Missouri child fatality study: Underreporting of maltreatment fatalities among children younger than five years of age, 1983 through 1986. *Pediatrics, 91,* 330-337.

Faller, K. C. (1990). *Child sexual abuse: An interdisciplinary manual for diagnosis, case management, and treatment.* New York: Columbia University Press.

Fazen, L. E., Lovejoy, F. H., & Crone, R. K. (1986). Acute poisoning in a children's hospital: A 2-year experience. *Pediatrics, 77,* 144-151.

Feldman, K. W. (1983). Help needed on hot water burns. *Pediatrics, 71,* 145-146.

Feldman, K. W. (1987). Child abuse by burning. In R. E. Helfer & R. S. Kempe (Eds.), *The battered child* (4th ed., pp. 197-213). Chicago: University of Chicago Press.

Feldman, K. W., & Brewer, D. K. (1984). Child abuse, cardiopulmonary resuscitation, and rib fractures. *Pediatrics, 73,* 339-342.

Finkelstein, J. L., Schwartz, S. B., Madden, M. R., Marano, M. A., & Goodwin, C. W. (1992). Pediatric burns. *Pediatric Clinics of North America, 39,* 1145-1163.

Fischler, R. S. (1983). Poisoning: A syndrome of child abuse. *American Family Physician, 28*(6), 103-108.

Fiser, R. H., Kaplan, J., & Holder, J. C. (1972). Congenital syphilis mimicking the battered child syndrome. *Clinical Pediatrics, 11,* 305-307.

Fitzpatrick, T. B., Polano, M. K., & Suurmond, D. (1983). *Color atlas and synopsis of clinical dermatology.* New York: McGraw-Hill.

Fleisher, G. R., & Ludwig, S. (1993). *Textbook of pediatric emergency medicine* (3rd ed.). Baltimore: Williams & Wilkins.

Fomon, S. J. (1974). *Infant nutrition* (2nd ed.). Philadelphia: W. B. Saunders.

Fontana, V. J., & Besharov, D. J. (1979). *The maltreated child: The maltreatment syndrome in children—a medical, legal, and social guide* (4th ed.). Springfield, IL: Charles C Thomas.

Fontana, V. J., Donovan, D., & Wong, R. J. (1963). The maltreatment syndrome in children. *New England Journal of Medicine, 269,* 1389-1394.

Frank, D. A., & Zeisel, S. H. (1988). Failure to thrive. *Pediatric Clinics of North America, 35,* 1187-1206.

Franklin, C., & Jordan, C. (1992). Teaching students to perform assessments. *Journal of Social Work Education, 28,* 222-241.

Franklin, W., & Klein, R. E. (1987). Severe asthma due to household pets: A form of child abuse or neglect. *New England Regional Allergy Proceedings, 8,* 259-261.

Freedman, L. (1990). *Understanding the medical aspects of physical abuse: A guide for child protective service workers.* Trenton, NJ: Division of Youth and Family Services.

Friedman, E. M. (1987). Caustic ingestions and foreign body aspirations: An overlooked form of child abuse. *Annals of Otology, Rhinology & Laryngology, 96,* 709-712.

Frisch, L., & Rhodes, F. (1982). Child abuse and neglect in children referred for learning evaluations. *Journal of Learning Disabilities, 15,* 583-586.

Frischiano, A. R. (1974). Triceps skin fold and upper arm muscle size norms for assessment of nutritional status. *American Journal of Clinical Nutrition, 27,* 1025-1058.

Gahagan, S., & Rimsza, M. E. (1991). Child abuse or osteogenesis imperfecta: How can we tell? *Pediatrics, 88,* 987-992.

Garbarino, J. (1977). The human ecology of child maltreatment: A conceptual model for research. *Journal of Marriage and the Family, 39,* 721-727.

Garbarino, J., & Stott, F. M. (1989). *What children can tell us.* San Francisco: Jossey-Bass.

Gaudin, J. M. (1993a). *Child neglect: A guide for intervention.* U.S. Department of Health and Human Services: Administration for Children and Families: National Center on Child Abuse and Neglect.

Gaudin, J. M. (1993b). Effective intervention with neglectful families. *Criminal Justice and Behavior, 20,* 66-89.

Gelles, R. J. (1982). Problems in defining and labeling child abuse. In R. H. Starr (Ed.), *Child abuse prediction: Policy implications* (pp. 1-30). Cambridge, MA: Ballinger.

Gennarelli, T. A., & Thibault, L. E. (1985). Biomechanics of head injury. In R. H. Wilkins & S. S. Rengachary (Eds.), *Neurosurgery* (pp. 1531-1536). New York: McGraw-Hill.

Gennarelli, T. A., Thibault, L. E., Adams, J. H., Graham, D. I., Thompson, C. J., & Marcincin, R. P. (1982). Diffuse axonal injury and traumatic coma in the primate. *Annals of Neurology, 12,* 564-574.

Germain, G. B. (1984). The helping process: Initial phase. In *Social work practice in health care: An ecological perspective* (pp. 89-124). New York: Free Press.

Gil, D. G. (1971). Violence against children. *Journal of Marriage and the Family, 11,* 637-648.

Gil, D. G. (1975). Unraveling child abuse. *American Journal of Orthopsychiatry, 45,* 346-358.

Gillespie, R. W. (1965). The battered child syndrome: Thermal and caustic manifestations. *Journal of Trauma, 5,* 523-533.

Giovannoni, J. M., & Becerra, R. M. (1979). *Defining child abuse.* New York: Free Press.

Glaser, K. (1949). Double contour, cupping and spurring in roentgenograms of long bones in infants. *American Journal of Roentgenology, 61,* 482-492.

Goetting, M. G., & Sowa, B. (1990). Retinal hemorrhage after cardiopulmonary resuscitation in children: An etiologic reevaluation. *Pediatrics, 85,* 585-588.

Goldbloom, R. B. (1982). Failure to thrive. *Pediatric Clinics of North America, 29,* 151-165.

Goldbloom, R. B. (1987). Growth failure in infancy. *Pediatrics in Review, 9*(2), 57-61.

Gordon, E. F., & Vasquez, D. M. (1986). Failure to thrive: An expanded conceptual method. In D. Drotar (Ed.), *New directions in failure to thrive* (p. 69). New York: Plenum.

Gotschall, C. S. (1993). Epidemiology of childhood injury. In M. R. Eichenberger (Ed.), *Pediatric trauma: Prevention, acute care, rehabilitation* (pp. 16-19). St. Louis, MO: Mosby Year Book, Inc.

Graham, C. B. (1972). Assessment of bone metabolism: Methods and pitfalls. *Radiologic Clinics of North America, 10,* 185.

Graziano, A. M., & Namaste, K. A. (1990). Parental use of physical force in child discipline: A survey of 679 college students. *Journal of Interpersonal Violence, 5,* 449-463.

Green, M. (1986). *Green and Richmond pediatric diagnosis: Interpretation of symptoms and signs in different age periods* (4th ed.). Philadelphia: W. B. Saunders.

Greene, P. E., Chisick, M. C., & Aaron, G. R. (1994). A comparison of oral health status and need for dental care between abused/neglected children and nonabused/non-neglected children. *Pediatric Dentistry, 16*(1), 41-45.

Grossman, D. C., Rauh, M. J., & Rivara, F. P. (1995). Prevalence of corporal punishment among students in Washington State schools. *Archives of Pediatrics & Adolescent Medicine, 149,* 529-536.

Guandolo, V. L. (1985). Munchausen syndrome by proxy: An outpatient challenge. *Pediatrics, 75,* 526-530.

Guthkelch, A. K. (1971). Infantile subdural hematoma and its relationship to whiplash injuries. *British Medical Journal, 2,* 430-431.

Haas, J. E., Taylor, J. A., Bergman, A. B., Van Belle, G., Felgenhauer, J. L., Siebert, J. R., & Banjamin, D. R. (1993). Relationship between epidemiologic risk factors and clinicopathologic findings in the sudden infant death syndrome. *Pediatrics, 91,* 106-112.

Hadley, M. N., Sonntag, V. K. H., Rekate, H. L., & Murphy, A. (1989). The infant whiplash-shake syndrome: A clinical and pathological study. *Neurosurgery, 24,* 536-540.

Hahn, Y. S., Raimondi, A. J., McLone, D. G., & Yamanouchi, Y. (1983). Traumatic mechanisms of head injury in child abuse. *Child's Brain, 10,* 229-241.

Haines, D. E., Harkey, H. L., & Al-Mefty, O. (1993). The "subdural" space: A new look at an outdated concept. *Neurosurgery, 32,* 111-120.

Halsted, C. C., & Shapiro, S. R. (1979). Child abuse: Acute renal failure from ruptured bladder. *American Journal of Diseases of Children, 133,* 861-862.

Hamill, P. V. V., Drizd, T. A., Johnson, C. L., Reed, R. B., Roche, A. F., & Moore, W. M. (1979). Physical growth: National Center for Health Statistics percentiles. *American Journal of Clinical Nutrition, 32,* 607-629.

Hamlin, H. (1968). Subgaleal hematoma caused by hair pulling. *Journal of the American Medical Association, 205,* 314.

Hammond, J., Perez-Stable, A., & Ward, G. (1991). Predictive value of historical and physical characteristics for the diagnosis of child abuse. *Southern Medical Journal, 84,* 166-168.

Hampton, R. L. (1985). Child abuse incidence and reporting by hospitals: Significance of severity, class, and race. *American Journal of Public Health, 75,* 56-60.

Han, D. P., & Wilkinson, W. S. (1990). Late ophthalmic manifestations of the shaken baby syndrome. *Journal of Pediatric Ophthalmology and Strabismus, 27,* 299-303.

Hanigan, W. C., Peterson, R. A., & Njus, G. (1987). Tin ear syndrome: Rotational acceleration in pediatric head injuries. *Pediatrics, 80,* 618-622.

Hathaway, W. E., Hay, W. W., Groothuis, J. R., & Paisley, J. W. (1993). *Current pediatric diagnosis and treatment.* Norwalk, CT: Appleton & Lange.

Heger, A. H. (1991). Interviewing the child. *Child sexual abuse, Report of the Twenty-Second Ross Roundtable on Critical Approaches to Common Pediatric Problems.* Columbus, OH: Ross Laboratories.

Heins, M. (1984). The battered child revisited. *Journal of the American Medical Association, 251,* 3295-3300.

Helfer, R. E. (1973). The etiology of child abuse. *Pediatrics, 51,* 777-779.

Helfer, R. E. (1977). Injuries resulting when small children fall out of bed. *Pediatrics, 60,* 533-535.

Helfer, R. E. (1987). The developmental basis of child abuse and neglect: An epidemiological approach. In R. E. Helfer & R. S. Kempe (Eds.), *The battered child* (4th ed., pp. 60-80). Chicago: University of Chicago Press.

Helfer, R. E., & Kempe, R. S. (1987). *The battered child* (4th ed.). Chicago: University of Chicago Press.

Hennes, H. M., Smith, D. S., Schneider, K., Hegenbarth, M. A., Duma, M. A., & Jona, J. Z. (1990). Elevated liver transaminase levels in children with blunt abdominal trauma: A predictor of liver injury. *Pediatrics, 86,* 87-90.

Hepler, B., Sutheimer, C., & Sunshine, I. (1986). Role of toxicology laboratory in suspected ingestions. *Pediatric Clinics of North America, 33,* 245-260.

Herndon, W. A. (1983). Child abuse in a military population. *Journal of Pediatric Orthopedics, 3*(1), 73-76.

Herzberger, S. D., & Tennen, H. (1988). Applying the label of physical abuse. In G. T. Hotaling, D. Finkelhor, J. T. Kirkpatrick, & M. A. Straus (Eds.), *Coping with family violence: Research and policy perspectives* (pp. 18-30). Newbury Park, CA: Sage.

Hight, D. W., Bakalar, H. R., & Lloyd, J. R. (1979). Inflicted burn in children: Recognition and treatment. *Journal of the American Medical Association, 242,* 517-520.

Himes, J. H., Roche, A. F., Thissen, D., & Moore, W. M. (1985). Parent-specific adjustments for evaluation of recumbent length and stature of children. *Pediatrics, 75,* 304-313.

Hiss, J., & Kahana, T. (1995). The medicolegal implications of bilateral cranial fractures in infants. *Journal of Trauma, 38,* 32-34.

Hobbs, C. J. (1984). Skull fracture and the diagnosis of abuse. *Archives of Diseases in Childhood, 59,* 246-252.

Hobbs, C. J., Hanks, H. G. I., & Wynne, J. M. (1993a). *Child abuse and neglect: A clinician's handbook.* New York: Churchill Livingstone.

Hobbs, C. J., Hanks, H. G. I., & Wynne, T. M. (1993b). Failure to thrive. In *Child abuse and neglect: A clinician's handbook* (pp. 17-45). New York: Churchill Livingstone.

Hodge, D., Schwartz, W., Sargent, J., Bodurtha, J., & Starr, S. (1982). The bacteriologically battered baby: Another case of Munchausen by proxy. *Annals of Emergency Medicine, 11*(4), 205-207.

Holton, J. B., et al. (1991). Inherited metabolic diseases in sudden infant death syndrome. *Archives of Diseases in Children, 66,* 1315-1317.

Homer, C., & Ludwig, S. (1981). Categorization of etiology of failure to thrive. *American Journal of Diseases of Children, 135,* 848-851.

Howing, P. T., & Wodarski, J. S. (1992). Legal requisites for social workers in child abuse and neglect situations. *Social Work, 37,* 330-335.

Hunt, C. E., & Brouillette, R. T. (1987). Sudden infant death syndrome: 1987 perspective. *Journal of Pediatrics, 110,* 669-678.

Hyman, I. (1990). *Reading, writing, and the hickory stick: The appalling story of physical and psychological abuse in American schools.* Lexington, MA: Lexington Books.

Hyman, I. A. (1994, March). *States which have abolished corporal punishment.* Philadelphia: The National Center for the Study of Corporal Punishment and Alternatives. (Affiliated with EPOCH-USA)

Hyman, I., & Lally, D. (1982). Discipline in the 1980's: Some alternatives to corporal punishment. *Children Today, 11*(1), 10-13.

Information on Civil Child Abuse and Neglect Statutes. (1993). Fairfax, VA: National Clearinghouse on Child Abuse and Neglect.

Information on Mandatory Reporting Laws. (1993). Alexandria, VA: American Prosecutors Research Institute.

Investigation and Prosecution of Child Abuse. (1993). Alexandria, VA: American Prosecutors Research Institute.

Jackson, D. M. (1953). The diagnosis of the depth of burning. *British Journal of Surgery, 40,* 588.

Joffe, M., & Ludwig, S. (1988). Stairway injuries in children. *Pediatrics, 82,* 457-461.

Johnson, C. F. (1990). Inflicted injury versus accidental injury. *Pediatric Clinics of North America, 37,* 791-814.

Johnson, C. F., & Coury, D. L. (1988). Bruising and hemophilia: Accident or child abuse? *Child Abuse & Neglect, 12,* 409-415.

Johnson, C. F., & Coury, D. L. (1992). Child neglect: General concepts and medical neglect. In S. Ludwig & A. E. Kornberg (Eds.), *Child abuse: A medical reference* (2nd ed., pp. 321-331). New York: Churchill Livingstone.

Johnson, C. F., & Showers, J. (1985). Injury variables in child abuse. *Child Abuse & Neglect, 9,* 207-215.

Jones, A. M., & Weston, J. T. (1976). The examination of the sudden infant death syndrome infant: Investigative and autopsy protocols. *Journal of Forensic Sciences, 21,* 833-841.

Justice, B., Calvert, A., & Justice, R. (1985). Factors mediating child abuse as a response to stress. *Child Abuse & Neglect, 9,* 359-363.

Justice, B., & Justice, R. (1976). *The abusing family.* New York: Human Sciences Press.

Kadushin, G., & Kulys, R. (1983). Discharge planning revisited: What do social workers actually do in discharge planning? *Social Work, 38,* 713-726.

Kahn, A., Blum, D., Rebuffat, E., Sottiau, M., Levitt, J., Bochner, A., Alexander, M., Grosswasser, J., & Muller, M. F. (1988). Polysomnographic studies of infants who subsequently died of sudden infant death syndrome. *Pediatrics, 82,* 721.

Kanter, R. K. (1985). Retinal hemorrhage after cardiopulmonary resuscitation or child abuse. *Journal of Pediatrics, 108,* 430-432.

Katcher, M. L. (1981). Scald burns from hot tap water. *Journal of the American Medical Association, 246,* 1219-1222.

Kaufman, J., & Ziegler, E. (1987). Do abused children become abusive parents? *American Journal of Orthopsychiatry, 57,* 186-192.

Kaufman, K. L., Coury, D., Pickrel, E., & McCleery, J. (1989). Munchausen syndrome by proxy: A survey of professionals' knowledge. *Child Abuse & Neglect, 13,* 141-147.

Keen, J. H., Lendrum, J., & Wolman, B. (1975). Inflicted burns and scalds in children. *British Medical Journal, 4,* 268-269.

Keens, T. G., & Davidson Ward, S. L. (1993). Apnea spells, sudden death, and the role of the apnea monitor. *Pediatric Clinics of North America, 40,* 897-911.

Kelly, T. (1989). Emotional support of the injured child. In J. Carrie (Ed.), *Pediatric trauma nursing* (pp. 223-243). Rockville, MD: Aspen.

Kemp, J. S., & Thach, B. T. (1991). Sudden death in infants sleeping on polystyrene-filled cushions. *New England Journal of Medicine, 324,* 1858-1864.

Kempe, R. S., Cutler, C., & Dean, J. (1980). The infant with failure-to-thrive. In C. H. Kempe & R. E. Helfer (Eds.), *The battered child* (3rd ed., pp. 163-182). Chicago: University of Chicago Press.

Kempe, R. S., & Goldbloom, R. B. (1987). Malnutrition and growth retardation ("failure to thrive") in the context of child abuse and neglect. In R. E. Helfer & R. S. Kempe (Eds.), *The battered child* (4th ed., pp. 312-335). Chicago: University of Chicago Press.

Kempe, R. S., Silverman, F. N., Steele, B. F., Droegmueller, W., & Silver, H. K. (1962). The battered child syndrome. *Journal of the American Medical Association, 181,* 17-24.

Kessler, D. B., & Hyden, P. (1991). Physical, sexual, and emotional abuse of children. *CIBA Foundation Symposium, 43*(2), 1-32.

Kleinman, P. K. (1987a). Bony thoracic trauma. In P. K. Kleinman (Ed.), *Diagnostic imaging of child abuse* (pp. 67-89). Baltimore: Williams and Wilkins.

Kleinman, P. K. (1987b). Extremity trauma. In P. K. Kleinman (Ed.), *Diagnostic imaging of child abuse* (pp. 29-66). Baltimore: Williams and Wilkins.

Kleinman, P. K. (1987c). Head trauma. In P. K. Kleinman (Ed.), *Diagnostic imaging of child abuse* (pp. 159-200). Baltimore: Williams and Wilkins.

Kleinman, P. K. (1987d). Skeletal trauma: General considerations. In P. K. Kleinman (Ed.), *Diagnostic imaging of child abuse* (pp. 5-28). Baltimore: Williams and Wilkins.

Kleinman, P. K. (1987e). Spinal trauma. In P. K. Kleinman (Ed.), *Diagnostic imaging of child abuse* (pp. 91-102). Baltimore: Williams and Wilkins.

Kleinman, P. K. (1987f). Visceral trauma. In P. K. Kleinman (Ed.), *Diagnostic imaging of child abuse* (pp. 115-158). Baltimore: Williams and Wilkins.

Kleinman, P. K., Blackbourne, B. D., Marks, S. C., Karellas, A., & Belanger, P. (1989). Radiologic contributions to the investigation and prosecution of cases of fatal infant abuse. *New England Journal of Medicine, 320,* 507-511.

Kleinman, P. K., Marks, S. C., & Blackbourne, B. (1986). The metaphyseal lesion in abused infants: A radiologic-histopathologic study. *American Journal of Radiology, 146,* 895-905.

Kleinman, P. K., Marks, S. C., Spevak, M. R., & Richmond, J. M. (1992). Fractures of the rib head in abused infants. *Radiology, 185*(1), 119-123.

Kleinman, P. K., & Spevak, M. R. (1992). Soft tissue swelling and acute skull fractures. *Journal of Pediatrics, 121,* 737-739.

Kogutt, M. S., Swischuk, L. E., & Fagan, C. J. (1974). Patterns of injury and significance of uncommon fractures in the battered child syndrome. *American Journal of Roentgenology, 121,* 143-149.

Korbin, J. E. (1987). Child abuse and neglect: The cultural context. In R. E. Helfer & R. S. Kempe (Eds.), *The battered child* (4th ed., pp. 23-41). Chicago: University of Chicago Press.

Kornberg, A. E. (1992). Skin and soft tissue injuries. In S. Ludwig & A. E. Kornberg (Eds.), *Child abuse: A medical reference* (2nd ed., pp. 91-104). New York: Churchill Livingstone.

Kriel, R. L., Krach, L. E., & Panser, L. A. (1989). Closed head injury: Comparison of children younger and older than 6 years of age. *Pediatric Neurology, 5,* 296-300.

Krischer, J. P., Fine, E. G., Davis, J. H., & Nagel, E. L. (1987). Complications of cardiac resuscitation. *Chest, 92,* 287-291.

Krugman, R. (1987). The assessment process of a child protection team. In R. E. Helfer & R. S. Kempe (Eds.), *The battered child* (4th ed., pp. 127-136). Chicago: University of Chicago Press.

Krugman, R. D. (1991). Closing remarks. In R. D. Krugman & J. M. Leventhal (Eds.), *Child sexual abuse: The twenty-second Ross roundtable on critical approaches to common pediatric problems* (pp. 100-101). Ross Laboratories: Columbus, OH.

Krugman, R. D. (1992). Commentary on child abuse and neglect. *Pediatric Annals, 21,* 475-476.

Lamphear, V. S. (1985). The impact of maltreatment on children's psychosocial adjustment: A review of the research. *Child Abuse & Neglect, 9,* 251-263.

Langlois, N. E. I., & Gresham, G. A. (1991). The aging of bruises: A review and study of the color changes with time. *Forensic Science International, 50,* 227-238.

Lazoritz, S. (1992). Child abuse: An historical perspective. In S. Ludwig & A. E. Kornberg (Eds.), *Child abuse: A medical reference* (2nd ed., pp. 85-90). New York: Churchill Livingstone.

Ledbetter, D. J., Hatch, E. I., Feldman, K. W., Ligner, C. L., & Tapper, D. (1988). Diagnostic and surgical implications of child abuse. *Archives of Surgery, 123,* 1101-1105.

Lenoski, E. F., & Hunter, K. A. (1977). Specific patterns of inflicted burn injuries. *Journal of Trauma, 17,* 842-846.

Leventhal, J. M. (1981). Risk factors for child abuse: Methodologic standards in case-control studies. *Pediatrics, 68,* 684-690.

Leventhal, J. M., Thomas, S. A., Rosenfield, N. S., & Markowitz, R. I. (1993). Fractures in young children: Distinguishing child abuse from unintentional injuries. *American Journal of Diseases of Children, 147,* 87-92.

Levin, A. (1990). Ocular manifestations of child abuse. *Ophthalmology Clinics of North America, 3,* 249-264.

Levin, H. S., Aldrich, E. F., Saydjari, C., Eisenberg, H. M., Foulkes, M. A., Bellefleur, M., Luerssen, T. G., Jane, J. A., Marmarou, A., & Marshall, L. F. (1992). Severe head injury in children: Experience of the Traumatic Coma Data Bank. *Neurosurgery, 31,* 435-444.

Levinson, D. (1989). *Family violence in cross-cultural perspective* (Vol. 1). Newbury Park, CA: Sage.

Liebert, R. M., & Wicks-Nelson, R. (1981). *Developmental psychology* (3rd ed.). Englewood Cliffs, NJ: Prentice Hall.

Light, R. J. (1973). Abused and neglected children in America: A study of alternative politics. *Harvard Educational Review, 43,* 556-598.

Ludwig, S. (1990). The abused patient: Family violence. In M. L. Callahan (Ed.), *Current therapy in emergency medicine* (2nd ed., pp. 319-323). Chicago: E. B. Decker.

Ludwig, S. (1992a). Defining child abuse. In S. Ludwig & A. E. Kornberg (Eds.), *Child abuse: A medical reference* (2nd ed., pp. 1-12). New York: Churchill Livingstone.

Ludwig, S. (1992b). Failure to thrive/starvation. In S. Ludwig & A. E. Kornberg (Eds.), *Child abuse: A medical reference* (pp. 303-320). New York: Churchill Livingstone.

Ludwig, S. (1993). Psychosocial emergencies: Child abuse. In G. R. Fleisher & S. Ludwig (Eds.), *Textbook of pediatric emergency medicine* (3rd ed., pp. 1429-1463). Baltimore: Williams and Wilkins.

Ludwig, S., & Rostain, A. (1992). Family function and dysfunction. In M. D. Levine, W. B. Carey, & A. C. Crocker (Eds.), *Developmental behavioral pediatrics* (2nd ed., pp. 147-159). Philadelphia: W. B. Saunders.

Ludwig, S., & Warman, M. (1984). Shaken baby syndrome: A review of 20 cases. *Annals of Emergency Medicine, 13,* 104-107.

Lyons, T. J., & Oates, K. (1993). Falling out of bed: A relatively benign occurrence. *Pediatrics, 92,* 125-127.

Malatack, H. H., Wiener, E. S., Gartner, J. C., Zitelli, B. J., & Brunetti, E. (1985). Munchausen syndrome by proxy: A new complication of central venous catheterization. *Pediatrics, 75,* 523-525.

Marino, T. A., & Langston, C. (1982). Cardiac trauma and the conduction system. *Archives of Pathology Laboratory Medicine, 106*, 173-174.

Martin, J. A., & Elmer, E. (1992). Battered children grow up: A follow-up study of individuals severely maltreated as children. *Child Abuse & Neglect, 16*, 75-87.

Martin, S. R., & Walker, W. A. (1990). Vasculitus. In F. A. Oski, C. D. DeAngelis, R. D. Feigin, & J. B. Warshaw (Eds.), *Principles and practice of pediatrics* (pp. 1720-1722). Philadelphia: J. B. Lippincott.

Maternal and Child Health Bureau. (1994). *Child Health USA '94* (DHHS Publication No. HRSA-MCH-94-1). Washington, DC: Government Printing Office.

McClain, P. W., Sacks, J. J., Ewigman, B. G., Smith, S. M., Mercy, J. A., & Sniezek, J. E. (1994). Geographic patterns of fatal abuse or neglect in children younger than 5 years old, United States, 1979-1988. *Archives of Pediatric and Adolescent Medicine, 148*, 82-86.

McClain, P. W., Sacks, J. J., Froehlke, R. G., & Ewigman, B. G. (1993). Estimates of fatal child abuse and neglect, United States, 1979 through 1988. *Pediatrics, 91*, 338-343.

McClelland, C. Q., Rekate, H., Kaufman, B., & Persse, L. (1980). Cerebral injury in child abuse: A changing profile. *Child's Brain, 7*, 225-235.

McCormick, K. F. (1992). Attitudes of primary care physicians toward corporal punishment. *Journal of the American Medical Association, 267*, 3161-3165.

McCort, J., & Vaudagna, J. (1964). Visceral injuries in battered children. *Radiology, 82*, 424-428.

McCullock Melnyk, K. A. (1988). Barriers: A critical review of recent literature. *Nursing Research, 37*(4), 196-200.

McCurd, K., & Daro, D. (1993). *Current trends in child abuse reporting and fatalities: The results of the 1992 annual fifty state survey.* Chicago: National Committee for Prevention of Child Abuse.

McDowell, H. P., & Fielding, D. W. (1984). Traumatic perforation of the hypopharynx: An unusual form of abuse. *Archives of Diseases of Childhood, 59*, 888-889.

McEniery, J., Hanson, R., Grigor, W., & Horowitz, A. (1991). Lung injury resulting from a nonaccidental crush injury to the chest. *Pediatric Emergency Care, 7*, 166-168.

McGuire, T. L., & Feldman, K. W. (1989). Psychologic morbidity of children subjected to Munchausen syndrome by proxy. *Pediatrics, 83*, 289-292.

McIntosh, T. K. (1992). Pharmacologic strategies in the treatment of experimental brain injuries. *Journal of Neurotrauma, 9*(Suppl. 1), S201-S209.

McLaurin, R. L., Isaacs, E., & Lewis, H. P. (1971). Results of nonoperative treatment in 15 cases of infantile subdural hematoma. *Journal of Neurosurgery, 34*, 753-759.

Meadow, R. (1977). Munchausen syndrome by proxy: The hinterland of child abuse. *Lancet, 2*, 343-345.

Meadow, R. (1990). Suffocation, recurrent apnea, and sudden infant death. *Journal of Pediatrics, 117*, 351-357.

Meadow, R. (1993). False allegations of abuse and Munchausen syndrome by proxy. *Archives of Disease in Childhood, 68*, 444-447.

Meagher, D. P. (1990). Burns. In J. G. Raffensperger (Ed.), *Swenson's pediatric surgery* (5th ed., pp. 317-337). Norwalk, CT: Appleton & Lange.

Mellick, L. B., & Reesor, K. (1990). Spiral tibial fractures of children: A commonly accidental spiral long bone fracture. *American Journal of Emergency Medicine, 8*(3), 234-237.

Mellion, B. T., & Narayan, R. K. (1992). Delayed traumatic intracerebral hematomas and coagulopathies. In D. Barrow (Ed.), *Complications and sequelae of head injury* (pp. 51-60). Park Ridge, IL: American Association of Neurologic Surgeons.

Merten, D. F., Cooperman, D. R., & Thompson, G. H. (1994). In R. M. Reece (Ed.), *Child abuse: Medical diagnosis and management* (pp. 23-53). Malvern, PA: Lea & Febiger.

Merten, D. F., & Osborne, D. R. S. (1984). Craniocerebral trauma in the child abuse syndrome: Radiological observations. *Pediatric Radiology, 14*, 272-277.

Merten, D. F., Radkowski, M. A., & Leonidas, J. C. (1983). The abused child: A radiological reappraisal. *Radiology, 146*, 377-381.

Meservy, C. J., Towbin, R., McLaurin, R. L., Myers, P. A., & Ball, W. (1987). Radiographic characteristics of skull fractures resulting from child abuse. *American Journal of Radiology, 149*, 173-175.

Meyer, F. B., Sundt, T. M., Fode, N. C., Morgan, M. K., Forbes, G. S., & Mellinger, J. F. (1989). Cerebral aneurysms in childhood and adolescence. *Journal of Neurosurgery, 70*, 420-425.

Miller, S. K. (1987). *Workbook on child abuse*. Philadelphia: Children's Hospital of Philadelphia.

Mollison, P. L. (1993). *Blood transfusions in clinical medicine* (9th ed., pp. 157-158). London: Blackwell Scientific.

Moritz, A. R., & Henriques, F. C. (1947). Studies of thermal injury: The relative importance of time and surface temperature in the causation of cutaneous burns. *American Journal of Pathology, 23*, 695-720.

Mukerji, S. K., & Siegel, M. J. (1987). Rhabdomyolysis and renal failure in child abuse. *American Journal of Radiology, 148*, 1203-1204.

Mulford, R. M. (1979). Protective services for children. In *Encyclopedia of social work*. Washington, DC: National Association of Social Workers.

Musemeche, C. A., Barthel, M., Cosentino, C., & Reynolds, M. (1991). Pediatric falls from heights. *Journal of Trauma, 31*, 1347-1349.

Myers, J. E. B. (1992a). *Evidence in child abuse and neglect cases, Vol. 2* (2nd ed., pp. 79-321). New York: Wiley.

Myers, J. E. B. (1992b). *Legal issues in child abuse and neglect*. Newbury Park, CA: Sage.

Myers, J. E. B., & Carter, L. E. (1988). Proof of physical child abuse. *Missouri Law Review, 53*, 189-225.

Myers, J. E. B., & Peters, W. D. (1987). Child abuse reporting in the 1980s. *The American Humane Society*, pp. 6-14.

National Center on Child Abuse and Neglect. (1981). *Study findings: Study of national incidence and prevalence of child abuse and neglect*. Washington, DC: U.S. Department of Health and Human Services.

National Center on Child Abuse and Neglect. (1988a). *Child neglect: A guide for intervention*. Washington, DC: U.S. Department of Health and Human Services.

National Center on Child Abuse and Neglect. (1988b). *Study findings: Study of national incidence and prevalence of child abuse and neglect*. Washington, DC: U.S. Department of Health and Human Services.

National Center on Child Abuse and Neglect. (1992a). *Child protective services: A guide for caseworkers* (DHHS Publication No. HHS 105-88-1702). Washington, DC: Government Printing Office.

National Center on Child Abuse and Neglect. (1992b). *A coordinated response to child abuse and neglect: A basic manual* (DHHS Publication No. ACF 92 30362). Washington, DC: Government Printing Office.

National Center on Child Abuse and Neglect. (1993). *National child abuse and neglect data system: Working paper 2—1991 summary data component*. Washington, DC: Government Printing Office.

Needleman, H. L. (1986). Orofacial trauma in child abuse: Types, prevalence, management, and the dental profession's involvement. *Pediatric Dentistry, 8*(SI1), 71-79.

Nelson, F. P. (1991). Corporal punishment versus child abuse. *AAP News*, p. 17.

Newberger, C. M., & Newberger, E. H. (1981). The etiology of child abuse. In N. S. Ellerstein (Ed.), *Child abuse and neglect* (pp. 11-20). New York: Wiley.

Newberger, E. H., & Hyde, J. N. (1975). Child abuse: Principles and implications of current pediatric practice. *Pediatric Clinics of North America, 22*, 695-699.

Nimityongskul, P., & Anderson, L. D. (1987). The likelihood of injuries when children fall out of bed. *Journal of Pediatric Orthopedics, 7*, 184-186.

Oates, K. (1982). *Child abuse—A community concern*. New York: Brunner/Mazel.

O'Connor, J. F., & Cohen, J. (1987). Dating fractures. In P. K. Kleinman (Ed.), *Diagnostic imaging of child abuse* (pp. 103-113). Baltimore: Williams and Wilkins.

Ogden, J. A. (1990). *Skeletal injury in the child* (2nd ed.). Philadelphia: W. B. Saunders.

Ommaya, A. K., Faas, F., & Yarnell, P. (1968). Whiplash injury and brain damage: An experimental study. *Journal of American Medical Association, 204*, 285-289.

Ommaya, A. K., & Gennarelli, T. A. (1974). Cerebral concussion and traumatic unconsciousness: Correlation of experimental and clinical observations on blunt head injuries. *Brain, 97*, 633-654.

Ommaya, A. K., & Yarnell, P. (1962). Subdural hematoma after whiplash injury. *Lancet, 2*, 237-239.

O'Neill, J. A. (1979). Burns in children. In C. P. Artz, J. A. Moncrief, & B. A. Pruitt (Eds.), *Burns: A team approach* (pp. 341-350). Philadelphia: W. B. Saunders.

O'Neill, J. A., Meacham, W. F., Griffin, P. P., & Sawyers, J. L. (1973). Patterns of injury in the battered child syndrome. *Journal of Trauma, 13*, 332-339.

Oren, J., Kelly, D., & Shannon, D. C. (1986). Identification of a high-risk group for sudden infant death syndrome among infants who were resuscitated for sleep apnea. *Pediatrics, 77,* 495-499.

Orenstein, D. M., & Wasserman, A. L. (1986). Munchausen syndrome by proxy simulating cystic fibrosis. *Pediatrics, 78,* 621-624.

Oski, F. A., DeAngelis, C. D., Feigin, R. D., & Warshaw, J. B. (1990). *Principles and practice of pediatrics.* Philadelphia: J. B. Lippincott.

Pang, D., & Pollack, I. F. (1989). Spinal cord injury without radiographic abnormality in children—the SCIWORA syndrome. *Journal of Trauma, 29,* 654-664.

Parent, A. D. (1992). Pediatric chronic subdural hematoma: A retrospective comparative analysis. *Pediatric Neurosurgery, 18,* 266-271.

Parish, R. A., Myers, P. A., Brandner, A., & Templin, K. H. (1985). Developmental milestones in abused children, and their improvement with a family-oriented approach to the treatment of child abuse. *Child Abuse & Neglect, 9,* 245-250.

Pascoe, J. M., Hildebrandt, H. M., Tarrier, A., & Murphy, M. (1979). Patterns of skin injury in nonaccidental and accidental injury. *Pediatrics, 64,* 245-247.

Pearson, H. A. (1983). Diseases of blood. In R. E. Behrman, V. C. Vaughn, & W. E. Nelson (Eds.), *Nelson textbook of pediatrics* (12th ed., pp. 1204-1257). Philadelphia: W. B. Saunders.

Pelton, L. H. (1978). Child abuse and neglect: The myth of classlessness. *American Journal of Orthopsychiatry, 48,* 608-617.

Pena, S. D. J., & Medovy, H. (1973). Child abuse and traumatic pseudocyst of the pancreas. *Journal of Pediatrics, 83,* 1026-1028.

Peterson, D. R. (1988). Clinical implications of sudden infant death syndrome epidemiology. *Pediatrician, 15*(4), 198-203.

Peterson, K. E., Rathbun, J. M., & Huerrera, M. A. (1985). Growth rate analysis in failure to thrive treatment & research. In D. Drotar (Ed.), *New directions in failure to thrive: Implications for research and practice.* New York: Plenum.

Peterson, M. S., & Urquiza, A. J. (1993). *The role of mental health professionals in the prevention and treatment of child abuse and neglect.* Washington, DC: U.S. Department of Health and Human Services.

Pless, J. E. (1983). The story of Baby Doe. *New England Journal of Medicine, 309,* 664.

Pokorny, N. J. (1990). Hemangioma. In F. A. Oski, C. D. DeAngelis, R. D. Feigin, & J. B. Warshaw (Eds.), *Principles and practice of pediatrics* (pp. 1609-1611). Philadelphia: J. B. Lippincott.

Ponsonby, A. L., Dwyer, T., Gibbons, L. E., Cochrane, J. A., Jones, M. E., & McCall, M. J. (1992). Thermal environment and sudden infant death syndrome: Case-control study. *British Medical Journal, 304*(6822), 277-282.

Poole, S. R., Ushkow, M. C., Nader, P. R., Bradford, B. J., Asbury, J. R., Worthington, D. C., Sanabria, K. E., & Carruth, T. (1991). The role of the pediatrician in abolishing corporal punishment in schools: Committee on school health, American Academy of Pediatrics. *Pediatrics, 88,* 162-167.

Prader, A., Tanner, J. M., & von Harnack, G. A. (1963). Catch-up growth following illness or starvation. *Journal of Pediatrics, 62,* 646-689.

Press, S., Grant, P., Thompson, V. T., & Milles, K. L. (1991). Small bowel evisceration: Unusual manifestation of child abuse. *Pediatrics, 88,* 807-809.

Purdue, G. F., & Hunt, J. L. (1992). Burn injuries. In S. Ludwig & A. E. Kornberg (Eds.), *Child abuse: A medical reference* (2nd ed., pp. 105-116). New York: Churchill Livingstone.

Purdue, G. F., Hunt, J. L., & Prescott, P. R. (1988). Child abuse by burning—An index of suspicion. *Journal of Trauma, 28,* 221-224.

Quinby, W. C. (1966). Fractures of the pelvis and associated injuries in children. *Journal of Pediatric Surgery, 1,* 353-364.

Radbill, S. X. (1987). Children in a world of violence: A history of child abuse. In R. E. Helfer & R. S. Kempe (Eds.), *The battered child* (4th ed., pp. 3-22). Chicago: University of Chicago Press.

Rapaport, S. I. (1983). Preoperative hemostatic evaluation: Which tests, if any? *Blood, 61,* 229-231.

Reece, R. M. (1993). Fatal child abuse and sudden infant death syndrome: A critical diagnostic decision. *Pediatrics, 91,* 423-429.

Rees, A., Symons, J., Joseph, M., & Lincoln, C. (1975). Ventricular septal defect in a battered child. *British Medical Journal, 1,* 20-21.

Ricci, L. R. (1991). Photographing the physically abused child. *American Journal of Diseases of Children, 145,* 275-281.

Richardson, A. C. (1994). Cutaneous manifestations of abuse. In R. M. Reece (Ed.), *Child abuse: Medical diagnosis and management* (pp. 167-184). Philadelphia: Lea & Febiger.

Rimer, R. L., & Roy, S. (1977). Child abuse and hemoglobinuria. *Journal of American Medical Association, 238,* 2034-2035.

Rivara, F. P., Parrish, R. A., & Mueller, B. A. (1986). Extremity injuries in children: Predictive value of clinical findings. *Pediatrics, 78,* 803-807.

Robson, M. C., & Heggers, J. P. (1988). Pathophysiology of the burn wound. In H. F. Carvajal & D. H. Parks (Eds.), *Burns in children: Pediatric burn management* (pp. 27-32). Chicago: Year Book.

Rogers, D. W., & Bentovim, A. (1981). Nonaccidental poisoning: The elusive diagnosis. *Archives of Diseases in Childhood, 56,* 156-157.

Rose, M., & Schwartz, R. (1992). Civil and criminal judicial intervention. In S. Ludwig & A. E. Kornberg (Eds.), *Child abuse: A medical reference* (2nd ed., pp. 423-440). New York: Churchill Livingstone.

Rosenberg, D. A. (1987). Web of deceit: A literature review of Munchausen syndrome by proxy. *Child Abuse & Neglect, 11,* 547-563.

Rosenberg, N. M., Singer, J., Bolte, R., Christian, C., & Selbst, S. M. (1994). Retinal hemorrhage. *Pediatric Emergency Care, 10,* 303-305.

Rosenthal, P. A., & Doherty, M. D. (1984). Serious sibling abuse by preschool children. *Journal of American Academy of Child Psychiatry, 23,* 186-190.

Sameroff, A., & Abbe, L. (1978). The consequences of prematurity: Understanding and therapy. In H. Pick (Ed.), *Psychology: From research to practice.* New York: Plenum.

Sandler, A. P., & Haynes, V. (1978). Nonaccidental trauma and medical folk belief: A case of cupping. *Pediatrics, 61,* 921-922.

Satler, E. (1990). Childhood feeding problems. In *Feelings and their medical significance.* Columbus, OH: Ross Laboratories.

Sato, Y., Yuh, W. T. C., Smith, W. L., Alexander, R. C., Kao, S. C. S., & Ellerbroek, C. J. (1989). Head injury in child abuse: Evaluation with MR imaging. *Radiology, 173,* 653-657.

Saulsbury, F. T., & Hayden, G. F. (1985). Skin conditions simulating child abuse. *Pediatric Emergency Care, 1,* 147-150.

Saywitz, K. J. (1990). Developmental considerations for forensic interviewing. *The Interviewer, 3*(2), 2, 5, 15.

Schechner, S. A., & Ehrlich, F. E. (1974). Gastric perforation and child abuse. *Journal of Trauma, 14,* 723-725.

Schmitt, B. D., Gray, J. D., & Britton, H. L. (1978). Car seat burns in infants: Avoiding confusion with inflicted burns. *Pediatrics, 62,* 607.

Schmitt, B. D., Grosz, C. A., & Carroll, C. A. (1976). The child protection team: A problem oriented approach. In R. E. Helfer & C. H. Kempe (Eds.), *Child abuse and neglect: The family and the community* (pp. 91-113). Cambridge, MA: Ballinger.

Schmitt, B. D., & Krugman, R. D. (1992). In R. E. Behrman, R. M. Kliegman, W. E. Nelson, & V. C. Vaughan (Eds.), *Nelson textbook of pediatrics* (14th ed., pp. 78-83). Philadelphia: W. B. Saunders.

Schmitt, B. D., & Mauro, R. D. (1989). Nonorganic failure to thrive: An outpatient approach. *Child Abuse & Neglect, 13,* 235-248.

Schreier, H. A., & Libow, J. A. (1993). *Hurting for love: Munchausen by proxy syndrome.* New York: Guilford.

Schulz, K. F., Murphy, F. K., Patamasucon, P., & Meheus, A. Z. (1990). Congenital syphilis. In K. K. Holmes, P. A. Mardh, P. F. Sparling, P. J. Wiesner, W. Cates, S. Lemon, & W. Stamm (Eds.), *Sexually transmitted diseases* (2nd ed., pp. 821-842). New York: McGraw-Hill.

Schwartz, A. J., & Ricci, L. R. (1996). How accurately can bruises be aged in abused children? Literature review and synthesis. *Pediatrics, 97,* 254-256.

Schwartz, P. J. (1987). The quest for the mechanisms for the sudden infant death syndrome: Doubts and progress. *Circulation, 75,* 677.

Schweich, P., & Fleisher, G. (1985). Rib fractures in children. *Pediatric Emergency Care, 1,* 187-189.

Schwengel, D., & Ludwig, S. (1985). Rhabdomyolysis and myoglobinuria as manifestations of child abuse. *Pediatric Emergency Care, 1*(4), 194-197.

Selbst, S. M., Baker, M. D., & Shames, M. (1990). Bunk bed injuries. *American Journal of Diseases of Children, 144*, 721-723.

Selye, H. (1956). *The stress of life*. New York: McGraw-Hill.

Sezen, F. (1970). Retinal hemorrhage in newborn infants. *British Journal of Ophthalmology, 55*, 248.

Showers, J., & Garrison, K. M. (1988). Burn abuse: A four-year study. *Journal of Trauma, 28*, 1581-1583.

Sibert, J. R., & Murphy, J. F. (1980). Child poisoning and child abuse. *Archives of Diseases in Childhood, 55*, 822.

Silence, D. O. (1983). Abnormalities of density or modeling of skeleton. In R. E. Behrman & V. C. Vaughan (Eds.), *Nelson textbook of pediatrics* (pp. 1645-1650). Philadelphia: W. B. Saunders.

Silence, D. O. (1988). Osteogenesis imperfecta nosology and genetics. *Annals of the New York Academy of Science, 543*, 1-15.

Silence, D. O., Barlow, K. K., Cole, W. G., Dietrich, S., Garber, A. P., & Rimoin, D. L. (1986). Osteogenesis imperfecta type III: Delineation of the phenotype with reference to genetic heterogeneity. *American Journal of Medical Genetics, 23*, 821-832.

Sills, R. H. (1978). Failure to thrive: The role of clinical and laboratory evaluation. *American Journal of Diseases of Children, 132*, 967-969.

Silver, L. B., Dublin, C. C., & Lourie, R. S. (1969). Child abuse syndrome: The "gray areas" in establishing a diagnosis. *Pediatrics, 44*, 594-600.

Silverman, F. N. (1953). The roentgen manifestations of unrecognized skeletal trauma in infants. *American Journal of Roentgenology, 69*, 413-426.

Sivit, C. J., Taylor, G. A., & Eichelberger, M. R. (1989). Visceral injury in battered children: A changing perspective. *Radiology, 173*, 659-661.

Slakieu, K. A. (1990). Crisis theory: A general framework. In K. A. Slakieu (Ed.), *Crisis intervention: A handbook for practice and research* (2nd ed., pp. 14-41). Needham Heights, MA: Allyn & Bacon.

Smialek, J. E., & Lambros, Z. (1988). Investigation of sudden infant deaths. *Pediatrician, 15*(4), 191-197.

Smialek, J. E., Smialek, P. Z., & Spitz, W. U. (1977). Accidental bed deaths in infants due to unsafe sleeping situations. *Clinical Pediatrics, 16*, 1031-1036.

Smistek, B. S. (1992). Photography of the abused and neglected child. In S. Ludwig & A. E. Kornberg (Eds.), *Child abuse: A medical reference* (pp. 467-477). New York: Churchill Livingstone.

Smith, N. J., & Ardern, M. H. (1989). More in sickness than in health: A case study of Munchausen by proxy in the elderly. *Journal of Family Therapy, 11*, 321-334.

Snyder, J. C., Hampton, R., & Newberger, E. H. (1983). Family dysfunction: Violence, neglect, and sexual misuse. In M. D. Levine, W. B. Carey, A. C. Crocker, & R. T. Gross (Eds.), *Developmental-behavioral pediatrics* (pp. 256-275). Philadelphia: W. B. Saunders.

Society for Adolescent Medicine. (1992). Corporal punishment in schools: A position paper of the Society for Adolescent Medicine. *Journal of Adolescent Health, 13*, 240-246.

Socolar, R. R. S., & Stein, R. E. K. (1995). Spanking infants and toddlers: Maternal belief and practice. *Pediatrics, 95*, 105-111.

Sognnaes, R. D. (1977). Forensic stomatology. *New England Journal of Medicine, 296*, 197-203.

Solomon, S. M., & Kirby, D. F. (1990). The refeeding syndrome: A review. *Journal of Parental and Enteral Nutrition, 14*, 90-97.

Solomon, T. (1973). History and demography of child abuse. *Pediatrics, 51*, 773-776.

Spevak, M. R., Kleinman, P. K., Belanger, P. L., Primack, C., & Richmond, J. M. (1994). Cardiopulmonary resuscitation and rib fractures in infants: A postmortem radiologic-pathologic study. *Journal of the American Medical Society, 272*, 617-618.

Spitz, R. A. (1945). Hospitalism: An inquiry into the genesis of psychiatric conditions in early childhood. *Psychoanalytic Study of the Child, 1*, 53-74.

Spitz, R. A. (1949). The role of ecological factors in emotional development in infancy. *Child Development, 20*(3), 145-155.

Sroufe, L. A., & Rutter, M. (1984). The domain of developmental psychopathology. *Child Development, 55*, 17-29.

Stanton, A. N., Scott, D. J., & Downham, M. A. P. S. (1980). Is overheating a factor in some unexpected infant deaths? *Lancet, 1*, 1054-1057.

Starr, R. H., Dubowitz, H., & Bush, B. A. (1990). The epidemiology of child maltreatment. In R. T. Ammerman & M. Hersen (Eds.), *Children at risk: An evaluation of factors contributing to child abuse and neglect* (pp. 23-51). New York: Plenum.

Statutory Compilations on Immunity for Mandated Reporters. (1993). Alexandria, VA: American Prosecutors Research Institute.

Statutory Compilations on Penalties for Failure to Report Child Abuse. (1993). Alexandria, VA: American Prosecutors Research Institute.

Steele, B. (1987). Psychodynamic factors in child abuse. In R. E. Helfer & R. S. Kempe (Eds.), *The battered child* (4th ed., pp. 81-114). Chicago: University of Chicago Press.

Stone, N. H., Rinaldo, L., Humphrey, C. R., & Brown, R. H. (1970). *Surgical Clinics of North America, 50,* 1419-1424.

Strait, R. T., Siegel, R. M., & Shapiro, R. A. (1995). Humeral fractures without obvious etiologies in children less than three years of age: When is it abuse? *Pediatrics, 96,* 667-671.

Straus, M. A. (1987). Is violence toward children increasing? A comparison of 1975 and 1985 national survey rates. In R. J. Gelles (Ed.), *Family violence* (2nd ed., pp. 78-88). Newbury Park, CA: Sage.

Straus, M. A., & Gelles, R. J. (1986). Societal change and change in family violence from 1975 to 1985 as related to two national surveys. *Journal of Marriage and the Family, 48,* 465-479.

Straus, M. A., & Gelles, R. J. (1988). How violent are American families? Estimates from the National Family Violence Survey and other studies. In G. T. Hotaling, D. Finkelhor, J. T. Kirkpatrick, & M. A. Straus (Eds.), *Family abuse and its consequences: New directions in research* (pp. 14-36). Newbury Park, CA: Sage.

Straus, M. A., Gelles, R. J., & Steinmetz, S. K. (1980). *Behind closed doors: Violence in American families.* Garden City, NY: Anchor.

Straus, M. A., & Kantor, G. K. (1987). Stress & child abuse. In R. E. Helfer & R. S. Kempe (Eds.), *The battered child.* Chicago: University of Chicago Press.

Subcommittee on 10th edition of the RDAs. (1989). *Recommended dietary allowances* (10th ed., p. 33). Washington, DC: National Academy Press.

Sussman, S. J. (1968). Skin manifestations of the battered child syndrome. *Journal of Pediatrics, 72,* 99-101.

Taitzs, L. S. (1987). Child abuse and osteogenesis imperfecta. *British Medical Journal, 295,* 1082-1083.

Tanner, J. M., Goldstein, H., & Whitehouse, P. H. (1970). Standards for children's height at age 2-9 years allowing for height of parents. *Archives of Diseases of Childhood, 45,* 755-762.

Thaler, M. M., & Krause, V. W. (1962). Serious trauma in children after external cardiac massage. *New England Journal of Medicine, 267,* 500-501.

Thomas, M., & Cameron, A. (1977). Rarity of non-accidental penetrating injury in child abuse. *British Medical Journal, 3,* 375-376.

Thomas, S. A., Rosenfield, N. S., Leventhal, J. M., & Markowitz, R. I. (1991). Long-bone fractures in young children: Distinguishing accidental injuries from child abuse. *Pediatrics, 88,* 471-476.

Tokoro, K., Nakajima, F., & Yamataki, A. (1988). Infantile chronic subdural hematoma with local protrusion of the skull in a case of osteogenesis imperfecta. *Neurosurgery, 22,* 595-598.

Tracy, T., O'Connor, T. P., & Weber, T. R. (1993). Battered children with duodenal avulsion and transection. *American Surgeon, 59,* 342-345.

Tunnessen, W. W. (1985). The girl with blue hands. *Contemporary Pediatrics, 2,* 55.

Tunnessen, W. W. (1988). *Signs & symptoms in pediatrics* (2nd ed.). Philadelphia: J. B. Lippincott.

Tunnessen, W. W. (1990). Pediatric dermatology. In F. A. Oski, C. D. DeAngelis, R. D. Feigin, & J. B. Warshaw (Eds.), *Principles and practice of pediatrics* (pp. 825-875). Philadelphia: J. B. Lippincott.

U.S. Department of Health and Human Services. (1995). *A report on the maltreatment of children with disabilities.* James Bell Associates, Inc., No. 105-89-16300. Washington, DC: Westat, Inc.

Valdez-Dapena, M. A., Greene, M., Basavanand, N., Catherman, R., & Truex, R. C. (1973). The myocardial conduction system in sudden death in infancy. *New England Journal of Medicine, 289,* 1179-1180.

Valentine, D. P., Acuff, D. S., Freeman, M. L., & Andreas, T. (1984). Defining child maltreatment: A multidisciplinary overview. *Child Welfare, 63,* 497-509.

Vowles, G. H., Scholtz, C. L., & Cameron, J. M. (1987). Diffuse axonal injury in early infancy. *Journal of Clinical Pathology, 40,* 185-189.

Wagner, G. N. (1986). Bitemark identification in child abuse cases. *Pediatric Dentistry, 8*(SI1), 96-100.

Walton, W. W. (1982). An evaluation of the Poison Prevention Packaging Act. *Pediatrics, 69,* 363-370.

Warner, J. E., & Hansen, D. J. (1994). The identification and reporting of physical abuse by physicians: A review and implications for research. *Child Abuse & Neglect, 18,* 11-25.

Wenstrop, R. J., Willing, M. C., Starman, B. J., & Byers, P. H. (1990). Distinct biochemical phenotypes predict clinical severity in nonlethal variants of osteogenesis imperfecta. *American Journal of Human Genetics, 46,* 975-982.

Wessel, M. A. (1980). The pediatrician and corporal punishment. *Pediatrics, 66,* 639-641.

West, M. P., & Yunghans, S. C. (1994). *Report of the Pennsylvania child fatality review task force.* Philadelphia: American Academy of Pediatrics.

Wetzel, R. C., Slater, A. J., & Dover, G. J. (1995). Fatal intramuscular bleeding misdiagnosed as suspected nonaccidental injury. *Pediatrics, 95,* 771-773.

White, R., Benedict, M. I., Wulff, L., & Kelly, M. (1987). Physical disabilities as risk factors for child maltreatment: A selected review. *Physical Disabilities, 57,* 93-101.

Whittaker, D. K. (1990). The principles of forensic dentistry: Two non-accidental injury, bite marks and archaeology. *Dental Update, 17,* 386-390.

Whyte, K. M., & Pascoe, M. (1989). Does "black" brain mean doom? Computed tomography in the prediction of outcome in children with severe head injuries: "Benign" vs. "malignant" brain swelling. *Australasian Radiology, 33,* 344-347.

Widom, C. S. (1989a). Child abuse, neglect, and adult behavior: Research design and findings on criminality, violence, and child abuse. *American Journal of Orthopsychiatry, 59,* 355-367.

Widom, C. S. (1989b). The cycle of violence. *Science, 244,* 160-166.

Wilde, J. A., & Pedroni, A. T. (1993). Privacy rights in Munchausen syndrome. *Contemporary Pediatrics, 12*(11), 83-91.

Wiley, J. F. (1991). Difficult diagnoses in toxicology: Poisons not detected by comprehensive drug screen. *Pediatric Clinics of North America, 38,* 725-737.

Wilkinson, W. S., Han, D. P., Rappley, M. D., & Owings, C. L. (1989). Retinal hemorrhage predicts neurologic injury in the shaking baby syndrome. *Archives of Ophthalmology, 107,* 1472-1474.

Williams, R. A. (1991). Injuries in infants and small children resulting from witnessed and corroborated free falls. *Journal of Trauma, 31,* 1350-1352.

Willinger, M., Hoffman, H. J., & Hartford, R. B. (1994). Infant sleep position and risk for sudden infant death syndrome: Report of meeting held January 13 and 14, 1994, National Institutes of Health, Bethesda, MD. *Pediatrics, 93,* 814-819.

Willinger, M., James, L. S., & Catz, C. (1991). Defining the sudden infant death syndrome (SIDS): Deliberations of an expert panel convened by the national institute of child health and human development. *Pediatric Pathology, 11,* 677-684.

Wilson, E. F. (1977). Estimation of the age of cutaneous contusions in child abuse. *Pediatrics, 60,* 750-752.

Wilson, E. P. (1992). Multidisciplinary approach to child protection. In S. Ludwig & A. E. Kornberg (Eds.), *Child abuse: A medical reference* (pp. 79-84). New York: Churchill Livingstone.

Wissow, L. S. (1990a). *Child advocacy for the clinician: An approach to child abuse and neglect.* Baltimore: Williams & Wilkins.

Wissow, L. S. (1990b). Child maltreatment. In F. A. Oski, C. D. DeAngelis, R. D. Feigin, & J. B. Warshaw (Eds.), *Principles & practice of pediatrics* (pp. 589-605). Philadelphia: J. B. Lippincott.

Wodarski, J. S., Kurtz, P. D., Gaudin, J. M., & Howing, P. T. (1990). Maltreatment and the school-age child: Major academic, socioemotional, and adaptive outcomes. *Social Work, 35,* 506-513.

Wolock, I., & Horowitz, B. (1984). Child maltreatment as a social problem: The neglect of neglect. *American Journal of Orthopsychiatry, 54,* 530-543.

Woolley, M. M., Mahour, G. H., & Sloan, T. (1978). Duodenal hematoma in infancy and childhood: Changing etiology and changing treatment. *American Journal of Surgery, 136,* 8-14.

Yeatman, G. W., & Dang, V. V. (1980). Cao gio (coin rubbing): Vietnamese attitudes toward health care. *Journal of the American Medical Association, 244,* 2748.

Ziegler, D. W., Long, J. A., Philippart, A. I., & Klein, M. D. (1988). Pancreatitis in childhood: Experience with 49 patients. *Annals of Surgery, 207,* 257-261.

Zimmerman, R. A., Bilaniuk, L. T., Bruce, D., Schut, L., Uzzell, B., & Goldberg, H. I. (1979). Computed tomography of craniocerebral injury in the abused child. *Radiology, 130,* 687-690.

Zinn, A. (1994). Genetic disorders that mimic child abuse or sudden infant death syndrome. In R. M. Reece (Ed.), *Child abuse: Medical diagnosis and management* (pp. 404-429). Philadelphia: Lea & Febiger.

Zitelli, B. J., Seltman, M. F., & Shannon, R. M. (1987). Munchausen's syndrome by proxy and its professional participants. *American Journal of Diseases of Children, 141,* 1099-1102.

Zuravin, S. J. (1989). The ecology of child abuse and neglect: Review of literature and presentation of data. *Violence and Victims, 4*(2), 101-120.

Index

Growth:
    measurement of, 175-178,
        203-209
    physical examination of,
        39, 176-178
Growth arrest lines, 111

Hands:
    burns of, 82
    fractures of, 120
Harm, definition of, 251
Head, measurement of, 177
Head trauma:
    data on, 147, 153, 167
    dating of, 163-165
    definitions for, 148-155
    history for, 157, 164, 165
    in older children, 165-166
    laboratory assessment for,
        160-161
    photos of, 193
    physical examination for,
        39, 158-160, 165
    prognosis for, 167-168
    radiology for, 44, 151-155,
        161-163, 165
    shaking impact syndrome
        and, 114, 115, 154,
        155-163
    treatment of, 150, 165-166
    X rays of, 113, 151, 152, 162
    See also Skull
Healing:
    of fractures, 103-104, 111,
        114, 115
    See also Folk healing;
        Treatment
Hearing impairments, 123
Hearsay evidence, 267-268
Heart, 143, 144
    failure to thrive and, 184
    physical examination of, 40
Height measurements,
    175-176, 177, 178, 203-209
Helfer, R. E., model of, 15
Hemangioma, 71
Hematologic disorders, and
    bruises, 70, 71-73
Hemoglobinuria, 45
Hemophilia, 70, 72
Henoch-Schönlein purpura, 73

Hepatic transaminases, 45
Hepatic trauma. See Liver
Hirschprung's disease, 184,
    199
Histories, 24-37
    false, and MSBP, 221,
        223-224
    for abdominal trauma, 130
    for bruises, 64-65
    for burns, 77-78, 87, 88
    for fractures, 98-99, 104
    for head trauma, 157, 164,
        165
    for neglect, 172, 174-176
    for poisonings, 220
    See also Interviews
Hollow visceral injuries, 140
Homicides, 227-228. See also
    Deaths
Hydrocephalus, 154, 155
    X ray of, 152
Hyperemia zone, 75
Hypoxic ischemic
    encephalopathy, 184

Idiopathic thrombocytopenia
    purpura, 70, 72
Ileum, 142. See also Intestines
Imaging techniques, 43-44.
    See also names of specific
    techniques
Immersion burns, 79-82
Immunodeficiency, 185
Incidence. See Data
Inflammatory bowel disease,
    184
Ingestions, injuries from, 140,
    141, 219-221
Inpatient vs. outpatient care,
    of FTT, 187-188
Institutional definitions, 6
Intentions, of perpetrators, 7
Interdisciplinary teams,
    242-245, 247, 248, 249
International bans, on
    corporal punishment, 8
Interpreter services, 237
Interviews, 38, 234-239
    documentation of, 255-260
    See also Histories
Intestines, 129, 132, 141-142

X ray of, 137
Intracerebral hemorrhage, 154
Intracranial hemorrhage, 149
Intracranial pressure, 153
Intrauterine growth
    retardation (IUGR),
    177-178, 183
Intraventricular hemorrhage,
    154
Investigation, by child
    protective services, 240,
    242
IUGR (intrauterine growth
    retardation), 177-178, 183

Jejunum, 142. See also
    Intestines
Jigsaw puzzle model, 14

Kempe, R. S., seminal work
    of, 212
Kidneys, 45, 134, 140
    failure to thrive and, 184
    radiology for, 135
Knowledge, about abuse,
    levels of, 10
Krugman, R. D., on child
    protection movement,
    213

Laboratory assessments, 41,
    43-46
    for abdominal trauma,
        45-46, 132-136
    for bite marks, 219
    for bruises, 70
    for burns, 87
    for child neglect, 172,
        178-179
    for fractures, 41-43,
        100-102, 116-118, 121-122
    for poisonings, 220-221
    for shaking impact
        syndrome, 160-161
    MSBP and, 225
Lacerations, 40, 61, 216. See
    also Bruises
Language interpreters, 237
Lead poisoning, 185

About the Authors

Angelo P. Giardino, MD, MSEd, is Vice President for Clinical Operations and Assistant Physician-in-Chief at the Children's Seashore House in Philadelphia, Pennsylvania, and Clinical Assistant Professor of Pediatrics at the University of Pennsylvania School of Medicine. He earned his medical degree at the University of Pennsylvania School of Medicine and completed his pediatric residency at the Children's Hospital of Philadelphia. He was named a Clinical Scholar at the Robert Wood Johnson Clinical Scholar's Program at the University of Pennsylvania School of Medicine and a research fellow in the Division of General Pediatrics at the Children's Hospital of Philadelphia. During fellowship training, he pursued specialized training in the evaluation of child sexual abuse. He holds a master's degree in health professions education and has co-developed a comprehensive resident curriculum on the evaluation of sexual abuse. Efforts are now underway to assess the impact of this curricular approach. In 1995, he co-founded the Abuse Referral Clinic for Children With Special Care Needs. This clinic provides interdisciplinary evaluations of children with disabilities suspected of having been abused.

Dr. Giardino serves on the Board of Directors of the Support Center for Child Advocates in Philadelphia, which is an advocacy organization providing social work services and legal support to children who have been maltreated. He serves as an expert witness of issues related to child abuse in the Court of Common Pleas in Philadelphia and Bucks County, Pennsylvania. He is coauthor of *A Practical Guide to the Evaluation of Sexual Abuse in the Prepubertal Child* (1992, Sage). He has served as a consultant to the U.S. Congress Office of Technology Assessment Currently, he is also a doctoral candidate at the Graduate School of Education at the University of Pennsylvania, where his work focuses on outcomes assessment in professional education.

Cindy W. Christian, MD, is Assistant Professor of Pediatrics at the University of Pennsylvania School of Medicine and Medical Director of the Child Abuse Program at the Children's Hospital of Philadelphia. Much of her clinical and academic work has been devoted to the care of the abused child. In addition to her clinical work, she conducts research on child abuse and has published numerous articles and book chapters on this subject. She also serves as a consultant for SCAN, Inc., an in-home treatment program for abused and neglected children. She is a member of the American Academy of Pediatrics Section on Child Abuse and Neglect, the Pennsylvania Governor's Community Partnership for Safe Children, the Pennsylvania Attorney General's Medical/Legal Advisory Board on Child Abuse, the Philadelphia County Children and Youth Agency Multidisciplinary Team, and the Law Enforcement Child Abuse Project of Philadelphia. She has lectured nationally on the problem of child abuse and neglect and has appeared in court on numerous occasions.

Eileen R. Giardino, PhD, RN, MSN, is Associate Professor and Interim Director of Undergraduate Programs at La Salle University in the School of Nursing She earned her master's degree in nursing at Widener University and her doctorate in education at the University of Pennsylvania. Her research interests focus on caring in nurse-client interactions, symptom manifestation and management, and the symptomatology of adult survivors of physical and sexual abuse. She has developed programs in health education and disease prevention in community-based health care and has facilitated support groups for adult survivors of child sexual abuse at Women Organized Against Rape. She serves on the board of the Children's Advocacy Center in Philadelphia, which works to promote multidisciplinary evaluation of children suspected of sexual abuse. She is completing course work for work as an Adult Nurse Practitioner. She is coauthor of *A Practical Guide to the Evaluation of Sexual Abuse in the Prepubertal Child* (Sage, 1992).

About the Contributors

Martha M. Cockerill, CRNP, MSN, is a pediatric nurse practitioner in the Primary Care Center at the Children's Hospital of Philadelphia. She is also an adjunct faculty member at Immaculata College, where she has lectured on child abuse and neglect. Her previous experience includes work as a pediatric nurse practitioner at the Medical College of Pennsylvania, where she was involved with drug treatment for mothers and follow-up of their children, follow-up with premature infants and newborns, and care of children with lead poisoning. She also served for many years as a staff nurse in the Intensive Care Nursery at the Hospital of the University of Pennsylvania.

Ann-Christine Duhaime, MD, is Associate Neurosurgeon at the Children's Hospital of Philadelphia, where she also serves as Associate Director of Trauma. Her research interests include the pathophysiology and treatment of head injury in infants and young children. Scientific publications include studies on the biomechanics of head injury in non-accidental injury, accidental mechanism and injury types in infants and toddlers, pathophysiology of subdural hematoma and mechanical trauma in the immature brain, and experimental treatments in severely head-injured children. She has served on several national committees related to head trauma, most recently the task force on guidelines for the treatment of severe head injuries in children.

Trude A. Haecker, MD, is Medical Director for Primary Care and Community Health Services at The Children's Hospital of Philadelphia. She is a Clinical Associate Professor of Pediatrics at the University of Pennsylvania School of Medicine. In her role as medical director she oversees three primary care centers providing comprehensive pediatric care to urban, medically underserved children and families.

Incorporated in those centers is the ambulatory education experience ("Continuity Clinic") for all of the pediatric residents of The Children's Hospital. Her prime area of interest is children with special needs, including follow-up care of high-risk neonates and the care of children in kinship or foster care.

Jennifer Diem Inglis, LSW, has been the Trauma Social Worker at The Children's Hospital of Philadelphia for the past six years. She provides assessment, intervention, support, and referrals for injured children and their families. She has extensive experience in assessing high-risk situations, including those of child abuse and neglect. She assists both families and staff in negotiating the legal and child welfare systems. She and the trauma clinical nurse specialist have worked closely to develop interdisciplinary collaborative social work and nursing interventions with a pediatric trauma population. She is active in social work and nursing education at The Children's Hospital and has served as a field instructor for graduate students in social work. She has presented at several local and national conferences on topics such as adolescent violence and family reactions to pediatric injury.

Stephen Ludwig, MD, is Professor of Pediatrics at the University of Pennsylvania School of Medicine and Associate Chairman for Medical Education at the Children's Hospital of Philadelphia, where he has also served as Director of the Emergency Department and Chief of the Division of General Pediatrics. He is an internationally recognized author on issues pertaining to graduate medical education, pediatric emergency medicine, and child abuse and neglect. He is the recipient of numerous national awards for teaching excellence, including the National Teaching Award from the Ambulatory Pediatric Association. He has published numerous articles in the ambulatory and emergency pediatric literature, including landmark investigation of child abuse and neglect. He is co-editor-in-chief of both the journal *Pediatric Emergency Care* and the *Textbook of Pediatric Emergency Medicine,* now in its third edition. He also edited *Child Abuse and Neglect: A Medical Reference* (1992). A tireless advocate for the welfare of children, he has been adviser to local, national, and international governments on issues of child health and safety.

Susan Perlis Marx, JD, is a consultant for the National Center, the U.S. Department of Justice, and other organizations, training prosecutors and other child abuse professionals. She served as an assistant district attorney in the Philadelphia District Attorney's office from 1985 through 1991 and was named Assistant Chief of the Child Abuse Unit in 1989. She joined the staff of the National Center for Prosecution of Child Abuse in November 1991. During her 2-year tenure at the National Center, she lectured to prosecutors and other professionals nationwide concerning the investigation and prosecution of child abuse, and she was the lead editor and a contributing author of the second edition of the center's authoritative manual, *Investigation and Prosecution of Child Abuse.* She also serves as an editorial board member and commentary coordinator for the *Journal of Child Sexual Abuse* and is a member of the executive board for the Maryland Center for Assault Prevention.